# Contemporary Advances in Sport Psychology

*Contemporary Advances in Sport Psychology* brings together leading international researchers to showcase some of the most important emerging topics in contemporary sport psychology. Each chapter offers a comprehensive review of current knowledge and research on a cutting-edge theme, followed by in-depth discussion of conceptual and methodological issues, and then outlines potential avenues for further research.

The book covers themes including:

- Contemporary personality perspectives
- Choking models of stress and performance
- Coping in sport
- Relational-efficacy beliefs
- Self-determination theory
- Transformational leadership
- Organisational psychology in sport
- Quantitative and qualitative methods in sport psychology

The review format provides the perfect entry point for all researchers, advanced students or practitioners looking to engage with the latest research themes in contemporary sport psychology, offering a greater depth of discussion than the typical journal article. Informing knowledge generation, applied research and professional practice, *Contemporary Advances in Sport Psychology* is an essential addition to any sport science library.

**Stephen D. Mellalieu** is an Associate Professor in Applied Sport Psychology in the Research Centre in Applied Sports, Technology, Exercise and Medicine (A-STEM) at Swansea University, UK, where he is Director of Postgraduate Studies and contributes to undergraduate and postgraduate programmes. He has published over 70 research papers in a wide range of international sport and social psychology journals and texts. He has also co-edited a number of acclaimed texts within the field of sport psychology with Professor Sheldon Hanton including: *Literature Reviews in Sport*

*Psychology* (2006), *Advances in Applied Sport Psychology: A Review* (2009) and the recent *Professional Practice in Sport Psychology: A Review* (2011). His current research interests lie in the area of athlete welfare, including stress and performance, psychological skills and behaviour change, and the organisational environment of elite sport. He is Associate Editor of the *Journal of Applied Sport Psychology* and a member of the Editorial Board of *The Sport Psychologist*. Stephen co-founded the *International Rugby Board Rugby Science Network* in 2011 of which he is Network Editor. He is also a Chartered Psychologist and an Associate Fellow of the British Psychological Society, a registered Practitioner Psychologist and Partner with the Health and Care Professions Council, a British Association of Sport and Exercise Sciences accredited Sport Scientist, and a Fellow of the Higher Education Academy. He has consultancy experience in a number of Olympic and professional sports. When he is not working or spending time with his family, Stephen can be found by, or in, an ocean taking part in numerous water-based pursuits, notably surfing.

**Sheldon Hanton** is a Professor of Sport Psychology at Cardiff Metropolitan University, UK, where he is the Pro Vice-Chancellor for Research. Sheldon is the Editor-in-Chief of *The Sport Psychologist* and sits on the Advisory Board for the *Journal of Sports Sciences*. He is also a member of the Editorial Board for the *Journal of Imagery Research in Sport and Physical Activity* and a former Board member for the *Journal of Applied Sport Psychology* and *Qualitative Research in Sport and Exercise*. He is also a member of the Economic and Social Research Council's Peer Review College. Professor Hanton lists his interests as competition stress and anxiety, mental toughness, organisational psychology, sports injury, and reflective practice. Sheldon has published over 250 peer-reviewed journal articles, edited texts, book chapters, and refereed conference papers. He has supervised or advised on 13 PhD completions, examined internationally and is currently supervising 11 Doctoral candidates. Sheldon is a Chartered Psychologist with the British Psychological Society and Registered with the Health and Care Professions Council. As a former National High Performance Centre Psychologist he advised the England Swim Team and consulted at international training camps and competitions.

# Contemporary Advances in Sport Psychology

A review

**Edited by**
**Stephen D. Mellalieu and**
**Sheldon Hanton**

Routledge
Taylor & Francis Group

LONDON AND NEW YORK

First published 2015
by Routledge
2 Park Square, Milton Park, Abingdon, Oxon OX14 4RN

and by Routledge
711 Third Avenue, New York, NY 10017

*Routledge is an imprint of the Taylor & Francis Group, an informa business*

*British Library Cataloguing-in-Publication Data*
A catalogue record for this book is available from the British Library

*Library of Congress Cataloging in Publication Data*
A catalog record for this book has been requested

ISBN: 978-0-415-74437-9 (hbk)
ISBN: 978-1-315-81305-9 (ebk)

Typeset in Baskerville
by Wearset Ltd, Boldon, Tyne and Wear

MIX
Paper from
responsible sources
FSC
www.fsc.org   FSC® C013056

Printed and bound in Great Britain by
TJ International Ltd, Padstow, Cornwall

# Contents

# Figures

# Tables

# Contributors

## Editors

**Stephen D. Mellalieu** is an Associate Professor in Applied Sport Psychology in the Research Centre in Applied Sports, Technology, Exercise and Medicine (A-STEM) at Swansea University, UK, where he is Director of Postgraduate Studies and contributes to undergraduate and postgraduate programmes. He has published over 70 research papers in a wide range of international sport and social psychology journals and texts. He has also co-edited a number of acclaimed texts within the field of sport psychology with Professor Sheldon Hanton including: *Literature Reviews in Sport Psychology* (2006), *Advances in Applied Sport Psychology: A Review* (2009) and the recent *Professional Practice in Sport Psychology: A Review* (2011). His current research interests lie in the area of athlete welfare, including stress and performance, psychological skills and behaviour change, and the organisational environment of elite sport. He is Associate Editor of the *Journal of Applied Sport Psychology* and a member of the Editorial Board of *The Sport Psychologist*. Stephen co-founded the *International Rugby Board Rugby Science Network* in 2011 of which he is Network Editor. He is also a Chartered Psychologist and an Associate Fellow of the British Psychological Society, a registered Practitioner Psychologist and Partner with the Health and Care Professions Council, a British Association of Sport and Exercise Sciences accredited Sport Scientist, and a Fellow of the Higher Education Academy. He has consultancy experience in a number of Olympic and Professional sports. When he is not working or spending time with his family, Stephen can be found by, or in, an ocean taking part in numerous water-based pursuits, notably surfing.

**Sheldon Hanton** is a Professor of Sport Psychology at Cardiff Metropolitan University, UK, where he is the Pro Vice-Chancellor for Research. Sheldon is the Editor-in-Chief of *The Sport Psychologist* and sits on the Advisory Board for the *Journal of Sports Sciences*. He is also a member of the Editorial Board for the *Journal of Imagery Research in Sport and*

*Physical Activity* and a former Board member for the *Journal of Applied Sport Psychology* and *Qualitative Research in Sport and Exercise*. He is also a member of the Economic and Social Research Council's Peer Review College. Professor Hanton lists his interests as competition stress and anxiety, mental toughness, organisational psychology, sports injury, and reflective practice. Sheldon has published over 250 peer-reviewed journal articles, edited texts, book chapters, and refereed conference papers. He has supervised or advised on 13 PhD completions, examined internationally and is currently supervising 11 Doctoral candidates. Sheldon is a Chartered Psychologist with the British Psychological Society and Registered with the Health and Care Professions Council. As a former National High Performance Centre Psychologist he advised the England Swim Team and consulted at international training camps and competitions.

## Authors

**Calum A. Arthur** is a Lecturer in the School of Sport at the University of Stirling in Scotland. He received his PhD in 2008 from Bangor University. Prior to his position at Stirling University he held a full time lecturing post at Bangor University from 2008 to 2013. He has worked extensively with the military, but has also worked across high-level sport and business. His research primarily focuses on the conceptualisation, measurement and training of leadership. He has published in a wide range of journals including *The Leadership Quarterly*, *Journal of Sport and Exercise Psychology*, *Psychology of Sport and Exercise*, and *Journal of Applied Sport Psychology*. He also regularly reviews for several journals and is currently serving on the Editorial Board of *The Sports Psychologist*.

**Mark R. Beauchamp** is an Associate Professor and Michael Smith Foundation for Health Research (MSFHR) scholar at the University of British Columbia, Canada. His research primarily focuses on group processes within health, exercise and sport settings. His research programme has received funding from agencies such as the Canadian Institutes of Health Research, Canadian Foundation for Innovation, and Social Sciences and Humanities Research Council of Canada. He is a Chartered Psychologist and Associate Fellow of the British Psychological Society (BPS), and is also an Associate Editor for the *Journal of Sport and Exercise Psychology* as well as *Psychology and Health*. He sits on the Editorial Boards for a number other journals including *Health Psychology* (APA) and *Sport, Exercise and Performance Psychology* (APA).

**Steven R. Bray** received his PhD in Kinesiology from the University of Waterloo. He is a Professor in the Department of Kinesiology at McMaster University in Hamilton, Canada. His research interests are on self-regulation of exercise as well as social perceptions that arise in interdependent contexts such as client-healthcare practitioner interactions and youth sport coaching/instruction and how those perceptions relate to the thoughts, feelings and behaviours of the participants. His research has been published in *The Journal of Sport and Exercise Psychology, Psychology of Sport and Exercise, Rehabilitation Psychology, Biological Psychology* and *Psychophysiology*. Steven teaches courses in Sport and Exercise Psychology as well as Health Behaviour Change.

**Nick Caddick** is a PhD Candidate in the Peter Harrison Centre for Disability Sport at Loughborough University, UK. Nick's research explores the effects of surfing on the health and well being of combat veterans experiencing post-traumatic stress disorder (PTSD). His work on this topic has been published in leading international journals including *Qualitative Health Research* and *Psychology of Sport and Exercise*. Nick has also published book chapters and journal articles on qualitative research methods and is currently involved in work exploring the uses of methodological pluralism in qualitative data analysis in psychological research.

**Peter R. E. Crocker** received his PhD from the University of Alberta after receiving a BA (Psychology) and a MSc (Kinesiology) from Simon Fraser University. He is a Professor in the School of Kinesiology and an associate member of the Department of Psychology at the University of British Columbia, Canada. A two-time president of the Canadian Society of Psychomotor Learning and Sport Psychology (SCAPPS), he is a fellow of SCAPPS and the Association for Applied Sport Psychology (AASP). He has served as an Editor of *The Sport Psychologist* and as an Associate Editor of the *Journal of Sport and Exercise Psychology*. His research focuses primary on adaptation in sport and exercise, with a special focus on stress, coping and emotion. He has published over 100 peer-reviewed papers and book chapters, with his research primarily funded by the Social Sciences and Humanities Research Council of Canada. He is married, with two adult children, and enjoys golfing, fishing and bridge.

**Patrick Gaudreau** is an Associate Professor in the School of Psychology at the University of Ottawa in Canada where he directs the Laboratory for research on Achievement, Motivation, and the Regulation of Action (LAMRA). His research programme examines the role of personality, motivation and self-regulation to predict achievement and psychological adjustment of individuals engaged in performance-related activities. Ongoing research includes the examination of performance of athletes and students as well as the creation of bridges between preventive science and educational psychology. Patrick is currently an Associate Editor for *Anxiety, Stress, and Coping*. The Social Sciences and Humanities Research Council of Canada and the Sport Canada Sport Participation Research Initiative are supporting his research programme. In his spare time, he can be found in the bushes searching for his golf balls and those of his two young children.

**Katharina Geukes** is a Lecturer and Research Scholar in the Department of Psychological Diagnostics and Personality Psychology at the West-fälische Wilhelms-University of Münster, Germany. She received her PhD jointly from the Ruhr University Bochum, Germany and the University of Queensland, Brisbane, Australia, focusing on the prediction of performance under pressure through personality. She teaches courses in psychological diagnostics and personality psychology with an emphasis on interpersonal perceptions and the measurement of personality characteristics (e.g. subclinical narcissism). In her research Katharina focuses on the interplay between persons and situations. She investigates situational influences on personality and behaviour in social contexts in general and in sports, performance and pressure particularly. Katharina works as a consultant (sport) psychologist and enjoys European handball, running, skiing and surfing.

**Dan Gould** is the Director of the Institute for the Study of Youth Sports and Professor in the Department of Kinesiology at the Michigan State University, USA. Dan teaches graduate courses in the area and is heavily involved in the graduate programme. During his career Dan has focused equal attention on research, teaching and service activities in applied sport psychology. He has consulted extensively with numerous athletes of all age and skill levels and involved in a wide range of sports. He has also served on the US Olympic coaching development committee for ten years and co-chaired the sport science and technology committee. Actively involved in research, Dan has studied the stress-athletic performance relationship, sources of athletic stress, stress and burnout in young athletes, athlete motivation, the psychology of coaching, talent development, parental influences in youth sports, and performance enhancement. He has over 100 scholarly publications and over 50 applied sport psychology research dissemination-service publications. He has been invited to speak on sport psychology topics in over 20 countries. Two research-based children's sports texts have been co-edited by Dan and he served as one of the founding Co-Editors of *The Sport Psychologist*. Dan has secured numerous external grants to support his research and sport psychology educational efforts. Dan has co-authored two books, *Foundations of Sport and Exercise Psychology* (with Bob Weinberg) and *Understanding Psychological Preparation for Sport: Theory and Practice of Elite Performers* (with Lew Hardy and Graham Jones). Dan is a certified consultant and active fellow in Association of Applied Sport Psychology (AASP).

**Lew Hardy** is Professor of Health and Human Performance in the School of Sport, Health and Exercise Sciences at Bangor University, UK. He is also the Chief Executive of the Institute for the Psychology of Elite

Performance (IPEP) at Bangor University. Lew was one of the first professors of sport psychology in the United Kingdom and is one of a very small number of people to have given keynote and invited addresses at all the major sport psychology conferences in the world. He has over 140 full-length research publications and served three Olympic cycles as chairperson of the British Olympic Association's Psychology Steering Group (from 1989 to 2000). His central research interest is the psychology of very high-level performance, including the effects of stress, mental toughness, motivation, the utility of psychological skills and strategies, transformational leadership, and teamwork. He has been responsible for over £1 million pounds of grant capture and has equal applied experience of working across military, business and sport domains. Lew has served, or is currently serving, as an Associate Editor or Editorial Board member of many of the most highly regarded journals within the subject field including *Psychology of Sport and Exercise, Journal of Sport and Exercise Psychology* and *The Sport Psychologist.* Lew is a Chartered Psychologist and a fellow of the British Association of Sport and Exercise Sciences (BASES) and an accredited Sport Scientist. He was awarded the inaugural Distinguished International Scholar Award by the Association of Applied Sport Psychology (AASP) in 1996, and the Distinguished Contribution to Sport and Exercise Psychology by the British Psychological Society in 2011.

**Timothy C. Howle** is a PhD Candidate in the School of Sport Science, Exercise and Health (SSEH) at the University of Western Australia, Australia. He received his MSc in sport psychology from Florida State University in 2012. Tim is broadly interested in studying interpersonal aspects of sport and exercise. The focus of his work has been on self-presentation processes, and he has published and presented work in this area. His current research is aimed at understanding self-presentation motives, the factors that lead individuals to adopt these motives, and the behavioural and cognitive outcomes the motives shape. In addition to his research, Tim serves as a peer-reviewer of journal articles and assists with teaching courses in sport and exercise psychology.

**Ben Jackson** received his doctoral degree from the University of Leeds in 2008, and is currently a Research Assistant Professor in the School of Sport Science, Exercise and Health (SSEH) at the University of Western Australia. Ben's work within the 'Psychology of Active, Healthy Living' group within SSEH is focused on (a) the study of group and relationship processes in health contexts, (b) issues associated with self-regulation, self-control and motivation, and (c) the role of persuasion models in promoting physical activity-related outcomes. Ben's current work is funded by the Australian Research Council, and in addition to his research programme, he teaches courses in Sport and Exercise Psychology, and serves on the Editorial Boards for *Journal of Sport and Exercise Psychology* and *Psychology of Sport and Exercise.*

**Paul Larkin** holds a research position in the Faculty of Education and Social Work at the University of Sydney, Australia. He received his PhD in 2013 from the University of Ballarat, Australia, focusing on the decision-making performance of Australian football umpires and was also awarded the Doctoral Thesis Award of Distinction for Australian Council for Health, Physical Education, and Recreation Victorian State Branch in the same year. Paul conducts research in the applied areas of talent identification and development, specifically, the perceptual-cognitive performance of elite youth soccer players and Australian football umpires. In his current position Paul is working on an Australian Research Council funded project in collaboration with Football Federation Australia.

**Rebecca J. Larner** is a PhD Researcher in the Department of Sport and Exercise Science at the University of Portsmouth, UK. Rebecca's research interests lie within the domain of organisational psychology in elite sport, with a particular focus on the areas of organisational stress, emotion and self-regulation, organisational development, and excellence. She regularly reviews for sport and exercise psychology journals and provides applied sport psychology services to a range of sport performers and organisations in the UK.

**Christopher Mesagno** is a Senior Lecturer in Exercise and Sport Psychology at Federation University, Australia. He received his PhD in 2006 from Victoria University, in Melbourne, Australia, after receiving his BS (Psychology) and MS (Exercise & Sport Science) both from the University of Florida, Gainesville, Florida, USA. In 2007, Christopher was a co-recipient of the prestigious Association for Applied Sport Psychology Dissertation Award for his PhD dissertation in which he introduced a Self-Presentation Model of choking under pressure. He has published in journals such as the *Journal of Sport and Exercise Psychology*, *Psychology of Sport and Exercise*, *Journal of Applied Sport Psychology*, *The Sport Psychologist*, *International Journal of Sport and Exercise Psychology* and *International Journal of Sport Psychology*. He is also on the Editorial Board of *Journal of Sport Psychology in Action*. With his expertise in anxiety, coping, attention and concentration skills, he has worked with a number of athletes within a range of team and individual sports to enhance performance.

**Athanasios Mouratidis** is an Assistant Professor at the Department of Psychology of the Hacettepe University of Ankara, Turkey. He received his PhD in social psychology and sport sciences at the Catholic University of Leuven, Belgium in 2009. His research focuses on motivational processes among children, adolescents and young adults in achievement settings such as schools and sport contexts. At present, he investigates the interplay between the context and the person – how the personal quality of motivation and the social environment interact to predict effective self-regulation. He has published peer-reviewed articles on the quality of motivation in educational, sport and social psychology journals and reviewed for a number of international peer-reviewed journals including the *Journal of Personality and Social Psychology*, *Developmental Psychology* and *Journal of Sport and Exercise Psychology*. Athanasios is an Editorial board member for the *Physical Education and Sport Pedagogy* Journal.

**Johan Y. Y. Ng** is a Postdoctoral Fellow in the Department of Sports Science and Physical Education, the Chinese University of Hong Kong. He received his PhD from the University of Birmingham, UK, in 2013. His research interest is in the area of sport and exercise psychology, with a particular focus on the motivation to exercise and other health-related behaviours. Johan has published in journals including *Perspectives on Psychological Science*, *Journal of Sport and Exercise Psychology* and *British Journal of Health Psychology*.

**Nikos Ntoumanis** is a Research Professor at the Centre of Health Psychology and Behavioural Medicine, School of Psychology and Speech Pathology, at Curtin University, Australia. His research examines personal and contextual factors that optimise motivation and promote performance, psychological well-being, and health-conducive behaviours in various physical activity settings. His research has been published in a variety of peer-reviewed journals (e.g. *Perspectives on Psychological Science*, *Developmental Psychology*, *Journal of Educational Psychology*, *Personality and Social Psychology Bulletin*, *Annals of Behavioural Medicine*), and has attracted considerable research funding from major UK research councils (ESRC, MRC, BBSRC, ARC), charities, local health authorities and the European Union. Dr Ntoumanis has authored a book on using SPSS for sport and exercise scientists that was published by Routledge in 2001. He is the Editor-in-Chief of *Psychology of Sport and Exercise*, the official publication of the European Federation of Sport Psychology, and he serves on the Editorial Board of several other journals (e.g. *Journal of Educational Psychology*, *Journal of Sport and Exercise Psychology*). He often engages with the media (*The Times, Independent, Men's Health*, etc.) in an effort to disseminate his research. Dr Ntoumanis is married and has two daughters. In his spare time, he enjoys swimming, watching soccer and following international politics.

**Ross Roberts** is a Lecturer in Sport and Exercise Psychology and Co-Director of the Institute for the Psychology of Elite Performance (IPEP) at Bangor University, UK. Although his PhD research examined the role of imagery in motor skill performance, his research interests now focus on personality and individual differences, with a particular interest in the role of personality (especially narcissism) in performance contexts. He has published in a wide range of journals including the *Journal of Sport and Exercise Psychology*, *Psychology of Sport and Exercise* and *Frontiers in Human Neuroscience*, and is also on the Editorial Board of *The Sport*

*Psychologist.* He has received research funding from the Wellcome Trust, the Sports Council for Wales and the Hospitality, Leisure, Sport and Tourism Network. Ross is an Associate Fellow of the British Psychological Society (BPS), is a chartered Sport and Exercise Psychologist with the BPS and is also accredited by the British Association of Sport and Exercise Sciences and has worked with a number of high level squads and athletes.

**Brett Smith** is a Reader in Qualitative Health Research and leads the psycho-social health and wellbeing strand in the Peter Harrison Centre for Disability Sport at Loughborough University, UK. His funded research on disability and qualitative inquiry has resulted in over 100 publications and 100 invited talks. He is Editor of the award-winning journal, *Qualitative Research in Sport, Exercise, and Health* (QRSEH). Brett is also Associate Editor of *Psychology of Sport and Exercise* and actively serves on seven Editorial Boards. He is co-author of the book *Qualitative Research Methods in Sport, Exercise, and Health: From Process to Product.* Currently Brett is co-editing the forthcoming *International Handbook of Qualitative Methods in Sport and Exercise* (2015, Routledge).

**Katherine A. Tamminen** is an Assistant Professor in the Faculty of Kinesiology and Physical Education at the University of Toronto, Canada. Her research focuses on two main areas: stress, coping and emotion in sport, and young athletes' experiences in sport. Her current research examines how adolescent athletes learn to cope with stressors in sport and how parents and coaches influence athletes' coping. She also conducts research on interpersonal emotion regulation and social processes of coping in team sports, to understand how athletes' coping impacts their teammates and how it contributes to sport enjoyment, commitment and team cohesion. Her research is supported by the Social Sciences and Humanities Research Council of Canada and has been published in journals such as *Psychology of Sport and Exercise, Journal of Sports Sciences* and *Qualitative Research in Sport, Exercise, and Health.*

**Ian Taylor** is a Senior Lecturer in the School of Sport, Exercise and Health Sciences at Loughborough University, UK. Ian employs a strong theoretical perspective in his research to investigate strategies that optimise the psychological health and motivation of individuals in a range of settings, including sport, leisure and education. This knowledge is subsequently used to inform health behaviour change and maximise sport performance. He has published extensively in internationally recognised journals and sits on the Editorial Board of *Psychology of Sport and Exercise.* Ian is a chartered psychologist with the British Psychological Society and a fellow of the Higher Education Academy. His signature dish is baked salmon in filo pastry and his running exploits are a practical example of the flaws in the theory of planned behaviour.

**Peter Tomsett** is currently under taking his PhD within the school of Sport, Health and Exercise Science at Bangor University, UK, funded as part of the Higher Education Academy Mike Baker doctoral scholarship programme. In his PhD, Peter is investigating transformational leadership behaviour in the context of research supervision in higher education, under the supervision of Dr Nichola Callow, Dr Calum Arthur and Dr James Hardy. He also lectures in group dynamics and remains involved in research in the sporting context working collaboratively on a number of projects with a focus on transformational leadership theory.

**Carme Viladrich** is Associate Professor in the Department of Psychobiology and Methodology of Health Science at Universitat Autònoma de Barcelona, Spain. She specialises in quantitative psychological methods, psychometrics and structural equation models. Her present research interests include the study of measurement and structural properties of psychological models applied to sport and exercise psychology. Carme is the co-author of more than 40 research papers and her research has been funded by the Spanish Government and the European Community. Presently, she is Editor of the Methodology section of the Spanish scientific journal *Revista de Psicología del Deporte*. Management responsibilities held include Head of the Department, Deputy Dean of the Faculty of Psychology and member of the Governing Council of the Universitat Autònoma de Barcelona.

**Chris R. D. Wagstaff** is a Senior Lecturer in Sport and Performance Psychology at the University of Portsmouth, UK. He received his PhD from the University of Wales Institute, Cardiff. He subsequently held teaching positions at Cardiff Metropolitan and Bangor Universities and also worked at the Institute of Psychology in Elite Performance (IPEP). Chris is a Chartered Psychologist and an Associate Fellow of the British Psychological Society, a registered Practitioner Psychologist and Partner with the Health and Care Professions Council, a British Association of Sport and Exercise Sciences accredited Sport Scientist, and a Fellow of the Higher Education Academy. He has a long-standing interest in the psychology of elite performance and publishes widely within this domain. Specifically, Chris's research examines how individuals and teams deliver sustained excellence in high-pressure environments. This research encapsulates the areas of organisational functioning, stress and emotion, self-regulation, and leadership. As an applied practitioner Chris has provided psychological consultancy to a diverse range of clients including international, Olympic and Paralympic athletes, teams, coaches and support staff, business executives, senior military officers, performing artists, adventurers and medical surgeons.

**Toni Williams** joined the Peter Harrison Centre for Disability Sport at Loughborough University, UK, after being awarded a Glendonbrook

Doctoral Fellowship. Her PhD explores the impact of activity-based rehabilitation on the health and well-being of people with spinal cord injury (SCI). Toni's research interests also include narrative inquiry, disability studies, psychology of injury and rehabilitation, and qualitative meta-synthesis. Her first meta-synthesis of qualitative research on SCI and physical activity has recently been published in *Health Psychology Review*. She is currently Editorial Assistant for the journal *Qualitative Research in Sport, Exercise and Health*, and co-chair of the *4th International Conference on Qualitative Research in Sport and Exercise*.

**Tim Woodman** is a Professor and Head of School at Bangor University's School of Sport, Health and Exercise Sciences, UK. He is also a Co-Director of the Institute for the Psychology of Elite Performance (IPEP). Tim has a long-standing interest in stress and performance and his recent research has examined personality markers of stress and performance and the processes that underpin risk-taking behaviours. He has published approximately 50 peer-reviewed research articles on these topics. He is an Associate Editor for *The Sport Psychologist* and on the Editorial Board of *Psychology of Sport and Exercise*. Tim is a chartered Sport and Exercise Psychologist and accredited by the British Association of Sport and Exercise Sciences. He has worked with a number of international performers, most notably with British Gymnastics.

# Foreword

Sport and exercise psychology is an academic discipline and like all disciplines is built upon a scholarly research base. Therefore, it is exciting that over the last four decades we have seen an expediential growth in research in the field as reflected in the fact that we have at least six scholarly journals devoted exclusively to sport and exercise psychology and a plethora of studies published each year. Long gone are the days when a sport psychologist could have a handle on all the original research in most of the major research areas in the field. Nowadays, it is difficult to keep up in only one or two areas.

While this explosion in sport psychology research has certainly helped advance knowledge in the field, one problem associated with it is the need to integrate and synthesise the ever-expanding research base. We need to understand what we know, what we don't know, theoretical explanations for the phenomena being studied, methodological strengths and limitations, and future research directions. It is for this reason I was excited to learn that noted sport psychology researchers, Stephen Mellalieu and Sheldon Hanton, have collaborated to edit *Contemporary Advances In Sport Psychology: A Review*.

Mellalieu and Hanton's goals were to assemble up-to-date reviews of the most contemporary topical areas within the current field of sport psychology, all the while doing so with a distinctive conceptual and theoretical focus. The reader will find reviews on topics that have been studied for some time like personality, coping, choking and motivation. At the same time topics of more recent origin in sport psychology like transformational leadership, relational-efficacy beliefs and organisational psychology in sport are included. Finally, chapters on quantitative and qualitative methodologies and data analysis techniques are contained. An additional distinctive feature of this text is the inclusion of a commentary, in the form of an epilogue, from one of the most eminent scholars within the discipline of sport psychology, and a very good colleague of mine, Professor Lew Hardy.

This book comprises nine chapters that cover the latest contemporary topics in the sport psychology field. In most chapters you will find a detailed review of the literature, summarising what is known at this point in time while at the same time providing a rigorous methodological and theoretical critique of what has been done. The chapters then finish with detailed future directions outlining the kind of methodological and theoretical improvements needed to advance each area of study. Not only is the format of this book strong, but also the authors are exceptional. Mellalieu and Hanton have identified leading researchers at the cutting edge of their respective subject areas in each of the nine content areas included, making for strong chapters throughout.

The first chapter is entitled, 'Contemporary personality perspectives in sport psychology'. Here, Ross Roberts and Tim Woodman provide a review of the literature relating to personality and performance with the aim of encouraging more careful consideration of personality and individual differences in performance-related research. Following a historical overview of personality research in sport, and the recent work involving the 'Big 5' personality traits, the authors discuss narcissism and alexithymia, two variables that have considerable applicability to sporting environments and which are starting to receive increased research attention in the field. The chapter concludes by challenging researchers to consider the importance of developing theoretically grounded personality research questions that examine how, when and why personality influences behaviour.

In the second chapter, Peter Crocker, Katherine Tamminen and Patrick Gaudreau review the recent theoretical and empirical advancements on the literature on coping in sport. The chapter includes a discussion of the emerging awareness that coping should be examined from both an intrapersonal and an interpersonal perspective. Several important issues in the sport coping literature are discussed including the conceptualisation and classification of coping, its assessment, statistical modelling procedures used to analyse the construct, and how coping change and stability can be examined over time. The review also discusses new perspectives in sport coping, such as communal coping, interpersonal emotional regulation and the role of culture.

In the third chapter in this volume, Ian Taylor discusses self-determination theory (SDT) and the five sub-theories that detail distinct processes related to motivation, personality and well being. The chapter describes each sub-theory in detail and appraises research in sports contexts associated with each mini-theory. Examples of how each theory can inform sporting practice are then provided with suggestions made as to how sport researchers can advance the wider SDT literature.

Christopher Wagstaff and Rebecca Larner, in Chapter 4, then proceed to review the recent developments in the literature relating to organisational psychology in sport. The authors initially delimit and demystify organisational psychology from similar concentrations of industrial and organisational psychology. Then, the chapter provides an organising structure to align existing and potential future lines of inquiry into four core dimensions of research and application. These include: emotions and attitudes in sport organisations, stress and well being in sport organisations, behaviours in sport organisations, and environments in sport organisations. The chapter concludes with a consideration of some of the key issues facing investigation of the proposed organising structure.

In Chapter 5, written by Ben Jackson, Steven Bray, Mark Beauchamp and Timothy Howle, recent work within diverse physical activity contexts (sport, exercise, physical education and rehabilitation) is discussed in order to provide an overview of the tripartite efficacy literature. In outlining the major developments that have taken place in this area over the past decade, the authors consider the ways in which the tripartite constructs may be related to, and predictive of, salient behavioural, affective and interpersonal outcomes in these settings. A number of conceptual and methodological considerations are then offered for future tripartite efficacy work in the physical activity domain.

The sixth chapter, by Christopher Mesagno, Katharina Geukes and Paul Larkin begins with a review of literature on choking under pressure in sport. Specific emphasis is placed upon on recent debates in choking, common personality characteristics that contribute to athlete choking-susceptibility, and contemporary choking under pressure models. Implications for applied and strategic interventions to help athletes improve performance under pressure are also discussed.

In Chapter 7, Calum Arthur and Peter Tomsett review the recent literature examining transformational leadership in the sporting context. A detailed overview of 14 empirical studies conducted in the sport psychology domain is provided with key findings and methodological limitations highlighted. The authors discuss measurement and analytical issues that dominate existing research, such as the application of multi-level analyses and the global and differentiated conceptualisations of the construct. The chapter concludes with a call for researchers to consider the antecedents and potential contextual moderators of transformational leader effectiveness, possible negative consequences of transformational leadership, and the need for greater methodological rigour.

Chapter 8, written by Brett Smith, Nick Caddick, and Toni Williams considers recent qualitative conceptual advances in sport psychology. First, the authors highlight the trend towards interviews as the dominant method of data collection in sport psychology research. Several criticisms are discussed that have been levelled at interview research in order to signal how interviews might be used better to conceptually advance the field of sport psychology. Several worthwhile but under-utilised methods of data collection are then outlined with suggestions provided as to how an expansion of these methods would advance the field of sport psychology conceptually. Finally, the authors offer some concluding thoughts on qualitative conceptual advances in sport psychology.

In the ninth chapter, Nikos Ntoumanis, Athanasios Mouratidis, Johan Ng and Carme Viladrich discuss recent advances and controversies in selected quantitative analyses that are either widely used or are becoming increasingly popular in the sport and exercise psychology field. Specifically, four topics are discussed that offer new opportunities for better testing of theories and conceptual models in the sport and exercise psychology field. These include new procedures for mediation analysis, exploratory structural equation modelling and bifactor models as alternatives to confirmatory factor analysis, multilevel modelling as an alternative to repeated (multivariate) analysis of variance for the analysis of longitudinal data, and the latest advances in meta-analysis.

In the Epilogue to the book Professor Lew Hardy highlights key issues from the preceding chapters with a view to guide direction taken by future research. Lew's previous commentaries (e.g. Hardy, 1997; Hardy and Jones, 1994; Hardy *et al.*, 1997), have, and are still making significant contributions to shaping thinking on research in the field. Here, in his inimitable style, Lew gives an honest and informed appraisal of the chapters, highlighting generic factors and issues specific to each domain covered.

So whether you are interested in better understanding the scholarly research in these areas to guide your professional practice, better teach your graduate courses, or help stimulate your thinking relative to your future research, you will find the forthcoming text extremely instructive.

Dan Gould

## References

Hardy, L. (1997). The Coleman Roberts Griffith Address: Three myths about applied consultancy work. *Journal of Applied Sport Psychology*, 9, 277–294.

Hardy, L. and Jones, J. G. (1994). Current issues and future directions for performance-related research in sport psychology. *Journal of Sports Sciences*, 12, 61–92.

Hardy, L., Jones, J. G. and Gould, D. (1996). *Understanding psychological preparation for sport: Theory and practice of elite performers.* Chichester: John Wiley.

# Preface

*Contemporary Advances in Sport Psychology: A Review* is the fourth book in our series within the domain of sport psychology and follows on from the successful texts: *Literature Reviews in Sport Psychology* (Nova Science, 2006), *Advances in Applied Sport Psychology: A Review* (Routledge, 2009) and *Professional Practice in Sport Psychology: A Review* (Routledge, 2011). This latest book is very much indicative of both our passions for bringing together bodies of work from within the sport psychology field to further the development and dissemination of knowledge of basic and applied research and professional practice.

One of the privileges both Sheldon and myself feel we are afforded as part of this process is in our current roles at the time of writing serving as *Editor in Chief* and *Associate Editor* respectively of two of the most respected academic international peer-review journals within the sport psychology field (*The Sport Psychologist* and *Journal of Applied Sport Psychology*). We are consistently exposed to the latest 'hot topics' in the field by researchers at the cutting edge of the discipline. Thus, our intention with *Contemporary Advances in Sport Psychology: A Review* has been to draw upon these experiences in order to compile a collection of up-to-date reviews of the most contemporary topic areas within the field of sport psychology, with a distinctive conceptual and theoretical focus. Within each chapter, leading and emerging academics from the sport psychology field 'review' the broader topic area and then use their knowledge and expertise to paint a picture of how they see their respective subject field in terms of key conceptual and methodological issues, and future research directions. Unlike many existing collections of reviewed works, we have explicitly given each chapter contributor the academic freedom to write about their choice of topic, and place their unique 'slant' on the 'state of play' of their respective topic area.

We hope you enjoy reading the text as much as we have had the pleasure of bringing this collection of works together.

Stephen D. Mellalieu
Sheldon Hanton

# References

Hanton, S. and Mellalieu, S. D. (eds), (2006). *Literature reviews in sport psychology.* Hauppauge, NY: Nova Science.

Hanton S. and Mellalieu S. D. (eds), (2011). *Professional practice in sport psychology: A review.* New York: Routledge.

Mellalieu, S. D. and Hanton, S. (eds), (2009). *Advances in applied sport psychology. A review.* New York: Routledge.

# Acknowledgements

We are very grateful to all the Authors for their contributions to this book. We appreciate the task was challenging and we hope you are as pleased with the result as we are – thank you. Our appreciation is also extended to Routledge for working with us once more, and specifically to all the staff at the Sport and Leisure Section of Routledge Publishing.

Lastly, we would like to give a special mention to our respective families for their ongoing love and support throughout the production of another book and our professional careers in general.

# 1 Contemporary personality perspectives in sport psychology

*Ross Roberts and Tim Woodman*

## Introduction

Although their lives are dominated by engagement in sport, first and foremost sportsmen and sportswomen are people and people are different from each other. Sport may attract certain individuals; however, in this chapter we are more interested in the differences between individuals *within* the sport domain and how those differences might affect performance. For example, some athletes thrive on the pressures of competition, yet they do not enjoy training. Others love to train but then fail to achieve their potential in the world of elite sport. Given that sportspeople are so different underscores the importance of considering the role of individual differences in performance. Unfortunately, sport psychology research has typically not accorded this level of attention to personality and individual differences. In fact, personality has had something of a troubled history in sport psychology research and has been somewhat neglected. This seems all the more odd when personality is flourishing in other domains of psychology including clinical psychology, health psychology, social psychology, and neuroscience (e.g. Carver *et al.*, 2010; Connor-Smith and Flaschbart, 2010; DeYoung *et al.*, 2010; Ferguson, 2013).

The purpose of this review is to underscore the importance of personality and to propose something of a paradigm shift for sport psychology researchers by giving personality a more central focus in the context of sport performance. We begin by providing a brief overview of personality conceptualisation and measurement, as well as coverage of early personality research in sport including some of the limitations of that research. We then present more contemporary findings that address some of the problems associated with this early research. Although we touch on the "Big 5" personality traits (Costa and McCrae, 1992), we do not cover this aspect of personality in great detail and interested readers are referred to Allen *et al.* (2013) for an excellent and detailed review of the Big 5 in relation to sport. Our review moves beyond these traits by focusing on two personality variables – narcissism and alexithymia – which are starting to receive increased research attention and have considerable potential applicability to sporting environments. Although we provide specific research directions at particular points in the chapter, we close with some broader research questions and challenges, as well as applied implications, for the role of personality in performance contexts. Purposefully, we concentrate our review at the level of the individual and thus the impact of personality on individual performance as opposed to the influence of personality in relation to team functioning and team performance. This is not to say that personality is not relevant in groups, indeed it is (e.g. Beauchamp *et al.*, 2007 for more on this issue). We refer interested readers to the emerging literature on group composition and group functioning (e.g. Barrick *et al.*, 1998; Peeters *et al.*, 2006) for more on this topic.

## Personality conceptualisation and measurement

Personality has been defined as the "psychological qualities that contribute to an individual's enduring and distinctive patterns of feeling, thinking, and behaving" (Cervone and Pervin, 2013, p. 8). From their definition, Cervone and Pervin highlight four key principles of personality: (1) its *enduring* nature means that it is reasonably consistent across time and situations, (2) it is *distinctive*, and thus can differentiate between individuals, (3) its *contribution* to behaviour allows for the collection of empirical data as well as theory building, (4) the focus on *feeling, thinking,* and *behaving* takes into account all aspects of a person, not just one particular domain of life (see Cervone and Pervin). Although personality has been discussed in writings as far back as ancient Greece, work by Freud in the latter half of the nineteenth century, and later continued by Adler, Jung, and Eysenck (amongst others) provided some of the initial impetus into understanding how basic differences in personality contributed to human functioning and health. For example, Freud's model of psychosexual development proposed oral, anal, and phallic personality types, each with their own aetiology. Although Freud's work has been the subject of considerable controversy (e.g. Horney, 1973), it remains the subject of substantial research efforts to the present day, where neuroscientific evidence is providing support for many of Freud's theoretical postulates (e.g. see Turnbull and Solms, 2007).

Following Freud, work by Hans Eysenck (e.g. Eysenck and Eysenck, 1985), Gray (1970; Gray and McNaughton, 2000) and later by Costa and McCrae and Goldberg (e.g. Costa and McCrae, 1992; Goldberg, 1992) has attempted to describe the major personality traits underlying human behaviour. Eysenck outlined the "Giant 3" traits of extraversion, neuroticism, and psychoticism (tough mindedness), while Costa and McCrae and Goldberg's conceptualisations involve the so called "Big 5" traits of extraversion, conscientiousness, openness to experience, agreeableness, and neuroticism (see Costa and McCrae; Goldberg). The Giant 3 and Big 5 share some commonality as they both include extraversion and neuroticism. Somewhat differently, Gray's work has sought to provide a biological basis for personality and has examined the neural underpinnings of fundamental individual differences in sensitivities to reward and punishment (see Corr, 2008 for a detailed overview of this work). In Gray's work, extraversion and neuroticism are conceptualised as behavioural expressions of the sensitivity to reward and punishment, respectively. Of these various approaches to personality it is the Big 5 that has received by far the most research attention and has been used as an underlying theoretical framework in a number of areas of personality psychology, including leadership (e.g. Judge *et al.*, 2003); decision making (e.g. Hilbig, 2008); responses to stress (Carver and Connor-Smith, 2010); work performance (e.g. Barrick *et al.*, 2001) and sport (e.g. Allen *et al.*, 2011; Woodman, Hardy, Zourbanos *et al.*, 2010).

## Personality research in sport

Personality was once a topic of major research interest for sport psychology researchers (see Eysenck *et al.*, 1982). Indeed, Morgan (1980) claimed that personality traits may account for between 20–45 per cent of the variance in performance, and suggested that their examination along with other theoretical approaches would be useful in predicting sporting behaviour. However, despite early burgeoning interest in personality research in sport, much of it was beset by a lack of theoretical rationale, methodological flaws and a failure to control for Type I error rates, amongst other problems (Eysenck *et al.*). For example, typical early studies in the sport domain (e.g. Davis and Mogk, 1994; Schurr *et al.*, 1977; Williams, 1980) compared differences between more and less successful athletes on measures such as the Profile of Mood States (McNair *et al.*, 1989), or compared large samples of athletes against non-athletes on various personality scales without any real underpinning theoretical rationale. Results often revealed, unsurprisingly, no overall personality differences between athletes and non-athletes, although team sport athletes were sometimes reported to be more extraverted and individual sportsmen less anxious than non-athletes (see Eysenck *et al.*). Such an atheoretical approach to research typified much of the sport personality research (see Vealey, 2002). Indeed, based on the sorts of problems evident in the early personality research some sport psychology researchers (e.g. Gill and Williams, 2008) have questioned the usefulness of personality approaches to sport, leading it to being seen as something of a backwater in sport psychology research.

However, some researchers have continued to pursue personality research in sport using more theoretically grounded approaches. For example, using the Big 5 as a theoretical basis, Piedmont *et al.* (1999) found that neuroticism (negatively) and conscientiousness (positively) predicted some variance in athletic performance. In addition, based on

Eysenck's (1985) Giant 3, Egan and Stelmack (2003) found that Mount Everest climbers were higher than average in psychoticism (tough mindedness) and lower in neuroticism, suggesting that the influence of these variables predicts mountaineers' greater ability to deal with the harsh reality of high altitude mountaineering. More recently, the Big 5 has continued to be used within the sport domain. Both Allen et al. (2011) and Kaiseler et al. (2012) explored relationships between the Big 5 and coping responses to stress and found that the Big 5 differentially predicted the use of coping strategies. For example, these studies found neuroticism to be associated with greater use avoidant coping strategies, and conscientiousness to positively predict approach coping.

Such "main effect" type studies (where the influence of personality on performance or related variables is tested in terms of a linear relationship) are undoubtedly useful in understanding personality's impact on performance. However, a much greater understanding is likely to be garnered by considering both main *and* interactive effects. Following Lewin (1936), most researchers would agree that behaviour is a result of the interaction between the person and environmental factors. Thus, considering how personality interacts with environmental factors (e.g. coach behaviours, psychological skill use, state anxiety, etc.) to predict behaviour (i.e. performance) is likely to provide more meaningful answers for performance focused sport psychology researchers, as it seems plausible to suggest that not all coach behaviours or psychological skills (for example) will have the same effect on performance for all personality types. A growing number of studies are now considering personality and performance in relation to such person × environment interactions. As an example, Woodman, Hardy, Zourbanos et al. (2010) examined the interaction between personality and psychological skills on the training behaviours of high-level gymnasts. Across two samples, conscientiousness was positively related to the quality of gymnasts' preparation for competition (i.e. indicating a main effect of personality). More interestingly, in the context of person × environment interactions, only extroverts (not introverts) benefited from goal-setting with a view to becoming less distracted in training (see Figure 1.1). Furthermore, the skill of emotional control buffered the negative effects of neuroticism on coping with adversity such that neurotic individuals were better able to cope with adversity when they were better able to control their emotions in training. Conversely, emotional control was of no benefit for athletes who were not neurotic. These findings are important because they illustrate that not all athletes respond to, and benefit from, psychological interventions in the same way.

As a second example of person × environment interactions, Bell et al. (2013) demonstrated that speed accuracy trade-offs in decision making do not apply to all athletes in the same way. Drawing from the principles of Attentional Control Theory (Eysenck et al., 2007), Bell et al. demonstrated that the speed-accuracy trade-off existed for emotionally stable (i.e. low

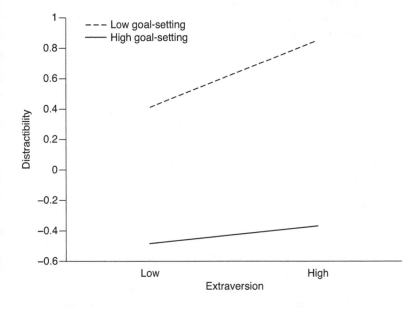

*Figure 1.1* Regression slopes of the interaction between extraversion and goal-setting on distractibility. Regression slopes are derived from regression equations with hypothetical individuals who are one standard deviation below the mean (low) or one standard deviation above the mean (high). Reproduced from Woodman, Hardy, Zourbanos *et al.* (2010).

neurotic) athletes' decision making, but that the opposite effect emerged for neurotic individuals. For neurotic individuals, more accurate decision making occurred when response time was low, and less accurate decision making was evident when response time was high. Neurotic individuals are stimulus driven and easily consumed by worry (cf. Eysenck *et al.*). Thus, rapid decision making might prevent them from being consumed with so-called "cognitive noise" (Robinson and Tamir, 2005), which impairs their attentional control.

## Beyond the Big 5

These studies show that there is considerable utility in thinking about how personality might impact performance when taking an interactive approach. The Big 5 have potential in this regard. However, there are other personality variables that deserve specific mention in the context of sport because of their theoretical and applied potential. These variables include perfectionism, optimism, mental toughness, narcissism, and alexithymia. In the sections that follow we briefly review perfectionism, optimism, and mental toughness. We then provide a more detailed account of narcissism and alexithymia, as these are two personality variables that may not be so familiar to sport psychology researchers despite their considerable research and applied potential for sport performance.

## Perfectionism

Perfectionism is a multi-dimensional construct that is characterised by the setting of extremely high personal standards alongside harsh criticism of one's own behaviour (Frost et al., 1990; Hewitt and Flett, 1991). Perfectionism has typically been conceptualised in two different ways. First, the Frost et al. approach comprises six dimensions: personal standards, organisation, concern over mistakes, doubts about actions, parental expectations, and parental criticism. In contrast, Hewitt and Flett's conceptualisation comprises three components: self-oriented perfectionism, socially prescribed perfectionism, and other-oriented perfectionism. There is a growing consensus in the literature that the various aspects of perfectionism can be incorporated into two broad dimensions: *perfectionistic striving*, a dimension related to having high personal standards and striving for perfection; and *perfectionistic concerns*, a dimension related to highly critical self-evaluation (e.g. see Dunkley et al., 2003; Gaudreau and Thompson, 2011; Stoeber and Otto, 2006). In line with this conceptualisation, perfectionistic striving, in the absence of perfectionistic concerns, has been related to positive outcomes such as Olympic performance (Gould et al., 2002), confidence (Hall, et al., 1998), lower levels of anxiety (e.g. Gotwals et al., 2010), and effective coping (Gaudreau and Antl, 2003). However, the combination of perfectionistic striving and perfectionistic concerns is associated with a number of maladaptive outcomes including burnout (e.g. Hill, 2013), the 'yips' (Roberts et al., 2013a), high anxiety (Koivula et al., 2002), and depression (Rice and Mirzadeh, 2000). As with the majority of personality findings reported in the previous section, the relationship between perfectionism and performance appears best viewed through an interaction lens (see also Gaudreau and Thompson). Specifically, the research to date suggests that perfectionistic striving might be adaptive only to the degree that it is not accompanied by the seemingly "ugly sister" of perfectionistic concerns; in combination, the two perfectionist tendencies can be rather more destructive, both in terms of performance and wellbeing.

## Optimism

Optimism is associated with a generalised positive expectancy about life as opposed to the generalised negative expectancy associated with pessimism (Carver and Scheier, 1992). Although optimism has yet to see a significant amount of research in the sport and performance domain it has a long history of research in personality and social psychology. This literature has consistently demonstrated that, across a wide range of significant and debilitating stressors, optimism is associated with greater physical and psychological well-being. This relationship has been found with stressors such as: quality of life following bypass surgery (e.g. Scheier *et al.*, 1989); recovery from missile attacks (e.g. Zeider and Hamner, 1992); recovery from breast cancer (e.g. Carver *et al.*, 1993); and adjustment to college (e.g. Brisette *et al.*, 2002). The benefits of optimism in these situations appear to be, at least in part, the result of optimists' making more effective use of coping strategies, and matching the more appropriate coping strategy to the situation (see Carver *et al.*, 2010). The handful of studies that have investigated optimism in performance settings have yielded results that are consistent with the previous findings on stress. In sporting situations optimism has been positively correlated with problem focused coping (Gaudreau and Blondin, 2004; Grove and Heard, 1992) and negatively associated with avoidant coping strategies such as resignation (Nicholls *et al.*, 2010). There is also some evidence to suggest that optimism can exert an indirect effect on performance via the use of task-oriented coping strategies (Gaudreau and Blondin).

To the best of our knowledge, research has yet to examine directly whether optimism should be associated with optimal performance under pressure. However, from an interaction perspective, a consideration of the tenets of Attentional Control Theory (ACT) suggests that such a relationship might be plausible. ACT suggests that, anxiety may not always have a detrimental effect on performance if a performer is reasonably confident in his/her ability to perform. This is because anxiety leads to an increase in effort, and this increase in effort is responsible for a maintained or increased level of performance under pressure (see Wilson, 2008, for a review of ACT in relation to competition). Effort is often conceptualised as a task oriented coping strategy, and is used by optimists (e.g. Gaudreau and Blondin, 2004). As such, when under pressure, optimists are more likely to increase their effort in order to bring about a good performance. With this theoretically derived framework for the relationship between optimism and performance, we encourage researchers to consider more closely this personality variable in relation to sport performance.

### Mental toughness

The precise conceptualisation and measurement of mental toughness is the subject of considerable, and at times heated, debate in the literature (e.g. see Clough *et al.*, 2012; Gucciardi *et al.*, 2012, 2014; Hardy *et al.*, 2014). However, it is generally agreed that mental toughness reflects a stable disposition that is associated with an ability to deal with a wide variety of stressors and obstacles, and yet still perform at a high level under pressure (see Bell *et al.*, 2013; Gucciardi *et al.*, 2014). For example, mental toughness predicts high level performance (Bell *et al.*) and is associated with Olympic success (Jones *et al.*, 2002). Historically, mental toughness research has been plagued by problems associated with self-report measures and atheoretical approaches (see Crust, 2008). Though many personality variables use self-report questionnaires, the reliance on self-report seems to be particularly problematic for mental toughness, given its ubiquitous standing as a desirable characteristic. Although self-report measures still tend to dominate the mental toughness literature there is evidence that researchers are at least beginning to utilise theoretical frameworks to underpin their research. For example, Clough and colleagues (e.g. Clough *et al.*) have used the construct of hardiness, (e.g. see Maddi and Khoshaba, 1994) as the basis for their mental toughness conceptualisation, Gucciardi and colleagues (e.g. Gucciardi *et al.*, 2009) have utilized Personal Construct Theory (Kelley, 1955), and most recently Hardy and colleagues (Bell *et al.*; Hardy *et al.*) have used existing personality and neuroscience theory (Revised Reinforcement Sensitivity Theory; Gray and McNaughton, 2000) to examine mental toughness. Hardy *et al.*'s work appears to be particularly noteworthy here for three reasons. First, like the work of Clough and Gucciardi, it uses an appropriate theoretical framework in the form of Revised Reinforcement Sensitivity Theory. Second, it offers the first psychometrically valid informant-rated measure of mentally tough behaviour, thereby foregoing the need to rely on self-report measures that are employed by others. Third, this work focuses on mental toughness in terms of behavioural outcome as opposed to an underlying set of cognitions. This behavioural approach is an important advance because cognition-based approaches offer no evidence that mentally tough behaviour (i.e. the ability to excel under pressure) has actually occurred. In their work, Hardy *et al.* demonstrated that mentally tough performers were high in punishment sensitivity and low in reward sensitivity. They were able to use this sensitivity to punishment to pick up threats in the environment, plan a response to these threats, and then execute the plan effectively to maintain or enhance performance. Future work in this area, using theoretically grounded conceptualisations of mental toughness such as this, will likely help to unravel the complex relationship between mental toughness and performance.

*Narcissism*

In clinical settings, narcissism is defined as "a pervasive pattern of grandiosity, need for admiration, and a lack of empathy" (*Diagnostic and Statistical Manual of Mental Disorders*, 5th edn text revision; American Psychiatric Association, 2013, p. 669). Research in normal (i.e. subclinical) settings has revealed that narcissism is associated with a grandiose, yet fragile, self-view and feelings of entitlement (see Brown *et al.*, 2009; Morf and Rhodewalt, 2001). In this chapter, we use *narcissists* or *high narcissists* interchangeably to describe "relatively 'normal' people who simply possess more narcissistic qualities than others" (Wallace *et al.*, 2005, p. 436). Such individuals score relatively highly on valid self-report measures of narcissism such as Raskin and Hall's (1979) Narcissistic Personality Inventory (NPI), as opposed to individuals with the more extreme narcissistic personality disorder defined by the American Psychiatric Association. The term *low narcissist* is used to describe individuals with relatively low scores on such self-report measures.

### Narcissism and performance

Narcissists consider themselves to be special people who are superior to others (Gabriel *et al.*, 1994), report high levels of confidence (Campbell *et al.*, 2004), and are self-focused and vain (Morf and Rhodewalt, 2001). However, such grandiose beliefs are typically not supported by behavioural reality. For example, in performance contexts, narcissists most often do not perform any better or worse than low narcissists, despite believing (very sincerely in some cases) that they have performed to a higher level than their non-narcissistic counterparts (e.g. Gabriel *et al.*; John and Robins, 1997; Judge *et al.*, 2006). The exception to this rule comes from a seminal set of studies that have provided convincing evidence that narcissists do perform particularly well in some situations, yet poorly in others (Wallace and Baumeister, 2002). Wallace and Baumeister reasoned that the performance of narcissists would be dependent on the level of self-enhancement opportunity available in the task. Because narcissists are so focused on demonstrating their (perceived) talents to the world, they should be acutely aware that different situations provide them with differing opportunities to gain such personal glory (see Wallace, 2011). Wallace and Baumeister hypothesised that narcissists would perform very well in situations where self-enhancement opportunity was high (e.g. performing a task under pressure or in front of an audience, or receiving public recognition for performance) as opposed to low (e.g. performing an easy task in a non-stressful situation). Across four laboratory studies Wallace and Baumeister consistently demonstrated that narcissists performed well when self-enhancement was high, but poorly when it was low. In short, this research demonstrates that when narcissists perceive an opportunity for self-enhancement they tend to excel; when such an opportunity is absent, they tend to under-perform.

The sporting environment provides an excellent medium via which to examine the effects of narcissism on performance, as it provides at least two ecologically valid situations where opportunity for self-enhancement is more or less present – namely competition and training, respectively. In fact, one would expect narcissists – all other things being equal – to perform better in competition than in training. This is because competition provides a greater opportunity for personal glory than training.

Recent findings support this position; both laboratory and field studies have demonstrated that narcissists perform well in competitive, pressurised settings (e.g. Guekes et al., 2012; 2013; Roberts et al., 2010, Roberts et al., 2013b; Woodman et al., 2011). Thus there appears to be clear evidence that narcissists thrive when there is an opportunity for self-enhancement.

Less well understood are the mechanisms underlying these effects. Wallace and Baumeister (2002) hypothesised that an increase in effort might explain narcissists' performance increases, yet provided no evidence to support this view. To date, only Woodman et al. (2011) have examined the possible role that effort might play in the narcissism-performance relationship. In a team-cycling task, where participants were asked to cycle as far as possible in a ten-minute period, narcissists cycled over a kilometre farther, had significantly higher heart rates, and significantly higher ratings of perceived effort when their individual performance was made identifiable in comparison to when it was not. Although this study provides some evidence that effort is one of the mechanisms explaining the effects of narcissism on performance only physical effort was measured. Thus no consideration was given to the role of mental effort, which is likely to be an important mechanism, at least in some situations (cf. Wilson et al., 2007). The role of effort may also be more complex than previously suggested, as it may be the case that narcissists are simply more efficient, and are able to exert the right *quality* of effort at the right time. The consideration of the potential difference between effort quantity and effort quality is an important avenue for future research to more fully understand the role that effort plays in performance. Multidisciplinary approaches that incorporate psychological, physiological and neuromuscular responses (cf. Cooke et al., 2011) will be required to address meaningfully these questions. Further to effort, there are likely other mechanisms at play in the narcissism–performance relationship. For example, narcissists' greater sensitivity to rewards (Foster and Trimm, 2008; Foster et al., 2009) may lead to more favourable cognitive appraisals (e.g. "I love competing in front of a crowd") and perceptions of control (e.g. "I feel good"), which may help them to perform well when it matters most.

*Narcissism, training, and competition*

The effect of self-enhancement on narcissists' performance leads to some interesting research and applied implications. As narcissists typically perform well in competition, psychological skills that are designed to aid performance (e.g. imagery, goal setting, and relaxation) might be of little use for narcissists. In fact, narcissists may not see the need to use these skills in competition, because they are performing in an environment that they find inherently enjoyable. In contrast, these strategies might be particularly useful for low narcissists. Evidence suggests that low narcissists often choke under the pressure of competition (e.g. Wallace and Baumeister, 2002). Thus, the use of psychological skills might reduce the likelihood of pressure-induced performance decrements for low narcissists. A recent study has examined these possibilities. Roberts *et al.* (2013b) examined the interaction between narcissism and three psychological skills (self-talk, relaxation, and emotional control) on competitive performance in a sample of elite figure skaters. They hypothesised that narcissists would be expected to perform well regardless of their use of psychological skills whereas low narcissists were hypothesised to perform better the more they reported using these skills. Some support was generated for these hypotheses as emotional control had the expected benefit on low narcissists' performance (i.e. low narcissists who were able to control their emotions performed better than those who were not, see Figure 1.2, bottom). However, for self-talk and relaxation, the nature of the effects was precisely counter to the hypotheses. That is, increases in the use of relaxation were associated with increases in performance *only* for narcissists (see Figure 1.2, top). Furthermore, increases in the use of self-talk were associated with an *increase* in performance for narcissists and a *decrease* in performance for low narcissists (see Figure 1.2 middle). It is clear from these findings that narcissism does impact the effectiveness of psychological skills and that "one size does not fit all" when it comes to psychological skills training. In other words, personality effects how beneficial psychological skills are likely to be for a performer. We return to this issue at the end of the chapter.

A question that has important applied value is: in order to further enhance their potential in competition, how can a coach get the best out of narcissists in situations that are important and yet lack an opportunity for self-enhancement (e.g. training)? Training provides very little, if any, opportunity for self-enhancement, yet it is where athletes spend 99 per cent of their time (McCann, 1995). In addition the quality of an athlete's training has a substantial impact on performance (Gould *et al.*, 2002; Hardy *et al.*, 1996). As such, narcissists might not be expected to work as hard as they might do in pressured situations (where the perceived value of their performance increases). Thus, establishing how best to maximise narcissists' training performance is certainly a worthwhile research avenue.

As coaches play a significant role in shaping how athletes perform (Gould *et al.*, 2002) considering the effects of coaching styles on the behaviour of narcissists, particularly in training, is worthwhile. Research in this area is limited, but there is some evidence to suggest that narcissists prefer different coaching styles to low narcissists. More specifically, Arthur *et al.* (2011) found that coach behaviours aimed at fostering a collective sense of unity within a group were not particularly effective for narcissists (although these behaviours did increase the effort of low narcissistic individuals). In contrast, coach behaviours that focused on treating athletes as individuals led to increases in

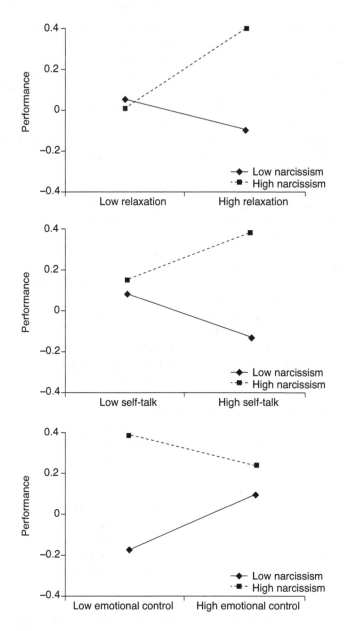

*Figure 1.2* Interactions between relaxation and narcissism (top), self-talk and narcissism (middle), and emotional control and narcissism (bottom), on performance. Regression slopes are derived from regression equations with hypothetical individuals who are one standard deviation below the mean (low) or one standard deviation above the mean (high). Performance refers to the difference between training and competition scores (higher scores indicate better performance in competition). Reproduced from Roberts *et al.* (2013b).

effort for low and high narcissists alike. Such findings provide a starting point to consider how coaches might influence narcissists' behaviour, especially to get the best out of them in situations where they might not normally be expected to perform well. In particular, because of their self-focused nature, narcissists are more likely to benefit from individually-focused coach behaviours, as opposed to ones that are directed a group as a whole. Further, narcissists' relentless pursuit of self-enhancement may see them respond more favourably to motivational climates that involve competition and ego-involvement as opposed to those that are task focused and emphasise the importance of self-referenced mastery (cf. Newton et al., 2000), as such ego-involving climates are likely to be more self-enhancing for the narcissist. Future research in this area is warranted to more fully understand the impact of coaching styles on narcissists' behaviour.

*The two faces of narcissism*

We have so far presented narcissism as a one-dimensional personality construct that is associated with a grandiose sense of self, which is often captured through the use of the NPI (the most widely used measure of narcissism in the social psychology literature). However, it is well established that there are two components of narcissism: narcissistic grandiosity and narcissistic vulnerability (see Campbell and Miller, 2011, for a review). What is not clear is whether these two components of narcissism are *two sides of the same coin* (i.e. the grandiose behaviours that narcissists display stem from a vulnerable core self-concept) or whether they are in fact *two different coins* with different underlying aetiologies. Considerable debate exists within the literature regarding the validity of each of these stances (e.g. Campbell and Miller; Morf and Rhodewalt, 2001; Ronningstam, 2011). However, regardless of these varying theoretical positions, most narcissism researchers agree that a more complete understanding of narcissism is only possible when both aspects of the construct are measured. Considering that the literature cited so far almost exclusively used the NPI as the measure of narcissism, it would be more appropriate to view this literature in terms of narcissistic grandiosity rather than narcissism per se. Although research has examined grandiosity and vulnerability in relation to various outcomes such as approach and avoidance motivation (Foster and Trimm, 2008), self-esteem (Zeigler-Hill *et al.*, 2008), and interpersonal behaviour (e.g. Miller *et al.*, 2011), no research has examined how grandiosity and vulnerability together predict performance. The impact of grandiosity and vulnerability on performance needs to be examined to ascertain the degree to which they exert independent or interactive effects. While grandiose narcissism appears clearly and positively associated with performance under pressure (e.g. Roberts *et al.*, 2013b; Wallace and Baumeister, 2002; Woodman *et al.*, 2011), grandiosity on its own might be unlikely to lead to the highest levels of performance.

Performing well under pressure offers an opportunity for the narcissist to buffer their fragile self-concept and so vulnerability might be the catalyst to achieving the highest levels of performance Therefore, performance might be best when both grandiosity and vulnerability are high as a result of the underlying fragility driving the narcissist to achieve the highest levels of performance. We encourage researchers to consider the effects of both grandiosity and vulnerability on performance, and the underlying mechanisms behind such performance effects, as these remain exciting research questions for this subject area.

### Alexithymia

Alexithymia refers to a trait deficit in emotion regulation (Mikolajczak and Luminet, 2006). Derived from the Greek for lack of (prefix "a-") words ("lex") for feelings ("thymia") and initially derived from clinical observations, alexithymia is characterised by the absence of words to express one's emotions and is typically viewed as a difficulty in acknowledging emotions and feelings coupled with an inability to express them to others (Sifneos, 1972; Taylor *et al.*, 1997). A substantial literature supports the relationship between alexithymia and a number of variables relating to poor mental health and emotion regulation including anxiety and depression (Corcos and Speranza, 2003; Lumley *et al.*, 1996), as well as difficulties in interpersonal relationships (Taylor *et al.*, 1997).

Recently, research in the performance domain has demonstrated that alexithymia appears to be a key antecedent of risk taking behaviours. More specifically, expeditionary mountaineers and ocean rowers, who spend considerable periods of time away from home, are higher in alexithymia in comparison to both population norms and matched control groups (Woodman, Hardy, Barlow *et al.*, 2010). In addition, skydivers high in alexithymia demonstrate higher state anxiety prior to jumps than their non-alexithymic counterparts (Woodman *et al.*, 2008, 2009a).

However, more importantly, this research demonstrates that more alexithymic individuals derive emotion regulation benefits as a result of engaging with high-risk sport. Woodman, Hardy, Barlow *et al.* (2010) reported that mountaineers and ocean rowers had greater difficulties in emotionally laden relationships (e.g. loving relationships) before expeditions, but felt better able to deal with these relationships post expedition. Furthermore, although the alexithymic skydivers in Woodman *et al.*'s (2008, 2009a) studies reported higher levels of anxiety before their jumps, they also enjoyed a greater reduction in anxiety after their jump compared to their non-alexithymic counterparts.

From a theoretical perspective, Fenichel's (1939) work on the counterphobic attitude provides a potential explanation for the emotion regulation benefits of high-risk environments. Fenichel suggested risk-taking environments provide an emotion regulation benefit because they allow the individual to experience, and subsequently to control, anxiety (hence why it is counter phobic; the individual actively seeks it out). Indeed, for individuals who have difficulty expressing their emotions in general, emotions such as anxiety are more easily identifiable in a risk-taking environment (being high up on an exposed ridge in the Himalaya in poor weather) than in another domain of life such as interpersonal relationships (Woodman, Hardy, Barlow *et al.*, 2010). According to Fenichel, most individuals experience generalised and internalised anxiety but are unable to identify the origin of that anxiety. Thus, risk-taking provides an opportunity to initiate and then to experience a very explicit and identifiable form of anxiety, with a view to mastering that anxiety-provoking situation and thus gaining a relative sense of well-being (i.e. a reduction in anxiety).

*Implications for performance*

The stressful nature of the competitive environment likely has a degree of similarity with the stressful nature of high-risk environments, which leads to the intriguing possibility that alexithymic individuals may be drawn to competitive settings. Indeed, although the competitive environment is not at the life-threatening end of the risk environment, the competitor's ego is under threat. That is, whereas in the high-risk activity domain the person's body is directly at risk, in the competitive sport domain the person's ego is at risk as evidenced by competitive state anxiety. Thus, competition environments may provide a pathway for gaining emotion regulation benefits, by experiencing high levels of anxiety, and then controlling that anxiety. To the best of our knowledge, despite its potential application in competitive environments, alexithymia research in sport has been limited to the high-risk domain. For example, it is well known that anxiety follows a specific temporal pattern, whereby it increases prior to performance (see Hanton *et al.*, 2004). Considering this effect alongside the anxiety responses in Woodman *et al.*'s (2008, 2009a) skydiving studies, it is possible that any pre-competition increases in anxiety would be further accentuated in alexithymics.

However, perhaps more interestingly, it is also possible that the performance of alexithymics might be less affected by high levels of anxiety. The stress and performance literature in sport has consistently demonstrated that anxiety can significantly impair performance (e.g. Hardy *et al.*, 1996; Wilson, 2008), although there appear to be a number of moderators of this effect including: confidence, perceptions of control, and cognitive appraisal (see Mellalieu *et al.*, 2006; Woodman and Hardy, 2001). Conversely, the exploration of personality and individual differences as moderators of the anxiety-performance relationship is unexplored research territory. However, alexithymics might rather enjoy the experience of, and subsequent control over, competitive anxiety, much like participants of some high-risk sports. In other words, alexithymics may appraise and approach stressful competition situations rather positively. As a result of these positive appraisals, they may subsequently perform well under pressure. Further, alexithymics' difficulty in describing emotions might also actually serve a direct performance benefit. That is, performing under pressure requires the effective control of emotions (Hardy *et al.*, 1996; Woodman *et al.*, 2009b) and individuals who have a somewhat blunted emotional response might in fact be in a better position to push themselves to the limits of their body. This opens up the intriguing possibility that a difficulty with emotion regulation (alexithymia) – which in normal circumstances would be somewhat of a hindrance (e.g. in personal relationships) – may in fact be transformed into an advantage in the high-pressure competition domain.

The potential "benefits" of alexithymia in relation to competitive environments may also mask a potentially more serious risk for such individuals. That is, the sense of well-being that is garnered from engaging in the high-risk activity appears to be only short-lived. For example, in Woodman *et al.*'s (2008) study with skydivers, although anxiety significantly dropped immediately following the jump, one hour later it had significantly risen back toward pre jump levels. In line with Fenichel's (1939) theoretical position this would be expected because the underlying cause of the alexithymic's difficulty with emotions has not been via the emotion-provoking situation; it has been addressed only as a proxy – the individual hasn't faced the underlying cause of his/her anxiety. As the high-anxiety environment serves only as a proxy for the confronting anxiety, the high-anxiety environment might become somewhat of a necessary "fix" for gleaning a sense of self. As such, alexithymics might continue to seek out stressful environments in order to gain emotion regulation benefits, and it is not known the extent to which this might have a negative impact, particularly on one's health. For example, given their need to experience emotion, alexithymics might be more likely to continue playing whilst ill or injured, thereby making any injuries worse and/or hampering the physical and psychological recovery from injury (cf. Evans and Hardy, 2002; Evans *et al.*, 2012). Furthermore, one can imagine how alexithymics might be tempted to take on more and more arduous types of sports (e.g. stepping up from a marathon to an ultra-marathon or 100-mile race) in order to continually experience anxiety, which might eventually become problematic to their health. We would encourage researchers to consider these types of questions in the future.

### The future for personality: research and applied implications

We believe personality plays a substantial role in performance. Referring back to Lewin's (1936) interactional approach to understanding behaviour, significant strides have been made in the sport psychology literature understanding the environmental impact on performance (as other chapters in this book demonstrate), yet the potential impact of the person or the interaction between the person and the environment has been lagging by comparison. We end with some final thoughts about the future for personality research (and applied work), and provide a summary of these thoughts in Table 1.1.

First, to avoid the limitations of the first wave of personality research it is imperative that the next wave of personality research be theoretically driven. Utilising theory to understand which personality variables might impact performance, in what way they might impact performance (i.e. a main and/or interactive effect), and why such impact might occur is key in this respect. Not all personality variables are likely to have the same effect on performance. Certainly, not all variables will affect performance by the same mechanisms. Therefore, teasing out particular individual effects is important. In this regard we believe there is a need to go beyond the simple trait approach espoused by the Big 5, to consider personality variables that have a strong theoretical basis, and to consider the inter-action between personality traits and between personality and environmental factors.

Despite their popularity, broad trait approaches to personality do not offer a comprehensive theoretical explanation for how such traits are developed and how they shape a person. The early personality theorists such as Freud, Adler, and Jung, considered the individual's development through early childhood, adolescence and adulthood, as they believed that early experiences shaped later thoughts and behaviours. In fact, such theories of "learning" are still prevalent today (cf. Bandura, 1986). However, many researchers became uncomfortable with subject matter of the research (i.e. Freud's focus on psychosexual development) and

*Table 1.1* Summary of the key issues for the future of personality in performance contexts

1  Personality research needs to be theoretically driven, utilising variables that have a strong theoretical basis.

2  Framing research questions in terms of person × environment interactions will likely be more fruitful than examining simple main effects between personality and particular performance-related outcomes. In this regard, considering how personality moderates the efficacy of psychological skills and also coaching behaviours has great relevance for researchers and applied practitioners alike.

3  Studies that investigate single personality variables in depth provide an opportunity to develop a deep understanding of the mechanisms underlying that variable.

4  There is potentially great value in incorporating multiple personality variables into the same model providing that researchers have a strong, theoretically derived, rationale for how these variables should interrelate.

gradually research started to move away from trying to understand individuals toward trait-based approaches. We believe that trying to understand a person by considering only five facets of their personality, although useful, will always be limited as this fails to consider what makes them individual and how they came to think and behave the way they do. Consequently, we encourage researchers to think beyond the Big 5, to consider personality variables with a strong theoretical basis, and to seek to understand the person more comprehensively.

Of the other personality variables that we have covered in this chapter, most have a strong theoretical basis. That is, a considerable body of work exists regarding the development of perfectionism (e.g. see Hewitt and Flett, 2002), narcissism (e.g. Kohut, 1977; Kernberg, 1977; Otway and Vignoles, 2006), and alexithymia (e.g. Taylor and Bagby, 2013) as a result of difficulties in childhood, and more specifically, in terms of difficulties in parent–child interactions. Although the precise nature of childhood experiences differ among these variables, they all share a degree of commonality in terms of parents not meeting their children's needs in some form or another. For example, narcissism develops as a result of either too much or not enough parental love (see Otway and Vignoles, 2006, for a useful overview). Perfectionism theorists have described the development of perfectionism in terms of a reaction to parental expectations or social learning (see Sapieja *et al.*, 2011, for a recent examination of the impact of parenting on the development of perfectionism in sport), and alexithymia develops as a result of insecure attachments and childhood trauma (see Taylor and Bagby, 2013, for a recent review). While parent–child difficulties have not been implicated in the development of optimism, parental behaviours do appear to be important. More specifically, Seligman and colleagues (e.g. Seligman *et al.*, 1995) have argued that children can develop optimistic beliefs by role modelling (optimistic) parental behaviour.

In contrast to the aforementioned personality variables, mental toughness has yet to receive research attention on its aetiology. However, the recent utilisation of Reinforcement Sensitivity Theory (Hardy *et al.*, 2014) as a theoretical basis for the construct helps to highlight the role of conditioning to various appetitive and aversive stimuli in the development of reward and punishment sensitivities (see Corr, 2008 for a review of RST), which might help to shed some light on how mental toughness might be developed. In addition, recent research (Lombardo *et al.*, 2012) has implicated foetal testosterone in the development of the reward system and approach related behaviour, which has potential implications for understanding how mental toughness is developed. Further work examining the development of mental toughness is certainly worthwhile.

The second issue to be considered in future research concerns the examination of personality variables in isolation or in combination. There is real merit in delving into specific personality variables in order to develop a fine-grained understanding of their mechanisms. However, performance is a multifaceted construct, and so multiple personality variables may well be "competing" at the same time to impact performance. Considering personality variables in combination may help to develop a comprehensive understanding of personality's effect on performance (see, for example, Castanier *et al.*, 2010; Otten, 2009, as examples of this approach) although this approach does run the risk of being subject to the problems associated with the early personality research unless genuinely theoretically-derived hypotheses are developed. Therefore we would suggest researchers be mindful of this potential issue, and develop theoretically sound questions if they take examine multiple personality variables in combination.

Third, the impact of personality on the efficacy of psychological skills (e.g. imagery, goal-setting) has great potential in both research and applied settings. From the data available in the literature it is clear that psychological skills are not equally effective for everyone, and can sometimes even negatively affect performance. This seriously questions the "one size fits all" approach to psychological skills training that seems to be the underpinning philosophical approach in many applied sport psychology interventions and texts (e.g. Williams, 2001; Weinberg and Gould, 2007). However, the evidence base, while consistent, is not exhaustive, and thus more work needs to be carried out to examine personality's influence on psychological skills, and when (but also why) various skills might be more or less effective. For example, we do not know whether various functions of self-talk might serve greater benefits for some people than others. Specifically, pessimistic individuals may find mastery of forms of self-talk particularly beneficial in dealing with stress; alternatively the use of these types of self-talk might have the paradoxical effect of increasing stress levels. Further, alexithymia is associated with reduced imagery ability (Mantani *et al.*, 2006), and so alexithymics may benefit more from verbal strategies than imaginal ones. These are just a few of the myriad of research questions that remain unexplored. We believe that researchers and practitioners interested in psychological skills certainly stand to learn a great deal by giving thought to the role of personality.

At an applied level, we echo the views of practitioners who advocate the importance of treating clients as individuals, building effective relationships with them, and developing interventions based on their specific needs (e.g. Fifer *et al.*, 2008), as opposed to taking a "one size fits all" approach to applied sport psychology consultancy. Individualised approaches might entail the practitioner spending more time getting to know the clients in detail, and trying to understand the sorts of personality characteristics of their clients, or a more selective and well thought out use of particular techniques available to the applied practitioner. To be clear, we are not suggesting that applied practitioners assess their clients with a myriad of personality measures, indeed athletes are known to hate paperwork (see Beckmann and Kellmann, 2003). Rather, establishing real trust and rapport through interviews, observations, and discussions with significant others can help to understand the athlete more fully.

We realise that our recommendations regarding consultancy are not new. For example, Rogers' (1957) now seminal work on humanistic approaches to counselling is based on the development of effective working relationships between clients and practitioners. In addition, the work of the most effective sport psychologists is built entirely around effective working relationships between clients and consultants (e.g. Fifer *et al.*, 2008; Giges and Petitpas, 2000). However, because such an approach takes time, it might be seen as the "difficult option", particularly for newly qualified practitioners wishing to be seen as effective (cf. Holt and Stream, 2001), given the desire for immediate impact that seems to dictate elite sport in the present day. Furthermore, this approach is perhaps not suited to the workshop format that many applied practitioners might have available to them. Nonetheless, it sits much more comfortably with the idea of athletes as individuals, rather than athletes as commodities.

## Conclusions

There is a wonderful opportunity for sport psychology researchers who are interested in performance to generate the next wave of knowledge of the role of personality in performance contexts. Given that sports men and women are people first and athletes second, spending more (research and applied) time thinking about the person that exists behind the athlete can only serve to help to advance our (psychological) understanding of the person and the link with the resultant performance.

## References

Allen, M. S., Greenlees, I., and Jones, M. (2011). An investigation of the five-factor model of personality and coping behaviour in sport. *Journal of Sports Sciences*, 29, 841–850.

Allen, M. S., Greenlees, I., and Jones, M. (2013). Personality in sport: A comprehensive review. *International Review of Sport and Exercise Psychology*, 6, 184–208.

American Psychiatric Association (2013). *Diagnostic and statistical manual of mental disorders (5th edn)*. Washington DC: Author.

Arthur, C. A., Woodman, T., Ong, C. W., Hardy, L., and Ntoumanis, N. (2011). The role of athlete narcissism in moderating the relationship between coaches' transformational leader behaviours and athlete motivation. *Journal of Sport and Exercise Psychology*, 33, 3–19.

Bandura, A. (1986). *Social foundations of thought and action: A social cognitive theory*. Englewood Cliffs, NJ: Prentice-Hall.

Barrick, M. R., Mount, M. K., and Judge, T. A. (2001). Personality and performance at the beginning of the new millennium: What do we know and where do we go next? *International Journal of Selection and Assessment*, 9, 9–30.

Barrick, M. R., Stewart, G. L., Neubert, M. J., and Mount, M. K. (1998). Relating member ability and personality to work-team processes and team effectiveness. *Journal of Applied Psychology*, 83, 43–51.

Beauchamp, M. R., Jackson, B. S., and Lavallee, D. (2007). Personality processes and intragroup dynamics in sport teams. In M. R. Beauchamp and M. A. Eys (eds), *Group dynamics in exercise and sport psychology* (pp. 25–41). London: Routledge.

Beckmann, J. and Kellmann, M. (2003). Procedures and principles of sport psychological assessment. *The Sport Psychologist*, 17, 338–350.

Bell, J. J., Hardy, L., and Beattie, S. (2013). Enhancing mental toughness and performance under pressure in elite young cricketers: A 2-year longitudinal intervention. *Sport, Exercise, and Performance Psychology*, 2, 281–297.

Bell, J. J., Mawn, L., and Poynor, R. (2013). Haste makes waste but not for all: The speed-accuracy trade-off does not apply to neurotics. *Psychology of Sport and Exercise*, 14, 860–864.

Brissette, I., Scheier, M. F., and Carver, C. S. (2002). The role of optimism in social network development, coping, and psychological adjustment during a life transition. *Journal of Personality and Social Psychology*, 82, 102–111.

Brown, R. P., Budzek, K., and Tamborski, M. (2009). On the measure and meaning of narcissism. *Personality and Social Psychology Bulletin*, 35, 951–964.

Campbell, W. K. and Miller, J. D. (2011). Narcissism and narcissistic personality disorder. Six suggestions for unifying the field. In W. K. Campbell and J. D. Miller (eds), *The handbook of narcissism and narcissistic personality disorder* (pp. 485–488). Hoboken NJ: John Wiley and Sons, Inc.

Campbell, W. K., Goodie, A. S., and Foster, J. D. (2004). Narcissism, confidence, and risk attitude. *Journal of Behavioural Decision Making*, 17, 297–311.

Carver, C. S. and Connor-Smith, J. (2010). Personality and coping. *Annual Review of Psychology*, 61, 679–704.

Carver, C. S., Pozo, C., Harris, S. D., Noriega, V., Scheier, M. F., Robinson, D. S., *et al.* (1993). How coping mediates the effect of optimism on distress: A study of women with early stage breast cancer. *Journal of Personality and Social Psychology*, 65, 375–390.

Carver, C. S., Scheier, M. F., and Segerstrom, S. C. (2010). Optimism. *Clinical Psychology Review*, 30, 879–889.

Castanier C., Le Scanff C., and Woodman T. (2010). Who takes risks in high-risk sports? A typological personality approach. *Research Quarterly for Exercise and Sport*, 81, 478–484.

Cervone, D. and Pervin, L. A. (2013). *Personality: Theory and research* (12th ed). Hoboken NJ: John Wiley and Sons Inc.

Clough, P., Earle, K., Perry, J. L., and Crust, L. (2012). Comment on "Progressing measurement in mental toughness: A case example of the Mental Toughness Questionnaire 48" by Gucciardi, Hanton, and Mallett (2012). *Sport, Exercise, and Performance Psychology*, 1, 283–287.

Connor-Smith, J. K. and Flachsbart, C. (2007). Relations between personality and coping: A meta-analysis. *Journal of Applied Psychology*, 93, 1080–1107.

Cooke, A., Kavussanu, M., McIntyre, D., Boardley, I. D., and Ring, C. (2011). Effects of competitive pressure on expert performance: Underlying psychological, physiological, and kinematic mechanisms. *Psychophysiology*, 48, 1146–1156.

Corcos, M. and Speranza, M. (2003). *Psychopathologie de l'alexithymie*. Paris: Dunod. [Psychopathology of alexithymia].

Corr, P. J. (2008). *The reinforcement sensitivity theory of personality.* Cambridge: Cambridge University Press.

Costa, P. T., Jr. and McCrae, R. R. (1992). Four ways five factors are basic. *Personality and Individual Differences,* 13, 653–665.

Crust, L. (2008). A review and conceptual re-examination of mental toughness: Implications for future researchers. *Personality and Individual Differences,* 45, 576–583.

Davis, C. and Mogk, J. P. (1994). Some personality correlates of interest and excellence in sport. *International Journal of Sport Psychology,* 25, 131–143.

DeYoung, C. G., Hirsch, J. B., Shane, M. S., Papademetris, X., Rajeevan, N., and Gray, J. R. (2010). Testing predictions from personality neuroscience: Brain structure and the Big Five. *Psychological Science,* 21, 820–828.

Dunkley, D. M., Zuroff, D. C., and Blankstein, K. R. (2003). Self-critical perfectionism and daily affect: Dispositional and situational influences on stress and coping. *Journal of Personality and Social Psychology,* 84, 234–252.

Egan, S. and Stelmack, R. M. (2003). A personality profile of Mount Everest climbers. *Personality and Individual. Differences,* 34, 1491–1494.

Evans, L. and Hardy, L. (2002). Injury rehabilitation: A qualitative follow-up study. *Research Quarterly for Exercise and Sport,* 73, 320–329.

Evans, L., Wadey, R., Hanton, S., and Mitchell, I. (2012). Stressors experienced by injured athletes. *Journal of Sports Sciences,* 30, 917–927.

Eysenck, H. J. and Eysenck, M. W. (1985). *Personality and individual differences: A natural science approach.* New York: Plenum Press.

Eysenck, M. W., Derakshan, N., Santos, R., and Calvo, M. G. (2007). Anxiety and cognitive performance: attentional control theory. *Emotion,* 7, 336–353.

Eysenck, M. W., Nias, D. K., and Cox, D. N. (1982). Sport and personality. *Advances in Behavioural Research and Therapy,* 4, 1–56.

Fenichel, O. (1939). The counter-phobic attitude. *International Journal of Psychoanalysis,* 20, 263–274.

Ferguson, E. (2013). Personality is of central concern to understand health: towards a theoretical model for health psychology. *Health Psychology Review,* 7, S32–S70.

Fifer, A. M., Henschen, K., Gould, D., and Ravizza, K. (2008). What works when working with athletes. *The Sport Psychologist,* 22, 356–377.

Foster, J. D. and Trimm, R. F. (2008). On being eager and uninhibited: Narcissism and approach-avoidance motivation. *Personality and Social Psychology Bulletin,* 34, 1004–1017.

Foster, J. D., Misra, T. A., and Reidy, D. E. (2009). Narcissists are approach-oriented toward their money and their friends. *Journal of Research in Personality,* 43, 764–769.

Frost, R. O., Marten, P., Lahart, C., and Rosenblate, R. (1990). The dimensions of perfectionism. *Cognitive Therapy and Research,* 14, 449–468.

Gabriel, M. T., Critelli, J. W., and Ee, J. S. (1994). Narcissistic illusions in self-evaluations of intelligence and attractiveness. *Journal of Personality,* 62, 143–155.

Gaudreau, P. and Antl, S. (2008). Athletes' broad dimensions of dispositional perfectionism: Examining changes in life satisfaction and the mediating role of sport-related motivation and coping. *Journal of Sport and Exercise Psychology,* 30, 356–382.

Gaudreau, P. and Blondin, J. P. (2004). Differential associations of dispositional optimism and pessimism with coping, goal attainment, and emotional adjustment during sport competition. *International Journal of Stress Management*, 11, 245–269.

Gaudreau, P. and Thompson, A. (2010). Testing a 2×2 model of dispositional perfectionism. *Personality and Individual Differences*, 48, 532–537.

Giges, B. and Petitpas, A. J. (2000). Brief contact interventions in sport psychology. *The Sport Psychologist*, 14, 176–187.

Gill, D. L. and Williams, L. (2008). *Psychological dynamics of sport and exercise* (3rd edn). Champaign, IL: Human Kinetics.

Goldberg, L. R. (1992). The development of markers for the Big-Five factor structure. *Psychological Assessment*, 4, 26–42.

Gotwals, J. K., Dunn, J. G. H., Causgrove-Dunn, J., and Gamache, V. (2010). Establishing validity evidence for the sport multidimensional perfectionism scale-2 in intercollegiate sport. *Psychology of Sport and Exercise*, 11, 423–432.

Gould, D., Dieffenbach, K., and Moffett, A. (2002). Psychological characteristics and their development in Olympic champions. *Journal of Applied Sport Psychology*, 14, 172–204.

Gould, D., Greenleaf, C., Chung, Y., and Guinan, D. (2002). A survey of US Atlanta and Nagano Olympians: Variables perceived to influence performance. *Research Quarterly for Exercise and Sport*, 73, 175–186.

Gray, J. A. (1970). The psychophysiological basis of introversion-extraversion. *Behaviour Research and Therapy*, 8, 249–266.

Gray, J. A. and McNaughton, N. (2000). *The Neuropsychology of anxiety: An enquiry into the functions of the septo-hippocampal system*. Oxford University Press, Oxford, UK.

Grove, J. R., and Heard, N. P. (1997). Optimism and sport confidence as correlates of slump-related coping among athletes. *The Sport Psychologist*, 11, 400–410.

Gucciardi, D. F., Gordon, S., and Dimmock, J. A. (2009). Advancing mental toughness research and theory using personal construct psychology. *International Review of Sport and Exercise Psychology*, 2, 54–72.

Gucciardi, D. F., Hanton, S., and Mallett, C. J. (2012). Progressing measurement in mental toughness: A case example of the Mental Toughness Questionnaire-48. *Sport, Exercise, and Performance Psychology*, 1, 194–214.

Gucciardi, D. F., Hanton, S., Gordon, S., Mallett, C. J., and Temby, P. (2014). The concept of mental toughness: Tests of dimensionality, nomological network, and traitness. *Journal of Personality*. Advance online publication.

Guekes, K., Mesagno, C., Hanrahan, S. J., and Kellmann, M. (2012). Testing an interactionist perspective on the relationship between personality traits and performance under public pressure. *Psychology of Sport and Exercise*, 13, 243–250.

Guekes, K., Mesagno, C., Hanrahan, S. J., and Kellmann, M. (2013). Activation of self-focus and self-presentation traits under private, mixed, and public pressure. *Journal of Sport and Exercise Psychology*, 35, 50–59.

Hall, H. K., Kerr, A. W., and Matthews, J. (1998). Precompetitive anxiety in sport: The contribution of achievement goals and perfectionism. *Journal of Sport and Exercise Psychology*, 20, 194–217.

Hanton, S., Thomas, O., and Maynard, I. (2004). Competitive anxiety responses in the week leading up to competition: The role of intensity, direction and frequency dimensions. *Psychology of Sport and Exercise*, 15, 169–181.

Hardy, L., Bell, J. J., and Beattie, S. (2014). A neuropsychological model of mentally tough behaviour. *Journal of Personality*, 82, 69–81.

Hardy, L., Jones, J. G., and Gould, D. (1996). *Understanding psychological preparation for sport: Theory and practice of elite performers.* Chichester: John Wiley.

Hewitt, P. L. and Flett, G. L. (1991). Perfectionism in the self and social contexts: Conceptualisation, assessment, and association with psychopathology. *Journal of Personality and Social Psychology*, 60, 456–470.

Hewitt, P. L. and Flett, G. L. (2002). Perfectionism and stress processes in psychopathology. In G. L. Flett and P. L. Hewitt (eds), *Perfectionism: Theory, research, and treatment* (pp. 255–284). Washington: American Psychological Association.

Hilbig, E. (2008). Individual differences in fast-and-frugal decision-making: Neuroticism and the recognition heuristic. *Journal of Research in Personality*, 42, 1641–1645.

Hill, A. P. (2013). Perfectionism and burnout in junior soccer players: A test of the 2×2 model of dispositional perfectionism. *Journal of Sport and Exercise Psychology*, 35, 18–29.

Holt, N. L. and Strean, W. B. (2001). Reflecting on initiating sport psychology consultation: A self-narrative of neophyte practice. *The Sport Psychologist*, 15, 188–204.

Horney, K. (1973). *The neurotic personality of our time.* New York: Norton.

Jones, G., Hanton, S., and Connaughton, D. (2002). What is this thing called mental toughness? An investigation of elite sport performers. *Journal of Applied Sport Psychology*, 14, 205–218.

Judge, T. A., LePine, J. A., and Rich, B. L. (2006). Loving yourself abundantly: Relationship of the narcissistic personality to self-and other perceptions of workplace deviance, leadership, and task and contextual performance. *Journal of Applied Psychology*, 91, 762–776.

Judge, T. A., Piccolo, R. F., and Kosalka, T. (2003). The bright and dark sides of leader traits: A review and theoretical extension of the leader trait paradigm. *The Leadership Quarterly*, 20, 855–875.

Kaiseler, M., Polman, R. C. J., and Nicholls, A. R. (2012). Effects of the big five personality dimensions on appraisal coping, and coping effectiveness in sport. *European Journal of Sport Science*, 12, 62–72.

Kernberg, O. F. (1975). *Borderline conditions and pathological narcissism.* New York: Aronson.

Kohut, H. (1977). *The restoration of the self.* Madison, CT: International Universities Press.

Koivula, N., Hassmén, P., and Fallby, J. (2002). Self-esteem and perfectionism in elite athletes: effects on competitive anxiety and self-confidence. *Personality and Individual Differences*, 32, 865–875.

Lewin, K. (1936) *Principles of topological psychology.* New York: McGraw-Hill.

Lombardo, M. V., Ashwin, E., Auyeun, B., Chakrabarti, B., Lai, M. C., Taylor, K., *et al.* (2012). Fetal programming effects of testosterone on the reward system and behavioural approach tendencies in humans. *Biological Psychiatry*, 72, 839–847.

Lumley, M. A., Stettner, L., and Wehmer, F. (1996). How are alexithymia and physical illness linked? A review and critique of pathways. *Journal of Psychosomatic Research*, 41, 505–518.

Maddi, S. R., and Khoshaba, D. M. (1994). Hardiness and mental health. *Journal of Personality Assessment*, 63, 265–274.

Mantani, T., Okamoto, Y., Shirao, N., Okada, G., and Yamawaki, S. (2005). Reduced activation of posterior cingulated cortex during imagery in subjects with high degrees of alexithymia: A functional magnetic resonance imaging study. *Biological Psychiatry*, 57, 982–990.

McCann, S. (1995). Overtraining and burnout. In S. M. Murphy (ed.), *Sport psychology interventions* (pp. 347–368). Champaign, IL: Human Kinetics.

McNair, D. M., Lorr, M., and Droppleman, L. (1971). *Manual for the Profile of Mood States*. San Diego, CA: Educational and Industrial Testing Service.

Mellalieu, S. D., Hanton, S., and Fletcher, D. (2006). A competitive anxiety review: Recent directions in sport psychology research. In S. Hanton and S. D. Mellalieu, (eds). *Literature reviews in sport psychology* (pp. 1–45). Hauppauge, NY: Nova Science.

Mikolajczak, M. and Luminet, O. (2006). Is alexithymia affected by situational stress or is it a stable trait related to emotion regulation? *Personality and Individual Differences*, 40, 1399–1408.

Miller, J. D., Hoffman, B. J., Gaughan, E. T., Gentile, B., Maples, J., and Campbell, W. K. (2011). Grandiose and vulnerable narcissism: A nomological network analysis. *Journal of Personality*, 79, 1013–1042.

Morf, C. C. and Rhodewalt, F. (2001). Unravelling the paradoxes of narcissism: A dynamic self-regulatory processing model. *Psychological Inquiry*, 12, 177–196.

Morgan, W. P. (1980). Trait psychology controversy. *Research Quarterly for Exercise and Sport*, *51*, 50–76.

Newton, M., Duda, J. and Yin, Z. (2000). Examination of the psychometric properties of the perceived motivational climate in sport questionnaire-2 in a sample of female athletes. *Journal of Sports Sciences*, 18, 275–290.

Nicholls, A. R., Polman, R. C. J., Levy, A. R., and Backhouse, S. H. (2008). Mental toughness, optimism, pessimism, and coping among athletes. *Personality and Individual Differences*, 44, 1182–1192.

Otten, M. (2009). Choking vs. clutch performance: A study of sport performance under pressure. *Journal of Sport and Exercise Psychology*, 31, 583–601.

Otway, L. J. and Vignoles, V. L. (2006). Narcissism and childhood recollections: A quantitative test of psychoanalytic predictions. *Personality and Social Psychology Bulletin*, 32, 104–116.

Peeters, A. G., Rutte, C. G., van Tuijl, H. F. J. M., and Reymen, I. M. M. J. (2006). The big five personality traits and individual satisfaction with the team. *Small Group Research*, 37, 187–211.

Piedmont, R. L., Hill, D. C., and Blanco, S. (1999). Predicting athletic performance using the five-factor model of personality. *Personality and Individual Differences*, 27, 769–777.

Raskin, R. N. and Hall, C. S. (1979). A narcissistic personality inventory. *Psychological Reports*, *45*, 590.

Rice, K. G. and Mirzadeh, S. A. (2000). Perfectionism, attachment, and adjustment. *Journal of Counselling Psychology*, 47, 238–250.

Robins, R. W. and John, O. P. (1997). Effects of visual perspective and narcissism on self-perception: Is seeing believing? *Psychological Science*, 8, 37–42.

Roberts, R., Callow, N., Hardy L., Woodman, T., and Thomas, L. (2010). Interactive effects of different visual imagery perspectives and narcissism on motor performance. *Journal of Sport and Exercise Psychology*, 32, 499–517.

Roberts, R., Rotheram, M., Maynard, I., Thomas, O., and Woodman, T. (2013a). Perfectionism and the 'yips': An initial investigation. *The Sport Psychologist*, 27, 53–61.

Roberts, R., Woodman, T., Hardy, L., Davis, L., and Wallace, H. W. (2013b). Psychological skills do not always help performance: The moderating role of narcissism. *Journal of Applied Sport Psychology*, 25, 316–325.

Robinson, D. M. and Tamir, M. (2005). Neuroticism as mental noise: A relation between neuroticism and reaction time standard deviations. *Journal of Personality and Social Psychology*, 89, 107–114.

Rogers, C. R. (1951). *Client-centred therapy*. London: Constable and Company.

Ronningstam, E. (2011). Psychoanalytic theories on narcissism and narcissistic personality. In W. K. Campbell and J. D. Miller (eds), *The handbook of narcissism and narcissistic personality disorder* (pp. 41–55). Hoboken NJ: John Wiley and Sons, Inc.

Sapieja, K., Dunn, J. G. H., and Holt, N. L. (2011). Perfectionism and perceptions of parenting styles in male youth soccer. *Journal of Sport and Exercise Psychology*, 33, 20–39.

Scheier, M. F. and Carver, C. S. (1992). Effects of optimism on psychological and physical well-being: Theoretical overview and empirical update. *Cognitive Therapy and Research*, 16, 201–228.

Scheier, M. F., Matthews, K. A., Owens, J. F., Magovern, G. J., Lefebvre, R. C., Abbott, R. A., *et al.* (1989). Dispositional optimism and recovery from coronary artery bypass surgery: The beneficial effects on physical and psychological well-being. *Journal of Personality and Social Psychology*, 57, 1024–1040.

Schurr, K. T., Ashley, M. A., and Joy, K. J. (1977). A multivariate analysis of male athlete personality characteristics: Sport type and success. *Multivariate Experimental Clinical Research*, 3, 53–68.

Seligman, M. E. P., Reivich, K., Jaycox, L., and Gillham, A. (1995). *The optimistic child: A revolutionary program that safeguards children against depression and builds lifelong resilience*. Boston: Hougthon Mifflin Hartcourt.

Sifneos, P. E. (1972). *The prevalence of "alexithymia" characteristics in psychosomaticpatients*. Topics of Psychosomatic Research. Basel, Switzerland: S. Karger.

Stoeber, J. and Otto, K. (2006). Positive conceptions of perfectionism: Approaches, evidence, challenges. *Personality and Social Psychology Review*, 10, 295–319.

Taylor, G. J. and Bagby, M. R. (2013). Psychoanalysis and empirical research: The example of alexithymia. *Journal of the American Psychoanalytic Association*, 61, 99–133.

Taylor, G. J., Bagby, R. M., and Parker, J. D. A. (1997). *Disorders of affect regulation: Alexithymia in medical and psychiatric illness*. Cambridge: Cambridge University Press.

Turnbull, O. and Solms, M. (2007). Awareness, desire, and false beliefs: Freud in the light of modern neuropsychology. *Cortex*, 43, 1083–1090.

Vealey, R. S. (2002). Personality and sport behaviour. In T. S. Horn (ed.), *Advances in sport psychology* (2nd edn, pp. 43–82). Champaign, IL: Human Kinetics.

Wallace, H. M. (2011). Narcissistic self-enhancement. In W. K. Campbell and J. D. Miller (eds), *The handbook of narcissism and narcissistic personality disorder* (pp. 309–318). Hoboken NJ: John Wiley and Sons, Inc.

Wallace, H. M. and Baumeister, R. F. (2002). The performance of narcissists rises and falls with perceived opportunity for glory. *Journal of Personality and Social Psychology*, 82, 819–834.

Wallace, H. M., Baumeister, R. F., and Vohs, K. D. (2005). Audience support and choking under pressure: A home disadvantage? *Journal of Sports Sciences*, 23, 429–438.

Weinberg, R. S. and Gould, D. (2007). *Foundations of sport and exercise psychology* (4th edn). Leeds: Human Kinetics.

Williams, J. M. (2009, ed.). *Applied sport psychology: Personal growth to peak performance* (6th edn). Maidenhead: McGraw-Hill.

Wilson, M. (2008). From processing efficiency to attentional control: A mechanistic account of the anxiety–performance relationship. *International Review of Sport and Exercise Psychology*, 1, 184–201.

Wilson, M., Smith, N. C., and Holmes, P. S. (2007). The role of effort in influencing the effect of anxiety on performance: Testing the conflicting predictions of processing efficiency theory and the conscious processing hypothesis. *British Journal of Psychology*, 98, 411–428.

Woodman, T. and Hardy, L. (2001). Stress and anxiety. In R. S. Singer, H. A. Hausenblas, and C. M. Janelle (eds), *Handbook of sport psychology* (pp. 290–318). New York: Wiley.

Woodman, T., Cazenave, N., and LeScanff, C. (2008). Skydiving as emotion regulation: the rise and fall of anxiety is moderated by alexithymia. *Journal of Sport and Exercise Psychology*, 30, 424–433.

Woodman, T., Davis, P. A., Hardy, L., Callow, N., Glasscock, I., and Yuill-Proctor, J. (2009). Emotions and sport performance. An exploration of happiness, hope and anger. *Journal of Sport and Exercise Psychology*, 31, 169–188.

Woodman, T., Hardy, L., Zourbanos, N., Beattie, S., and McQuillan, A. (2010). Do performance strategies moderate the relationship between personality and training behaviours? An exploratory study. *Journal of Applied Sport Psychology*, 22, 183–197.

Woodman, T., Hardy, L., Barlow, M., and Le Scanff, C. (2010). Motives for participation in prolonged engagement high-risk sports: An agentic emotional regulation perspective. *Psychology of Sport and Exercise*, 11, 345–352.

Woodman, T., Huggins, M., LeScanff, C., and Cazenave, N. (2009). Alexithymia determines the anxiety experienced in skydiving. *Journal of Affective Disorders*, 116, 134–138.

Woodman, T., Roberts, R., Hardy, L., Callow, N., and Rogers, C. H. (2011). There is an "I" in TEAM: Narcissism and social loafing. *Research Quarterly for Exercise and Sport*, 82, 285–290.

Zeidner, M., and Hammer, A. L. (1992). Coping with missile attack: Resources, strategies, and outcomes. *Journal of Personality*, 60, 709–746.

Zeigler-Hill, V., Clark, C. B., and Pickard, J. D. (2008). Narcissistic subtypes and contingent self-esteem: Do all narcissists base their self-esteem on the same domains? *Journal of Personality*, 76, 753–774.

# 2 Coping in sport

*Peter R. E. Crocker, Katherine A. Tamminen, and Patrick Gaudreau*

## Introduction

Success in high performance sport requires continual management of constantly changing challenges. When we consider many of the recent outstanding Olympic champions, such as Bradley Wiggins (cycling; Great Britain), Usain Bolt (athletics; Jamaica), Missy Franklin (swimming; USA), and Alexandre Bilodeau (ski moguls; Canada), it seems clear that achievement striving involves not only physical skills but also strong psychological and emotional skills over extended periods of time (Hanin, 2010; Uphill and Jones, 2012). Athletes may face many stressors in the pursuit of excellence such as difficult opponents, injury, performance plateaus, performance slumps, troubled coach–athlete relationships, media scrutiny, excessive personal and social expectations, and organisational politics (Hanton *et al.*, 2005; Mosewich *et al.*, 2013; Nicholls and Polman, 2007). Such threats and challenges can easily derail an athlete's pursuit of excellence as well as overall physical and mental well being.

Researchers and practitioners have long recognised that successful adaptation in any achievement setting requires effective cognitive, behavioural, and emotional self-regulation skills (see Hoar *et al.*, 2006; Lazarus, 1999; Uphill and Jones, 2012). A critical process in self-regulation is coping (Lazarus, 1999; Skinner and Zimmer-Gembeck, 2007), which involves volitional thoughts and actions to manage physically and psychologically demanding situations. Common coping strategies in sport include increasing effort, seeking social support, avoidance, wishful thinking, changing tactics, problem-solving, confrontation, relaxation or arousal control, and planning. These and other coping strategies are part of an athlete's overall self-regulation repertoire that facilitates successful adaptation in high performance sport. The purpose of this chapter is to critically review the sport coping literature, focusing primarily on the last ten years of research. It is not possible to cover all the key issues in detail or all the sport coping literature. We will, however, focus on some key topics such as conceptualisation, coping as both an individual and group level construct, quantitative and qualitative assessment, modelling, coping over time, and communal coping and interpersonal emotion regulation. We also consider research in regards to gender, culture, and coping effectiveness. Within various sections we also provide guidance towards future research.

## Coping conceptualisation

Coping in sport has typically been conceptualised within a stress and emotion framework, primarily guided by the early work of Lazarus and Folkman (1984) and later by Lazarus' cognitive-motivational-relational framework (Lazarus, 1991, 1999; see Hoar *et al.*, 2006; Nicholls and Thelwell, 2010). Lazarus's framework holds that stress is a process that involves a dynamic transactional relationship between the athlete and the environment. An athlete will evaluate specific demands (stressors) in terms of personal meaning based on what is at stake in respect to goals, commitments, and values (this evaluation is termed primary appraisal). In addition, the athlete also evaluates coping options, future expectancies, and agency (termed secondary appraisal). These appraisals are thought to influence an athlete's coping actions (thoughts and behaviours) that can actively change the person-environment transaction and/or regulate emotional experience. The way that an athlete copes with specific demands will presumably influence personal and social outcomes (Lazarus, 2000).

Stress can also be viewed as part of an adaptation process in which people need to continually regulate to changing conditions as well as to develop and enhance new personal and social resources to handle future demands (Hobfoll, 2001; Lazarus, 1999). Adaptation in sport "involves athletes' appraisal of stressors, their cognitive, emotional, behavioural, and physiological responses, and adjustment to appraised conditions through automatic self-regulatory processes as well as through rational, planned behaviours and coping responses" (Tamminen *et al.*, 2014, p. 143). Thus, coping is one of the processes that can facilitate athletes' self-regulation and be a critical factor in determining if athletes can successfully meet the demands of difficult athletic competitions (Hanin, 2000; Lazarus, 2000; Nicholls and Thelwell, 2010). An adaptation framework recognises that coping is not only a response to problems and negative emotions but can also involve planful and proactive cognitions and behaviours to facilitate positive psychological and emotional growth (Tamminen *et al.*).

There has been recent debate in the sport literature whether coping should include both conscious and automatic cognitive and behavioural actions (Nicholls and Thelwell, 2010; Uphill and Jones, 2009). Although this controversy is complex and not new (see Lazarus and Folkman, 1984; Skinner, 1995), our position in this chapter is that coping only involves *voluntary effortful* responses that have the purpose of cognitive, emotional, and behavioural regulation. It is possible that through practice and experience, some coping skills may require reduced attentional resources and become routines. These routines are often referred to as management skills (Aldwin, 2007). Also, consistent with the position of Hoar *et al.* (2006), coping does not include involuntary emotional reactions (crying; trembling). Thus, based on the foundational work of Folkman and Lazarus (1980), our working definition of coping is that it shall include all effortful cognitions and behaviours an athlete employs to manage constantly changing perceived important adaptation challenges.

Sport research has generally emphasised coping as a within-person or intrapersonal process, although athletes' stress and adaptation processes are often influenced by others and influence others (Friesen *et al.*, 2013; Tamminen and Gaudreau, 2014). This interpersonal aspect recognises that coping can be a group level construct in that teams, or groups within a team, are often collectively coping with demands. From the interpersonal perspective it is possible to examine how an athlete copes and how this coping influences the coping of others, as well as to consider teams' coping with shared challenges and demands (Tamminen and Gaudreau, 2014). Research has examined the linkage between social contextual factors (i.e. social support, coach–athlete relationships, parent–athlete relationship) and athletes' coping and emotional regulation (see Lafferty and Dorrell, 2006; Tamminen and Gaudreau, 2014; Tamminen and Holt, 2012). However, this research has generally emphasised coping by the athlete at the individual level. Later in the chapter we will consider an emerging area of research, called communal coping, which considers coping and emotional regulation at the group level.

Whether considered at an intrapersonal or interpersonal level, coping is a response to adaptation challenges. It is clear from the literature that these challenges can involve multiple stressors of varying intensity, frequency, and duration, in various sports contexts, across different temporal periods, and be expected or unexpected (Hoar *et al.*, 2006; Nicholls and Thelwell, 2010). Coping will also be impacted by the constraints and opportunities afforded by cultural beliefs, social-development considerations, as well as social and gender roles and expectations (Aldwin, 2007; Anshel, 2010; Hoar and Evans, 2010; Kaiseler and Polman, 2010). Thus, it is not surprising that the literature has found that athletes use a multiplicity of cognitive and behavioural coping actions. The next section will consider how researchers attempt to classify these individual coping actions into meaningful analytic units to examine the potential antecedents and consequences of coping.

## Classifying coping

Given the vast array of coping strategies athletes and groups can use to manage stress and facilitate adaptation, it is not surprising there are various ways to classify coping (Hoar *et al.*, 2006; Nicholls and Thelwell, 2010). Most of these classifications systems, ranging from micro-analytical to macro-analytical, were developed in associated fields in social and clinical psychology and sociology. Micro-analytic approaches involve identifying specific types of coping strategies. These strategies can include arousal control, turning to religion, increasing effort, problem-solving, positive or negative self-talk, learning reflection, seeking social support, imagery, planning, relaxation, logical analysis, reappraisal, mental disengagement, behavioural disengagement, acceptance wishful thinking, humour, resignation, confrontation, venting, and suppression of competing activities (see Gaudreau and Blondin, 2004; Hoar *et al.*, 2010; Gould *et al.*, 1993; McDonough *et al.*, 2013; Reeves *et al.*, 2009).

Macro-analytic approaches involve grouping similar coping strategies together and can vary widely (Nicholls and Thelwell, 2010). One approach is to categorise coping into various functions such as problem-focused and emotion-focused coping (Lazarus, 1999; Lazarus and Folkman, 1984). Problem-focused coping refers to cognitive and behavioural efforts to change the environmental demands or the actions of the athlete (or group). Emotion-focused coping involves strategies to regulate emotion processes. Some authors also include avoidance coping as a function that involves actively not dealing with the stressful transaction (Kowalski and Crocker, 2001). Another macro-analytic approach involves grouping coping strategies into higher order ways of coping such as engagement and disengagement coping (Ebata and Moss, 1991; Gaudreau and Blondin, 2004), behavioural and cognitive coping (Compas *et al.*, 2001), and approach and avoidance coping (Roth and Cohen, 1986; Anshel *et al.*, 2000). A further approach involves classifying coping according to whether the person is anticipating and taking proactive steps to manage stressful transactions (Aspinwall and Taylor; 1997; Tamminen and Holt, 2010). The specific approach taken to classify coping is often shaped by a specific theoretical position and has a profound impact on the specific measurement procedures and data analysis and interpretation used in sport coping research (Aldwin, 2007; Crocker *et al.*, 2010; Nicholls and Ntoumanis, 2010).

## Coping assessment

Sport coping researchers have employed various measurement and assessment techniques such as questionnaires, interviews, diaries, concept maps, and think aloud protocols (see Crocker *et al.*, 1998; Hoar *et al.*, 2006; Nicholls and Ntoumanis, 2010). These techniques, along with subsequent analytic techniques, are rooted in methodological assumptions as well as theoretical conceptualisations (Crocker *et al.*, 2010). A detailed discussion of measurement and analytic issues is far beyond the purpose of this chapter. However, we will review some key quantitative and qualitative assessment methods commonly used in the last decade by sport researchers.

### Quantitative methods: questionnaires

The most common coping assessment method is questionnaires. The advantages of questionnaires are that researchers can (a) evaluate the validity evidence for scores for specific populations, (b) compare results across studies, and (c) use various analytical strategies to modelling and evaluate specific theoretical questions (Crocker *et al.*, 2010). There are numerous sport-specific and sport-modified questionnaires reported in the literature including the Ways of Coping Checklist for Sport (WCCS; Madden *et al.*, 1989), Modified Ways of Coping Checklist (MWCC; Crocker, 1992), Coping Style Inventory (CSI; Kaissidis-Rodafinos and Anshel, 2000), the Coping Style in Sport Survey (CSSS; Anshel *et al.*, 2000), the Modified COPE (MCOPE; Crocker and Graham, 1995), the Athletic Coping Skills Inventory 28 (ACS-28; Smith *et al.*, 1995), the Coping Function Questionnaire (CFQ; Kowlaski and Crocker, 2001) and the Inventaire des Stratégies de Coping en Compétition Sportive (ISCCS; Gaudreau and Blondin, 2002). A description most of these instruments, including psychometric properties and relative strengths and weaknesses has been discussed extensively (see Crocker *et al.*, 1998; Hoar *et al.*, 2006; Nicholls and Ntoumanis, 2010; Lidor *et al.*, 2012). Therefore, we will only focus on the four most prominent sport coping instruments: the ACSI-28, MCOPE, CFQ, and the ISCCS. It should be noted that all of these instruments assess coping at the individual but not group level.

### Athletic Coping Skills Inventory-28 (ACSI-28)

The Athletic Coping Skills Inventory-28 (ACSI-28; Smith *et al.*, 1995) is a sport-specific measure that assesses psychological skills. The ACSI-28 contains seven subscales (1) Coping with Adversity, (2) Peaking under Pressure, (3) Goal Setting/Mental Preparation, (4) Concentration, (5) Freedom from Worry, (6) Confidence and Achievement Motivation, and (7) Coachability. The items consist of statements about the experiences of other athletes and athletes are asked to rate how often they have had the same experiences on a 4-point Likert-type scale (0 = almost never, to 3 = almost always). Researchers can chose to examine individual sub-scales or to combine the seven sub-scales into a total composite measure.

There is good validity evidence of ACSI-28 scores for various high school and university sporting populations (see Hoar *et al.*, 2006; Smith *et al.*, 1995). All subscales have acceptable test-retest reliability as well as internal consistency. The individual scales and total composite measure typically show theoretically meaningful relations with other coping scales, anxiety, and performance ratings. The ACSI-28 has also been translated into other languages such as Greek and Spanish (Goudas *et al.*, 1998; Sanz *et al.*, 2011). It has recently been used to examine various applied and theoretical questions such as predicting sport injuries (Johnson and

Ivarsson, 2011), examining relationships of coping with perfectionism and motivation (Mouratidis and Michous, 2011), and linking coping to mental toughness and distinguishing between levels of expertise in cricket batsmen (Weissensteiner *et al.*, 2012).

Although the ACSI-28 has much strength, researchers should be aware of some potential conceptual and measurement limitations (Lidor *et al.*, 2012). First, several reviews have suggested that the ACSI-28 is more a measure of relatively stable psychological skills than a measure of coping skills (Crocker *et al.*, 1998; Hoar *et al.*, 2006). Nevertheless, psychological skills are an important feature of coping and are often included in coping skills training for athletes (Hoar *et al.*, 2006). At a measurement level, there has not been any systematic evaluation of gender or group invariance. Thus comparisons between groups on ASCI-28 scores should be treated with caution. Finally, since the instructions to participants assume that psychological skills are relatively stable, the ACSI-28 will not be able to capture changes in coping over time and across situations (Lidor *et al.*, 2012).

## Modified COPE

Crocker and Graham (1995) examined coping with performance difficulties in sport using a questionnaire that combined modifications to selected scales from Carver and Scheier's (1989) COPE inventory as well as additional scales from sport modifications to the Ways of Coping Checklist (see Crocker, 1992). This resulting questionnaire, termed the Modified COPE (MCOPE), consisted of 12 coping scales: active coping, seeking social support for instrumental reasons, planning, seeking social support for emotional reasons, denial, humour, behavioural disengagement, venting of emotion, suppression of competing activities, self-blame, wishful thinking, and increasing effort. Participants indicate how much they use a particular coping action during a stressful performance situation, with items scored on a 5-point scale ranging from 1 (used not at all/very little) to 5 (used very much). Although Crocker and colleagues (Crocker and Graham, 1995; Crocker and Isaack, 1997) assessed sport coping using this pooled instrument primarily because of perceived weaknesses of other coping measures, many sport coping researchers have adopted the MCOPE (Nicholls and Polman, 2007).

The MCOPE has demonstrated acceptable validity evidence of scores for various sporting populations using both situational and dispositional coping instructions (Giacobbi and Weinberg, 2000; Hoar *et al.*, 2006; Lidor *et al.*, 2012). Across many studies, the MCOPE reveals sound scale reliability (except for denial scale), factor structure, and construct validity (see Eklund *et al.*, 1998; Nicholls and Ntoumanis, 2010), with specific MCOPE scales demonstrating meaningful theoretical relationships with motivation, emotion/affect, and athletic goals. The MCOPE has also been translated to French (Gaudreau *et al.*, 2001). Recent research with the MCOPE has examined how coping and coping effectiveness was related to hardiness and anxiety interpretation (Hanton *et al.*, 2013), as well as examining various hypotheses related to gender differences in coping by soccer players (Kaiseler *et al.*, 2012).

There are a number of limitations with the MCOPE. First, since the MCOPE is a hybrid questionnaire combining scales from two instruments, it does not have a solid conceptual or theoretical foundation. Second, it has not been subjected to rigorous psychometric evaluation such as gender and group invariance. Thus caution is warranted in interpreting results. Nicholls and Ntoumanis (2010) also argued that the hierarchical structure of the MCOPE has not been evaluated. This assumes the MCOPE scales can be combined into higher order dimensions such as problem-focused, emotion-focused, and avoidance. We do not believe, however, that the MCOPE implies or requires such a hierarchical structure. Lastly, it is possible that the specific scales in the MCOPE cannot capture specific types of coping, such as arousal control or spiritual reflection.

### Coping Function Questionnaire

The Coping Function Questionnaire (CFQ) is a sport-specific instrument developed to assess problem-focused, emotion-focused, and avoidance coping functions (Kowalski and Crocker, 2001). Athletes are asked to respond to how frequency they used each coping item in response to a self-reported stressful situation. The CFQ consists of 18 items scored on a five point Likert-type scale (1 = not at all; 5 = very much). Although originally developed through a multi-step process for adolescent athletes, the CFQ has been used in university and young adult populations (Hanton *et al.*, 2008; Poliseo and McDonough, 2012). We are not aware of any attempts to translate the CFQ to other languages.

The CFQ has generally demonstrated good validity evidence for scores in various athletic populations. In the original work, Kowalski and Crocker (2001) reported acceptable scale reliability, with confirmatory factor analysis revealing modest evidence of model fit for the three-factor model as well as gender invariance. Although other researchers have not examined the CFQ psychometric properties in any detail, the three scales typically demonstrated good scale reliability. Evidence for construct validity of scores include meaningful relationships with control beliefs, trait anger, perceived stress as well as correlations with other conceptually related coping scales such as the MCOPE (Bolgar *et al.*, 2008; Kowalski and Crocker, 2001; Kowalski *et al.*, 2005). Recent studies utilising the CFQ have examined coping function in relationship to types of perfectionism (Crocker *et al.*, 2014) and personality in sport (Allen *et al.*, 2011).

Despite its strengths as sport-specific measures with acceptable measurement properties, researchers need to be aware of some important limitations in the CFQ. First, since the CFQ only assesses coping function, it does not provide information on the specific types of coping strategies used to manage competitive stress and adaptation. It has been suggested that the CFQ might be best used concurrently with sport-specific measures that assess coping at the strategy level to provide a more complete depiction of the coping process (Hoar *et al.*, 2006). Second, rather than athletes simply reporting what strategies they used to cope, the CFQ requires that athletes make inferences about the actual function of their coping efforts (Lidor *et al.*, 2012). Third, the CFQ could likely be improved through item modification, reduction of redundant items, as well as more thorough psychometric evaluation and validation across various sporting populations (Lidor *et al.*, 2012; Nicholls and Ntoumanis, 2010).

*Inventaire des Stratégies de Coping en Compétition Sportive (ISCCS)*

The ISCCS is a sport-specific instrument designed to assess coping in competition situations (Gaudreau and Blondin, 2002). Conceptually rooted in engagement and disengagement conceptualisations of coping, the ISCCS was originally developed in French and is also known in English as the *Coping Inventory for Competitive Sport* (CICS). Developed through a multistep instrument construction and evaluation process, the ISCCS is composed of 39 items, with 10 scales that can be combined into three higher order coping dimensions: task-oriented coping, distraction-oriented coping, and disengagement-oriented coping. Task-oriented coping includes the scales of mental imagery, relaxation, thought control, logical analysis, effort expenditure, and seeking social support. Distraction-oriented coping consists of the scales of mental distraction and distancing. Disengagement coping includes the scales of disengagement/resignation and venting of unpleasant emotions. Athletes rate the extent to which each item represents their actions or thoughts during a stressful competition on a 5-point scale (1 = does not correspond at all, 5 = corresponds very strongly). Although developed for sport competition, the ISCSS has been modified to assess coping in sport training (Schellenberg *et al.*, 2013). There is also a dispositional version of the ISCCS (Hurst *et al.*, 2011).

The ISCCS has shown good validity evidence for scores in various sporting populations. Typically scale reliability is acceptable, although some studies have shown that some items or scales have been problematic (e.g. Gaudreau *et al.*, 2005). Several studies have demonstrated the ISCCS has solid factorial validity, with acceptable model fit for the 10-factor model, support for the higher order 3-factor model, and evidence of factorial invariance across individual and team sport subsamples (Gaudreau and Antl, 2008; Gaudreau and Blondin, 2002, 2004). Several studies have also shown theoretically meaningful relationships between the three higher order dimensions of the ISCCS and other coping scales, goal attainment, motivation, and personality (Gaudreau and Antl, 2008; Gaudreau and Blondin, 2002; Nicholls *et al.*, 2008). The ISCCS has become an increasingly popular measure in sport, with recent studies examining the mediating role of coping in passion and burnout relationships (Schellenberg *et al.*, 2013), decision-making and coping (Laborde *et al.*, 2014), and associations between affective profiles and coping (Martinent *et al.*, 2013).

The ISCCS has a number of conceptual and measurement strengths as a sport-specific measure of coping during the competition process. Researchers need, however, to be aware of some specific limitations. First, because the ISCCS was developed for competition related stress, it has limited effectiveness to assess coping during other types of sport related stress such as interpersonal conflict, injury, performance plateaus, and organisational stress. Second, Nicholls and Ntoumanis (2010) argue there is a need to provide additional evidence for the hierarchical structure of the ISCCS in various sporting populations. Third, the higher-order dimensions assume that specific types of coping captured by the ten scales can be nested only under one of three higher-order functional dimensions (Lidor *et al.*, 2012). However, as noted by Lazarus (1991), it is possible that some strategies might serve multiple functions. Fourth, given the complexities of coping, it is possible that the ten scales do not capture all aspects of coping possible in competition setting. Notwithstanding these limitations, Lidor *et al.* (2012) have suggested that the ISCCS may be the best instrument for examining coping in competition using quantitative methods.

## Qualitative methods

Many studies on coping have used qualitative research methods to understand how individuals interpret and make sense of their athletic experiences. Qualitative researchers may use a variety of methods such as interviews, observations, or athletes' personal journals or diaries to collect data within broader methodological approaches such as case studies, grounded theory, ethnography, or phenomenological approaches (Tamminen and Holt, 2010a; Nicholls and Ntoumanis, 2010). Richard Lazarus (2006) argued that researchers "need to go back to a much more idiographic perspective and seek rich in-depth descriptions of the lives of individuals over time and diverse conditions" (p. 42). The potential richness of qualitative approaches can provide information about athletes' goals and motivations, appraisal processes, responses to stressors, and descriptions of ways in which they attempted to cope with stressors in sport.

While each qualitative approach and method used for data collection can produce different results and forms of knowledge, qualitative studies of athletes' coping in sport psychology have generally used interviews as the primary methods of data collection to understand athletes' perceptions of stressors, emotions, coping, and coping effectiveness (e.g. Gould *et al.*, 1993; McDonough *et al.*, 2013; Nicholls *et al.*, 2005; Thatcher and

Day, 2008). Early qualitative studies exploring high performance athletes' coping strategies revealed that athletes used thought control, task focus strategies, emotional control strategies, and behavioural strategies such as following a routine, distraction, or attempting to control the environment to deal with stressors in sport (Gould *et al.*, 1993). Gould and colleagues noted that athletes often used multiple coping strategies in combination to deal with stressors, supporting additional research which suggested that athletes' coping strategy use depended on the nature of the athletes' stressor appraisals (Anshel, 2001; Dale, 2000; Holt and Hogg, 2002). These findings are supported by subsequent research adopting a phenomenological approach to explore athletes' perceptions of effective coping in sport. Nicholls and colleagues (2005) reported that athletes used a number of cognitive and behavioural strategies which were deemed to be effective in dealing with stress in sport, including rationalising, reappraising, blocking, positive self-talk, following a routine, breathing exercises, physical relaxation, and seeking social support. The athletes also reported some strategies that were deemed to be ineffective in dealing with stressors (trying too hard, speeding up, routine changes, negative thoughts), and the athletes also reported that a lack of coping was associated with ineffective coping.

Longitudinal qualitative research has provided insight into athletes' process of coping over time. For example, to examine athletes' expected and actual use of coping strategies during a championship tournament, Holt *et al.* (2007) conducted pre- and post-tournament interviews with collegiate volleyball players regarding their competition appraisals of stressors and coping strategies. This study revealed that the athletes generally did not anticipate many of the stressors they actually encountered during the tournament and similarly there was little consistency in athletes' anticipated coping compared to their actual coping strategy use. The athletes who reported more effective coping had greater consistency between their pre- and post-competition coping reports, suggesting that athletes who were better able to anticipate and deploy coping strategies were more satisfied with their coping efforts.

Other longitudinal research studies investigating athlete's coping processes have used diary approaches to document athletes' stressors and coping over periods of 28 and 31 days (Nicholls *et al.*, 2005, 2006). These studies have demonstrated that athletes' stressors fluctuated over the course of a month and a small number of stressors (injury, mental errors, physical errors, observing opponents play well, and weather) accounted for the majority of the athletes' concerns. Athletes reported greater numbers of stressors during more competitive periods (e.g. stressor frequencies coincided with most important competitions). Athletes' coping also increased when they reported more stressors, although athletes' use of particular coping strategies changed depending on the appraised stressor.

Building on these longitudinal approaches, researchers have sought to examine adolescent athletes' stressors and coping over entire competitive seasons. Tamminen and Holt (2010b) collected data through observations, interviews, and weekly audio diaries with a team of female adolescent basketball players to document stressors and coping over an entire competitive season. Findings showed that athletes' reported stressors and coping strategies changed over the course of the season and analysis of athletes' coping profiles demonstrated that some athletes were more proactive in their approach to dealing with stressors, whereas other athletes were more reactive in coping with stressors. In a similar study, McDonough *et al.* (2013) interviewed eight competitive swimmers before and after swim meets across an entire season, and athletes were grouped into profiles based on the way they generally appraised and dealt with stressors. Some athletes tended to report that stressors were something to be avoided and they reported not anticipating upcoming stressors, and used cognitive and behavioural avoidance and distraction to deal with stressors. Other athletes reported that stressors were viewed as problems to be solved, and they used multiple strategies to deal with stressors, including emotion-focused coping, avoidance, seeking support, reappraisal, increasing effort, and focusing on strategy, technique, or opponents. The final group of athletes generally perceived swimming as fun and minimally stressful, and they anticipated and reported few stressors during competitions. This research has illustrated differences in the way athletes approach competitions and appraise stressors, which may help to explain differences in the way that athletes cope with stressors. Taken together, these longitudinal qualitative studies have proved valuable in advancing our understanding of athletes' processes of stressor appraisal and coping over time. Broadly, these studies have illustrated Lazarus' (1999) recursive and transactional process of coping in sport contexts, demonstrating how athletes' stressors and coping change over time and across different situations.

Researchers have also drawn on a variety of qualitative methodologies such as case studies, grounded theory, ethnography, and phenomenological approaches to advance our understanding of athletes' coping in sport. For example, Nieuwenhuys and colleagues (Nieuwenhuys *et al.*, 2008, 2011) conducted case studies with elite athletes to explore the athletes' meta-experiences – that is, their knowledge, attitudes, and preferences – about emotions and coping during competitions. The researchers produced detailed sequential analysis of the athletes' experiences, thoughts, and coping actions during successful and unsuccessful experiences. The results suggested that athletes' meta-experiences (their attitudes about their coping and past performances) influence how, when, and which coping strategies are used to deal with performance-related stressors. Such research is valuable in understanding why athletes use particular coping strategies to deal with stressors in sport. This approach to understanding athletes' knowledge about their coping can serve as a basis for future research and interventions to help athletes reflect on their coping and help athletes to adopt new or different approaches to cope effectively with stressors in sport.

Another case-study approach was used to explore two national trampoline coaches' experiences of coping with vicarious trauma (witnessing a trampolinist's traumatic injury: Day *et al.*, 2013). Through multiple interviews and narrative analyses, the researchers provided accounts of the coaches' efforts to cope with the trauma they witnessed through making meaning, re-experiencing the trauma, and by using acceptance and avoidance coping. The in-depth analysis of the coaches' experience supported Lazarus' (1999) CMRT and demonstrated the individual nature of coping with the traumatic event based on each coach's appraisal of the situation. This research underscored the value in understanding each individual's experience of dealing with stressors rather than making broad generalisations about what may constitute effective or ineffective coping, particularly when dealing with traumatic events in sport contexts.

Grounded theory research is a methodology for researchers seeking to produce a theory that is "grounded" in the participants' data (Corbin and Strauss, 2008). One example of grounded theory methodology used to explore aspects of coping in sport was the development of a theory describing adolescent athletes' process of learning about coping with stressors in sport (Tamminen and Holt, 2012). The grounded theory described adolescent athletes' learning about effective coping as a process that unfolded over time with exposure to increasing challenges and stressors in sport, and the results highlighted the role of parents and coaches in facilitating athletes' learning. Findings indicated that parents and coaches could adopt particular strategies to help athletes learn to cope with stressors (e.g. questioning and reminding athletes about past coping efforts, initiating informal conversations about coping, sharing experiences, providing perspective about stressors and coping), however participants emphasised the importance of developing a supportive environment in which to learn about coping. Grounded theory can be a valuable methodological approach to identify processes that may influence the development of athletes' coping and strategies for helping athletes to cope with stressors in sport.

Qualitative research approaches have advanced our understanding of athletes' stressors and coping in sport, they have helped to identify antecedents and consequences of athletes' coping, and qualitative research has also highlighted factors that influence athletes' coping and the complexity of coping in sport contexts. While many studies have primarily used interviews and content analyses to explore athletes' stressors and coping in sport contexts, researchers have embraced qualitative methodologies which have produced in-depth descriptions of athletes' coping process.

## Modelling coping: basic issues

The theoretical and empirical literature indicates that coping is part of a complex process involved in stress and adaptation (Aldwin, 2007; Lazarus, 1999; Nicholls, 2010a). Previous reviews have attempted to highlight the antecedents and consequences of coping in sport (see Hoar *et al.*, 2006; Nicholls and Polman, 2006). Situational antecedents could include specific sport related demands, social and sport constraints and opportunities, and culture. Personal antecedents could include personality, motivational orientations, personal sporting goals, coping styles, self-esteem, athletic identity, social-cognitive development, and personal resources to name a few (see Hoar *et al.*, 2006; Nicholls, 2010a). Many of these situational and personal antecedents will interact to impact cognitive appraisals that could influence coping before, during, and after a stressful sport transaction (Lazarus, 1999; Aldwin, 2007). There are also many adaptive and maladaptive outcomes of coping including enhanced or diminished sport performance and athletic goal attainment, changes in emotions, burnout, psychological well being, alterations in interpersonal relationships and social functioning, and susceptibility to injury (see Hoar *et al.*, 2006; Jordet, 2010; Tamminen *et al.*, 2014). These outcomes are discussed in more detail in the section on coping effectiveness.

We believe it might be informative to highlight representative studies that demonstrate how researchers have attempted to model the complexity of the coping process. There are many research designs and analysis techniques that can model the antecedents and consequences of coping. These range from simple predictive models, to more complex mediation and moderation models, some involving longitudinal designs (see Crocker *et al.*, 2010). To a large extent, the specific design and analysis procedures will depend on specific research questions. Many of the early studies on coping in sport were descriptive or exploratory in nature (using both quantitative and qualitative procedures), which revealed that athletes used many different types of coping strategies to manage a variety of stressful competitive demands, often using a combination of problem-focused and emotion-focused coping strategies (e.g. Madden *et al.*, 1988; Crocker, 1992). These were followed by numerous simple predictive studies based on cross-sectional designs in which researchers tried to establish relationships between specific antecedents and types of coping or to predict the effects of coping on specific outcomes (see Crocker and Graham, 1998; Nicholls and Polman, 2007). Other sport researchers used group designs to establish if there were coping differences based on specific groups such as gender, culture, level of sport expertise, and age to name a few (see Anshel 2010; Kaisler and Polman, 2010). In the last decade, sport researchers have increasing utilised more sophisticated designs such as mediation and moderation models and prospective longitudinal designs to examine more complex theoretical questions.

Mediation models propose the effects of an independent variable on a dependent variable are caused by one or more mediator variables (Hoyle and Kenny, 1999). In the coping literature, there are many examples of mediator analysis. For example, in a study of American and Mexican high-school tennis players, Puente-Diaz and Anshel (2005) found that perceived controllability mediated the relationship between nationality and active coping during a stressful competition. Meditation models can also look at the effects of multiple meditators. For example, Gaudreau and Antl (2008) examined relationships among perfectionism, goal attainment, life satisfaction, motivation, and coping in French Canadian athletes. They found that that disengagement-oriented coping mediated the negative relationship between evaluative concerns perfectionism (tendency to engage in negative social evaluation and high self-criticism) and change in life satisfaction. Furthermore, self-determined and non-self-determined motivation partially mediated the relationships between different dimensions of perfectionism and coping.

Recent studies have examined the potential mediating effects of coping between personality dimensions and athletes' emotional and achievement behaviours. Hill *et al.* (2010) examined whether the relationship between dimensions of perfectionism and burnout was mediated by different coping styles in junior elite athletes. They found that higher levels of socially prescribed perfectionism (similar to evaluative concerns perfectionism) was positively related to higher avoidance coping, which was subsequently positively correlated with higher levels of athlete burnout. In contrast, self-oriented perfectionism (tendency to set high personal performance standards and engage in self-oriented striving) was positively related to higher problem-focused coping and negatively related to avoidance coping. Both of these types of coping subsequently predicted athlete burnout scores. Hill and colleagues argued that coping may explain why there are differences in the relationships between dimensions of perfectionism and burnout. Recently, Schellenberg *et al.* (2013) examined whether coping mediated the relationships between types of passion and burnout and athlete goal attainment in collegiate volleyball players over the course of a season. The authors suggested that their findings supported that types of passion were indirectly related to changes in burnout and goal attainment over the season by means of different coping dimensions. Harmonious passion (a more positive form of activity engagement) was positively related to task-oriented coping, which was subsequently associated with change in goal attainment. Obsessive passion (a potentially more negative form of activity engagement) was positively associated with disengagement-oriented coping, which, in turn, was positively associated with changes in burnout and negatively associated with changes in goal attainment. Schellenberg *et al.* (2013) suggested that task oriented strategies help athletes develop skills and resources to facilitate achievement striving whereas disengagement strategies inhibit such processes and make athletes more prone to failure and burnout. Although both the Hill *et al.* and the Schellenberg *et al.* (2013) studies suggest the potential mediating effects of coping in personality-athletic outcomes relationships as suggested by specific conceptual frameworks, the passive observation nature of the designs makes it is difficult to establish causal relationships among variables. Nevertheless, mediation models allow researchers to more carefully examine the potential effects of coping as a mechanism in many psychological variables-outcome relationships in sport.

The sport coping literature identifies several moderators that could influence coping-outcome relationships including personality, gender, and culture (see Kaiseler and Polman, 2010; Anshel, 2010; Polman *et al.*, 2010). Moderation holds that the relationship between an independent variable (such as coping) and a dependent variable (such as an emotion) varies across levels of a moderator variable (such as gender). For example, the relationship between disengagement coping and anxiety could be significantly different between males and female athletes. There are some very good examples of studies that have examined moderator effects in sport related coping. For example, Ntoumanis and Biddle (1998) examined whether perceived coping effectiveness moderated the effects of coping strategies on emotional experience in British athletes. They reported moderator effects (coping effectiveness X coping strategy use) for several relationships including the coping strategies of seeking social support, venting of emotions, and behavioural disengagement. For example, athletes who reported high levels of seeking social support reported high positive affect. However, positive affect was highest when the strategy was combined with high effectiveness, compared to all other combinations of coping usage and effectiveness. Recently, Deroche *et al.* (2011) examined if pain coping (ignoring pain) could moderate the negative effect of pain intensity on combat athletes' desire to play through pain. Their findings supported moderation effects as the negative effects of pain intensity on the desire to play through the pain decreased as athletes engaged in pain coping. Another example of moderation was a study by Hanton *et al.* (2013) who examined if the personality construct of hardiness moderated the effects of anxiety direction (facilitators vs. debilitators) on coping usage and effectiveness in collegiate and club athletes. Significant interaction effects for hardiness and anxiety direction indicated that athletes high in hardiness and who perceived anxiety as facilitative used more planning, active coping, and increased effort coping and, furthermore, found these strategies to be more effective compared to other combinations of hardiness and anxiety direction.

There are several challenges in examining moderator effects involving coping. First, the ideal moderator should be unrelated to the other independent variable. This seldom occurs. For example, sport researchers often find that potential moderator variables such as personality dimensions, gender, and culture are related to coping and appraisal processes in sport-related stress (Kaiseler *et al.*, 2012a, 2012b; Anshel, 2010). Second, moderator analysis requires large sample sizes, since interaction effects are often small. Third, it is critical to conduct moderated analysis to examine moderation effects. Recently, Kaiseler *et al.* (2012a) claimed that gender moderated coping in soccer players. Their analysis found gender differences in coping in responses to three stress scenarios, after statistically controlling for the appraisals of stress intensity and perceived control. However, they never conducted moderated analysis to determine if gender interacted with appraisal to predict coping. In conclusion, moderator analysis is a useful way to examine the complex interactions that are likely to exist involving coping and other key variables in stress and adaption models.

## Coping over time: assessing change and stability

Years before the popularization of intensive longitudinal designs, Lazarus and Folkman (1984, p. 297) outlined the many advantages of measuring the "actual or momentary utilization of coping strategies in a particular situation at a particular point in time". Defining coping as a "constantly changing process" has encouraged many researchers and practitioners to measure coping across multiple points in time, situations, and contexts. More importantly, this recommendation has proven to be pivotal to show that coping combines the inherent characteristics of a trait and a process (Gaudreau and Miranda, 2010).

On the one hand, the coping responses of an athlete substantially vary across measurement points (i.e. days, competitions, trainings). On the other hand, each athlete has a typical coping response that can either be inferred using dispositional a coping measure or average of the specific coping responses obtained across multiple measurement occasions. The focus of dispositional coping is typically at the *between-person level of analysis* where researchers examine the extent to which athletes are coping differently from one another. Individual differences in coping can be seen as the structure or the blueprint of coping (Lazarus and Folkman, 1984). As eloquently stated by Carver *et al.* (1989, p. 270), "people do not approach each context anew, but rather bring to bear a preferred set of coping strategies that remains relatively fixed across time and circumstances". In mathematical parlance, dispositional coping is the average of the coping distribution of an athlete across multiple coping episodes. "Structure and process are both necessary for an understanding of coping" (Lazarus and Folkman, (1984) p. 298) because the mean and standard deviations of a person offer complementary information about his or her coping distribution. As such, the focus of a process-centred approach is typically at the *within-person level of analysis* where researchers examine how the coping of an athlete varies across time, situations, and contexts. Both levels of analysis are needed because inter-individual differences and intra-individual differences are likely to explain for whom and under which circumstances certain coping actions are associated to better psychological, emotional, and functional outcomes.

Recent research provided evidence that the variance of coping responses collected across multiple time points is attributable to substantial between-person differences and within-person variability. In a study of 107 male soccer players followed across three competitions, 48 per cent of the variance in task-oriented coping and disengagement-oriented coping and 51 per cent of the variance in distraction-oriented coping was attributable to between-person differences (Louvet *et al.*, 2007). Similar findings were reported with a sample of 329 soccer referees across three competitions over a 10-month season. A total of 59 per cent, 52 per cent, and 50 per cent of the variance in their problem-focused coping, emotion-focused coping, and seeking social support was attributable to between-person differences (Louvet *et al.*, 2009). The amount of between-person differences in the coping of 54 male golfers across six consecutive golf rounds ranged from 49 per cent for disengagement-oriented coping to 75 per cent for task-oriented coping (Gaudreau *et al.*, 2010). Across ten consecutive days of a summer basketball training camp, 45 per cent of the daily effort (a task-oriented coping strategy) of 63 adolescents was attributable to between-person differences (Mouratidis and Michou, 2011). A total of 36 per cent of the variance in the episodic task-oriented coping of 16 elite women saber fencers was explained by between-person differences in a study in which coping was measured after each point during a fencing match (Doron and Gaudreau, 2014). All of these results indicate that coping responses of sport participants can be described as showing both within-person variability (e.g. change, inconsistency) and between-person differences (e.g. stability, consistency).

Within-person variability in coping should not be interpreted as a random phenomenon merely attributable to measurement error because recent research has provided evidence for the longitudinal factorial invariance of coping questionnaires. Fletcher (2008) surveyed a sample of 219 female athletes across four sport competitions using the Coping Inventory for Competitive Sport (Gaudreau and Blondin, 2002). Results of longitudinal confirmatory factor analysis performed on each of the ten coping strategies supported the configural, metric, and scalar invariance of most of the parameters constrained to equality. Similar findings have been reported on the longitudinal factor invariance of the Ways of Coping Questionnaire with a sample of soccer referees (Louvet *et al.*, 2009). Longitudinal factor invariance of coping responses is important insofar as it demonstrates that the conceptual properties of the coping construct are *qualitatively invariant* and *structurally stable* across measurement points.

Despite the substantial within-person variability in coping, most research has relied on cross-sectional or prospective designs in which coping strategies are measured on a single occasion. Although much has been learned from these studies, little theoretical and empirical efforts have been made to examine the antecedents and consequences of coping at the within-person level of analysis. Mouratidis and Michou (2011) have recently examined the daily association between situational autonomous motivation and effort expenditure (a task-oriented coping strategy) during training sessions. Results of multilevel modelling analyses have shown that adolescents are likely to expend significantly more effort than their own average on days during which their level of situational autonomous motivation is higher than their own average. Results of a multilevel study of coping and sport performance (Gaudreau *et al.*, 2010) have also revealed that amateur golfers improved their score by 1.77 strokes compared to their average during golf rounds in which they used more task-oriented coping than their own average. In contrast, golfers took 2.22 more strokes during rounds in which they used more disengagement-oriented coping than their own average. These results appear to be consequential insofar as a within-person variation of two strokes can certainly explain why golfers sometimes qualify or not (i.e. earn money or not) for weekend rounds in high-level amateur and professional golf tournaments.

Future research is needed to examine the separate and combined effects of coping at the between- and within-person levels of analysis. *Homology* – or the generalisability of the associations between coping and athletic outcomes across levels of analysis – is not to be taken for granted (Chen *et al.*, 2005). Homology is empirically demonstrated when the direction (i.e. positive or negative) and the strength of the association between coping and coping effectiveness is invariant across level of analysis. In a recent study of Doron and Gaudreau (2014), the results of a Bayesian multilevel structural equation model revealed important differences in the association between episodic coping and performance across levels of analysis. Sabers fencers were more likely to increase their perceived control and task-oriented coping immediately after winning a point during the match (within-person level). In contrast, winning more points on average during the match was not significantly associated with higher average of perceived control and task-oriented coping (between-person level). Overall, such results point out to the necessity of empirically examining the invariance of theoretically-driven antecedents and consequences of coping across within- and between-person levels of analysis.

## Interpersonal coping: communal coping and interpersonal emotion regulation

### Communal coping

Much of the literature examining coping in sport has typically focused on athletes' efforts to deal with stressors individually (Tamminen and Gaudreau, 2014), although athletes' stressors, emotions, and efforts to cope are frequently social in nature (Campo *et al.*, 2012). Communal coping (Lyons *et al.*, 1998) represents a novel perspective through which to examine athletes' collective efforts to deal with stressors in a team or group context. Communal coping refers to a process whereby stressors are appraised and acted upon in the context of close relationships, and it describes the efforts of individuals as they cope with stressors collectively as a group or team (Lyons *et al.*, 1998). The three main components of communal coping include: (a) a communal coping orientation, (b) communication about the stressor, and (c) cooperative action to deal with the stressor (Lyons *et al.*, 1998). A communal coping orientation refers to members of the team holding the belief that joining together to deal with the stressor is necessary and beneficial. Communication about the stressor refers to modes of communication, patterns, and strategies to discussing and dealing with the stressor. Cooperative action to deal with the stressor can include strategies such as compensatory assistance, where individuals make up for their own deficits by drawing on others' strengths. While Lyons and colleagues have noted that the value of communal coping for achieving success is "obvious in team sport" (p. 592), there are no studies to date which have used a communal coping perspective to investigate athletes' collective coping as a team. Nonetheless, communal coping is emerging as a valuable approach for understanding processes of coping and accounts for the social context in which coping takes place.

There is some sport-related research that is connected to the concept of communal coping. "We-talk" is thought to be indicative of communal coping (Sillars *et al.*, 1997) and researchers have begun to explore the relationship between individuals' use of we-talk, perceptions of collective efficacy, and individual performance tasks. Researchers investigating the effects of group-focused self-talk (e.g. "we are confident performers") on a dart-throwing task showed that participants using group-focused self-talk had greater improvement in performance compared to a neutral self-talk condition (e.g. "I am a student"; Son *et al.*, 2011). The authors speculated that task performance improvements in the group-referent self-talk condition may have been due to improved perceptions of the group's ability to perform, which may have decreased individual performers' anxiety. While these relationships remain to be tested, the findings suggest that perceptions of the team's ability to perform (e.g. collective efficacy; Chow and Feltz, 2014) is related to individuals' task performance, which supports previous research regarding the positive relationship between perceptions of collective efficacy and team performance (Myers *et al.*, 2004). Future research may seek to investigate the use of we-talk as an indicator of communal coping and athletes' perceptions that their team can collectively deal with stressors to achieve positive team performances. Moving beyond lab-based experimental settings, qualitative research of communal coping in naturalistic settings where athletes practice and compete together on a regular basis may provide valuable information about athletes' use of "we-talk" within team settings.

Future research examining communal coping in sport should first seek to establish the main processes and features of communal coping within teams of athletes. This would include investigations of how stressors are appraised as a team and how athletes' shared appraisals may be congruent or incongruent from their teammates' appraisals; investigating athletes' communal coping orientations and beliefs about dealing with stressors individually or collectively; examining how athletes communicate about stressors and communal coping; and exploring how athletes engage in communal coping to deal with stressors and determining what strategies constitute communal coping actions in sport.

### Interpersonal emotional regulation

While communal coping deals with the way individuals come together to deal with stressors collectively, a complementary area of research that warrants further attention in sport is interpersonal emotion regulation. Emotion regulation refers to the "processes by which individuals influence which emotions they have, when they have them, and how they experience and express these emotions" (Gross, 1998, p. 275), while interpersonal emotion regulation focuses on understanding how individuals influence and regulate their own and others' emotions (Niven *et al.*, 2009; Zaki and Williams, 2013). Interpersonal emotion regulation (also called extrinsic emotion regulation; Gross, 2013) provides a framework for integrating several areas of research concerning interpersonal interactions when dealing with emotions and coping with stressors in sport. First, emotion regulation and coping often involves seeking and providing support from, and to others, for assistance to deal with stressors in sport. There is evidence that athletes seek support when dealing with competitive and organisational stressors (Kristiansen and Roberts, 2010), injuries (Rees *et al.*, 2010), burnout (DeFreese and Smith, 2013), and sport withdrawal and retirement (Park *et al.*, 2013). Second, athletes' emotions and emotion regulation or coping can potentially influence other people around them. Athletes' celebratory emotional displays have been associated with their team's eventual success (Moll *et al.*, 2010), there is evidence that athletes' emotions converge among teammates (Totterdell, 2000), and athletes report that their emotions and performance is influenced by the content of coaches' pre-game and intermission speeches (Breakey *et al.*, 2009; Vargas-Tonsing and Guan, 2007). Third, athletes report being aware that their own emotional displays influence others and they report deliberately attempting to regulate teammates' emotions in sport contexts. For example, an ethnographic study among high performance curlers revealed that athletes were aware of their emotional displays and attempted to regulate their own emotions to avoid upsetting teammates, and they also reported trying to regulate their teammates' emotions to benefit the team's performance (Tamminen and Crocker, 2013).

Additional research within a national sport organisation provided evidence that individuals perceived their use of emotion regulation strategies was influenced by their emotion abilities and also the social norms regarding emotion expression within the sport organisation (Wagstaff *et al.*, 2012; see also Wagstaff and Larner, this volume). Furthermore, directors, administrators, coaches, and athletes perceived that educational workshops and one-on-one training were useful in improving their emotion regulation abilities and improved perceptions of relationship quality and closeness within the organisation, suggesting that interventions to improve interpersonal emotion regulation could be valuable in sport organisations (Wagstaff *et al.*, 2013).

In light of calls to examine coping and emotions from an interpersonal perspective in sport (Friesen *et al.*, 2013; Tamminen and Gaudreau, 2014) and to situate coping within a social context (Carpenter and Scott, 1992), communal coping and interpersonal emotion regulation may be valuable perspectives for conceptualising the interpersonal processes of coping and emotion regulation within teams. Communal coping could help to describe how individual athletes appraise stressors as a member of a team, even if the stressor does not appear affect the athlete directly. For example, communal coping may be useful for understanding how athletes appraise another teammate's performance problems as they influence the rest of the team (e.g. how and when does "your problem" become "our problem"?). Communal coping would provide a framework for describing how athletes' coping within teams occurs as a process of coordinated strategies to deal with stressors collectively (e.g. how do athletes collectively deal with "our problems" as a team?). Interpersonal emotion regulation provides a perspective for integrating research on support seeking, emotional displays and emotional contagion, and efforts to regulate one's own emotions and others' emotions (Zaki and Williams, 2013). While researchers have only begun to explore interpersonal emotion regulation in sport, it provides a promising perspective for investigating how athletes interact with others when dealing with emotions and stressors in sport, and it allows researchers to account for the social consequences of emotion regulation in teams and groups. Moving forward, these approaches will require research methods that are sensitive to social processes and changes that affect multiple members of a team (e.g. ethnographic qualitative methods, social network analysis, interdependence models). These perspectives may help to advance our understanding of how athletes' efforts to deal with emotions and stressors influence others around them, rather than viewing emotion regulation and coping as an isolated process occurring within the athlete.

## Culture differences in coping

Culture has been relatively neglected in the study of the coping process in sport (Anshel, 2010). Although there are many definitions, culture typically refers to beliefs and values that shape thinking, behaving, and emoting by a particular group of people. Culture will determine what events are important, the potential consequences and benefits of sporting success and failure, and often constrain the ways to manage specific sporting demands. Thus, cultural should impact how athletes from various groups appraise, cope, and adapt to sport-related stress.

Sport research has typically focused on nationality differences in appraisal and coping (Anshel, 2010). This typically involves comparing athletes from different countries that are thought to have cultural differences. For example, Hoedaya and Anshel (2003) found that Indonesian and Australian athletes not only perceived the stressfulness of competitive situations differently, there were also nationality differences in how athletes coped with specific stressors. For example, Australian athletes perceived a bad call by a referee to be more stressful then Indonesian athletes. Indonesian athletes were also more likely to use denial, restraint, and active coping during the game compared to Australian athletes. Another example is a study by Laborde *et al.* (2012) who examine the effects of culture, emotional intelligence, and stressor situation on task oriented coping (TOC) and disengagement oriented coping (DOC). They reported that Chinese table tennis players were more likely than French players to use higher levels of DOC and TOC to manage stress from three stressor situations; however, culture did not moderate the effects of either situations or emotional intelligence on coping.

There are many fundamental limitations in most sport research on culture and coping. First, researchers often use nationality as a proxy measure of culture. This is problematic because it assumes that all athletes from a particular country shared the same culture and does not recognise important ethnic and religious differences that may exist within a country. Without identifying and measuring key cultural values within a study, researchers are often left to speculate about why there are nationality differences. Second, most studies fail to determine the underlying mechanisms that may lead to cultural differences in coping. Cultural beliefs may cause individuals to have different appraisals of importance, control, and coping options for particular stressful situations (Anshel, 2010). However, few studies evaluate these appraisals directly and then systematically analyse their relationships with coping to examine specific direct, mediation, or moderator models. Nevertheless, in multicultural societies researchers and practitioners must be sensitive to potential cultural differences that may influence how athletes attempt to manage and adapt to stressful sport encounters.

## Gender differences in coping

Gender differences in coping in sport are not well understood (Kaiseler and Polman, 2010). Although some reviews have suggested that there are robust gender differences (Hoar *et al.*, 2006), a close examination indicates inconsistent findings across studies. A recent systematic analysis of sport studies from 1990 to 2009 by Kaiseler and Polman (2010) found only 12 studies that explicitly analysed gender differences. Their analysis indicated only partial support for gender differences. However, results were equivocal; in some studies, males used more problem-focused coping compared to females (e.g. Hammermeister and Burton, 2004), some studies found no such differences (e.g. Crocker and Graham, 1995) and others found that females used more problem-focused coping (e.g. Nicholls *et al.*, 2007). There was more evidence (seven of 12 studies) that females used more emotion-focused strategies compared to males.

Much of the recent research on gender differences has been shaped by a meta-analysis of coping in multiple domains (Tamres *et al.*, 2002). Their analysis showed that women were more likely than men to engage in most types of coping, but that the nature of the stressor was an important moderator of gender differences. Tamres *et al.* (2002) indicated there are two primary views to explain potential gender differences. The situational hypothesis holds that gender differences occur because males and females are often confronting and reporting different stressors and also appraise the same stressors differently. This hypothesis was developed from the Role Constraint Theory (Rosario *et al.*, 1988), which holds that society/culture necessitates that males and females have specific gendered roles. These roles constrain the types of stressor sources that males and females predominantly face as well as shape the appraisal of similar stressors. Thus, if stressor source and appraisals are controlled, gendered coping should disappear. An alternative hypothesis, the dispositional hypothesis, holds that general differences will exist even when men and women are presented with the same stressor and have similar cognitive appraisals. Thus, gendered coping research in sport needs to consider the stressor type and the appraisal of the stressor (Hoar *et al.*, 2010; Kaiseler and Polman, 2010).

Two recent sport studies have attempted to examine the dispositional and situational hypotheses by considering stressor types and appraisals (Hoar *et al.*, 2010; Kaiseler *et al.*, 2012). Hoar *et al.* asked adolescent athletes to report how they appraised and coped with the most stressful interpersonal situation in sport. Using a combination of qualitative and quantitative methods, these authors identified five main themes of interpersonal stress sources relating to difficulties with: (a) personal social behaviour (athlete's social behaviour is the perceived source of stress); (b) coach; (c) teammates and opponents; (d) referee; and (e) family. For each of these stressors, instances of coping on 11 coping strategies were examined for gender differences. Results revealed that the odds of an athlete selecting aggression, cognitive reappraisal, and seeking social support to manage interpersonal stress sources was significantly related to gender after controlling for stress appraisal intensity. But the results indicated several key findings. First, there were more similarities than differences in coping between genders across stressors. Second, gender differences in coping were not robust across sources of interpersonal stress. For example, female athletes reported using more instances of seeking social support in the context of coach and personal social behaviour interpersonal stress sources. Female athletes also reported using more cognitive reappraisal than males only for the referee stress event. Male athletes used more aggression in the context of a peer stressor. Third, these gender differences did not disappear after controlling for stressor intensity. The Hoar *et al.* (2010) findings, however, need to be treated with caution because of limitations in methods such as self-reported recall over a long time period (up to 12 months), use of only coping instances to assess coping strategy usage, and only controlling for stressor intensity. Nevertheless, their findings do suggest that stressor type is an important consideration when examining gendered coping.

To address some key limitations in the gendered coping literature, Kaiseler *et al.* (2012) examined gender differences in soccer players for 12 coping strategies in response to three experimenter defined scenarios (wrong call from the referee, observing an opponent cheating, and technical error), and they also assessed appraisals of stress intensity and perceived control. Although multivariate analysis indicated no significant gender effect for appraisals, univariate analysis indicated that females appraised higher stress and lower control. However, gender differences were not robust across all three situations and effect sizes were very small. After controlling for appraisals, there was evidence of significant gender differences in coping. Across all three situations, females reported higher levels of seeking social support and wishful thinking. Females also reported higher levels of active coping for the stressors of wrong referee call and opponent cheating scenarios, as well as higher levels of self-blame for wrong referee calls. All effects were small. Kaiser *et al.* interpreted their findings as support for the dispositional hypothesis and that gender moderated appraisal-coping relationships. Although a promising study as it attempted to control for type of sport, specific types of stressors, and two types of appraisal, the study was still limited in its analytic strategy. The authors failed to conduct interaction analysis involving the three situations and gender, and also did not conduct moderated analysis of gender.

In summary, there is still much to be learned about gender differences in coping in sport. The literature points out that there are more similarities than differences in gendered coping. Kaiseler and Polman (2010) suggested that using broad dimension of coping, instead of more distinct coping strategies, may be obscuring gender differences. Also, recent empirical studies suggest that researchers must consider differences in stressors as well as cognitive appraisals to specific stressors. Nevertheless, given the interacting multitude of stress and adaption factors that can influence coping, there is a need for strong theoretical frameworks to direct research in this area

## Coping effectiveness

Much has been written and many meanings have been given to the notion of coping effectiveness during the last decade (e.g. Nicholls, 2010). The consideration of coping effectiveness typically within a stress process model has led Nicholls to define coping effectiveness in sport as "the degree in which a coping strategy or combination of strategies is or are successful in alleviating stress" (p. 264). We believe the definition can be more wide-ranging by replacing "alleviating stress" with "promoting successful adaptation". As such, time has come to step back and clarify the definitional roots of coping effectiveness.

To be effective implies the capacity to generate desirable outcomes. Given the multifinality of coping efforts, it is our understanding that effectiveness implies that a coping effort has been successful in promoting task success and emotional regulation rather than any one of these in isolation. It is generally held that effective coping can enhance sport performance as well as psychological well being (Lazarus, 2000). This idea, which was clearly summarised by Lazarus and Folkman (1984, p. 188), appears to have been long forgotten by coping researchers:

> A person who manages a problem effectively but at great emotional cost cannot be said to cope effectively.... Similarly, a person who regulates his or her emotions successfully but does not deal with the source of the problem cannot be said to be coping effectively.

Although task success and emotional regulation often correlate to a moderate degree, not all individuals appear to benefit from the salubrious emotional effects of task success. Synchronicity between task success and emotional adjustment can be indirectly inferred when a coping strategy positively correlates with valid indicators of task success and emotional adjustment. Synchronicity would be difficult to directly measure using traditional self-reported questionnaires but nonetheless appears to be the hallmark of what coping theorists have traditionally considered as the indicator of coping effectiveness.

So far, researchers have used two approaches to measure coping effectiveness in the sport literature. Several researchers have measured perceived coping effectiveness with items capturing a subjective evaluation of the extent to which a particular coping effort has been effective (Nicholls and Polman, 2007), effective at reducing stress (Nicholls *et al.*, 2009), effective at managing worries/concerns (Nicholls *et al.*, 2007), or effective at managing stress (Hanton *et al.*, 2008). A distinction has sometimes been made between short-term coping effectiveness (i.e. reducing, managing, or countering the psychological and performance problems during a competition) and long-term effectiveness (i.e. degree of satisfaction, enjoyment, and intention to continue in one's sport, Kim and Duda, 2003).

Researchers have typically reported higher perceived effectiveness for task-oriented coping strategies compared to disengagement-oriented strategies (e.g. Kaiseler *et al.*, 2009). Athletes with more experience and those currently competing at the elite levels tend to perceived both task-oriented and emotion-oriented coping as more effective than athletes with less experience and those who no longer compete at the elite levels (Hanton *et al.*, 2008). Athletes regardless of their experience and level of expertise, in contrast, perceive avoidance-oriented coping, as relatively ineffective.

Perceived coping effectiveness has also been assessed globally in relation to one's coping efforts during sport competition rather than in relation to each specific coping strategy used during the stress encounter (Levy *et al.*, 2011). In these studies, task-oriented coping and disengagement-oriented coping have been positively and negatively associated with global perceived coping effectiveness, respectively (Levy *et al.*, (2011); Nicholls *et al.*, 2010). Despite their respective strengths, each of these methods measured coping effectiveness in the eye of the beholder without determining whether coping can actually predict consequential athletic outcomes. This approach is somewhat comparable to a process evaluation in which the effect of an intervention is entirely assessed through the perceived effectiveness reported by the participants themselves (Melnyk and Morrison-Beedy, 2012). Therefore, several researchers have preferred an empirical outcome approach in which coping effectiveness is inferred when a coping strategy positively correlates with desirable outcomes and/or negatively correlates with undesirable outcomes.

Much evidence has been garnered for the positive and negative association of task-oriented coping and disengagement-oriented coping with and indicators of task success of athletes in the sport domain, respectively. Sport achievement has either been evaluated subjectively by the athletes themselves (Amiot *et al.*, 2004; Gaudreau and Antl, 2008; Nicolas *et al.*, 2011; Smith *et al.*, 2011), semi-objectively using a performance-goal discrepancy index (e.g. Gaudreau and Blondin, 2004; Gaudreau *et al.*, 2002), or objectively with the results obtained in a sport competition (e.g. Bois *et al.*, 2009; Gaudreau *et al.*, 2010). Despite their contributions, most of these studies have adopted cross-sectional or prospective designs in which performance was measured at a single point in time. The results of a recent study conducted with 438 collegiate volleyball players have shown that task-oriented coping and disengagement-oriented coping were positively and negatively associated with true change in goal attainment from the middle to the end of a competitive season (Schellenberg *et al.*, 2013). Both coping and performance can rapidly fluctuate across performance episodes during the course of a competitive match. Results of a recent study (Doron and Gaudreau, 2014) have demonstrated that episodic task-oriented coping was significantly more likely after winning versus losing the previous point in the match. Although task-oriented coping did not significantly predict the likelihood of winning the subsequent point in the match, it was nonetheless associated with a significantly greater likelihood of winning points in succession (i.e. winning streaks) in comparison to either losing points in succession (i.e. losing streaks) or winning a point outside of a streak.

Most researchers in the sport domain have adopted correlational research designs that preclude strong (if any) affirmations about the causal role of coping in predicting consequential outcomes in the lives of athletes. Results of a recent systematic review of the stress management literature have provided stronger support for the positive effects of stress management interventions to reduce the stress of competitive athletes (Rumbold *et al.*, 2012). Twenty-two of the 23 studies tested in a randomised control trial have shown that stress management interventions can be effective to reduce stress of participants. However, only 7 of the 13 studies examining stress and performance outcomes have shown that stress management interventions can be effective to simultaneously improve performance and stress-related outcomes. Recent experimental studies – one conducted with tennis players (Achtziger *et al.*, 2008) and one conducted with research participants in the lab (Stern *et al.*, 2013) – have highlighted the potential of short but theoretically-driven stress interventions to improve sport performance. Participants who were trained to identify potential stressors and to proactively create if-then coping plans were significantly more likely to obtain better task performance compared to individuals randomised in a goal setting control condition. They were also less likely to experience anxiety and to perceive the target (golf hole, dartboard) to be significantly closer which, in turn, explained their advantages in how they achieved on golf putting and dart throwing tasks (Stern *et al.*, 2013). Although some experimental studies have highlighted the potential of intervening on coping to facilitate both performance and emotional adjustment, more research is needed outside of the lab before we can recommend real-life implementation of these psycho-educational activities to coaches and sport associations.

Perceived coping effectiveness and empirically measured outcomes are often only modestly correlated. In a study conducted with a large sample of 414 athletes (Levy *et al.*, 2011), the correlation between athletes' subjective performance evaluation after a sport competition and their perceived coping effectiveness was significant but weak (r=0.15). Sometimes, this correlation has been much higher (r=0.45, Poliseo and McDonough, 2012). Although achievement-related outcomes have high consequential validity in the sport domain, they appear to be only one of the many indicators taken into account by athletes in their judgments of perceived coping effectiveness. Perceived coping effectiveness in sport could be evaluated in multiple ways, including reducing unwanted emotional states, enhancing positive or facilitative emotions, broadening and building resources, controlling cognitions and decision making, reducing stress intensity, managing physiological symptomology, redirection of motivational processes, facilitating performance, enhancing social functioning, and augmenting psychological well being (Tamminen *et al.*, 2014; Hanin, 2010; Nicholls, 2010; Ziedner and Saklofske, 1996). Overall, athletes' perceived coping effectiveness and measurable empirical outcomes (e.g. task success) of coping should not necessarily be taken as synonyms.

Intervention researchers rarely evaluate the objective effectiveness of an intervention without considering the perceived satisfaction of their participants (Melnyk and Morrison-Beedy, 2012). Using this analogy, we believe that much could be learned by integrating the perceived coping effectiveness approach which asks the athlete whether they believe their coping efforts have been effective and the empirical outcome approach which evaluates objective outcomes of coping efforts. The study by Ntoumanis and Biddle (1998) has provided a convincing example of the potential benefits of this combined measurement approach. The level to which a coping strategy was used and the extent to which it was perceived as effective both made a unique contribution in the prediction of affective states of athletes. Furthermore, perceived coping effectiveness moderated the relationship between coping usage and affective states of athletes in the case of behavioural disengagement and seeking support. For athletes who perceived behavioural disengagement as highly effective, the negative relationship between behavioural disengagement and positive affect was significantly attenuated. For athletes who perceived seeking support as highly effective, the negative association between seeking support and positive affect was entirely buffered whereas the positive association with negative affect was significantly attenuated.

Most sport researchers would probably agree with Lazarus's (1999) assertion that most coping strategies are neither inherently effective nor ineffective. That is, a strategy might be effective in one situation but ineffective in another situation because of differences in the actual demands faced by the athletes. For example, confronting teammates over lack of effort could lead to better team performance whereas confronting a referee over a bad call might lead to expulsion. Furthermore, some strategies might provide short-term effectiveness but be maladaptive in the long term (see Folkman and Moskowitz, 2004; Nicholls, 2010). For example, avoiding some difficult technical skills in figure skating might reduce short-term anxiety but using these same avoidance strategies over time will likely lead to diminished performance. Despite the heuristic value of this theoretical assumption, sport researchers have typically found that some forms of coping, such as task oriented or problem-focused coping, are more effective than other forms of coping. We believe that these results should not be taken as evidence for the argument that task-oriented coping always lead to adaptive outcomes or to coping effectiveness. Closer attention should be allocated to the sport context to offer a trustworthy interpretation of these findings and to determine the "boundary conditions" of when and in what contexts certain coping strategies are likely to be effective.

The context of sport is inherently achievement driven. Although individual differences do exist, athletes are trained to believe they are responsible for and accountable of their sport performance. The standards and goals of competitive sport environments create a dialectical person-environment transaction in which task-oriented efforts are likely to be socially reinforced and personally valued. In such contexts, task-oriented efforts are likely to facilitate goal attainment and positive affectivity for most athletes under most competitive situations. Therefore, it is not surprising that task-oriented coping efforts positively correlate with indicators of task success because they reciprocate, match or fit with the agendas that constrain and shape the situational demands and the social identity of competitive athletes (Lazarus and Folkman, 1984, p. 188). Task-oriented coping efforts create the needed conditions to facilitate the demonstration of competence and mastery over time (e.g. learning, self-improvement) and the building up of a social network (e.g. peer support, coach support). As demonstrated in the work of Van Yperen (2009), it is likely to foster the development of expertise and long-term survival in the competitive sport domain.

Contextual features of the sport environment are limiting the likelihood of empirically demonstrating that task-oriented coping is ineffective to promote desirable performance and emotional outcomes. Stretching out our experimental conditions to delineate the boundary conditions of the effectiveness of task-oriented coping is an area of particular importance to inform applied sport psychologists about for whom and under which conditions task-oriented coping stops being associated with desirable outcomes. A developmental approach might be useful in that regard (Heckhausen *et al.*, 2010). Task-oriented efforts are likely to become less efficient when something interferes with the typical dialectical person-environment transaction of being an athlete. Exhaustion, injuries, sport–life conflicts, and new developmentally appropriate commitments (e.g. friends, romantic relationships, and retirement intention) are likely to momentarily interfere with the dominant dialectic transaction in ways that will likely disrupt the effectiveness of task-oriented coping during training and sport competition. Mismatch between the new situation and the typical coping efforts – which have been reinforced by the context and valued by the athlete for years – will create an emerging life agenda in which sport-related task-oriented coping might stop significantly predicting sport success and positive affectivity about one's sport. Recurrent or accelerated reappearance of unexpected linkages between task-oriented efforts and task failure will set the tone for modification in goals, values, commitments, priorities, and social network in ways that might encourage athletes to mentally and/or behaviourally disengage from one's sport in order to incorporate and prioritise other social identities. For some athletes under some particular life circumstances, cumulative null associations between task-oriented coping and sport success might constitute a developmentally appropriate process likely to generate both continuity and change. The disengagement and re-engagement processes likely to result when sport-related goals become unattainable (Wrosch *et al.*, 2013) could eventually help the athletes to progressively transfer their personal coping skills acquired in sport (i.e. continuity) to start exploring other personally relevant activities (i.e. changes).

During stressful and challenging situations typically experienced in the daily training and competition of competitive athletes, the activation of task-oriented coping efforts is likely to maximize the likelihood of task success. However, athletes need to strike a balance between their coping efforts and the need for coping. Using high levels of task-oriented coping might be effective but inefficient when there is nothing or very few things to cope with. Deploying one's total repertoire of task-oriented coping would be unnecessary for a top-ranked tennis players playing against an opponent ranked 500th in the world. Task-oriented coping might be significantly associated with task success even during such episodes of minimal stress and challenge. However, one could expect a diminishing rate of return because, in such situations, the athlete could succeed even while using minimal amount of task-oriented coping. Overactivation of the task-oriented coping efforts when there is little to cope with is inefficient because it forces the athlete to utilise too much resource compared to what is actually needed to succeed in the current situation. Success in that particular episode might be costly insofar as it might hinder the conservation of resources needed to successfully cope with subsequent situations involving higher levels of stress and challenges. Recurrent inefficiency in task-oriented coping might result in higher allostatic load that could "wear and tear" (Dhabhar, 2011, p. 57) the mental and physical resources of the athletes. Future research should pay more attention to coping efficiency (relative outcomes of coping in comparison to resource allocation) in order to understand, for example, why task-oriented coping only weakly diminishes the likelihood of experiencing symptoms of athletic burnout over time (Schellenberg *et al.*, 2013).

On a final note, Lazarus and Folkman (1984) have argued that the association between coping and psychological outcomes should be moderated by cognitive appraisals as well as a by personality dispositions. For example, the goodness of fit hypothesis specifies that task-oriented coping should be most effective in situations that are perceived as challenging and controllable. In contrast, task-oriented coping might become ineffective in situations that are perceived as uncontrollable and threatening. Although research has found direct positive association between challenge appraisals and task-oriented coping, on the one hand, and between threat appraisals and disengagement-oriented coping, on the other hand (e.g. Kowalski *et al.*, 2005; Poliseo and

McDonough, 2012), a goodness of fit hypothesis would be supported only if cognitive appraisals moderate the relationship between coping and outcomes. Empirical support has yet to emerge for the goodness of fit hypothesis in the sport domain. In a recent study conducted with 139 collegiate level athletes, cognitive appraisals did not significantly interact with coping to predict coping effectiveness, positive affect, negative affect, and goal attainment (Poliseo and McDonough, 2012). Lazarus and Folkman (1984) never suggested that individuals with higher challenge appraisals should benefit more from task-oriented coping in comparison to individuals with lower levels of challenge appraisals. Testing the goodness of fit hypothesis using traditional between-person statistical analyses is unlikely to yield conclusive evidence (Park *et al.*, 2004) because the hypothesis requires a within-person comparisons of coping and cognitive appraisals across several coping episodes in the lives of the participants. To our knowledge, studies have yet to examine the goodness of fit hypothesis using a proper within-person design allowing the effects of coping to be properly compared according to within-person fluctuations in cognitive appraisals.

## Summary

Coping is part of a complex process require for successful adaptation in sport achievement settings. Sport researchers have generally investigated coping within a stress and emotion framework to examine how athletes deal with competitive stressors, although we believe it can be extended to investigate how athletes develop and acquire new resources to manage future demands. There is emerging research that holds that coping should be considered both at the intrapersonal and interpersonal level. Although most sport research focuses on the intrapersonal nature of coping, there are exciting developments in interpersonal coping areas such as communal coping and interpersonal emotional regulation.

Sport researchers, using both qualitative and quantitative methods, have demonstrated that coping is influenced by a number of key factors such as cognitive appraisals of stressors and coping resources, personality, gender, and culture. Coping also demonstrates both dispositional and dynamic properties over time. It is also evident that coping impacts many athletic outcomes such as performance, emotion and cognitive regulation, as well as psychological well-being. Understanding how and why coping is effective in the short and long-term adaptation process is a stimulating area of study. We stressed throughout the chapter, however, that the coping process is complicated. There are no simple "if-then" propositions to be made. Although there are still many gaps in our knowledge, we have identified both strengths and limitations in our measurement and conceptual approaches and have made many suggestions for future research.

# References

Achtziger, A., Gollwitzer, P. M., and Sheeran, P. (2008). Implementation intentions and shielding goal striving from unwanted thoughts and feelings. *Personality and Social Psychology Bulletin*, 34, 381–393. doi: 10.1177/0146167207311201.

Aldwin, C. M. (2007). *Stress, coping, and development: An integrative approach* (2nd ed.). New York: Guilford.

Allen, M. S., Greenlees, I., and Jones, M. (2011). An investigation of the five-factor model of personality and coping behaviour in sport. *Journal of Sports Sciences*, 29, 841–850.

Amiot, C. E., Gaudreau, P., and Blanchard, C. M. (2004). Self-determination, coping, and goal attainment in sport. *Journal of Sport and Exercise Psychology*, 26, 396–411.

Anshel, M. H. (2001). Qualitative validation of a model for coping with acute stress in sport. *Journal of Sport Behaviour*, 24, 223–246.

Anshel, M. H. (2010). Cultural differences in coping with stress in sport. In A. R. Nicholls (ed.), *Coping in sport: Theory, methods, and related constructs* (pp. 119–138). Hauppauge, NY: Nova Science.

Anshel, M. H., William, L. R., and Williams, S. M. (2000). Coping style following acute stress in competitive sport. *The Journal of Social Psychology*, 140, 751–73.

Aspinwall, L. G. and Taylor, S. E. (1997). A stitch in time: Self-regulation and proactive coping. *Psychological Bulletin*, 121, 417–436.

Bolgar, M. R., Janelle, C., and Giacobbi, P. R. (2008). Trait anger, appraisal, and coping differences among adolescent tennis players. *Journal of Applied Sport Psychology*, 20, 73–87.

Bonnano, G. A., Papa, A., Lalande, K., Westphal, M., and Coifman, K. (2004). The importance of being flexible: The ability to both enhance and suppress emotional expression predicts long-term adjustment. *Psychological Science*, 15, 482–487. doi: 10.1111/j.0956-7976.2004.00705.x.

Bois, J. E., Sarrazin, P., Southon, J., and Boiche, C. S. (2009). Psychological characteristics and their relation to performance in professional golfers. *The Sport Psychologist*, 23, 252–270.

Breakey, C., Jones, M. I., Cunningham, C. T., and Holt, N. L. (2009). Female athletes' perceptions of a coach's speeches. *Journal of Sport Science and Coaching*, 4, 489–504.

Campo, M., Mellalieu, S. D., Ferrand, C., Martinent, G., and Rosnet, E. (2012). Emotions in team contact sports: A systematic review. *The Sport Psychologist*, 26, 62–97.

Carpenter, B. N. and Scott, S. N. (1992). Interpersonal aspects of coping. In B. N. Carpenter (ed.), *Personal coping: Theory, research, and application* (pp. 93–109). Westport, CT: Praeger.

Carver, C. S., Scheier, M. F., and Weintraub, J. K. (1989). Assessing coping strategies: A theoretically based approach. *Journal of Personality and Social Psychology*, 56, 267–283.

Chen, G., Bliese, P. D., and Mathieu, J. E. (2005). Conceptual framework and statistical procedures for delineating and testing multilevel theories of homology. *Organisational Research Methods*, 8, 375–409.

Chow, G. M. and Feltz, D. L. (2014). Collective efficacy beliefs and sport. In M. Beauchamp and M. Eys (eds), *Group dynamics in exercise and sport psychology* (2nd edn, pp. 298–316). New York: Routledge.

Compas, B. E., Connor-Smith, J. K., Saltzman, H., Thomsen, A. H., and Wadsworth, M. E. (2001). Coping with stress during childhood and adolescence: Problems, progress, and potential in theory and research. *Psychological Bulletin*, 127, 82–127.

Corbin, J. and Strauss, A. (2008). *Basics of qualitative research: Techniques and procedures for developing grounded theory* (3rd edn). Thousand Oaks, CA: Sage.

Crocker, P. R. E. (1992). Managing stress by competitive athletes: Ways of coping. *International Journal of Sport Psychology*, 23, 161–175.

Crocker, P. R. E. and Graham, T. R. (1995). Coping by competitive athletes with performance stress: Gender differences and relationships with affect. *The Sport Psychologist*, 9, 325–338.

Crocker, P. R. E. and Isaak, K. (1997). Coping during competitions and training sessions: Are youth swimmers consistent? *International Journal of Sport Psychology*, 28, 355–369.

Crocker, P. R. E., Kowalski, K. C., and Graham, T. R. (1998). Measurement of coping strategies in sport. In J. L. Duda (ed.), *Advances in sport and exercise psychology measurement* (pp. 149–161). Morgantown, WV: Fitness Information Technology.

Crocker, P. R. E., Gaudreau, P., Mosewich, A. D., and Kljajic, K. (2014). Perfectionism and the stress process in intercollegiate athletes: Examining the 2×2 model of perfectionism in sport competition. *International Journal of Sport Psychology*. Special issue on perfectionism, 45, 325–348.

Crocker, P. R. E., Mosewich, A. D., Kowalski, K. C., and Besenski, L. J. (2010). Coping: Research design and analysis issues. In A. R. Nicholls (ed.), *Coping in sport: Theory, methods, and related constructs* (pp. 53–76). Hauppauge, NY: Nova Science.

Dale, G. (2000). Distractions and coping strategies of elite decathletes during their most memorable performances. *The Sport Psychologist*, 14, 17–41.

Day, M. C., Bond, K., and Smith, B. (2013). Holding it together: Coping with vicarious trauma in sport. *Psychology of Sport and Exercise*, 14, 1–11.

DeFreese, J. D. and Smith, A. (2013). Teammate social support, burnout, and self-determined motivation in collegiate athletes. *Psychology of Sport and Exercise*, 14, 258–265. doi:10.1016/j.psychsport.2012.10.009.

Deroche, T., Woodman, T., Stephan, Y., Brewer, B. W., and Le Scanff, C. (2011). Athletes' inclination to play through pain: A coping perspective. *Anxiety, Stress and Coping: An International Journal*, 24, 579–587.

Doron, J. and Gaudreau, P. (2014). A point-by-point analysis of performance in a fencing match: Psychological processes associated with winning and losing streaks. *Journal of Sport and Exercise Psychology*, 36, 3–13. doi: 10.1123/jsep. 2013–0043.

Ebata, A. T. and Moss, R. H. (1991). Coping and adjustment in healthy and distressed adolescents. *Journal of Applied Development Psychology*, 12, 33–54.

Eklund, R. C., Grove, J. R., and Heard, N. P. (1998). The measurement of slump-related coping: Factorial validity of the COPE and modified-COPE inventories. *Journal of Sport and Exercise Psychology*, 20, 157–175.

Evans, M. B., Hoar, S. D., Gebotys, R. J., and Marchesin, C. A. (2013). Endurance athletes' coping function use during competitive suffering episodes. *European Journal of Sport Science*. Published online DOI:10.1080/17461391.2013.832803.

Fletcher, R. (2008). Longitudinal factorial invariance, differential, and latent mean stability of the Coping Inventory for Competitive Sports. In M. P. Simmons and L. A. Foster (eds), *Sport and Exercise Psychology Research Advances* (pp. 293–306). New York: Nova Science.

Folkman, S. and Lazarus, R. S. (1980). An analysis of coping in a middle-aged community sample. *Journal of Health and Social Behaviour*, 21, 219–239.

Folkman, S., and Lazarus, R. S. (1985). If it changes it must be a process: Study of emotion and coping during three stages of a college examination. *Journal of Personality and Social Psychology*, 48, 150–170.

Folkman, S. and Moskowitz, J. (2004). Coping: Pitfalls and promise. *Annual Review of Psychology*, 55, 745–774.

Fredrickson, B. L. (2001). The role of positive emotions in positive psychology: The broaden and build theory of positive emotions. *American Psychologist*, 56, 218–226.

Gaudreau, P. and Antl, S. (2008). Athletes' broad dimensions of dispositional perfectionism: Examining changes in life satisfaction and the mediating role of sport related motivation and coping. *Journal of Sport and Exercise Psychology*, 30, 356–382.

Gaudreau, P. and Blondin, J. P. (2002). Development of a questionnaire for the assessment of coping strategies employed by athletes in competitive sport settings. *Psychology of Sport and Exercise*, 3, 1–34.

Gaudreau, P. and Blondin, J. P. (2004a). Different athletes cope differently: A cluster analysis of coping. *Personality and Individual Differences*, 36, 1865–1877.

Gaudreau, P. and Blondin, J.P. (2004b). The differential effect of dispositional optimism and pessimism on athletes' coping, goal attainment, and emotional adjustment during a sport competition. *International Journal of Stress Management*, 11, 245–269.

Gaudreau, P. and Miranda, D. (2010). Coping across time, situations, and contexts: A conceptual and methodological overview of stability, consistency, and change. In A. R. Nicholls (ed.), *Coping in sport: Theory, methods, and related constructs* (pp. 15–32). New York, NY: Nova.

Gaudreau, P., Blondin, J. P., and Lapierre, A. M. (2002). Athletes' coping during a competition: Relationship of coping strategies with positive affect, negative affect, and performance-goal discrepancy. *Psychology of Sport and Exercise*, 3, 125–150.

Gaudreau, P., El Ali, M., and Marivain, T. (2005). Factor structure of the Coping Inventory for Competitive Sport with a sample of participants at the 2001 New York Marathon. *Psychology of Sport and Exercise*, 6, 271–288.

Gaudreau, P., Lapierre, A. M., and Blondin, J. P. (2001). Coping at three phases of competition: Comparison between precompetitive, competitive, and postcompetitive utilization of the same strategy. *International Journal of Sport Psychology*, 32, 369–385.

Gaudreau, P., Nicholls, A., and Levy, A. R. (2010). The ups and downs of coping and sport achievement: An episodic process analysis of within-person associations. *Journal of Sport and Exercise Psychology*, 32, 298–311.

Giacobbi Jr., P. R. and Weinberg, R. S. (2000). An examination of coping in sport: Individual trait anxiety differences and situational consistency. *The Sport Psychologist*, 14, 42–62.

Gould, D., Eklund, R. C., and Jackson, S. A. (1993). Coping strategies used by U.S. Olympic wrestlers. *Research Quarterly for Exercise and Sport*, 64, 83–93.

Goudas, M., Theodorakis, Y., and Karamousalidis, G. (1998). Psychological skills in basketball: Preliminary study for the development of a Greek form of the Athletic Coping Skills Inventory-28. *Perceptual and Motor Skills*, 86, 59–65.

Goyen, M. J. and Anshel, M. H. (1998). Sources of acute competitive stress and use of coping strategies as a function of age and gender. *Journal of Applied Developmental Psychology*, 19, 469–486.

Gross, J. J. (1998). The emerging field of emotion regulation: An integrative review. *Review of General Psychology*, 2, 271–299.

Gross, J. J. (2013). Emotion regulation: Taking stock and moving forward. *Emotion*, 13, 359–365.

Hammermeister, J. and Burton, D. (2004). Gender differences in coping with endurance sports: Are men from Mars and women from Venus? *Journal of Sport Behaviour*, 27, 148–164.

Hanin, Y.L. (2000). Successful and poor performance and emotions. In Y. L. Hanin (ed.), *Emotions in sport* (pp. 157–187). Champaign, IL: Human Kinetics.

Hanin, Y. L. (2010). Coping with anxiety in sport. In A. R. Nicholls (ed.), *Coping in sport: Theory, methods, and related constructs* (pp. 159–175). New York: Nova Science.

Hanton, S., Fletcher, D., and Coughlan, G. (2005). Stress in elite sport performers: A comparative study of competitive and organisational stressors. *Journal of Sports Sciences*, 23, 1129–1141.

Hanton, S., Neil, R., and Evans, L. (2013). Hardiness and anxiety interpretation: An investigation into coping usage and effectiveness. *European Journal of Sport Science*, 13, 96–104.

Hanton S., Neil R., Mellalieu, S. D., and Fletcher, D. (2008). Competitive experience and performance status: An investigation into multidimensional anxiety and coping. *European Journal of Sport Science*, 8, 143–152.

Heckhausen, J., Wrosch, C., and Schulz, R. (2010). A motivational theory of life-span development. *Psychological Review*, 117, 32–60. doi: 10.1037/a0017668.

Hill, A. P., Hall, H. K., and Appleton, P. R. (2010). Perfectionism and athlete burnout in junior elite athletes: The mediating role of coping tendencies. *Anxiety, Stress and Coping*, 23, 415–430. doi:10.1080/10615800903330966.

Hoar, S. D., Crocker, P. R. E., Holt, N. L., and Tamminen, K. A. (2010). Gender differences in adolescent athletes' coping with interpersonal stressors in sport: More similarities than differences? *Journal of Applied Sport Psychology*, 22, 134–149.

Hoar, S. D., Kowalski, K. C., Gaudreau, P., and Crocker, P. R. E. (2006). A review of coping in sport. In S. Hanton and S. D. Mellalieu (eds), *Literature reviews in sport psychology* (pp. 53–103). Hauppauge, NY: Nova Science.

Hobfoll, S. (2001). The influence of culture, community, and the nest-self in the stress process: Advancing conservation of resources theory. *Applied Psychology: An International Review*, 50, 337–421.

Holt, N. L. and Hogg, J. M. (2002). Perceptions of stress and coping during preparations for the 1999 women's soccer world cup finals. *The Sport Psychologist*, 16, 251–271.

Holt, N. L., Berg, K. J., and Tamminen, K. A. (2007). Tales of the unexpected: Coping among female collegiate volleyball players. *Research Quarterly for Exercise and Sport*, 78, 117–132.

Hurst, J. R., Thompson, A., Visek, A. J., Fisher, B., and Gaudreau, P. (2011). Towards a dispositional version of the coping inventory for Competitive Sport. *International Journal of Sport Psychology*, 42, 167–185.

Hoedaya, D. and Anshel, M. H. (2003). Sources of stress and coping strategies among Australian and Indonesian athletes. *Australian Journal of Psychology*, 55, 159–165.

Johnson, U. and Ivarsson, A. (2011). Psychological predictors of sport injuries among junior soccer players. *Scandinavian Journal of Medicine and Science in Sports,* 21, 129–136.

Jordet, G. (2010). Choking under pressure as self-destructive behaviour. In A. R. Nicholls (ed.), *Coping in sport: Theory, methods, and related constructs* (pp. 239–259). Hauppauge, NY: Nova Science.

Kaiseler, M. and Polman, R. C. J. (2010). Gender and coping in sport: Do male and female athletes cope differently? In A. R. Nicholls (ed.), *Coping in sport: Theory, methods, and related constructs* (pp. 79–93). New York: Nova Science Publishers.

Kaiseler, M., Polman, R. C. J., and Nicholls, A. R. (2009). Mental toughness, stress, stress appraisal, coping and coping effectiveness in sport. *Personality and Individual Differences,* 47, 728–733.

Kaiseler, M., Polman, R. C. J., and Nicholls, A. R. (2012). Gender differences in appraisal and coping: An examination of the situational and dispositional hypothesis. *International Journal of Sport Psychology,* 43, 1–14.

Kaissidis-Rodanfinos, A. N. and Anshel, M. H. (2000). Psychological predictions of coping responses among Greek basketball referees. *Journal of Social Psychology,* 140, 329–344.

Kim, M. S. and Duda, J. L. (2003). The coping process: Cognitive appraisals of stress, coping strategies, and coping effectiveness. *The Sport Psychologist,* 17, 406–425.

Kowalski, K. C. and Crocker, P. R. E. (2001). Development and validation of the Coping Function Questionnaire for adolescents in sport. *Journal of Sport and Exercise Psychology,* 23, 136–155.

Kowalski, K. C., Crocker, P. R. E., Hoar, S. D., and Niefer, C. B. (2005). Adolescents' control beliefs and coping with stress in sport. *International Journal of Sport Psychology,* 36, 257–272.

Kristiansen, E. and Roberts, G. C. (2010). Young elite athletes and social support: Coping with competitive and organisational stress in "Olympic" competition. *Scandinavian Journal of Medicine and Science in Sports,* 20, 686–695.

Laborde, S., You, M., Dosseville, F., and Salinas, A. (2012). Culture, individual differences, and situation: Influence on coping in French and Chinese table tennis players. *European Journal of Sport Science,* 12, 255–261.

Laborde, S., Dosseville, F., and Kinrade, N. P. (2014). Decision-specific reinvestment scale: An exploration of its construct validity, and association with stress and coping appraisals. *Psychology of Sport and Exercise,* 15, 238–246.

Lazarus, R. S. (1991). *Emotion and adaptation.* New York: Oxford University Press.

Lazarus, R. S. (1999). *Stress and emotion: A new synthesis.* New York: Springer Publishing.

Lazarus, R. S. (2000). Cognitive-motivational-relational theory of emotion. In Y. L. Hanin (ed.), *Emotions in sport* (pp. 39–63). Champaign, IL: Human Kinetics.

Lazarus, R. S. (2006). Emotions and interpersonal relationships: Toward a person-centered conceptualization of emotions and coping. *Journal of Personality,* 74, 9–46. doi:10.1111/j.1467–6494.2005.00368.x.

Lazarus, R. S. and Folkman, S. (1984). *Stress, appraisal, and coping.* New York: Springer Publishing.

Levy, A. R., Nicholls, A., and Polman, R. (2011). Pre-competitive confidence, coping, and subjective performance in sport. *Scandinavian Journal of Medicine and Science in Sports,* 21, 721–729. doi: 10.1111/j.1600–0838.2009.01075.x.

Lidor, R., Crocker, P. R. E., and Mosewich, A. D. (2012). Measuring coping skills and self-regulation. In G. Tenenbaum, R. Eklund, and A. Kamata (eds), *Measurement in sport and exercise psychology* (pp. 393–407). Champaign, IL: Human Kinetics.

Louvet, B., Gaudreau, P., Menaut, A., Genty, J., and Deneuve, P. (2007). Longitudinal patterns of stability and change in coping across three competitions: A latent class growth analysis. *Journal of Sport and Exercise Psychology*, 29, 100–117.

Louvet, B., Gaudreau, P., Menaut, A., Genty, J., and Deneuve, P. (2009). Revisiting the changing and stable properties of coping utilization using latent class growth analysis: A longitudinal investigation with soccer referees. *Psychology of Sport and Exercise*, 10, 124–135.

Lyons, R. F., Mickelson, K. D., Sullivan, M. J. L., and Coyne, J. C. (1998). Coping as a communal process. *Journal of Personal and Social Relationships*, 15, 579–605.

Madden, C. C., Kirkby, R. J., and McDonald, D. (1989). Coping styles of competitive middle distance runners. *International Journal of Sport Psychology*, 20, 287–296.

Martinent, G., Nicolas, M., Gaudreau, P., and Campo, M. (2013). A cluster analysis of affective states before and during competition. *Journal of Sport and Exercise Psychology*, 35, 600–611.

Melnyk, B. and Morrison-Beedy, D. (2012). *Intervention research: Designing, conducting, analyzing, and funding.* New York: Springer Publishing.

Moll, T., Jordet, G., and Pepping, G. J. (2010). Emotional contagion in soccer penalty shootouts: Celebration of individual success is associated with ultimate team success. *Journal of Sports Sciences*, 29, 983–992.

Mosewich, A. D., Kowalski, K. C., and Crocker, P. R. E. (2013). Managing injury and other setbacks in sport: Experiences of (and resources for) high performance women athletes. *Qualitative Research in Sport, Exercise and Health* (available on-line Feb 2013) DOI:10.1080/2159676X.2013.766810.

Mouratidis, A. and Michou, A. (2011). Perfectionism, self-determined motivation, and coping among adolescents. *Psychology of Sport and Exercise*, 12, 355–367.

Myers, N. D., Payment, C., and Feltz, D. L. (2004). Reciprocal relationships between collective efficacy and team performance in women's ice hockey. *Group Dynamics: Theory, Research, and Practice*, 8, 182–195.

Nicholls, A. R. (2007). A longitudinal phenomenological analysis of coping effectiveness among Scottish international adolescent golfers. *European Journal of Sport Science*, 7, 169–178.

Nicholls, A. R. (2010). Effective versus ineffective coping in sport. In A. R. Nicholls (ed.), *Coping in sport: theory, methods, and related constructs* (pp. 263–276). New York: Nova Science.

Nicholls, A. R. and Ntoumanis, N. (2010). Traditional and new methods of assessing coping in sport. In A. R. Nicholls (ed.), *Coping in sport: Theory, methods and related constructs* (pp. 35–51). New York: Nova Science.

Nicholls, A. R. and Polman, R. C. J. (2007). Coping in sport: A systematic review. *Journal of Sport Sciences*, 25, 11–31.

Nicholls, A. R. and Polman, R. C. J. (2008). Think aloud: Acute stress and coping strategies during golf performances. *Anxiety, Stress, and Coping*, 21, 283–294.

Nicholls, A. R. and Thelwell, R. C. (2010). Coping conceptualised and unravelled. In A. R. Nicholls (ed.), *Coping in Sport: Theory, methods, and related constructs* (pp. 3–14). New York: Nova Science.

Nicholls, A. R., Holt, N. L., and Polman, R. C. J. (2005). A phenomenological analysis of coping effectiveness in golf. *Sport Psychologist*, 19, 111–131.

Nicholls, A. R., Holt, N. L., Polman, R. C. J and Bloomfield, J. (2006). Stressors,
coping, and coping effectiveness among professional rugby union players. *The
Sport Psychologist*, 20, 314–329.

Nicholls, A. R., Holt, N. L., Polman, R. C. J., and James, D. W. (2005). A longitudinal idiographic analysis of an international adolescent golfer's stress and
coping. *Journal of Sports Sciences*, 23, 167–168.

Nicholls, A. R., Levy, A. R., Grice, A., and Polman, R. (2009). Stress appraisals,
coping, and coping effectiveness among international cross-country runners
during training and competition. *European Journal of Sport Science*, 9, 285–293.

Nicholls, A. R., Polman, R. C. J., Levy, A. R., and Backhouse, S. H. (2008). Mental
toughness, optimism, pessimism, and coping among athletes. *Personality and Individual Differences*, 44, 1182–1192.

Nicholls, A. R., Polman, R., Levy, A. R., and Borkoles, E. (2010). The mediating
role of coping: A cross-sectional analysis of the relationship between coping self-
efficacy and coping effectiveness among athletes. *International Journal of Stress
Management*, 17, 181–192. doi: 10.1037/a0020064.

Nicholls, A. R., Polman, R. C. J., Levy, A. R., Taylor, N. J., and Cobley, S. (2007).
Stressors, coping, and coping effectiveness: Gender, type of sport, and skill differences. *Journal of Sports Sciences*, 25, 1521–1531.

Nicholls, A. R., Polman, R. C. J., Morley, D., and Taylor, N. J. (2009). Coping and
coping effectiveness in relation to a competitive sport event: Pubertal status,
chronological age, and gender among adolescent athletes. *Journal of Sport and
Exercise Psychology*, 31, 299–317.

Nicolas, M., Gaudreau, P., and Franche, V. (2011). Perception of coaching behaviours, coping, and achievement in a sport competition. *Journal of Sport and Exercise Psychology*, 33, 460–468.

Nieuwenhuys, A., Hanin, Y. L., and Bakker, F. C. (2008). Performance-related
experiences and coping during races: A case of an elite sailor. *Psychology of Sport
and Exercise*, 9, 61–76. doi:10.1016/j.psychsport.2006.12.007.

Nieuwenhuys, A., Vos, L., Pijpstra, S., and Bakker, F. C. (2011). Meta experiences
and coping effectiveness in sport. *Psychology of Sport and Exercise*, 12, 135–143.

Niven, K., Totterdell, P., and Holman, D. (2009). A classification of controlled
interpersonal affect regulation strategies. *Emotion*, 4, 498–509.

Ntoumanis, N. and Biddle, S. J. H. (1998). The relationship of coping and its perceived effectiveness to positive and negative affect in sport. *Personality and Individual Differences*, 24, 773–788.

Ntoumanis, N. and Biddle, S. J. H. (2000). Relationship of intensity and direction
of competitive anxiety with coping strategies. *The Sport Psychologist*, 14, 360–371.

Park, C. L., Armeli, S., and Tennen, H. (2004). Appraisal-coping goodness of fit: A
daily internet study. *Personality and Social Psychology Bulletin*, 30, 558–569.

Park, S., Lavallee, D., and Tod, D. (2013). Athletes' career transition out of sport:
A systematic review. *International Review of Sport and Exercise Psychology*, 6, 22–53.

Poliseo, J. M. and McDonough, M. H. (2012). Coping effectiveness in competitive
sport: Linking goodness of fit and coping outcomes. *Sport, Exercise, and Performance Psychology*, 1, 106–119.

Rees, T., Mitchell, I., Evans, L. and Hardy, L. (2010). Stressors, social support and
psychological responses to sport injury in high- and low-performance standard
participants. *Psychology of Sport and Exercise*, 11, 505–512.

Reeves, C. W., Nicholls, A. R. and McKenna, J. (2009). Stressors and coping strategies among early and middle adolescent premier league academy soccer players: Differences according to age. *Journal of Applied Sport Psychology*, 21, 31–48.

Rosario, M., Shinn, M., Morch, H. and Huckabee, C. B. (1988). Gender differences in coping and social supports: Testing socialization and role constraint theories. *Journal of Community Psychology*, 16, 55–69.

Roth, S. and Cohen, L. J. (1986). Approach, avoidance, and coping with stress. *American Psychologist*, 41, 813–819.

Rumbold, J. L., Fletcher, D., and Daniels, K. (2012). A systematic review of stress management interventions with sport performers. *Sport, Exercise, and Performance Psychology*, 1, 173–193. doi: 10.1037/a0026628.

Sanz, J. L. G, Pérez, L. M. R., Coll, V. G., and Smith, R. E. (2011). Development and validation of a Spanish version of the Athletic Coping Skills Inventory, ACSI-28. *Psicothema*, 23, 495–502.

Schellenberg, B., Gaudreau, P., and Crocker, P. R. E. (2013). Passion and coping: Relationships with changes in burnout and goal attainment in collegiate volleyball players. *Journal of Sport and Exercise Psychology*, 35, 270–280.

Skinner, E. A. (1995). *Perceived control, motivation, and coping: Individual differences and development*. Thousand Oaks, CA: Sage.

Skinner, E. A. and Zimmer-Gembeck, M. J. (2007). The development of coping. *Annual Review of Psychology*, 58, 119–144.

Smith, A. L., Ntoumanis, N., Duda, J. L., and Vansteenkiste, M. (2011). Goal striving, coping, and well-being: A prospective investigation of the self-concordance model in sport. *Journal of Sport and Exercise Psychology*, 33, 124–145.

Smith, R. E., Schutz, R. W., Smoll, F. L., and Ptacek, J. T. (1995). Development and validation of a multidimensional measure of sport-specific psychological skills: The Athletic Coping Skills Inventory-28. *Journal of Sport and Exercise Psychology*, 17, 379–398.

Son, V., Jackson, B., Grove, J. R., and Feltz, D. L. (2011). "I am" versus "we are": Effects of distinctive variations of self-talk on efficacy beliefs and motor performance. *Journal of Sports Sciences*, 29, 1417–1424.

Stern, C., Cole, S., Gollwitzer, P. M., Oettingen, G., and Balcetis, E. (2013). Effects of implementation intentions on anxiety, perceived proximity, and motor performance. *Personality and Social Psychology Bulletin*, 39, 623–635.

Tamminen, K. A. and Gaudreau, P. (2014). Coping, social support, and emotion regulation in teams. In M. Beauchamp and M. Eys (eds), *Group dynamics in exercise and sport psychology: Contemporary themes* (2nd edn, pp. 222–239). New York: Routledge.

Tamminen, K. A. and Holt, N. L. (2010a). A meta-study of qualitative research examining stressor appraisals and coping among adolescents in sport. *Journal of Sport Sciences*, 28, 1563–1580.

Tamminen, K. A. and Holt, N. L. (2010b). Female adolescent athletes' coping: A season long investigation. *Journal of Sports Sciences*, 28, 101–114.

Tamminen, K. A. and Holt, N. L. (2012). Adolescent athletes' learning about coping and the roles of parents and coaches. *Psychology of Sport and Exercise*, 13, 69–79.

Tamminen, K. A. and Crocker, P. R. E. (2014). Simplicity does not always lead to enlightenment: A critical commentary on "Adaptation processes affecting performance in elite sport." *Journal of Clinical Sport Psychology*, 7, 75–91.

Tamminen, K. A. and Crocker, P. R. E. (2013). "I control my own emotions for the sake of the team": Emotional self-regulation and interpersonal emotion regulation among female high-performance curlers. *Psychology of Sport and Exercise*, 14, 737–747.

Tamminen, K. A., Crocker, P. R. E., and McEwen, C. E. (2014). Emotional experiences and coping in sport: How to promote positive adaptational outcomes in sport. In R. Gomes (ed.), *Positive human functioning from a multidimensional perspective* (pp. 143–162). Nova Science.

Tamminen, K. A., Holt, N. L., and Neely, K. C. (2013). Exploring adversity and the potential for growth among elite female athletes. *Psychology of Sport and Exercise*, 14, 28–36. doi: 10.1016/j.psychsport.2012.07.002.

Tamres, L. K., Janicki, D., and Helgeson, V. S. (2002). Sex differences in coping behaviour: A meta-analytic review and an examination of relative coping. *Personality and Social Psychology Review*, 6, 2–30.

Thelwell, R. C., Weston, N. J. V., and Greenlees, I. A. (2007). Batting on a sticky wicket: Identifying sources of stress and associated coping strategies for professional cricket batsmen. *Psychology of Sport and Exercise*, 8, 219–232.

Totterdell, P. (2000). Catching moods and hitting runs: Mood linkage and subjective performance in professional sport teams. *Journal of Applied Psychology*, 85, 848–859.

Vargas-Tonsing, T. and Guan, J. (2007). Athletes' preferences for informational and emotional pre-game speech content. *International Journal of Sports Science and Coaching*, 2, 171–180.

Uphill, M. A. and Jones, M. V. (2012). The consequences and control of emotions in elite athletes. In J. Thatcher, M. V. Jones, and D. Lavallee (eds), *Coping and emotion in sport* (2nd edn, pp. 213–235). London: Routledge.

Van Yperen, N. W. (2009). Why some make it and others do not: Identifying psychological factors that predict career success in professional adult soccer. *The Sport Psychologist*, 23, 317–329.

Wagstaff, C. R. D., Fletcher, D., and Hanton, S. (2012). Exploring emotion abilities and regulation strategies in sport organisations. *Sport, Exercise and Performance Psychology*, 1, 262–282.

Wagstaff, C. R. D., Hanton, S., and Fletcher, D. (2013). Developing emotion abilities and regulation strategies in a sport organisation: An action research intervention. *Psychology of Sport and Exercise*, 14, 476–487.

Weissensteiner, J. R., Abernethy, B., Farrow, D., and Gross, J. (2012). Distinguishing psychological characteristics of expert cricket batsmen. *Journal of Science and Medicine in Sport*, 15, 74–79.

Wrosch, C., Scheier, M. F., and Miller, G. E. (2013). Goal adjustment capacities, subjective well-being, and physical health. *Social and Personality Psychology Compass*, 7, 847–860. doi: 10.1111/spc3.12074.

Zaki, J. and Williams, W. C. (2013). Interpersonal emotion regulation. *Emotion*, 13, 803–810.

Zeidner, M. and Saklofske, D. (1996). Adaptive and maladaptive coping. In M. Zeidner and N. Endler (eds), *Handbook of coping: Theory, research, applications* (pp. 505–531). New York, NY: Wiley.

# 3 The five self-determination mini-theories applied to sport

*Ian Taylor*

## Introduction

Motivation is a key component of maintaining successful and worthwhile sports participation, irrespective of whether sport refers to a sociable game of tennis between friends or an Olympic final with a global audience watching. Scholarly attempts to understand motivational phenomena in sporting contexts have, therefore, gained considerable momentum and a framework that often underpins these endeavours is self-determination theory (SDT). SDT's empirical beginnings are observable in research concerning 'the effects of externally mediated rewards on intrinsic motivation' (Deci, 1971) and the theory began to be applied to sports and competitive settings in the following years (e.g. Vallerand, 1983; Weinberg, 1979). Partly due to this early work, SDT is commonly described as a theory of motivation; however, its expansion to include five complementary mini-theories now encompasses motivation, human development, well-being, and personality. These theories are presented in subsequent sections of this chapter and relevant sport-based research is evaluated. Sporting applications are integrated within this commentary and potential future research questions are raised in the hope of stimulating novel and groundbreaking research.

## Cognitive evaluation theory

A central principle of SDT is that humans are active organisms that are fundamentally inclined towards growth, which manifests itself as an innate tendency to engage in activity for its own sake and without external prompts (Deci and Ryan, 2000). This *intrinsic motivation* is evidenced through inherent enjoyment, interest and curiosity during activity (Vansteenkiste *et al.*, 2010). Cognitive evaluation theory (CET) is the oldest of the self-determination theories and was developed from investigation into the impact of external rewards on the human predisposition towards intrinsic motivation. In initial studies, monetary rewards were found to reduce subsequent intrinsic motivation for puzzle solving and headline writing tasks, whereas verbal approval and positive feedback enhanced intrinsic motivation (Deci, 1971). The specific nature of rewards and contingencies has subsequently been shown to be important in moderating the undermining effect, for example, unexpected rewards do not damage intrinsic motivation and performance-contingent rewards have a diminished effect (Deci *et al.*, 1999a, 1999b).

CET can explain these consequences as it proposes that intrinsically motivated action can only flourish in contexts that support individuals' fundamental needs for autonomy and competence. Autonomy reflects the feeling of volition, self-organisation, and the experience of behaviour as congruent with one's integrated sense of self (deCharms, 1968; Deci and Ryan, 2000). Despite some misconceptions, autonomy is distinct from control, independence, or individualism (Chirkov *et al.*, 2003; Vansteenkiste *et al.*, 2010). Competence refers to a propensity to be effective and attain valued outcomes within an environment (White, 1959). Environments do not cause intrinsic motivation, but support or thwart it via controlling and informational facets. If controlling aspects of the environment are perceived salient, an individual will feel induced or coerced into action. Autonomy is, therefore, undermined because the true origin of behaviour (i.e. locus of causality) shifts from internal to external prompts. In contrast, informational contexts facilitate autonomy and competence because optimal challenges and aptitude-relevant feedback are prevalent (Deci and Ryan, 1985a). Although supported by decades of research, investigators should be aware that the theory is not without debate (e.g. Byron and Khazanchi, 2012).

These theoretical tenets have significance for sport, particularly the competitive ethos embedded within sport. Competition can be an enjoyable opportunity to gauge how one has improved or bring intense pressure from external (e.g. pressure from parents to win a tournament) or internal sources described as ego-involvements (e.g. an athlete believing they must win to be successful and valued by their team; Ryan, 1982). In non-sports contexts, winning a puzzle-solving competition has unsurprisingly been shown to enhance competence and, therefore, intrinsic motivation (Reeve and Deci, 1996). In the same study, when informing participants prior to the task that the only thing that matters is to win created a controlling environment, autonomy and intrinsic motivation were diminished. The type of sport played may influence these effects of competition as participants in a hand-grip endurance task reported greater enjoyment (a prototypical indicator of intrinsic motivation) in team versus individual competitions (Cooke *et al.*, 2013). Tauer and Harackiewicz (2004) reported similar findings during basketball free-throw tasks and suggested that team competition may provide a context where feelings of relatedness are supported, which may increase enjoyment. Indeed, the ongoing development of CET incorporated the need to care for others and to be cared for as a third, albeit more distal, antecedent of intrinsic motivation (Deci and Ryan, 2000). In other words, feelings of relatedness may make intrinsic motivation more likely but it is not essential.

CET has also been employed to investigate the influence of athletic scholarships on intrinsic motivation, with equivocal findings reported. On the one hand, track and field scholarship holders have been shown to be less intrinsically motivated compared to non-scholarship holders (Cremades *et al.*, 2012). Similarly, Kingston *et al.* (2006) were able to distinguish between scholarship and non-scholarship athletes based on their motives for participation, with intrinsic motivation contributing to this discrimination. On the other hand, scholarship athletes have been shown to be more intrinsically motivated than their non-scholarship counterparts (Amorose and Horn, 2000), and scholarship status was not related to changes in intrinsic motivation over the course of a season (Amorose and Horn, 2001). These mixed results highlight the potential dual influence of external contingencies on intrinsic motivation. Scholarships may suppress autonomy (e.g. 'I must perform because I'm a scholarship athlete') or they may enhance competence (e.g. 'I must be good because they gave me a scholarship'). Longstanding research has outlined that it is the functional significance, or the subjective meaning of the contextual feature that is the decisive component in shaping motivation and regulating behaviour (Deci and Ryan, 1987). Moreover, the degree to which one is predisposed to seek out autonomy may moderate the undermining effect of contextual features on intrinsic motivation (Hagger and Chatzisarantis, 2011).

A third application of CET to sport demonstrates the influence of feedback on athletes' intrinsic motivation. Predictably, positive feedback has consistently been linked to intrinsic motivation, because it is competence enhancing (Mouratidis *et al.*, 2008; Vallerand and Reid, 1984). What is perhaps more useful to coaches and professionals working with athletes is how to communicate remedial feedback without disturbing intrinsic motivation. Corrective feedback provided in an autonomy-supportive fashion has been correlated with higher autonomy, competence, and intrinsic motivation in athletes from a range of sports (Carpentier and Mageau, 2013; Mouratidis *et al.*, 2010). Hence, coaches should provide a meaningful (from the athlete's perspective) reason why the feedback may help the athlete, ask the athlete's opinion on the feedback provided, and provide a choice of solutions (Mageau and Vallerand, 2003).

Building on this knowledge, sport could be a fruitful context to advance CET in several important ways. From a broad perspective, Vansteenkiste *et al.* (2010) highlighted that most research has examined the influence of a single event on individuals' intrinsic motivation. The impact of multiple events (e.g. winning or losing streaks, continual performance evaluation) on intrinsic motivation over a sustained period of time, such as a competitive season, would enhance knowledge. The identification of potential moderators of the relationship between competition and intrinsic motivation would also seem worthy. It is possible, for example, that a positive athletic disposition (e.g. resilience, optimism) or certain adaptive contexts (e.g. a socially supportive environment) may buffer athletes against the potentially negative effects of competitive losses. Relatedly, is the perceived threat or challenge of an upcoming competition most influential for intrinsic motivation or is the outcome (e.g. winning or losing) more significant? It seems plausible that reductions in intrinsic motivation via controlling aspects of competition may precede the competitive event, whereas declines in intrinsic motivation through competence deprivation may be more likely to occur after the event.

A further route of enquiry may explore the proposal that feelings of relatedness are helpful for the facilitation of intrinsic motivation, but not a requisite. Some individuals enjoy their particular sport to get away from the world and be alone, while others love sport because it provides opportunity to socialise and identify with a team. Are there circumstances in which relatedness is particularly significant for intrinsic motivation, compared to other instances where relatedness has very little importance? Is intrinsic motivation more fragile and susceptible to controlling external events when relatedness is not experienced? For instance, the impact of feedback or rewards from a coach may be different if a sense of relatedness is felt between athlete and coach, as opposed to an emotionally distant relationship. These questions could be explored in training situations where relatedness and external contingencies are manipulated or by adopting ecologically valid designs examining the interaction between relatedness need satisfaction and external contingencies.

## Organismic integration theory

Sporting activities are not always driven by eudaimonic enjoyment, attentiveness, and natural inquisition that is associated with intrinsic motivation, particularly when one considers the higher echelons of competitive sport. Sports participation, training, and competition are often driven by contingent motives, such as the importance of training for successful performance, the yearning to impress others, or the desire to win competitions. These multiple extrinsic motives vary in quality (Deci and Ryan, 2000) and are reflected in the second theory encompassed within SDT; namely organismic integration theory (OIT). CET explains one manifestation of the human innate growth tendency, intrinsic motivation, whereas OIT focuses on a second. All individuals are predisposed to internalise extrinsically driven behaviour so that it becomes integrated with one's true sense of self (i.e. become self-determined; Deci and Ryan). The degree to which these extrinsic motivations are self-determined allows these motives to reside on a continuum.

Motives that are devoid of self-determination are termed external regulations and reflect intentions to attain an external reward or to avoid a threatened punishment (Deci and Ryan, 2000). Taking part in sport to collect as many medals as possible or putting effort in during training to avoid the threat of an extra hard fitness session are examples of external regulation. If an athlete is only motivated by these stimuli, then removal of the contingency will limit maintenance of the behaviour (Deci and Ryan, 1985a). Next on the continuum lies introjected regulation, which denotes participation in an activity due to self-administered contingencies, such as enhancing self-esteem, pride, or avoiding guilt or shame (Deci and Ryan, 2000). Introjected regulations are, therefore, more self-determined compared to external regulations; however, they represent only partial internalisation and are low in self-determination. Expressions of introjected regulation in sport may include needing to beat competitors to feel good about oneself, or a child from a particularly athletic family participating in sport to avoid shaming the family name.

Identified regulations are next on the continuum, which reflect motivation for behaviour because one values and endorses the significance and meaning of the activity (Deci and Ryan, 2000). Participating in training because one personally values the subsequent impact upon performance is an example of identified regulation. These motives are relatively self-determined because one recognises the behaviour's value, and has more fully accepted it as their own compared to introjected regulations. Finally, integrated regulation represents the most self-determined of extrinsic motives, and typifies a state where various identified motives have been assimilated into one congruent representation of the self (Deci and Ryan). An individual who participates in sport because he or she identifies as being an athlete, and lives all aspects of their life in line with becoming a better athlete would be an example of this regulation. Although not strictly explicated in OIT, researchers often explore the full range of motives described by the wider self-determination meta-theory by considering intrinsic motivation, which represents wholly self-determined functioning, and amotivation. This latter construct embodies a complete absence of motivation. An amotivated individual lacks intention to engage in activity, and perceives no link between his or her efforts and outcomes associated with the activity (Deci and Ryan). Overall, intrinsic motivation, integrated regulation, and identified regulation are considered self-determined or autonomous motives, whereas introjected and external regulations are considered low self-determined or controlling motives.

There are three primary self-report inventories that tap into sport participants' motivational regulations in English speaking samples; the Behavioural Regulation in Sport Questionnaire (BRSQ; Lonsdale *et al.*, 2008), the Revised Sport Motivation Scale (SMS-II; Pelletier *et al.*, 2013), and the Situational Motivational Scale (SiMS; Guay *et al.*, 2000). The latter inventory aims to assess motivation at any given moment and has frequently been employed in sports settings (e.g. Conroy *et al.*, 2006), whereas the BRSQ and SMS-II tap into general motives within the sports context. Scores from these questionnaires can used in several ways, for instance, researchers may choose to examine overall self-determination using a relative index. This is achieved by multiplying each regulation subscale score by an assigned weight according to its location on the self-determination continuum. These product terms are then summed to form an index of self-determination. The weights to be used if employing the BRSQ or SMS-II are: 3 (intrinsic motivation); 2 (integrated regulation); 1 (identified regulation); –1 (introjected regulation); –2 (external regulation); and –3 (amotivation). The SiMS aims to be a brief inventory that taps into fluctuating motives; therefore, it does not measure integrated or introjected regulation. As a result, the weights to be used are 2 (intrinsic motivation), 1 (identified regulation), –1 (external regulation), and –2 (amotivation).

Researchers may also examine each regulation independently or adopt a person-oriented approach where profiles of the various motivations are explored. Each method has advantages and disadvantages; however, adopting the self-determination index may hide important information regarding overall levels of motivation. For example, an athlete possessing low levels of self-determined and controlling motivation would receive the same overall score as an athlete possessing high levels of self-determined and controlling motivation, yet clearly these profiles are meaningfully different (see Ullrich-French and Cox, 2009, for a discussion of this topic in physical education settings). Adopting a person-oriented, rather than a variable-oriented approach may allow researchers to overcome this limitation and identify combinations of motives that are adaptive. As an example of this type of approach, Gillet *et al.* (2013) demonstrated that national tennis players displaying a motivational profile with moderate self-determined motivation and high controlling motivation performed worse in a tennis competition, compared to players with high self-determination and low controlling motivation (study 1 and 2), and players high in self-determined and controlled motivation (study 2). The enhanced performance associated with high levels of both types of motivation may, however, come at a cost. Long distance runners displaying this profile reported higher levels of emotional and physical exhaustion, despite superior levels of performance, compared to athletes displaying other motivational profiles (Gillet *et al.*, 2012).

Irrespective of the measurement approach, a significant quantity of sport-based research generally suggests that adaptive outcomes are associated with self-determined regulations, whereas maladaptive consequences are associated with controlling regulations and amotivation. For example, a recent meta-analysis demonstrated that intrinsic motivation and self-determined extrinsic motivation negatively predicted indices of burnout, whereas amotivation positively predicted burnout. Introjected and external regulation showed no association, or very small positive correlations with burnout (Li *et al.*, 2013). This lack of relationship may be due to the different measurement of motivation, as studies employing the BRSQ tended to find stronger positive associations between controlling regulations and burnout (Li *et al.*, 2013).

Other recent examples of the benefits of self-determined motivation include evidence that self-determination towards sport is associated with pro-social behaviours (Lonsdale and Hodge, 2011), vitality, positive emotions and satisfaction (Blanchard *et al.*, 2009; Vansteenkiste *et al.*, 2010), flow (Lonsdale *et al.*, 2008), intentions to participate in sport (Vansteenkiste *et al.*, 2008), objective sport performance (Gillet *et al.*, 2010), but not coach-rated performance (Mouratidis *et al.*, 2008). Theoretically expected relationships have also been observed among controlling regulations and sport dropout in a large sample of youth athletes (Garcia-Calvo *et al.*, 2010), susceptibility to drug use via moral disengagement processes (Hodge *et al.*, 2013), anti-social behaviour (Lonsdale and Hodge, 2011), and negative affect (Vansteenkiste *et al.*, 2010). Self-determination towards other activities related to sport has also been shown to be beneficial. Specifically, Chan and Hagger (2012) revealed that self-determined motivation towards sport injury prevention was positively associated with adherence to injury prevention behaviours and beliefs regarding safety in sport. Autonomous motives underlying ideographic goal strivings within sport (as opposed to autonomous motivation towards sport in general) have also been linked to effort, goal attainment, and well-being in cross-sectional and longitudinal research (Smith *et al.*, 2007, 2010, 2011).

In addition to the motivation of athletes, recent work has begun to consider the motivation of sports coaches and athletic directors. Self-determination towards these roles has been positively associated with coaches' perceived support of their athletes' psychological needs (Rocchi *et al.*, 2013) and negatively related to burnout (Sullivan *et al.*, 2014. This focus on coaches should continue with the recent development of the Coach Motivation Questionnaire (McLean *et al.*, 2012), which is undergirded by the self-determination continuum.

These studies have built on considerable earlier work offering general support for the benefits of self-determined behavioural regulation in relation to a variety of outcomes, including persistence (e.g. Pelletier *et al.*, 2001), dropout (e.g. Sarrazin *et al.*, 2001), morality (e.g. Ntoumanis and Standage, 2009), and well-being (e.g. Gagné *et al.*, 2003). Similar to the maintenance of intrinsic motivation described by CET, OIT proposes that the internalisation growth tendency also requires autonomy, competence, and relatedness to be gratified (Deci and Ryan, 2000). This premise has received substantial, albeit largely cross-sectional support in sport settings (Amorose and Anderson-Butcher, 2007; Blanchard *et al.*, 2009; Hollembeak and Amorose, 2005; McDonough and Crocker, 2007; Ntoumanis and Standage, 2009).

This OIT-informed sports research provides preliminary foundations that research with improved methodologies offering conceptual advancements can build upon. Researchers should now take this opportunity to diversify from cross-sectional, self-report tests of the general postulates of OIT (see Baumeister *et al.*, 2007, for a critique of the over-emphasis on self-reported outcomes within psychology). For example, internalisation is a *process*, yet no research has considered the influence of psychological need satisfaction over a sustained period to identify if athletes become *more* self-determined towards sport participation over time. This is particularly important when considering how to engage new sports participants who may join sports teams for non-self-determined reasons (e.g. because their friends attend, because they feel compelled to because it's cool). Another interesting research question is whether the internalisation process is linear, whereby individuals are generally driven by external regulations, followed by introjected regulations, and so on, or can certain contextual factors lead to significant step changes in internalisation? Longitudinal approaches would also allow for the analysis of the temporal ordering of constructs associated with OIT and various outcomes. For instance, Lonsdale and Hodge (2011) used cross-lagged panel models to explore the direction (not causality) of effects between self-determined regulations and burnout in elite rugby players. Analysis revealed that amotivation and controlling motivation (particularly introjected regulation) preceded burnout, whereas, burnout preceded decreases in autonomous motivation. Such findings explicate important information on the motivational processes that occur in sport. Similar analysis could be adopted to examine reciprocal effects of psychological need satisfaction and motivation. It is plausible, for example, that increases in external regulation may lead an athlete to seek less opportunities to experience autonomy and competence, leading to lower need satisfaction.

Competitive sport also offers an appropriate context to further study the impact of extrinsic motivational regulations because training is sometimes punishing, repetitive, and unenjoyable. Athletes may not always rely on autonomous motives, but instead be motivated to not let teammates down or by the knowledge that rivals are training on Christmas day. These introjected regulations may be necessary and effective determinants of maximal sporting performance in certain situations. Focusing on controlling regulations further, the distinction between approach and avoidance components might be worth investigating. In a sample of Belgian sport students, approach-based introjected motives (e.g. impressing others or attaining self-worth) were unrelated to well-being and performance indicators. However, avoidance-based introjected regulation (e.g. avoiding shame or guilt) was a positive predictor of depressive feelings and negative affect, and a negatively predictor of overall well-being and coach-rated performance (Assor *et al.*, 2009; Study 2). Extrapolating from this research it is likely that approach and avoidance components of external regulation may also have different outcomes. For example, being motivated to win a trophy may elicit different behavioural, cognitive, and emotional outcomes, compared to a verbal threat of being dropped from the team.

## Basic psychological needs theory

In the description of CET and OIT, the fundamental processes of intrinsically motivated behaviour and internalisation were facilitated by satisfaction of autonomy, competence, and relatedness. Basic psychological needs theory (BPNT) focuses on these three needs in more detail and explains that satisfaction of these fundamental needs will lead to psychological health, optimal functioning and well-being (Ryan and Deci, 2000). Importantly, all three needs are necessary and functional costs or substitute processes transpire without sufficient support for any of the needs. These processes may have some value in inadequate circumstances, such as self-worth protection, but are nonetheless associated with suboptimal human functioning (Ryan and Deci, 2000).

BPNT has received significant attention within sports settings; however, this research has often employed self-report outcome variables, which makes firm conclusions hard to draw due to potential common method variance (see, Arthur and Tomsett, this volume; Lindell and Whitney, 2001; Podsakoff *et al.*, 2003). Notwithstanding this fact, cross-sectional and longitudinal designs using a composite score of need satisfaction or examining the three needs individually has generally supported BPNT. Specifically, psychological need satisfaction has been positively correlated with subjective vitality (Adie *et al.*, 2008; Mack *et al.*, 2011; Reinboth and Duda, 2006; Reinboth *et al.*, 2004), intrinsic satisfaction (Reinboth *et al.*, 2004), positive affect (Gaudreau *et al.*, 2009; Mack *et al.*, 2011; Quested and Duda, 2010), positive developmental experiences (Taylor and Bruner, 2012), self-esteem (Amorose *et al.*, 2009; Coatsworth and Conroy, 2009), enjoyment (Quested *et al.*, 2013), and well-being and adaptive interpersonal behaviour in coaches (Stebbings *et al.*, 2011, 2012). Relatedness need satisfaction, however, was not correlated with the outcomes in some of the work (Amorose *et al.*, 2009; Reinboth *et al.*, 2004; Stebbings *et al.*, 2011), and also demonstrated limited predictive power in a sample of injured athletes (Podlog *et al.*, 2010).

Longitudinal investigations have also taken place, exploring within-person change in psychological need satisfaction. This refers to fluctuations from each individual's normal levels, which represents an important distinction from between-person differences because absolute levels are made irrelevant in the analysis (Curran and Bauer, 2011). In a sample of youth soccer players over two competitive seasons, Adie *et al.* (2012) demonstrated that within-person changes in competence and relatedness (but not autonomy) satisfaction positively predicted subjective vitality. Gagné *et al.* (2003) also examined within-person changes in young gymnasts over a four-week period. Increases in the satisfaction of all three needs were consistently linked with indicators of well-being (i.e. positive affect, vitality, self-esteem). Each psychological need was entered into multilevel regression equations separately due to high correlations among the three needs, which may explain the additional predictive utility, compared to Adie *et al.* Interestingly, Adie and colleagues also examined individual differences and found no associations among psychological needs and outcomes. The authors attributed these null findings to statistical artifacts or measurement issues. If researchers choose to adopt this explanation for null findings, they must also consider that the acceptance of alternative hypotheses may also be spurious.

One exception to the self-report focus concerns a study of recreational basketball players. Participants with higher pre-game autonomy and competence demonstrated greater frequency and better quality shooting, compared to players with lower autonomy and competence (Sheldon *et al.*, 2013). Surprisingly, players experiencing high relatedness performed worse in some elements of shooting, which the authors explained by suggesting less aggressive play and greater distribution of shots to teammates occurred in players with high relatedness satisfaction.

Based on the above review, satisfying psychological needs may lead to well-being and potentially superior performance. Conversely, low levels of need satisfaction have been frequently explored as a potential antecedent of negative outcomes in sport. For example, a meta-analysis synthesising 18 studies concluded that all three psychological needs were inversely related to burnout (Li *et al.*, 2013). Composite psychological need satisfaction has also been inversely related to subsequent cortisol responses (a physiological indicator of stress) in vocational dancers (Quested *et al.*, 2011), and negative affect in volleyball players (Gaudreau *et al.*, 2009). When exploring the three needs independently, young gymnasts reported all three needs to be inversely associated with negative affect (Gagné *et al.*, 2003). However, vocational dancers only reported competence and relatedness satisfaction to be correlated with negative affect (Quested and Duda, 2010). Again, the analytic strategy using by Gagné *et al.* may explain this difference in predictive utility.

Despite these findings relating low need satisfaction to negative outcomes, it has been pointed out that low need satisfaction has not always been related to ill-being (Bartholomew, Ntoumanis, Ryan and Thøgesen-Ntoumani, 2011). For example, changes in satisfaction of psychological needs were unrelated to physical and emotional exhaustion (Adie *et al.*, 2012) and physical symptoms of illness (Reinboth and Duda, 2006). Bartholomew and colleagues (2011) explain these null findings by suggesting that low scores on inventories measuring psychological need satisfaction do not adequately capture the intensity of active psychological need frustration. These authors provide the example of a female athlete feeling incompetent because she does not have the necessary skills (i.e. low need satisfaction) versus feeling incompetent because her coach is demeaning and critical of her (i.e. need thwarting).

As a result, psychological need thwarting has been argued to be conceptually distinct from low need satisfaction (Bartholomew *et al.*, 2011). Following psychometric validation of a measurement scale (Bartholomew *et al.*, 2011), three studies showed that need thwarting was a better predictor of maladaptive outcomes (e.g. disordered eating, burnout, depression) compared to psychological need satisfaction (Bartholomew, Ntoumanis, Ryan, Bosch, and Thorgersen-Ntoumani, 2011).

This scholarly avenue certainly warrants further attention, as considerably more research and development should be conducted before the distinction between need thwarting and low need satisfaction is a well-supported postulate of BPNT. For example, an almost exclusive reliance on self-report instruments exists; therefore, the distinctive correlations among thwarting, satisfaction and outcomes may simply be a measurement artifact (e.g. positive valence need satisfaction items correlating with positive valence outcome items, and negative valence need thwarting items correlating with negative valence outcome items). Moreover, the lone non-self-report outcome variable adopted in the introductory work, secretory immunoglobulin A (SIgA), was used as an immunological indicator of stress and maladaptive human functioning. However, immunoglobulins directly neutralise bacteria and viruses or initiate other immune processes to eliminate infections (Moser and Leo, 2010). Measuring these proteins in saliva, therefore, is an indicator of adaptive immunity (Brandtzaeg, 1998). At best, using SIgA as an indicator of stress and poor health is a complex issue (Bosch *et al.*, 2002).

The second area of future advancement lies in clarifying the conceptual distinction between psychological need thwarting and dissatisfaction. Currently, arguments for the discrepancy are founded on contextual influences on psychological needs, rather than the organismic experience of need thwarting. For instance, Bartholomew, Ntoumanis, Ryan, Bosch and Thorgersen-Ntoumani's (2011) example of need thwarting described above focuses on the actions of the athlete's coach and an emphasis on the active thwarting of psychological needs *by significant others* was sought during measurement development (Bartholomew *et al.*, 2011). It seems at present, therefore, that the current conceptualiseation of need thwarting may represent the antithesis of contextual support for human psychological needs, rather than the antithesis of need satisfaction.

As well as the conceptual and methodological issues associated with psychological need thwarting, several other future research directions may be pursued. Recruiting young athletes into long-term developmental research would be appropriate for the life-span validation of BPNT that is necessary. The sports context also provides opportunity to explore whether potential deficits in need satisfaction (e.g. lower competence after a competitive loss, lower autonomy after interactions with a coach, less relatedness after training alone) lead to enhanced drives to fulfill those needs in other contexts. Preliminary evidence of this *needs as motives* hypothesis has been observed (Sheldon and Gunz, 2009), however, at what stage do the deficits in need satisfaction become chronic and lead to the development of need substitutes, maladaptive protective mechanisms, or psychopathology?

There are many instances described in previous sections when satisfaction of a particular need has not been associated with the respective outcome variables. When this occurs, researchers often provide ad hoc explanations that do not do justice to the complexities of the issue. For example, often relatedness need satisfaction has been shown to be uncorrelated with well-being and it is subsequently suggested that this might be expected because relatedness plays a distal role in the process under investigation (e.g. Reinboth *et al.*, 2004). According to SDT, relatedness only plays a secondary role in the maintenance of intrinsic motivation, not the promotion of well-being. In fact, alternative theories would suggest that relatedness is a critical psychological need (e.g. Leary and Baumeister, 2005). Quested *et al.* (2013) tested the salience of the three needs for vocational dancers across three different contexts; namely during class, dance rehearsal, and performances. Several differences existed across situations, for example, only daily levels of competence predicted positive and negative affect in performance settings, whereas all three needs were predictive to different degrees in class and rehearsal settings. Future research may wish to continue exploring situations in which the salience of the three psychological needs may vary. Rather than adopting an exploratory approach, it is recommended that researchers formulate a priori hypotheses to be tested, rather than relying on post-hoc speculations.

As demonstrated, psychological need satisfaction is critical for the development of well-being, as well as internalisation and intrinsic motivation processes discussed in the previous sections. Based on the organismic-dialectical perspective of SDT, the environment can facilitate or forestall these processes; hence, researchers have focused on the role of the coach in supporting or thwarting psychological needs. The majority of this research has considered autonomy support, which refers to taking the other person's perspective, acknowledging their feelings, providing choice and information, and minimising pressure (Mageau and Vallerand, 2003). Conroy and Coatsworth (2007a) advocate that demonstrating interest in athletes input and praising autonomous behaviour are also autonomy supportive behaviours. Autonomy support has been positively related to all three psychological needs (e.g. Amorose and Anderson-Butcher, 2007), intrinsic motivation (Joesaar *et al.*, 2012), and self-determination towards sport (Gillet *et al.*, 2012). Most of the research has, however, used self-report measures of perceived autonomy supportive behaviours. Work has also begun to define and investigate psychologically controlling coaching, which undermines athletes' psychological needs through the use of tangible rewards, feedback to reinforce expected behaviours, excessive surveillance, intimidation, promoting ego-involvement, and conditional regard (Bartholomew *et al.*, 2009). Research has found that coach control was negatively associated with autonomy need satisfaction (Blanchard *et al.*, 2009; Isoard-Gautheur *et al.*, 2012) and positively associated with changes in need thwarting (Balaguer *et al.*, 2012), controlling motivation and amotivation (Pelletier *et al.*, 2001), and fear of failure (Conroy and Coatsworth, 2007b).

Early work conceptualised control as the opposite of autonomy support (e.g. Deci and Ryan, 1987), however, it has been recently argued that the two types of behaviour may be independent in sports contexts and should be analysed separately (Bartholomew *et al.*, 2010). If this stance is taken in future research, one must be careful that the measurement chosen is reflective of this approach. For example, often researchers have adapted the Health Care Climate Scale (Williams *et al.*, 1996) to measure autonomy support in sport, however, one item taps into control and is reverse scored to assess autonomy support (e.g. 'I don't feel very good about the way my coach talks to me'). Another consideration is whether one conceptualises autonomy support and control as a set of behaviours or more general interpersonal styles. In sports and education contexts, there is an emphasis on a behavioural perspective whereby lists of autonomy supportive behaviours have been created (e.g. Mageau and Vallerand, 2003; Reeve, 2002). However, this approach may lack contextual sensitivity, as different behaviours may be more or less appropriate in given situations. In a case study of soccer coaching for socially disadvantaged adolescents, providing opportunity for initiative and leadership did not reap benefits for one of the recipients. On the other hand, examples of controlling coaching (e.g. using punishments, making fun of the participants) produced many beneficial motivational outcomes (Cowan *et al.*, 2012). To adapt a common phrase, it's not what you do; it's the way that you do it and the way that it is perceived (Deci and Ryan, 1987).

## Causality orientations theory

The bulk of early work within CET investigated the effects of different controlling or informational events on intrinsic motivation. The same event can however be experienced differently by assorted individuals (i.e. functional significance; Deci and Ryan, 1987). Causality orientations theory (COT) proposes that these individual differences can be explained by three general propensities to orient toward environments and regulate behaviour (Deci, 1980; Deci and Ryan, 1985b). Those with a dominant autonomy orientation have a tendency to seek out interesting activities, find value in events, and to act volitionally. Such an athlete may take the initiative in training, interpret feedback as important for improvement, and live according to their long-term athletic goals. In contrast, individuals with a foremost control orientation tend to construe events as controlling and pressurising, and focus on rewards, gains, and approval. An athlete oriented in this way would rely on the coach to tell them what to do and train hard only when something tangible can be gained. Finally, a prevailing impersonal orientation is characterised by perceptions of incompetence and experiencing behaviour as out of one's control. Athletes with this outlook would see most aspects of their sport as too difficult, and perceive outcomes of training or competition to be disassociated with their behaviour (e.g. 'winning this match had nothing to do with me').

During the development of the general causality orientations scale, autonomy orientation was positively correlated with adaptive outcomes (e.g. positive ego development and self-esteem) and inversely associated with negative outcomes (e.g. self-derogation, hostility, and guilt). The reverse pattern of associations was observed with a control orientation and to a greater extent with impersonal orientation (Deci and Ryan, 1985b). Examining parents of children participating in sport revealed that a control orientation was positively associated, and an autonomy orientation was negatively related to parents' ego defensiveness, which in turn led to anger and aggressive spectator behaviour (Goldstein and Iso-Ahola, 2008). Chan *et al.* (2011) asked athletes to consider a time when they were injured and found that an autonomy orientation positively predicted self-determination towards sport, self-determination towards injury treatment and perceived autonomy support from the coach. A control orientation negatively predicted autonomy support from the coach, and positively predicted controlled sport motivation and controlled treatment motivation.

Apart from some exceptions, there is a lack of COT-based research in sport, which presents a wide opportunity for future exploration within this context. The theorised outlook on life seen in autonomy-oriented individuals seems to preclude these individuals to the demands of competitive sport. For example, researchers may wish to scrutinise whether autonomously oriented athletes perform better and show greater talent development over a period of time, compared to individuals with dominant control or impersonal orientations. Participants whose autonomy orientation was primed in a laboratory displayed better performance on a rowing machine compared to control-primed participants, and impersonal-primed participants performed worse still (Hodgins *et al.*, 2006, Study 3). Sport is also full of potential threats to one's sense of self, such as competitive losses, normative evaluations, and public performances. Autonomy oriented athletes may experience these threats, but respond in more adaptive ways, compared to control and impersonal oriented athletes (Hodgins and Knee, 2002).

## Goal contents theory

The newest theory to be added to the self-determination framework is goal contents theory (GCT), which distinguishes between intrinsic and extrinsic goals and their influence on motivation and well-being. Intrinsic goals, such as close relationships and personal growth, are likely to satisfy one's basic psychological needs and lead to greater well-being. Contrastingly, extrinsic goals, such as financial wealth and popularity are unrelated or negatively related to psychological needs and well-being (Kasser and Ryan, 1996). Extrinsic goals are viewed as compensatory pursuits that people place importance on during periods of need deprivation (Vansteenkiste *et al.*, 2010), whereas intrinsic goals promote an inward orientation and are more likely to satisfy innate psychological needs (Vansteenkiste *et al.*, 2008).

Intrinsic and extrinsic goals are distinct from autonomous and controlling motivation, as either type of goal can be pursued for autonomous or controlling reasons. A sports star may pursue trophies, fame, and celebrity (extrinsic goals) because they value doing so (autonomous motivation). The same sport star could wish to volunteer his or her time to meet sick children at the local hospital (intrinsic goals) because his or her club demands it (controlling motivation). Sheldon *et al.* (2004) demonstrated that the negative effects of pursuing materialistic goals were not explained by the underlying motive for pursuing the goals.

Substantial evidence exists outside of sport to corroborate the theory. For example, the imaginary or real pursuit of materialistic goals has been negatively related to self-actualisation, happiness, affect, life satisfaction, vitality, and change in well-being over one year, as well as positively related to anxiety and physical symptoms of ill-being (e.g. Kasser and Ahuvia, 2002; Kasser and Ryan, 1996; Sheldon *et al.*, 2004). Similar results have been found when examining intrinsic versus extrinsic goal attainment, rather than the pursuit of such goals (Kasser and Ryan, 2001; Niemiec *et al.*, 2009; Ryan *et al.*, 1999; Sheldon and Kasser, 1998; Taylor and Stebbings, 2012). Within this collection of work, the attainment of materialistic desires is proposed to be unrelated or negatively associated with well-being because one's sense of self becomes unstable due to a reliance on attaining external rewards and affirmative evaluations by others (Kasser and Ryan, 2001).

In one of the isolated tests of extrinsic and intrinsic goal pursuit in sport, partial support for the theory was found. Competence need satisfaction was associated with intrinsic goal pursuit in Singaporean student athletes, yet autonomy and competence need satisfaction were positively associated with extrinsic goal pursuit. Relatedness need satisfaction was negatively associated with extrinsic goal pursuit (Wang *et al.*, 2011). The authors proposed that the sport environment, in which winning and attaining trophies is emphasised, makes the pursuit of extrinsic goals and rewards less harmful. This argument seems particularly relevant in sports contexts, and debate exists as to whether the pursuit of extrinsic goals is harmful in environments that emphasise such goals (e.g. Sagiv and Schwartz, 2000; Vansteenkiste *et al.*, 2006). Hence, researchers may wish to deliberate on this topic in more detail.

In addition to the goal-environment match, other future research directions are apparent. As has been done for the exercise domain (Sebire *et al.*, 2008), the development of a sport-specific assessment of goals is necessary. For example, pursuing sport for financial wealth may be irrelevant to all but elite athletes in some sports. Once sound instrumentation has been established, researchers may wish to further explore whether the development of extrinsic goals in sport is a function of innate psychological need deprivation (Williams *et al.*, 2000). In other words, do athletes focus on extrinsic goals because their needs are not satisfied in sporting contexts? Relatedly, it may be interesting to see if need deprivation in another context (e.g. controlling parents at home) leads to the development of extrinsic goals in the sporting context. Finally, the effects of intrinsic and extrinsic goal pursuit may vary in certain contexts, in a similar vein to performance, process, and outcome goals in traditional goal setting research (Burton *et al.*, 2001). For example, a swimmer may need to rely on the motivational benefits of imagining medaling at a world championship when preparing for his or her early morning training session. In comparison, intrinsic goal pursuit (e.g. personal improvement) during the training session may be most beneficial.

## Conclusion

The above review distinguishes between five different theories that form the self-determination meta-theory. Moving forward, it is important to consider the nuances of each theory and the underlying principles from classic SDT work that each theory is grounded upon. Suggesting that relatedness is a distal antecedent of well-being is an example of blurring the boundaries of the five theories that should be avoided in future investigation. Within sports contexts, OIT and BPNT are the most researched of the five theories and researchers should attempt to move beyond cross-sectional research using wholly self-report methods if they only replicate well-established tenets of these theories. Rather than applying the postulates of SDT to sport, scholars should use the sports context to advance new knowledge concerning SDT using robust and innovative research methods. Researchers may also wish to take advantage of the very little attention paid to testing and advancing CET, COT, and GCT within sporting milieus. It is hoped that this book chapter provides some inspiration and ideas to advance these theories.

## References

Adie, J. W., Duda, J. L., and Ntoumanis, N. (2008). Autonomy support, basic need satisfaction and the optimal functioning of adult male and female sport participants: A test of basic needs theory. *Motivation and Emotion*, 32, 189–199.

Adie, J. W., Duda, J. L., and Ntoumanis, N. (2012). Perceived coach-autonomy support, basic need satisfaction and the well- and ill-being of elite youth soccer players: A longitudinal investigation. *Psychology of Sport and Exercise*, 13, 51–59.

Amorose, A. J. and Anderson-Butcher, D. (2007). Autonomy-supportive coaching and self-determined motivation in high school and college athletes: A test of self-determination theory. *Psychology of Sport and Exercise*, 8, 654–670.

Amorose, A. J. and Horn, T. S. (2000). Intrinsic motivation: Relationships with collegiate athletes' gender, scholarship status, and perceptions of their coaches' behaviour. *Journal of Sport and Exercise Psychology*, 22, 63–84.

Amorose, A. J. and Horn, T. S. (2001). Pre- and post-season changes in intrinsic motivation of first year college athletes: Relationships with coaching behaviour and scholarship status. *Journal of Applied Sport Psychology*, 13, 355–373.

Amorose, A. J., Anderson-Butcher, D., and Cooper, J. (2009). Predicting changes in athletes' well-being from changes in need satisfaction over the course of a competitive season. *Research Quarterly for Exercise and Sport*, 80, 386–392.

Assor, A., Vansteenkiste, M., and Kaplan, A. (2009). Identified versus introjected approach and introjected avoidance motivations in school and in sports: The limited benefits of self-worth strivings. *Journal of Educational Psychology*, 101, 482–497.

Balaguer, I., Gonzales, L., Fabra, P., Castillo, I., Merce, J., and Duda, J. L. (2012). Coaches' interpersonal style, basic psychological needs and the well- and ill-being of young soccer players: A longitudinal analysis. *Journal of Sports Sciences*, 30, 1619–1629.

Bartholomew, K. J., Ntoumanis, N., Ryan, R. M., Bosch, J. A., and Thøgersen-Ntoumani, C. (2011). Self-determination theory and diminished functioning: The role of interpersonal control and psychological need thwarting. *Personality and Social Psychology Bulletin*, 37, 1459–1473.

Bartholomew, K. J., Ntoumanis, N., Ryan, R. M., and Thogersen-Ntoumani, C. (2011). Psychological need thwarting in the sport context: Assessing the darker sides of athletic experience. *Journal of Sport and Exercise Psychology*, 33, 75–102.

Bartholomew, K. J., Ntoumanis, N., and Thøgersen-Ntoumani, C. (2009). A review of controlling motivational strategies from a self-determination theory perspective: Implications for sports coaches. *International Review of Sport and Exercise Psychology*, 2, 215–233.

Bartholomew, K. J., Ntoumanis, N., and Thøgersen-Ntoumani, C. (2010). The controlling interpersonal style in a coaching context: Development and initial validation of a psychometric scale. *Journal of Sport and Exercise Psychology*, 32, 193–216.

Baumeister, R. F., Vohs, K. D., and Funder, D. C. (2007). Psychology as the science of self-reports and finger movements: Whatever happened to actual behaviour? *Perspectives on Psychological Science*, 2, 396–403.

Blanchard, C. M., Amiot, C. E., Perreault, S., Vallerand, R. J., and Provencher, P. (2009). Cohesiveness and psychological needs: Their effects on self-determination and athletes' subjective well-being. *Psychology of Sport and Exercise*, 10, 545–551.

Bosch, J. A., Ring, C., de Geus, E. J., Veerman, E. C., and Amerongen, A. V. (2002). Stress and secretory immunity. *International Review of Neurobiology*, 52, 213–253.

Brandtzaeg, P. (2003). Role of secretory antibodies in the defence against infections. *International Journal of Medical Microbiology*, 293, 3–15.

Burton, D., Naylor, S., and Holliday, B. (2001). Goal setting in sport: Investigating the goal effectiveness paradox. In R. Singer, H. A. Hausenblas, and C. M. Janelle (eds), *Handbook of research on sport psychology* (2nd edn, pp. 497–528). New York: Wiley.

Byron, K. and Khazanchi, S. (2012). Rewards and creative performance: A meta-analytic test of theoretically derived hypotheses. *Psychological Bulletin*, 138, 809–830.

Chirkov, V. I., Ryan, R. M., Kim, Y., and Kaplan, U. (2003). Differentiating autonomy from individualism and independence: A self-determination theory perspective on internalization of cultural orientations and well-being. *Journal of Personality and Social Psychology*, 84, 97–110.

Carpentier, J. and Mageau, G. A. (2013). When change-oriented feedback enhances motivation, well-being and performance: A look at autonomy-supportive feedback in sport. *Psychology of Sport and Exercise*, 14, 423–435.

Chan, D. K. C. and Hagger, M. S. (2012). Trans-contextual motivation in sport injury prevention among elite athletes. *Journal of Sport and Exercise Psychology*, 34, 661–682.

Chan, D. K. C., Spray, C., and Hagger, M. S. (2011). Treatment motivation for rehabilitation after a sport injury: Application of the trans-contextual model. *Psychology of Sport and Exercise*, 12, 83–92.

Coatsworth, J. D. and Conroy, D. E. (2009). The effects of autonomy-supportive coaching, need satisfaction and self-perceptions on initiative and identity in youth swimmers. *Developmental Psychology*, 45, 320–328.

Conroy, D. E. and Coatsworth, J. D. (2007a). Assessing autonomy-supportive coaching strategies in youth sport. *Psychology of Sport and Exercise*, 8, 671–684.

Conroy, D. E. and Coatsworth, J. D. (2007b). Coaching behaviours associated with changes in fear of failure: Changes in self-talk and need satisfaction as potential mechanisms. *Journal of Personality*, 75, 384–419.

Conroy, D. E., Kaye, M. P. and Coatsworth, J. D. (2006). Coaching climate and the destructive effects of mastery-avoidance goals on situational motivation. *Journal of Sport and Exercise Psychology*, 28, 69–92.

Cooke, A., Kavussanu, M., McIntyre, D. and Ring, C. (2013). The effects of individual and team competitions on performance, emotions and effort. *Journal of Sport and Exercise Psychology*, 35, 132–143.

Cowan, D., Taylor, I. M., McEwan, H. and Baker, J. S. (2012). Bridging the gap between self-determination theory and coaching soccer to disadvantaged youth. *Journal of Applied Sport Psychology*, 24, 361–374.

Cremades, J., Flournoy, B., and Gomez, C. B. (2012). Scholarship status and gender differences in motivation among U.S. collegiate track and field athletes. *International Journal of Sport Science and Coaching*, 7, 333–344.

Curran, P. J. and Bauer, D. J. (2011). The disaggregation of within-person and between-person effects in longitudinal models of change. *Annual Review of Psychology*, 62, 583–619.

deCharms, R. (1968). *Personal causation*. New York: Academic.

Deci, E. L. (1971). Effects of externally mediated rewards on intrinsic motivation. *Journal of Personality and Social Psychology*, 18, 105–115.

Deci, E. L. and Ryan, R. M. (1985a). *Intrinsic motivation and self-determination in human behaviour*. New York: Plenum Publishing Co.

Deci, E. L. and Ryan, R. M. (1985b). The general causality orientations scale: Self-determination in personality. *Journal of Research in Personality*, 19, 109–134.

Deci, E. L. and Ryan, R. M. (1987). The support of autonomy and the control of behaviour. *Journal of Personality and Social Psychology*, 53, 1024–1037.

Deci, E. L. and Ryan, R. M. (2000). The 'what' and 'why' of goal pursuits: Human needs and the self-determination of behaviour. *Psychological Inquiry*, 11, 227–268.

Deci, E. L., Koestner, R., and Ryan, R. M. (1999a). A meta-analytic review of experiments examining the effects of extrinsic rewards on intrinsic motivation. *Psychological Bulletin*, 125, 627–668.

Deci, E. L., Koestner, R., and Ryan, R. M. (1999b). The undermining effect is a reality after all: Extrinsic rewards, task interest, and self-determination. *Psychological Bulletin*, 125, 692–700.

Gagné, M., Ryan, R. M., and Bargmann, K. (2003). Autonomy support and need satisfaction in the motivation and well-being of gymnasts. *Journal of Applied Sport Psychology*, 15, 372–390.

Garcia-Calvo, T., Cervello, E., Jimenez, R., Iglesias, D., and Moreno-Murcia, J. A. (2010). Using self-determination theory to explain sport persistence and dropout in adolescent athletes. *Spanish Journal of Psychology*, 13, 677–684.

Gaudreau, P., Amiot, C., and Vallerand, R. J. (2009). Trajectories of affective states in adolescent hockey players: Turning point and motivational antecedents. *Developmental Psychology*, 45, 307–319.

Gillet, N., Berjot, S., Vallerand, R. J., and Amoura, S. (2012). The role of autonomy support and motivation in the prediction of interest and dropout intentions in sport and education settings. *Basic and Applied Social Psychology*, 34, 278–286.

Gillet, N., Berjot, S., Vallerand, R. J., Amoura, S., and Rosnet, E. (2012). Examining the motivation-performance relationship in competitive sport: A cluster-analytic approach. *International Journal of Sport Psychology*, 43, 79–102.

Gillet, N., Vallerand, R. J., Amoura, S., and Baldes, B. (2010). Influence of coaches' autonomy support on athletes' motivation and sport performance: A test of the hierarchical model of intrinsic and extrinsic motivation. *Psychology of Sport and Exercise*, 11, 155–161.

Gillet, N., Vallerand, R. J., and Paty, B. (2013). Situational motivational profiles and performance with elite performers. *Journal of Applied Social Psychology*, 43, 1200–1210.

Goldstein, J. D. and Iso-Ahola, S. (2008). Determinants of parents' sideline-rage emotions and behaviours at youth soccer games. *Journal of Applied Social Psychology*, 38, 1442–1462.

Guay, F., Vallerand, R. J., and Blanchard, C. M. (2000). On the assessment of situational intrinsic and extrinsic motivation: The Situational Motivation Scale (SIMS). *Motivation and Emotion*, 24, 175–213.

Hagger, M. S. and Chatzisarantis, N. L. (2011). Causality orientations moderate the undermining effect of rewards on intrinsic motivation. *Journal of Experimental Social Psychology*, 47, 485–489.

Hodge, K., Hargreaves, E., Gerrard, D., and Lonsdale, C. (2013). Psychological mechanisms underlying doping attitudes in sport: Motivation and moral disengagement. *Journal of Sport and Exercise Psychology*, 35, 419–432.

Hodgins, H. S. and Knee, C. R. (2002). The integrating self and conscious experience. In E. L. Deci and R. M. Ryan (eds), *Handbook of self-determination research* (pp. 87–100). Rochester, NY: University of Rochester Press.

Hodgins, H. S., Yacko, H. A., and Gottlieb, E. (2006). Autonomy and non-defensiveness. *Motivation and Emotion*, 30, 283–293.

Hollembeak, J. and Amorose, A. J. (2005). Perceived coaching behaviours and college athletes' intrinsic motivation: A test of self-determination theory. *Journal of Applied Sport Psychology*, 17, 20–36.

Isoard-Gautheur, S., Guillet, E., and Lemyre, P. N. (2012). A prospective study of the influence of perceived coaching style on burnout propensity in elite adolescent athletes: Using a self-determination theory perspective. *The Sport Psychologist,* 26, 282–298.

Jõesaar, H., Hein, V., and Hagger, M. S. (2012). Youth athletes' perception of autonomy support from the coach, peer motivational climate and intrinsic motivation in sport setting: One-year effects. *Psychology of Sport and Exercise,* 13, 257–262.

Kasser, T. and Ahuvia, A. C. (2002). Materialistic values and well-being in business students. *European Journal of Social Psychology,* 32, 137–146.

Kasser, T. and Ryan, R. M. (1996). Further examining the American dream: Differential correlates of intrinsic and extrinsic goals. *Personality and Social Psychology Bulletin,* 22, 280–287.

Kasser, T. and Ryan, R. M. (2001). Be careful what you wish for: Optimal functioning and the relative attainment of intrinsic and extrinsic goals. In P. Schmuck and K. M. Sheldon (eds), *Life goals and well-being: Towards a positive psychology of human striving* (pp. 116–131). Ashland, OH: Hogrefe and Huber Publishers.

Kingston, K., Horrocks, C., and Hanton, S. (2006). Do multidimensional intrinsic and extrinsic motivation profiles discriminate between athletic scholarship status? *European Journal of Sport Science,* 6, 53–63.

Leary, M. R. and Baumeister, R. F. (2000). The nature and function of self-esteem: Sociometer theory. In M. P. Zanna (ed.), *Advances in experimental social psychology* (Vol. 32, pp. 1–62). San Diego, CA: Academic Press.

Li, C., Wang, C. K., Pyun, D. Y., and Kee, Y. H. (2013). Burnout and its relations with basic psychological needs and motivation among athletes: A systematic review and meta-analysis. *Psychology of Sport and Exercise,* 14, 692–700.

Lindell, M. K. and Whitney, D. J. (2001). Accounting for common method variance in cross-sectional research designs. *Journal of Applied Psychology,* 86, 114–121.

Lonsdale, C. and Hodge, K. (2011). Temporal ordering of motivational quality and athlete burnout in elite sport. *Medicine and Science in Sports and Exercise,* 43, 913–921.

Lonsdale, C., Hodge, K. and Rose, E. (2009). Athlete burnout in elite sport: A self-determination perspective. *Journal of Sports Sciences,* 27, 785–795.

Mack, D. E., Wilson, P. M., Oster, K. O., Kowalski, K. C., Crocker, P. R. E., and Sylvester, B. D. (2011). Well-being in volleyball players: Examining the contributions of independent and balanced psychological need satisfaction. *Psychology of Sport and Exercise,* 12, 533–539.

Mageau, G. A. and Vallerand, R. J. (2003). The coach-athlete relationship: A motivational model. *Journal of Sports Sciences,* 21, 883–904.

McDonough, M. H. and Crocker, P. R. E. (2007). Testing self-determined motivation as a mediator of the relationship between psychological needs and affective and behavioural outcomes. *Journal of Sport and Exercise Psychology,* 29, 645–663.

McLean, K., Mallett, C., and Newcombe, P. (2012) Assessing coach motivation: The development of the Coach Motivation Questionnaire (CMQ). *Journal of Sport and Exercise Psychology,* 34, 184–207.

Moser, M. and Leo, O. (2010). Key concepts in immunology. *Vaccine,* 28, C2–C13.

Mouratidis, A., Lens, W., and Vansteenkiste, M. (2010). How you provide corrective feedback makes a difference: The motivating role of communicating in an autonomy-supportive way. *Journal of Sport and Exercise Psychology,* 32, 619–637.

Mouratidis, M., Vansteenkiste, M., Lens, W., and Sideridis, G. (2008). The motivating role of positive feedback in sport and physical education: Evidence for a motivational model. *Journal of Sport and Exercise Psychology*, 30, 240–268.

Niemiec, C. P., Ryan, R. M., and Deci, E. L. (2009). The path taken: Consequences of attaining intrinsic and extrinsic aspirations in post-college life. *Journal of Research in Personality*, 43, 291–306.

Ntoumanis, N. and Standage, M. (2009). Prosocial and antisocial behaviour in sport: A self-determination theory perspective. *Journal of Applied Sport Psychology*, 21, 365–380.

Pelletier, L. G., Fortier, M. S., Vallerand, R. J., and Brière, N. M. (2001). Associations among perceived autonomy support, forms of self-regulation, and persistence: A prospective study. *Motivation and Emotion*, 25, 279–306.

Pelletier, L. G., Rocchi, M. A., Vallerand, R. J., Deci, E. L., and Ryan, R. M. (2013). Validation of the revised sport motivation scale (SMS-II). *Psychology of Sport and Exercise*, 14, 329–341.

Podlog, L., Lochbaum, M., and Stevens, T. (2010). Need satisfaction, well-being and perceived return-to-sport outcomes among injured athletes. *Journal of Applied Sport Psychology*, 22, 167–182.

Podsakoff, P. M., MacKenzie, S. M., Lee, J., and Podsakoff, N. P. (2003). Common method variance in behavioural research: A critical review of the literature and recommended remedies. *Journal of Applied Psychology*, 88, 879–903.

Quested, E. and Duda, J. L. (2010). Exploring the social-environmental determinants of well- and ill-being in dancers: A test of basic needs theory. *Journal of Sport and Exercise Psychology*, 32, 39–60.

Quested, E., Bosch, J. A., Burns, V. E., Cumming, J., Ntoumanis, N., and Duda, J. L. (2011). Basic psychological need satisfaction, stress-related appraisals, and dancers' cortisol and anxiety responses. *Journal of Sport and Exercise Psychology*, 33, 828–846.

Quested, E., Duda, J. L., Ntoumanis, N., and Maxwell, J. P. (2013). Daily fluctuations in the affective states of dancers: A cross-situational test of basic needs theory. *Psychology of Sport and Exercise*, 14, 586–595.

Quested, E., Ntoumanis, N., Viladrich, E., Haug, E., Ommundsen, Y., Van Hoye, A., Merce, J., Hall, H. K., Zourbanos, N., and Duda, J. L. (2013). Intentions to drop-out of youth soccer: A test of the basic needs theory among European youth from five countries. *International Journal of Sport and Exercise Psychology*, 11, 395–407.

Reeve, J. (2002). Self-determination theory applied to educational settings. In E. L. Deci and R. M. Ryan (eds), *Handbook of self-determination research* (pp. 183–203). Rochester, NY: University of Rochester Press.

Reeve, J. and Deci, E. L. (1996). Elements within the competitive situation that affect intrinsic motivation. *Personality and Social Psychology Bulletin*, 22, 24–33.

Reinboth, M. and Duda, J. L. (2006). Perceived motivational climate, need satisfaction and indices of well-being in team sports: A longitudinal perspective. *Psychology of Sport and Exercise*, 7, 269–286.

Reinboth, M., Duda, J. L., and Ntoumanis, N. (2004). Dimensions of coaching behaviour, need satisfaction, and the psychological and physical welfare of young athletes. *Motivation and Emotion*, 28, 297–313.

Rocchi, M. A., Pelletier, L. G., and Couture, A. L. (2013). Determinants of coach motivation and autonomy supportive behaviours. *Psychology of Sport and Exercise*, 14, 852–859.

Ryan, R. M. (1982). Control and information in the intrapersonal sphere: An extension of Cognitive Evaluation Theory. *Journal of Personality and Social Psychology*, 43, 450–461.

Ryan, R. M. and Deci, E. L. (2000). Self-determination theory and the facilitation of intrinsic motivation, social development, and well-being. *American Psychologist*, 55, 68–78.

Ryan, R. M., Chirkov, V. I., Little, T. D., Sheldon, K. M., Timoshina, E., and Deci, E. L. (1999). The American dream in Russia: Extrinsic aspirations and well-being in two cultures. *Personality and Social Psychology Bulletin*, 25, 1509–1524.

Sagiv, L. and Schwartz, S.H. (2000). A new look at national culture: Illustrative applications to role stress and managerial behaviour. In N. N. Ashkanasy, C. Wilderom, and M. F. Peterson (eds), *The handbook of organisational culture and climate* (pp. 417–436). Newbury Park, CA: Sage.

Sarrazin, P., Vallerand, R. J., Guillet, E., Pelletier, L., and Cury, F. (2001). Motivation and dropout in female handballers: A 21-month prospective study. *European Journal of Social Psychology*, 31, 1–24.

Sebire, S. J., Standage, M., and Vansteenkiste, M. (2008). Development and validation of the Goal Content for Exercise Questionnaire. *Journal of Sport and Exercise Psychology*, 30, 353–377.

Sheldon, K. M. and Gunz, A. (2009). Psychological needs as basic motives, not just experiential requirements. *Journal of Personality*, 77, 1467–1492.

Sheldon, K. M. and Kasser, T. (1998). Pursuing personal goals: Skills enable progress but not all progress is beneficial. *Personality and Social Psychology Bulletin*, 24, 1319–1331.

Sheldon, K. M., Ryan, R. M., Deci, E. L., and Kasser, T. (2004). The independent effects of goal contents and motives on well-being: It's both what you pursue and why you pursue it. *Personality and Social Psychology Bulletin*, 30, 475–486.

Sheldon, K. M., Zhaoyang, R., and Williams, M. (2013). Psychological need-satisfaction and basketball performance. *Psychology of Sport and Exercise*, 14, 675–681.

Smith, A. L., Ntoumanis, N., and Duda, J. L. (2007). Goal striving, goal attainment, and well being: An adaptation of the self-concordance model in sport. *Journal of Sport and Exercise Psychology*, 29, 763–782.

Smith, A. L., Ntoumanis, N., and Duda, J. L. (2010). An investigation of coach behaviours, goal motives, and implementation intentions as predictors of well being in sport. *Journal of Applied Sport Psychology*, 22, 17–33.

Smith, A., Ntoumanis, N., Duda, J. L., and Vansteenkiste, M. (2011). Goal striving, coping, and well-being in sport: A prospective investigation of the self-concordance model. *Journal of Sport and Exercise Psychology*, 33, 124–145.

Stebbings, J., Taylor, I. M., and Spray, C. M. (2011). Antecedents of perceived coach autonomy supportive and controlling behaviours: Coach psychological need satisfaction and well-being. *Journal of Sport and Exercise Psychology*, 33, 255–272.

Stebbings, J., Taylor, I. M., Spray, C. M., and Ntoumanis, N. (2012). Antecedents of perceived coach interpersonal behaviours: The coaching environment and coach psychological well- and ill-being. *Journal of Sport and Exercise Psychology*, 34, 481–502.

Sullivan, G. S., Lonsdale, C., and Taylor, I. M. (2014). Burnout in high school athletic directors: A self-determination perspective. *Journal of Applied Sport Psychology*, 26, 256–270.

Tauer, J. M. and Harackiewicz, J. M. (2004). The effects of cooperation and competition on intrinsic motivation and performance. *Journal of Personality and Social Psychology*, 86, 849–861.

Taylor, I. M. and Bruner, M. W. (2012). The social environment and developmental experiences in elite youth soccer. *Psychology of Sport and Exercise*, 13, 390–396.

Taylor, I. M. and Stebbings, J. (2012). Disentangling within-person changes and individual differences among fundamental need satisfaction, attainment of acquisitive desires, and psychological health. *Journal of Research in Personality*, 46, 623–626.

Ullrich-French, S. and Cox, A. E. (2009). Using cluster analysis to examine the combinations of motivation regulations of physical education students. *Journal of Sport and Exercise Psychology*, 31, 358–379.

Vallerand, R. J. (1983). The effect of differential amounts of positive verbal feedback on the intrinsic motivation of male hockey players. *Journal of Sport Psychology*, 5, 100–107.

Vallerand, R. J. and Reid, G. (1984). On the causal effects of perceived competence on intrinsic motivation: A test of cognitive evaluation theory. *Journal of Sport Psychology*, 6, 94–102.

Vansteenkiste, M., Duriez, B., Simons, J., and Soenens, B. (2006). Materialistic values and well-being among business students: Further evidence for their detrimental effect. *Journal of Applied Social Psychology*, 36, 2892–2908.

Vansteenkiste, M., Mouratidis, A., and Lens, W. (2010). Detaching reasons from aims: Fair play and well being in soccer as a function of pursuing performance-approach goals for autonomous or controlling reasons. *Journal of Sport and Exercise Psychology*, 32, 217–242.

Vansteenkiste, M., Niemiec, C. P., and Soenens, B. (2010). The development of the five mini-theories of self-determination theory: An historical overview, emerging trends, and future directions. In T. C. Urdan and S. A. Karabenick (eds), *Advances in motivation and achievement, v. 16A—The decade ahead: Theoretical perspectives on motivation and achievement* (pp. 105–165). London: Emerald Group Publishing Limited.

Vansteenkiste, M., Soenens, B., and Duriez, B. (2008). Presenting a positive alternative to strivings for material success and the thin-ideal: Understanding the effects of extrinsic relative to intrinsic goal pursuits. In S. J. Lopez (ed.), *Positive psychology: Exploring the best in people* (pp. 57–86). Westport, CT: Praeger.

Wang, J., Sproule, J., McNeill, M., Martindale, R., and Lee, K. S. (2011). Impact of talent development environment on achievement goals and life aspirations in Singapore. *Journal of Applied Psychology*, 23, 263–276.

Weinberg, R. (1979). Intrinsic motivation in a competitive setting. *Medicine and Science in Sports*, 11, 146–149.

White, R. W. (1959). Motivation reconsidered: The concept of competence. *Psychological Review*, 66, 297–333.

Williams, G. C., Cox, E. M., Hedberg, V., and Deci, E. L. (2000). Extrinsic life goals and health risk behaviours in adolescents. *Journal of Applied Social Psychology*, 30, 1756–1771.

Williams, G. C., Grow, V. M., Freedman, Z., Ryan, R. M., and Deci, E. L. (1996). Motivational predictors of weight loss and weight-loss maintenance. *Journal of Personality and Social Psychology*, 70, 115–126.

# 4 Organisational psychology in sport

## Recent developments and a research agenda

*Christopher R. D. Wagstaff and Rebecca J. Larner*

## Introduction

In the latter part of the twentieth century, elite sport was host to substantial commercialisation and globalisation (see Fletcher and Wagstaff, 2009). Thus far, during the twenty-first century there has been little indication that these complex, turbulent, and volatile changes will slow or desist. Indeed, an implication of these changes has been a growing demand for the establishment of organisational systems that instantly and consistently deliver success. In response to such requirements, there has been an increasing technologicalisation, medicalisation, and scientisation of elite sport performance environments as organisations seek a competitive edge (Wagstaff *et al.*, 2015). Such actions echo the observations of sport management scholars who have described the current state of unrest as a "global sporting arms race" (see Bingham and Shibli, 2008) exemplified by the creation of isomorphic institutions with hierarchically-structured bodies, coordinated policies and processes, democratised authority, and shared collective goals. Given this changing landscape of elite sport, psychologists have increasingly emphasised the importance of exploring the organisational contexts in which performers operate (see, for reviews, Fletcher and Wagstaff, 2009; Wagstaff *et al.*, 2012a). Indeed, given the pivotal role of human performance for optimising the functioning of sport organisations (see Wagstaff *et al.*, 2012b), the domain of organisational psychology has much to contribute to the changing face of elite sport (see Fletcher and Wagstaff, 2009).

## Defining, delimiting, and demystifying organisational psychology in sport

The foundations of organisational psychology lie with the confluence of industrial and organisational (I/O) psychology and the changing landscape of elite sport environments. I/O psychology has been defined as "a general practice specialty of professional psychology with a focus on scientifically-based solutions to human problems in work and other organisational settings. In these contexts, I/O psychologists assess and enhance the effectiveness of individuals, groups, and organisations" (American Psychological Association, 2011). Hence, I/O psychologists recognise the interdependence of individuals, organisations and society and consider problems such as employee turnover, absenteeism, and productivity; succession planning and development of managers and executives; organisational restructuring; workplace stress and well being; and employee motivation and performance (Wagstaff *et al.*, 2012a).

Scholars have typically distinguished between three concentrations of I/O psychology (e.g. Landy and Conte, 2009): personnel psychology, organisational psychology, and human engineering. Personnel psychology is often integrated within human resources in many workplaces and addresses issues such as recruitment, selection, training, performance appraisal, promotion, transfer, and termination. This work typically relates to the methods and principles used to select and evaluate potential employees and would have overlap with talent identification and team composition procedures in sport organisations. However, traditionally such roles have been performed by individuals responsible for the performance department (i.e. manager, performance director, director of sport), with input from scouts and performance analysts. The value of psychological input regarding these issues lies in the view that individuals have fluctuating work behaviours and attitudes and that information relating to these changes can help predict, maintain and increase performance and satisfaction.

Organisational psychology integrates research foundations in social psychology and organisational behaviour to address emotional and motivational aspects of organisational life. The main aim of this work is the evaluation of what motivates employees to have a successful, productive, satisfying work environment to help organisations function more effectively. Consequently, organisational psychologists commonly focus on topics such as attitudes, fairness, motivation, stress, leadership, teams, and broader aspects of organisational and work design. Given its emphasis on the reactions of people to work and their resultant action tendencies and responses, both the organisation and the people within its sphere of influence are of importance. Hence, organisational psychologists might also seek to achieve a fit between people, the work demands they might face and the organisation's idiosyncratic characteristics. Indeed, we propose that organisational psychology principles can advance sport performance through two means: the development of optimally functioning sport organisations and though the enhancement of the quality of work life for those that operate within their sphere of influence.

Human engineering refers to the study of human limitations with respect to the design of products, technology, systems, and environments that optimise performance. Whilst personnel psychology aims to find the best individual for the work, and organisational psychology aims to match the best person to relevant roles, human engineering aims to develop environments and systems that are compatible with the characteristics of the worker. According to Landy and Conte (2009) the diverse environmental aspects of this work may include tools, workspaces, information displays, shift work, work pace, machine controls, and safety. This approach integrates cognitive science, ergonomics, physiology, anatomy, and biomechanics. The role of human engineering psychologists in sport could incorporate the optimal understanding, functionality, and integration of medical, technological, and scientific advances by sport performers.

Although we perceive value in each of the three concentrations of I/O psychology, it is our belief that the biggest potential benefit to sport is the optimisation of organisational psychology factors, much of which will fall under the rubric of *positive* organisational psychology in sport (POPS; Wagstaff *et al.*, 2012a). Hence, our focus here is on the second concentration outlined above. Before providing a review and organising structure for research organisational psychology in sport we give consideration to the salience of this area.

## Vacuums and the myth of individualism

Advocates of organisational psychology in sport (see, e.g. Fletcher and Wagstaff, 2009) have frequently used an oft-quoted passage from Hardy *et al.*'s (1996) early sport psychology text; borrowing from Shaw's work on social environments (1981) Hardy *et al.* concluded their book by noting "elite athletes do not live in a vacuum; they function within a highly complex social and organisational environment, which exerts major influences on them and their performances" (pp. 239–240). Allied with Hardy *et al.*'s analogy of the environments in which elite sport performers prepare and perform, there are many dangers of what we would label a "myth of individualism". That is, a fallacy that sporting success or failure is wholly determined by individual effort or ability has prevailed for some time in society. The power of this myth lies in its promotion of a social fixation on talent and eliding of the salience of a wealth of interpersonal, team, and organisational level factors that impact performance. This is not to say that elite sport performers do not require talent, or that this cannot be nurtured and supplemented with individual effort. Indeed, such factors are pivotal for initial success and might be largely responsible for fugacious underdog triumphs. However, *sustained* success in high performance domains is not solely predicated on the embodied competence of individual performers, but how effectively these individuals build and maintain working relationships with a network of stakeholders (e.g. coaches, managers, selectors, performers) and organisations (e.g. sport institutions, bodies, organisations) in addition to those who provide informational (e.g. scientific, medical, and technological expertise), financial (e.g. sponsors), and social (e.g. friends, family) supports to optimise day-to-day productivity in preparation for and performance at major competitions (see Wagstaff *et al.*, 2012b).

In addition to the importance of dispelling the myth of individualism for sporting success, there is also a need to view sport organisations as workplaces that must ensure the well being of their employees rather than merely systematised collectives aimed at promoting success. That is, examining the psychological states of individuals during their engagement with organisations and at home (i.e. their work–life balance) might allow for a better understanding the well being of sport performers. Well being considers a wide range of experiences (e.g. demands and functioning), and incorporates positive (e.g. enthusiasm) and negative (e.g. anxiety) affective states and outcomes (e.g. psychosomatic health, job satisfaction), as well as the processes (e.g. communication) that facilitate these ends. Hence, the value of organisational psychology in sport lies with its examination and facilitation of performance factors (i.e. the development of optimally functioning sport organisations and debunking of the myth of individualism) and well being (i.e. the enhancement of the quality of work life and view sport organisations as places of work requiring considerations for sportspeople as employees with requisite rights and needs).

In line with the growing acknowledgement of the importance of organisational issues in elite sport, two recent reviews have summarised the emergence, application and potential futures for this domain. Specifically, in 2009 an article by Fletcher and Wagstaff was published in *Psychology of Sport and Exercise* that reviewed a (then) nascent body of research concerned with the emergence of organisational psychology in elite sport. Fletcher and Wagstaff reviewed six lines of inquiry pointing to the salience of these issues: factors affecting Olympic performance (see, for a review, Gould and Maynard, 2009); organisational stress (see, for a review, Arnold and Fletcher, 2012a); perceptions of roles (see, e.g. Reid *et al.*, 2004); organisational success factors (see, e.g. Weinberg and McDermott, 2002); performance environments in elite sport (see, e.g. Jones *et al.*, 2009); and organisational citizenship behaviour (see, e.g. Aoyagi *et al.*, 2008). More recently, Wagstaff *et al.* (2012a) reviewed the literature relating to the *positive* organisational psychology research in sport. In their review, Wagstaff *et al.* defined and delimited relevant concepts, including organisational psychology and positive organising, with a particular emphasis on extant research relating to organisational functioning in sport (i.e. positive environments, positive behaviours, and positive outcomes) and a call for attention to be paid to topics such as culture, climate and change, in addition to those aligned with positive organisational behaviour and scholarship (see Wagstaff *et al.*, 2012). Our intention is not to repeat the work presented in these reviews but to acknowledge recent developments and simulate new inquiry.

## A research agenda for organisational psychology in sport

In the remainder of this chapter we outline a structure for organisational psychology research in sport. This structure organises many extant (see, for reviews, Fletcher and Wagstaff, 2009; Wagstaff *et al.*, 2012a) and possible future lines of inquiry into four core dimensions of research and application; emotions and attitudes in sport organisations, stress and well being in sport organisations, behaviours in sport organisations, and environments in sport organisations.

### Emotions and attitudes in sport organisations

Due to their impact on a range of psychosocial variables associated with performance and well being (cf. Hanin, 2007) perhaps the most promising dimension of organisational psychology in sport relates to the inter-related areas of emotional and attitudinal phenomena. While a full review of these topics is beyond the scope of this chapter we consider a selection below.

### Emotions in sport organisations

Wagstaff *et al.* (2012b) stated that emotions play an essential role in sport organisations by providing feedback and stimulating retrospective appraisal of actions, promoting learning, and altering guidelines for future behaviour and self-management. Indeed, due to a recent proliferation of research attention exploring emotion and affect in organisations, Barsade *et al.* (2003) have termed the current era an "affective revolution". Importantly, this revolution has stimulated research on affective concepts for promoting team (e.g. Friesen *et al.*, 2013; Tamminen and Crocker, 2013) and organisational functioning (e.g. Wagstaff *et al.*, 2012b, 2012c, 2013) in sport. This growing body of research has generally indicated that emotional experience, regulation strategy use, and ability have important implications for individual, team, and organisational outcomes in sport.

Although the study of emotional experience has firmly established its place in sport psychology, almost all of this research has focused on the examination of negative emotions in competitive environments such as anxiety (see, for a review, Wagstaff, Neil *et al.*, 2012). Indeed, there is a relative dearth of research examining the daily affective experiences of sport performers within their organisations or the value of emotion-based interventions to improve psychological well being and organisational performance. McCarthy (2011) recently argued that the benefits of positive emotions have hitherto not been wholly realised in sport, especially in their capacity to generate greater self-efficacy, motivation, attention, problem-solving, and coping with adversity. Interestingly, beyond the context of sport, happiness has been the emotion of principal interest in organisations (Totterdell *et al.*, 2013). Indeed, a wide array of happiness-related concepts has been studied in the workplace and typically focuses on state-level variables (e.g. fluctuations in momentary happiness). Indeed, there is evidence that momentary happiness has positive consequences for employee well being, creativity, proactivity, task performance, and goal attainment (see Fisher, 2000). Such findings align with Frederickson's (2001) broaden and build theory of positive emotion which proposes that momentary emotional experiences engender success by broadening ones thought-action repertoires and building social, personal, and psychological resources to deal with or undo the deleterious effects of negative events.

In addition to the recent calls for a shift in extant emotion experience research to incorporate positive emotions, scholars have also acknowledged the importance of regulating emotions in sport organisations (e.g. Lane *et al.*, 2012; Wagstaff *et al.*, 2012b, 2012c). For example, Wagstaff *et al.* (2012b) conducted a nine-month ethnography in an Olympic national sport organisation (NSO), highlighting the development and maintenance of interpersonal relationships to be the critical building blocks for optimal organisational functioning. Moreover, individuals better able to monitor and manage their emotions were more likely to forge and maintain successful relationships. That is, participants used emotion-related abilities for managing conflict, communicating emotion, and managing and expressing emotion to maintain the psychological contract, engaging in contagious emotion regulation, and emotion regulation to aid the building and maintenance of relationships. The use of these emotion abilities and regulation strategies increased what Wagstaff *et al.* (2012b) termed "psychosocial capital" (i.e. enhanced levels of engagement and social relationships) and displays of prosocial behaviour within the organisation. Conversely, the absence of such abilities appeared to put a strain on interpersonal relationships, reduced individuals' social standing, and gave way to power struggles. In an attempt to extend the ethnographic work of Wagstaff *et al.* (2012b), Wagstaff *et al.* (2012c) used a semi-structured interview approach to identify key emotion abilities (i.e. identifying, processing and comprehending, and managing emotions) associated with the use of specific experience and expression regulation strategies (e.g. forward-tracking, back-tracking, reappraisal, suppression, and impulse control). To elaborate, Wagstaff *et al.* (2012c) found emotion abilities to influence regulation strategy selection through sociocultural norms present within organisations. For example, participants reported that adhering to expectations and norms relating to emotional expression to be a major contributing factor in regulation strategy selection. Based on these findings, Wagstaff *et al.* proposed a socio-cognitive model of emotion regulation in organisations to explain the antecedents to and consequences of emotion regulation (see Figure 4.1).

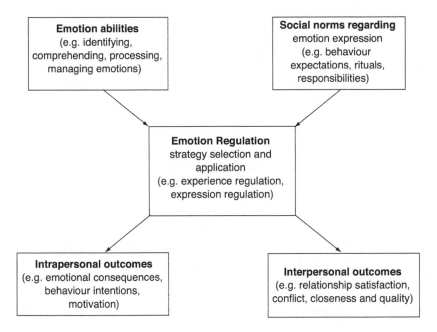

*Figure 4.1* A socio-cognitive model of emotion ability, regulation and inter- and intra-personal outcomes (Reproduced from Wagstaff *et al.*, 2012c).

Initial support has emerged for Wagstaff *et al.*'s (2012c) socio-cognitive model of emotion regulation in organisations (e.g. Friesen *et al.*, 2013; Tamminen and Crocker, 2013; Wagstaff *et al.*, 2013). For example, using a two-phase action research intervention, Wagstaff *et al.* (2013) showed emotion regulation and ability workshops to improve the practice of participants, their regulation strategy use, and perceptions of relationship quality and closeness. Moreover, participants receiving an extended one-to-one coaching intervention showed improvement in emotional intelligence ability scores in addition to the benefits demonstrated via workshops. The findings indicated that short-term generic interventions to promote the use of adaptive emotion regulation strategies might be effective in sport organisations, but the purposive development of emotional intelligence might require more longitudinal and idiographic approaches. Tamminen and Crocker (2013) recently provided additional support for Wagstaff *et al.*'s (2012c) model by highlighting the interpersonal emotion regulation undertaken by a team of curlers. Specifically, the authors found performers to be aware of and consider social and contextual factors (e.g. social norms and role on team) when regulating emotions in team meetings, practices, and games toward the achievement of multiple goals (e.g. positive performances, positive social relationships). In light of the fruitful body of work reviewed above, it would appear that the requirement for emotion regulation and emotional intelligence abilities have been underestimated in sport and reflect a pervasive necessity of organisational life.

In addition to the extant lines of emotion-related inquiry reviewed above, researchers have increasingly highlighted the potential value of examining emotional contagion (e.g. Moll *et al.*, 2010; O'Neil, 2008; Totterdell, 2000; Wagstaff *et al.*, 2012b, 2012c, 2013) and emotional labour (e.g. Wagstaff *et al.*, 2012b, 2012c, 2013) in sport organisations. Schoenewolf (1990) defined emotional contagion as a "process in which a person or group influences the emotions or behaviour of another person or group through the conscious or unconscious induction of emotion states and behavioural attitudes" (p. 50). In a first exploration of contagion in sport, Totterdell explained how the mood of individual players was linked to the collective mood of other players within a cricket team. Further, O'Neill (2008) proposed that emotional contagion mechanisms might be responsible for decreased performances by alpine skiers after witnessing an injury. Moll *et al.* (2010) also proposed emotional contagion to explain the association between goal celebrations and team performance in association football.

In addition to emotional contagion, sport psychologists have increasingly noted the importance of emotional labour in sport organisations (e.g. Wagstaff *et al.*, 2012b, 2012c). Morris and Feldman (1996) defined emotional labour as "the effort, planning and control needed to express organisationally desired emotions during interpersonal interactions" (p. 987). It is possible that the efforts associated with engaging in emotional labour might have intrapersonal or interpersonal costs for sport performers. Indeed, two recent studies have attempted to examine the interplay between emotional experience, regulation and psychosocial and task outcomes in performance domains. Specifically, in a study with a military performance team during a two-month Antarctic mountaineering expedition, Wagstaff and Weston (2014) found maladaptive emotion regulation strategies (e.g. suppression) to be rated as effective despite their use being correlated with negative intrapersonal (e.g. mental fatigue) and interpersonal (e.g. cohesion) outcomes. The authors concluded that the demanding expedition environment influenced participants' perceptions of emotion regulation requirements, regulation strategy selection, and effectiveness, which, in turn, were associated with greater levels of mental fatigue, instances of conflict, and decreased team performance. In a related study, Wagstaff (2014) used a laboratory-based repeated measures design to examine the relationship between emotional self-regulation and individual cycling performance. When participants suppressed their emotional reactions to an upsetting video prior to completing a 10k cycle time trial (suppression condition) they completed the task slower, generated lower mean power outputs, and reached a lower maximum heart rate and perceived greater physical exertion than when they were given no self-regulation instructions during the video (non-suppression condition) or received no video treatment (control condition). Wagstaff concluded that emotion regulation demands affected perceived exertion, pacing and sport performance; however, research is required to ascertain if such outcomes impact the team or organisational level outcomes and the extent to which chronic demands for emotion regulation influence any such relationships.

It is apparent from the discourse above that researchers must consider the level of analysis of the emotion concepts they study in sport organisations. Indeed, informed by the work of Ashkanasy (2003) we propose a five-level model for situating emotion research in sport organisations. The first level of analysis is related to understanding the within-person ebb and flow of daily emotional processes. This is characterised by the idiosyncratic experience of emotions such as anxiety, anger, and happiness. Such experiences are likely to be influenced by state affect, events, discrete emotions, moods, attitudes and behaviours in sport organisations. The second level of analysis relates to individual differences in emotion-related phenomena and provides between-person level understanding. This level is characterised by trait affectivity, emotion abilities and regulation strategies and attitudes towards the environment such as satisfaction, commitment, and identification burnout. At the third or dyadic, interpersonal, level of analysis, the communication of and with emotion is likely to influence relational dynamics. This is characterised by the coach-athlete relationship or performance partnerships. Such factors might relate to the exploration of emotional labour in emotional exchanges, interpersonal conflict and negotiation, interpersonal influence and power. At the fourth level of analysis, group and team level emotional dynamics are likely to impact a host of psychosocial and performance outcomes. This is characterised by the collective affective climate and environmental factors that define performance teams or sport science and medicine departments. At the fifth level of analysis, the creation of positive organisational policies, structures and cultures that minimise stress and promote well being might be of interest. For example, the wider organisational cultural and climatic behaviours are likely to influence affective phenomena at various other levels of analysis.

## Attitudes in sport organisations

In a study of performers' responses to organisational stressors, Fletcher *et al.* (2012) showed performers to respond in numerous emotional, attitudinal, and behavioural ways. Hence, and in view of the review of emotion phenomena above, of attitude-related topics in sport organisations are worthy of closer examination.

## Organisational commitment

Of the many attitudinal concepts of potential interest to sport psychologists seeking to optimise organisational functioning, one of the most promising is organisational commitment. In research conducted outside of sport, Mowday *et al.* (1979) proposed that organisational commitment was comprised of three components: acceptance and belief in an organisation's goals and values; a willingness to exert effort on behalf of the organisation to help meet the goals or values of that organisation; and, a strong desire to remain in the organisation. More recently, Meyer *et al.* (1993) extended Mowday and colleagues' work and argued that individuals can be committed to entities, objects or their profession rather than the organisation per se. Subsequently, Meyer and Allen (1997) proposed that organisational commitment could be based on any one of three elements: an emotional or affective commitment to an organisation (i.e. they want to stay); an element representing the perceived cost of leaving the organisation or continuance commitment (i.e. they have to stay), and; an element representing an obligation to remain in the organisation, or normative commitment (i.e. they feel they ought to stay). In an attempt to summarise the vast literature on organisational commitment outside of sport, several meta-analysis have been conducted (see Matthew and Zajoc, 1990; Meyer *et al.*, 2002) which have pointed to numerous antecedents (e.g. role ambiguity, role conflict, investment), correlates (e.g. job involvement, satisfaction), and consequences (e.g. turnover and withdrawal cognition, absenteeism, job performance, OCB, stress and work-family conflict) relating to affective, continuance, and normative commitment to one's organisation.

Recently, in a first exploration of organisational commitment in sport, Jackson *et al.* (2014) examined the role of this concept in explaining attrition rates in adolescent groups. In doing so, Jackson *et al.* (2014) drew on Meyer and Allen's (1997) three-factor model of organisational commitment to provide validity evidence for capturing adolescent athletes' commitment to their coach–athlete relationship or their team along with relations between commitment dimensions and relevant correlates (e.g. satisfaction, return intentions, cohesion) that were largely consistent with extant organisational theory.

The development of a sport-specific measure of organisational commitment provides an excellent opportunity to understand engagement, and intentions to or actual turnover in sport organisations in sport. One benefit of such research lies in the identification, management, or avoidance of what Ghiselli (1974) labelled the "hobo" syndrome, attributed to individuals more prone to changing organisations than others. In sport, such "hobo" or "journeyman" behaviours are increasingly apparent. For example in a 19-year career, association footballer Steve Claridge was involved in no fewer than 28 transfers between 22 different clubs. In comparison, Ryan Giggs has played almost 1000 games for Manchester United, in a career spanning 24 years. Interestingly, Giggs' commitment was espoused with Sir Alex Ferguson's 27-year tenure as manager at the same organisation. Indeed, organisational commitment is a variable of importance for a variety of roles in sport organisations and we should not limit its examination to sport performers. Elsewhere, in the Indian Premier League (IPL) where pro rata salaries are second only to the NBA, commitment of both cricketers to their respective franchises and that of franchises to their players is weak. Prior to the start of each IPL season, a player auction occurs where marquee players are sold with a base price of US$320,000. Amazingly, for the 2014 IPL, franchises were allowed to retain a maximum of five players from their squad of 27 from the 2013 IPL with the buying back of additional members at auction possible via a "first refusal" clause. Moreover, the substantial financial rewards available to performers transferring between franchises further destabilises commitment foundations. Thus, it appears that there is much potential in examining the antecedents and consequences of organisational commitment in sport given that those who have been with an organisation for a short period of time are likely to have weaker commitment foundations. Indeed, organisations might invest resources in socialisation processes for new members to promote the retention of desirable individuals until commitment foundations are established and stabilised.

*Organisational engagement and identification*

In addition to the value of examining commitment within sport organisations, other related affect-centred attitude variables of potential interest include organisational engagement and identification. We might consider engagement in sport to reflect the extent to which individuals cognitively, emotionally, and physically express themselves during the fulfilment of their roles within their organisation (cf. May *et al.*, 2004). Britt *et al.* (2007) have proposed a model of antecedents (e.g. clarity of job guidelines, personal control over job performance, personal relevance of job to identity and training, importance of job) and consequences (e.g. absorption, effort, persistence, health and well being and performance) of job engagement that might provide a point of departure for sport-specific examinations of this concept. Interestingly, a number of the proposed antecedents have overlap with roles variables highlighted as salient for group dynamics in sport such as role clarity, identification, and acceptance (see, for review, Martin *et al.*, 2014) and therefore offer a appealing confluence of research foci.

In addition to engagement, researchers might consider the extent to which individuals identify with their sport organisation. Research on identity in sport has largely focused on athletic identity (Brewer *et al.*, 1993) and coping with transitions out of sport (see, for review, Wylleman *et al.*, 2004). However, researchers have recently expanded their study of identity to include a range of variables at multiple levels of analysis. Generally, this research has shown a number of antecedents (e.g. justice and coach behaviour) to predict team identification and for this to be related to various positive (e.g. athlete satisfaction, task and social cohesion) and negative (e.g. adherence to unambitious team goals) outcomes (e.g. Burns *et al.*, 2012; De Backer *et al.*, 2011; Tauber and Sassenberg, 2012). Such findings indicate that organisational identity presents a fruitful avenue for research in sport.

### Stress and well being in sport organisations

The highly complex social and organisational environment of elite sport imposes numerous demands on the performers and personnel that function within it (i.e. preparation, expectations, interpersonal relationships), with advice frequently sought from psychologists on dealing with the pressures that accompany participation (Fletcher and Wagstaff, 2009; Mellalieu *et al.*, 2007). Indeed, the area of stress and well being has received more research attention than any other dimension within organisational psychology in sport. Much of this research has focused on the organisational stressors encountered by sport performers. Arnold and Fletcher (2012a) recently provided a synthesis of this research and developed a taxonomic classification of stressors. The authors concluded that a four category (namely leadership and personnel, cultural and team, logistical and environmental, and performance and personal issues) taxonomy provided the most accurate, comprehensive, and parsimonious classification of organisational stressors to date given their validity, generalisablility, and applicability to a large number of sport performers of various ages, genders, nationalities, sports, and standards. In considering measurement issues in this domain, Arnold and Fletcher (2012b) argued that the most fundamental and significant hindrance to examining organisational stress in sport has been the lack of a valid and reliable means of assessing the phenomena. In response to this observation, and using Arnold and Fletcher's (2012a) taxonomy of stressors, Arnold *et al.* (2013) presented a series of studies describing the development and validation of the Organisational Stressor Indicator for Sport Performers (OSI-SP).

In addition to the stressor taxonomic and measurement development work by Fletcher and colleagues, research has also emerged exploring performers' responses to general (Fletcher *et al.*, 2012; Levy *et al.*, 2009; Mellalieu *et al.*, 2013) and specific organisational stressors (e.g. Knight and Harwood, 2009; Kristiansen, Roberts *et al.*, 2011). For example, a series of articles Kristiansen and colleagues have examined the impact of negative media (e.g. Kristiansen, Roberts *et al.*, 2011), journalist–athlete relationships (e.g. Kristiansen and Hanstad, 2012; Kristiansen, Hanstad *et al.*, 2011) and use of mastery climates for dealing with media stressors (e.g. Kristiansen, *et al.*, 2012). In other research, Mellalieu *et al.* (2013) conducted a preliminary exploration of athlete, management, and support staff experiences of interpersonal conflict during a major international competition. Approximately 70 per cent of the sample reported experiencing conflict, with the majority of these instances occurring at the practice and competition venue or athlete village and more than 50 per cent being attributed to breakdowns in interaction and communication and power struggles between people. The authors highlighted that such findings were consistent with Wagstaff *et al.*'s (2012b) findings regarding the importance of communication in avoiding power struggles and conflict.

Despite the general themes associating organisational stressors with negative psychosocial and performance outcomes (e.g. interpersonal conflict), it is likely that these sources of strain could impact sport performance in both positive (e.g. motivation) and negative (e.g. anxiety) ways. Indeed, Fletcher *et al.* (2012) found athletes to respond to organisational stressors in a wide range of positive and negative emotional, behavioural, and attitudinal ways. Elsewhere, Tabei *et al.* (2012) found organisational stressors to be associated with dimensions of burnout. In order to better understand why performers report different responses to similar organisational stressors, Hanton *et al.* (2012) conducted a longitudinal daily diary study of stress appraisals with sport performers. The findings revealed individuals to appraise sources of organisational strain as predominantly threatening or harmful, with little perceived control, and few coping resources available. In a follow-up study, Didymus and Fletcher (2012) found harm/loss and threat appraisals to be associated with subsequent negative emotions and behaviours but the appraisal of stressors as a challenge to be associated with more positive outcomes (e.g. increased motivation and effort). Hence, organisational stressors appear to have the potential to harm individual's well being and performance, with individual differences in cognitive appraisal likely to be a pivotal factor in determining emotional, behavioural, and attitudinal responses to such demands. Hence, future research might devote greater attention to the role of appraisal in the organisational stress process. Further, individual differences that might mediate the stress process (e.g. hardiness, mental toughness, resilience), the strategies that individuals employ to manage responses to stressors (e.g. coping), and the performance and well-being outcomes following such processes (e.g. burnout, depression) warrant further research. Future explorations of organisational stress and well being in sport might also consider the mediating role of various emotional and attitudinal phenomena reviewed in this chapter (e.g. emotional labour) as well as the efficacy of preventative (i.e. primary) and reactive (i.e. secondary, tertiary) interventions targeted at individual, team, and organisational levels (see Fletcher *et al.*, 2006).

### Behaviours in sport organisations

The third proposed dimension of organisational psychology research inquiry encompasses the diverse topics aligned with organisational behaviour and relates to the impact of individual, group, and organisation-wide behaviour on performance and well being.

*Organisational citizenship behaviour (OCB)*

OCB has been defined as, "individual behaviour that is discretionary, not directly or explicitly recognised by the formal rewards system, and that in the aggregate promotes the effective functioning of the organisation" (Organ, 1988, p. 4). That is, OCB helps or benefits others to go beyond the requirements of their role, and support the social environment within organisations. While OCB has received considerable research attention in other fields of organisational psychology there has only been one study examining this concept in sport. Aoyagi *et al.* (2008) examined OCB, athlete satisfaction, team cohesion, and leadership behaviours among US athletes. Results showed that leadership was associated with cohesion, satisfaction, and OCB; cohesion was related to OCB; and satisfaction with cohesion. While research is needed to replicate and extend Aoyagi *et al.*'s findings, it would appear that increasing OCB could enhance indicators of organisational functioning in sport.

Two variables of interest that have been studied in association with OCB are prosocial and antisocial behaviours. Prosocial behaviours are carried out to produce and maintain the well being and integrity of others and might include congratulating teammates or helping an injured opponent (Kavussanu *et al.*, 2013). Conversely, antisocial behaviours are carried out to harm or disadvantage another and might include cheating or trying to injure an opponent (Kavussanu *et al.*, 2013). Thus, prosocial and antisocial behaviours have the potential to help or hinder others' performance and physical and mental well being. Research has highlighted numerous predictors of prosocial behaviour in sport, including; autonomy-supportive coaching styles (Hodge and Lonsdale, 2011), task orientation and mastery climate (Kavussanu, 2006), and characteristics of the sporting environment such as relational support from the coach, positive team attitude toward fair play, and exposure to high levels of socio-moral reasoning (Rutten *et al.*, 2008). However, more research is needed to better understand the interplay between these behaviours and organisational functioning.

*Leadership in sport organisations*

Sport organisations offer an excellent context for the examination of leadership. In an investigation of performance leadership and management in Olympic performance directors, Arnold and Fletcher (2011) highlighted four main areas of best practice: vision (e.g. vision development, influences on the vision, and sharing the vision, operations (e.g. financial management, strategic competition and training planning, athlete selection for competition, and upholding rules and regulations), people (e.g. staff management, lines of communication, and feedback mechanisms), and culture (e.g. establishing role awareness, and organisational and team atmosphere). In a follow-up study, Fletcher *et al.* (2012)

provided recommendations, advice and suggestions for enhancing performance leadership and management in elite sport. Specifically, five themes emerged for leaders and managers (namely establishing an approach, understanding roles within the team, developing contextual awareness, enhancing personal skills and strengthening relationships) and sport organisations (namely employing the most appropriate individual, creating the optimal environment, implementing systems and structures, developing an inclusive culture and providing appropriate support).

In addition to performance leadership and management research, a growing body of leadership research in sport has examined transformational leadership theory (see Arthur and Tomsett, this volume), which posits that leaders should inspire their followers through emotional appeals to adopt high goals and perform above the level of their normal expectations (Bass, 1985). Recently, Callow *et al.* (2009) examined peer leadership, team cohesion, and performance, finding task cohesion to be predicted by some transformational leadership behaviours (i.e. fostering acceptance of group goals, promoting teamwork, showing high performance expectations, and having consideration for individuals) and social cohesion to be predicted by other transformational behaviours (e.g. fostering acceptance of group goals and promoting teamwork). Further, the relationships between transformational leadership behaviours and cohesion were moderated by performance level of the teams. Other research on transformational leadership in sport has shown these behaviours to be positively associated with leader effectiveness (e.g. Rowold, 2006), leader-inspired extra effort (e.g. Arthur *et al.*, 2011), satisfaction with leadership (e.g. Gomes *et al.*, 2011), and task and social cohesion (Price and Weiss, 2011). Using transformational theory as a foundation, Arthur *et al.* (2012) proposed a sport-specific meta-cognitive model of leadership that centers on inspiring others by creating an inspirational vision of the future; providing the necessary support to achieve the vision; and challenging others to achieve the vision. Despite the promising findings, much remains to be examined within the domain of leadership within sport, including greater conceptual refinement and delineation from similar concepts (e.g. coaching and instruction behaviours) and examination of the efficacy of leadership interventions at multiple levels of sport organisations.

### Coaching in sport organisations

Coaching is present in almost every organisational domain and generally refers to attempts to improve performance by facilitating the acquisition of new knowledge, skills, and abilities. Indeed, coaching behaviours reflect a collection of transferable and interchangeable actions that include observing others by analysing performance, using effective and insightful questioning, assisting goal setting, and the provision of feedback to develop performance and enhance motivation. There is a rich history of using coaching methodologies as a vehicle for performance enhancement in sport as well as other high performance domains such as business, performing arts, and military (e.g. Gould and Wright, 2012). However, much of the recent research on coaching in sport has focused on holistic models of the coaching setting to enhance coach effectiveness and efficacy, none of this work has examined the utility of applying coaching behaviours in other areas of sport organisations. In an attempt to ascertain the general value of such practices across a breadth of organisational domains, a recent meta-analysis by Theeboom *et al.* (2013) showed coaching interventions to have a significant positive effect on outcomes such as coping ($g$=.43) and goal-directed self-regulation ($g$ =.74). Further, Wagstaff *et al.* (2013) recently found a one-to-one coaching intervention in an Olympic NSO to facilitate improvements in measures of individual (e.g. emotional abilities), dyadic and group (e.g. relationship quality and closeness), and organisational (e.g. organisational functioning) level variables. Further research is required to replicate and extend these findings and provide greater conceptual clarity regarding coaching behaviours in performance domains; however, coaching interventions might benefit organisations by impacting emotions (e.g. experience of positive emotion), attitudes (e.g. satisfaction, commitment, and identification) stress and well being (e.g. developing resilience, coping), and environments (e.g. coaching leaders to shape culture change).

### Environments in sport organisations

Sport organisations are characterised by multiple stakeholder groups (e.g. departments, teams) that must share resources in the pursuit of individual, team and organisational goals. The environments in which such work is done are likely to impact the effectiveness of this work. Therefore, a greater understanding of such environment-related factors will benefit functioning at various organisational levels.

### High performance environments in sport organisations

Research on high performance environments focuses on the athletes' surroundings and psychosocial factors that may affect a performer's mood, emotion, or motivation with an emphasis on what characterises a high performance environment and the development of these factors. Jones *et al.* (2009) presented a model of the psychological and social factors within a performance environment that impact organisational performance. They recognised individual-, group-, and organisational-level variables associated with high performance environments, which were conceptualised within the areas of leadership, performance enablers, people, and organisational climate to form the key components of the high performance environment (HPE) model.

Pain *et al.* (2012) found that the use of performance environment survey data and the coach's reflections of that data were beneficial in managing the performance environment in a soccer team. Further, team feedback meetings helped to improve athlete ownership and cohesiveness by encouraging athletes to share information and discuss issues with team preparation. The findings suggest that detailed attention to, and management of, the performance environment should help to improve team and organisation functioning and performance (Pain *et al.*, 2012). In related research, Mills *et al.* (2014) examined coaches' perceptions of the factors underpinning optimal development environments within elite soccer. From the results, the authors developed a conceptual framework that explained how a number of factors interact and contribute to an optimal performance environment. The main components of this framework were: psychosocial architecture (e.g. player welfare, key stakeholder relationships), organisational functioning (e.g. adaptability, effective communication), physical environment (e.g. material provisions), and operating system (e.g. organisational core). The findings suggest that practitioners should focus on creating a strong, dynamic organisational culture in order to develop an optimal performance environment for elite player development. Given these general findings practitioners should adopt a holistic view of the performance environment in order to provide a more coordinated approach to developing high performance. Moreover, practitioners attempting to effectively intervene at an environmental level in elite sport will need to be able to coach leaders, facilitate performance enablers, engage people, and shape cultural change.

*Climate, culture, and change*

In their call for a research agenda on POPS, Wagstaff *et al.* (2012a) highlighted that three variables were of particular interest to those attempting to intervene at the environment-level in sport organisations. These variables were climate, culture, and change.

The examination of climate in sport has typically focused on the illumination of the motivational climates surrounding sport performers by investigating the behaviours of coaches, peers, and parents perceived to be motivationally relevant to athlete performance and the extent to which athletes perceive their psychological needs to be supported (Keegan *et al.*, 2014). This literature has invariably demonstrated correlations between athletes' perceptions of the climate (e.g. a mastery climate) and individual-level outcomes such as self-determined motivation, affect, enjoyment, and persistence. Indeed, Keegan *et al.* recently highlighted that there may be a "complex, interactive, and multifaceted motivational atmosphere around sports performer, which contains within it the broad spectrum of influences exerted by coaches, parents, peers and others across a variety of contexts and settings" (p. 98). The exploration of such atmospheres will likely be of great interest to organisational psychologists in sport.

In line with calls for research on culture (see Schroeder, 2010; Wagstaff *et al.*, 2012a) researchers have recently considered the application of culture change management theories in elite sport performance team environments. That is, Cruickshank and Collins (2012) recently called for a focus on the knowledge surrounding the creation of high-performing cultures in on-field elite teams. The same authors suggested that culture change is context-dependent (i.e. employee agreement with change); context-shaped (i.e. the needs of high-ego performers, support staff, board members, fans, and media); and context-specific (i.e. scenarios of manager takeover). More recently, Cruickshank *et al.* (2013) reported a case study examining the key mechanisms and processes of a successful culture change programme at Leeds Carnegie. Interviews with team management, a specialist coach, players, and the CEO, showed culture change to be facilitated by subtly and covertly shaping the physical, structural, and psychosocial context in which support staff and players made performance-impacting choices, and regulating the to and fro of power.

In addition to the emergence and value of research on climate and culture in sport organisations, Wagstaff *et al.* (2015) recently explored sport medicine and science practitioners' experiences of organisational change using a two-year longitudinal design. The findings indicated that change occurred over four distinct stages (namely anticipation and uncertainty, upheaval and realization, integration and experimentation, normalization and learning). The findings highlighted salient emotional, behavioural, and attitudinal experiences of medics and scientists, the existence of poor employment practices, and direct (e.g. emotions, attitudes) and indirect (e.g. performance, turnover) implications for on-field performance following organisational change. Such findings have implications for preparing prospective sport medics and scientists for the realities of elite sport environments, sport organisations as employers and managers of change, and professional bodies responsible for the training and development of practitioners.

*Social environments in sport organisations*

Further to the emerging research on climate, culture and change, a body of literature exists representing social environments (see, for review, Martin *et al.*, 2014) of relevance to organisational psychology in sport. In his seminal text on group dynamics, Shaw (1981) described the social environment as the interpersonal relationships that come to be established once members have assembled and begin to interact. We review research on selected topics aligned with the social environment below.

*Organisational socialisation*

In many ways, the experiences of transitioning within or between sport organisations are likely to be similar to those experienced by employees in other professions. Indeed, newcomers or rookies in sport organisations must quickly navigate various social, emotional, behavioural, language, and cultural boundaries as they transition from an outsider to in-group member, which might result in ambiguity and anxiety regarding how they should behave. Hence, sport organisations should make efforts to optimise the processes through which individuals come to understand the politics, power dynamics, history, responsibilities, norms, and cliques of the various in-groups within their environment.

Researchers have typically distinguished between institutionalised (e.g. collective, formal, sequential, fixed, serial, investiture) and individualised (e.g. individual, informal, disjunctive, variable, random, divestiture) socialisation processes (see Jones, 1986), with the former associated with a range of positive intrapersonal outcomes. Such outcomes include reductions in negative role perceptions (e.g. role ambiguity and role conflict), desirable psychosocial outcomes for the individual (e.g. social acceptance, self-efficacy, job satisfaction), and more committed group members that have greater intentions to remain (see, for meta-analyses, Bauer *et al.*, 2007; Saks *et al.*, 2007). Such findings are relevant to sport organisations in view of the importance of managing such environments to optimise functioning through communication and interpersonal relationships (see Wagstaff *et al.*, 2012b). Indeed, many elite sport organisations use athlete liaison or welfare and education officers to assist with the transition from organisation to organisation (see Fitzpatrick, 2014). Much of the work done by liaison and welfare officers appears to include psychological strategies to manage emotional difficulties and the use of counselling skills (see Fitzpatrick, 2014). Hence, organisations might seek to recruit to such positions individuals with sport psychology backgrounds, or provide training and development opportunities to those employed in such roles to adequately and ethically prepare them for dealing with the psychological demands performers face during socialisation processes.

It should be noted that not all socialisation processes are functional for the individual or organisation performance and well being. While many socialisation processes within team environments such as initiations, rites of passage and group-bonding activities are innocuous, in extremis, these activities can be life threatening. That is, the phenomena of "hazing" relates to activities expected of someone joining a group that humiliates, degrades, abuses, or endangers, regardless of the person's willingness to participate (Hoover, 1999). One account of hazing activities by Farrey (2003) relates to a high-school wrestler in Conneticut, USA, being hog-tied and sexually assaulted with the blunt end of a plastic knife. In examining the impact of such socialisation processes, Waldron and Krane (2005) have argued that athletes will often do whatever it takes, not only to enhance performance, but also to fit into the social structure of a team by zealously adhering to norms without critically considering the consequences of this for their behaviour or health. Elsewhere, Waldron *et al.*

(2011) have found associations between such deviant over conformity and leaving organisations and sport.

## Status and power in sport organisations

Whilst an individual's position within a team or organisation might reflect their relative standing with respect to dimensions such as power, leadership, and attractiveness (Shaw, 1981), status refers to the evaluation of that position. That is, status reflects the rank or prestige allocated to one's position by members of a given social group. This perceived variable has potential implications for behaviour in sport organisations because of its importance for defining social environment and adjustment. Indeed, a body of research indicates that high status individuals select culturally-valued spatial positions within groups, conform to norms both more and less that low status team members depending on the situation, and are more likely to have a greater influence on the team's performance than low status individuals (see Shaw). In an early study, Hollander (1958) noted that high status individuals were often afforded "idiosyncratic credit" to deviate from norms within teams according to previous contribution to the group's goals. Moreover, status has been found to influence communication patterns and content (Kelly, 1951), perceptions, attributions, and satisfaction (Smith and Bordnaro, 1975), and the reactions of group members to deviant behaviour (Wahman, 1977). Hence, it would appear that status associated with an individual's position within a team is likely to have consequences for their behaviour toward others and the behaviour of others to the individual (Shaw). Unfortunately, little of this research has been conducted in sport contexts and we must examine whether the importance of status in performance teams and organisations extends to sport.

Another environmentally determined concept of potential interest to organisational psychologists – and one that is often used interchangeably with status – is power (Shaw, 1981). Bass (1960) defined power as control over others through the use of rewards and punishments. As power is likely to be influenced by subjective perceptions (i.e. who is powerful), the impact of this variable on behaviour will likely fluctuate across social environments (e.g. dyads and teams) within a given organisation. That is, the influence of any individual's behaviour within a sport organisation is likely to be mediated by their relative power and the power structure of their social environment. Indeed, one might hypothesise similar emotional, attitudinal, and behavioural correlates to be associated with power as those with status. Further, the extent to which individuals employ power in order to enhance compliance with their desires and the implications of such dynamics are likely to be of interest to organisational scholars. Interestingly, the use of behaviours associated with the dark triad of personality traits (i.e. narcissism, machiavellianism, psychopathy; cf. Paulhus and

Williams, 2002) have increasingly been highlighted within sport psychology research (e.g. Cruickshank and Collins, 2012; Wagstaff *et al.*, 2012b; Arthur *et al.*, 2011; Fletcher and Arnold, 2011). Hence, researchers seeking to optimise the environments in which individuals operate within sport might also benefit by examining the prevalence and potential influence of sub-clinical psychopathologies of individuals in the composition and leadership of teams and organisations.

*Roles in sport organisations*

An individual's role represents the set of responsibilities he or she holds, which is a function of the position occupied within the group and is interdependent with other members (Carron and Eys, 2012). Scholars (e.g. Carron and Eys, 2012) have distinguished between task (e.g. captain), social (e.g. comedian), formal (e.g. elected or elected, with prescribed behaviours), and informal (e.g. more natural, without prescribed behaviours) roles within sport organisations. In another recent review of roles in sport teams, Martin *et al.* (2014) highlighted that research has typically focused on the responses to formal role processes such as behavioural manifestations (i.e. role performance) and cognitions (i.e. role ambiguity and efficacy). For example, role ambiguity is related to cohesion, coaching competency, cognitive state anxiety, and athlete satisfaction (see Martin *et al.*, 2014). However, Martin *et al.*, 2014 also acknowledged that researchers have begun to investigate informal role processes and other role perceptions held by athletes (e.g. role acceptance). It is likely that research on roles within sport teams will continue to provide important insights into the behaviours and cognitions of those operating within them. Martin *et al.*, 2014 called for future research on roles that extends the theoretical underpinning of such topics and seeks to develop validated measures of roles concepts, and interventions to optimize such phenomena within organisations.

*Psychological contracts in sport organisations*

Wagstaff *et al.* (2012b) highlighted the importance of managing behaviour in line with norms to optimise functioning in sport organisations. Expectations regarding such behaviours might be influenced by psychological contracts or implicit subjective beliefs regarding perceived agreements or obligations regarding exchanges between employees and their organisation (see Rousseau, 1989; Conway and Briner, 2005). The breech of such contracts are likely to have significant implications for individual emotions (e.g. anger, sadness, betrayal), and attitudes (e.g. satisfaction, intention to turnover, organisational commitment, and organisational citizenship behaviours (cf. Conway and Briner, 2005). Indeed, the examination of psychological contracts offers a potentially fruitful vehicle for better understanding expectations and consequences of norms in sport organisations.

**Conclusion**

The changing landscape of elite sport has stimulated a burgeoning body of research examining organisational psychology in sport. Particular strengths within this domain relate to the elucidation of an understanding of emotional and attitudinal phenomena, stress and well being, key behaviours associated with optimal functioning, and environments which facilitate elite performance. This research also benefits by sampling individuals who directly and indirectly impact the functioning of sport organisations and quality of work life within them. Indeed, the research reviewed here has begun to provide insights into the predictors of sustained organisational performance and well being in sport that might be controlled and influenced through empirically grounded intervention. Despite these fruitful endeavours, it would appear that there remains much to be understood regarding organisational psychology in sport and we have pointed to numerous potential future lines of inquiry. In providing a structure to support this research agenda, our intention here has not been to provide a comprehensive list of concepts of interest, to be used to prescribe or regulate what should be examined. Instead, our aim has been to better situate extant and potential lines of inquiry in the hope of stimulating more systematic programmes of research to advance the field.

A salient point for consideration that has emerged from this review relates to the complexity of organisational dynamics, and the apparent intertwined and hierarchically nested nature of the core dimensions and topics they encompass. For example, extant literature has highlighted many variables of interest that appear to transcend dimensions and areas of influence (e.g. leadership, roles). Such issues might be explained by multilevel theory and research designs (see House *et al.*, 1995; Klein and Kozlowski, 2000). Indeed, a distinguishing feature of organisational psychology research is its examination of variables that occur naturally at several levels (e.g. individual, dyadic, team, and organisational, and sport). Only by acknowledging such features can we address effectively the complexities of how team and organisational environments influence individuals' performance and well being and are influenced in return. For example, according to the research presented here, the implementation of an intervention aimed at creating a high performance environment within a sport organisation would require concerted efforts across individual, team, organisational levels of analysis through the optimisation of leadership, performance enablers, people, and the organisational climate. Therefore, researchers must ensure consistency between conceptualisation and research design by integrating multilevel theory and research design or risk the pitfalls of developing incomplete and missspecified models and the exacerbation of a myth of individualism in the pursuit of ongoing sporting success.

In this chapter, our focus has been on research aligned with organisational psychology. However, as alluded to in our introductory sentiments, this reflects just one of three general I/O psychology concentrations. Indeed, we have given no space to a discourse on the importance of personnel psychology or human engineering factors. Research on such concentrations might focus on employment practices within sport organisations and their implications for the performance and well being of employees. Indeed, issues relating to poor employment practices in elite football have been highlighted by sport scholars (e.g. Waddington *et al.*, 2001; Wagstaff *et al.*, 2015), but have not been directly examined through an organisational psychology lens. Such applied research might benefit by using techniques commonly associated with personnel psychology, including the use of exit interviews when seeking to make improvements in organisational functioning. Human engineering research within sport organisations might prove the most problematic of the three, given the advanced development of sport biomechanics and technology and the work of practitioners to enhance the interface between individuals in organisations and these supports. However, it is possible that psychologists can optimise the understanding and integration of such supports if they are afforded such a role by organisations.

Finally, it is important to note that despite the nascent state of many areas of inquiry within this domain, much of the research reviewed here has used inductive research designs, grounded in the sport context to examine phenomena with divergent origins. Indeed, the recent use of ecologically valid designs to examine organisational psychology concepts in sport such as ethnography (e.g. Wagstaff *et al.*, 2012b), action research (e.g. Wagstaff *et al.*, 2013), and grounded theory (Cruickshank *et al.*, 2013) are highly suitable for research in its infancy. Moreover, it is reassuring to observe that researchers have begun to develop sport-specific measures of organisational-related variables (e.g. Fletcher and Arnold, 2012; Jackson *et al.*, 2014) as these lines of inquiry have blossomed. We hope future research in this domain will continue these good practices of scientific study.

# References

American Psychological Association. (2011). *Defining the practice of sport and performance psychology*. Division 47, Exercise and Sport Psychology, Practice Committee. www.apa.org/ed/graduate/specialize/industrial.aspx.

Aoyagi, M. W., Cox, R. H., and Mcguire, R. T. (2008). Organisational citizenship behaviour in sport: Relationships with leadership, team cohesion, and athlete satisfaction. *Journal of Applied Sport Psychology*, 20, 25–41.

Arnold, R. and Fletcher, D. (2012a). A research synthesis and taxonomic classification of the organisational stressors encountered by sport performers. *Journal of Sport and Exercise Psychology*, 34, 397–429.

Arnold, R. and Fletcher, D. (2012b). Psychometric issues in organisational stressor research: A review and implications for sport psychology. *Measurement in Physical Education and Exercise Science*, 16, 81–100. doi:10.1080/1091367X.2012.639608.

Arnold, R., Fletcher, D., and Daniels, K. (2013). Development and validation of the organisational stressor indicator for sport performers (OSI-SP). *Journal of Sport and Exercise Psychology*, 35, 180–196.

Arnold, R., Fletcher, D., and Molyneux, L. (2012). Performance leadership and management in elite sport: Recommendations, advice and suggestions from national performance directors. *European Sport Management Quarterly*, 12, 317–336.

Arthur, C., Hardy, L., and Woodman, T. (2012). Realising the Olympic dream: Vision, support and challenge. *Reflective Practice*, 13, 399–406.

Arthur, C. A., Woodman, T., Ong, C. W., Hardy, L., and Ntoumanis, N. (2011). The role of athlete narcissism in moderating the relationship between coaches' transformational leader behaviours and athlete motivation. *Journal of Sport and Exercise Psychology*, 33, 3–19.

Ashkanasy, N. M. (2003). Emotions in organisations: a multi-level perspective. *Research in Multi Level Issues*, 2, 9–54. doi:10.1016/S1475-9144(03)02002-2.

Barsade, S. G., Brief, A. P., and Spataro, S. E. (2003). The affective revolution in organisational behaviour: the emergence of a paradigm. In J. Greenberg (ed.), *Organisational behaviour: State of the science* (pp. 3–50). Mahwah, NJ: Lawrence Erlbaum.

Bass, B. M. (1960). *Leadership, psychology, and organisational Behaviour*. New York: Harper.

Bass, B. M. (1985). *Leadership and performance beyond expectations*. Collier Macmillan.

Bauer, T. N., Bodner, T., Erdogan, B., Truxillo, D. M., and Tucker, J. S. (2007). Newcomer adjustment during organisational socialization: a meta-analytic review of antecedents, outcomes, and methods. *Journal of Applied Psychology*, 92, 707–721.

Brewer, B. W., van Raalte, J. L., and Linder, D. E. (1993). Athletic identity: Hercules' muscles or Achilles heel? *International Journal of Sport Psychology*, 24, 237–254.

Britt, T. W., Dickinson, J. M., Green, T. M., and McKibben, E. S. (2007). Self-engagement at work. In D. Nelson and C. L. Cooper (eds), *Positive organisational behaviour* (pp. 143–158). London: Sage.

Burns, G. N., Jasinski, D., Dunn, S., and Fletcher, D. (2012). Athlete identity and athlete satisfaction. *Personality and Individual Differences*, 52, 280–284.

Callow, N., Smith, M. J., Hardy, L., Arthur, C. A., and Hardy, J. (2009). Measurement of transformational leadership and its relationship with team cohesion and performance level. *Journal of Applied Sport Psychology*, 21, 395–412. doi:10.1080/10413200903204754.

Carron, A.V. and Eys, M. A. (2012). *Group dynamics in sport* (4th edn). Morgantown, WV: Fitness Information Technology.

Conway, N. and Briner, R. B. (2005). *Understanding psychological contracts at work: A critical evaluation of theory and research*. Oxford: Oxford University Press.

Cruickshank, A. and Collins, D. (2012). Culture change in elite sport performance teams. *Journal of Applied Sport Psychology*, 24, 338–355.

Cruickshank, A., Collins, D., and Minten, S. (2013). Culture change in a professional sports team: Shaping environmental contexts and regulating power. *International Journal of Sports Science and Coaching*, 8, 319–326.

De Backer, M., Boen, F., Ceux, T., De Cuyper, B., Hoigaard, R., Callens, F., Fransen, K., and Vande Broek, G. (2011). Do perceived justice and need support of the coach predict team identification and cohesion? Testing their relative importance among top volleyball and handball players in Belgium and Norway. *Psychology of Sport and Exercise*, 12, 192–201.

Didymus, F. F. and Fletcher, D. (2012). Getting to the heart of the matter: A diary study of swimmers' appraisals of organisational stressors. *Journal of Sports Sciences*, 30, 1375–1385.

Farrey, T. (2003). *Athletes abusing athletes*. Retrieved December 8, 2011, from http://espn.go.com/otl/hazing/monday.html.

Fisher, C. D. (2000). Mood and emotions while working: Missing pieces of job satisfaction? *Journal of Organisational Behaviour*, 21, 185–202.

Fitzpatrick, R. (2014, February 13). Football transfers: How to help a multi-million pound star settle in. *British Broadcasting Company*. Retrieved from www.bbc.co.uk.

Fletcher, D. and Arnold, R. (2012). A qualitative study of performance leadership and management in elite sport. *Journal of Applied Sport Psychology*, 23, 223–242.

Fletcher, D. and Wagstaff, C. R. D. (2009). Organisational psychology in elite sport: Its emergence, application and future. *Psychology of Sport and Exercise*, 10, 427–434.

Fletcher, D., Hanton, S., and Mellalieu, S. D. (2006). An organisational stress review: Conceptual and theoretical issues in competitive sport. In S. Hanton and S. D. Mellalieu (eds), *Literature reviews in sport psychology* (pp. 321–374). New York, NY: Nova Science.

Fletcher, D., Hanton, S., and Wagstaff, C. R. D. (2012). Performers' responses to stressors encountered in sport organisations. *Journal of Sports Sciences*, 30, 349–58.

Fredrickson, B. L. (2001). The role of positive emotions in positive psychology: The broaden-and-build theory of positive emotions. *American Psychologist*, 56, 218–226.

Friesen, A. P., Lane, A. M., Devonport, T. J., Sellars, C. N., Stanley, D. N., and Beedie, C. J. (2013). Emotion in sport: Considering interpersonal regulation strategies. *International Review of Sport and Exercise Psychology*, 6, 139–154.

Ghiselli, E. E. (1974). Some perspectives for industrial psychology. *American Psychologist*, 29, 80–87.

Gomes, A. R., Lopes, H., and Mata, R. T. (2011). Leadership, cohesion and satisfaction: Differences between swimming and handball Portuguese teams. *Revista Mexican de Psicologia*, 28, 31–42.

Gould, D. and Maynard, I. (2009). Psychological preparation for the Olympic Games. *Journal of Sports Sciences*, 27, 1393–1408. doi:10.1080/02640410903081845.

Gould, D. and Wright, E. M. (2012). The psychology of coaching. In S. M. Murphy (ed.), *The Oxford handbook of sport and performance psychology* (pp. 343–362). Oxford University Press.

Hanin, Y. L. (2007). Emotions in sport: Current issues and perspectives. In G. Tenenbaum and R. C. Eklund (eds), *Handbook of Sport Psychology* (3rd edn, pp. 31–58). Hoboken, NJ: John Wiley and Sons.

Hanton, S., Wagstaff, C. R. D., and Fletcher, D. (2012). Cognitive appraisals of stressors encountered in sport organisations. *International Journal of Sport and Exercise Psychology*, 10, 276–289. doi:10.1080/1612197X.2012.682376.

Hardy, L. J., Jones, G., and Gould, D. (1996). *Understanding psychological preparation for sport: Theory and practice of elite performers*. John Wiley and Sons.

Hatfield, E., Cacioppo, J., and Rapson, R. (1994). *Emotional contagion*. New York: Cambridge University Press.

Hodge, K. and Lonsdale, C. (2011). Prosocial and antisocial behaviour in sport: The role of coaching style, autonomous vs. controlled motivation, and moral disengagement. *Journal of Sport and Exercise Psychology*, 33, 527–547.

Hollander, E. P. (1958). Conformity, status, and idiosyncrasy credit. *Psychological Review*, 65, 117–127.

Hoover, N. C. (1999). *Initiation rites and athletics: A national survey of NCAA sports teams. Final report*. Alfred, NY: Alfred University.

Jackson, B., Gucciardi, D., and Dimmock, J. A. (2014). Toward a multidimensional model of athletes' commitment to coach-athlete relationships and interdependent sport teams: A substantive-methodological synergy. *Journal of Sport and Exercise Psychology*, 36, 52–68.

Jones, G., Gittins, M., and Hardy, L. (2009). Creating an environment where high performance is inevitable and sustainable: the high performance environment model. *Annual Review of High Performance Coaching and Consulting*, 1, 139–150.

Jones, G. R. (1986). Socialization tactics, self-efficacy, and newcomers' adjustments to organisations. *Academy of Management Journal*, 29, 262–279.

Kavussanu, M. (2006). Motivational predictors of prosocial and antisocial behaviour in football. *Journal of Sports Sciences*, 24, 575–588. doi:10.1080/02640410500190825.

Kavussanu, M., Stanger, N., and Boardley, I. D. (2013). The prosocial and antisocial behaviour in sport scale: Further evidence for construct validity and reliability. *Journal of Sports Sciences*, 31, 1208–1221. doi:10.1080/02640414.2013.77547.

Keegan, R. J., Harwood, C., Spray, C. M., and Lavallee, D. E. (2014). A qualitative investigation of the motivational climate in elite sport participants. *Psychology of Sport and Exercise*, 15, 97–107.

Kelly, H. H. (1951). Communication in experimentally created hierarchies. *Human Relations*, 4, 39–56.

Klein K. J. and Kozlowski, S. W. J. (2000). From micro to meso: Critical steps in conceptualising and conducting multilevel research. *Organisational Research Methods*, 3, 211–236. doi:10.1177/109442810033001.

Knight, C. J. and Harwood, C. G. (2009). Exploring parent-related coaching stressors in British tennis: A developmental investigation. *International Journal of Sports Science and Coaching*, 4, 545–565. doi:10.1260/174795409790291448.

Kristiansen, E. and Hanstad, D. (2012). Journalists and Olympic athletes: A Norwegian case study of an ambivalent relationship. *International Journal of Sport Communication*, 5, 231–245.

Kristiansen, E., Halvari, H., and Roberts, G. C. (2012). Organisational and media stress among professional football players: Testing an achievement goal theory model. *Scandinavian Journal of Medicine and Science in Sports*, 22, 569–579.

Kristiansen, E., Hanstad, D. V., and Roberts, G. C. (2011). Coping with the media at the Vancouver Winter Olympics: "We all make a living out of this." *Journal of Applied Sport Psychology*, 23, 443–458. doi:10.1080/10413200.2011.598139.

Kristiansen, E., Roberts, G. C., and Sisjord, M. K. (2011). Coping with negative media content: The experiences of professional football goalkeepers. *International Journal of Sport and Exercise Psychology*, 9, 295–307. doi:10.1080/1612197X.2011.623451.

Landy, F. J. and Conte, J. M. (2009). *Work in the 21st century: An introduction to industrial and organisational psychology*. Hoboken, NJ: John Wiley and Sons.

Lane, A. M., Beedie, C. J., Jones, M. V., Uphill, M. A., and Devonport, T. J. (2012). The BASES expert statement on emotion regulation in sport. *Journal of Sports Sciences*, 30, 1189–1195.

Levy, A., Nicholls, A., Marchant, D., and Polman, R. (2009). Organisational stressors, coping, and coping effectiveness: A longitudinal study with an elite coach. *International Journal of Sports Science and Coaching*, 4, 31–45.

Martin, L., Bruner, M., Eys, M. A., and Spink, K. (2014). The social environment in sport: Selected topics. *International Review of Sport and Exercise Psychology*, 7, 87–105.

Mathieu, J. E. and Zajac, D. M. (1990). A review and meta-analysis of the antecedents, correlates, and consequences of organisational commitment. *Psychological Bulletin*, 108, 171–194.

May, D. R., Gilson, R. L. and Harter, L. M. (2004). The psychological conditions of meaningfulness, safety and availability and the engagement of the human spirit at work. *Journal of Occupational and Organisational Psychology*, 77, 11–37.

McCarthy, P. J. (2011). Positive emotion in sport and exercise performance: Current status and future directions. *International Review of Sport and Exercise Psychology*, 4, 50–69.

Mellalieu, S. D., Hanton, S., Neil, R., Fletcher, D., and Wagstaff, C. R. D. (2007). Competition and organisation stress. *Journal of Sports Sciences*, 25, 33–36.

Mellalieu, S., Shearer, D. A., and Shearer, C. (2013). A preliminary survey of interpersonal conflict at major games and championships. *The Sport Psychologist*, 27, 120–129.

Meyer, J. P. and Allen, N. J. (1997). *Commitment in the workplace: Theory, research, and application*. London: Sage.

Meyer, J. P., Allen, N. J., and Smith, C. A. (1993). Commitment to organisations and occupations: extension and test of a three-component conceptualisation. *Journal of Applied Psychology*, 78, 538–551.

Meyer, J. P., Stanley, D. J., Herscovitch, L., and Topolnytsky, L. (2002). Affective, continuance, and normative commitment to the organisation: A meta-analysis of Antecedents, correlates, and consequences. *Journal of Vocational Behaviour*, 61, 20–52.

Mills, A., Butt, J., Maynard, I., and Harwood, C. (2014). Toward an understanding of optimal development environments within elite soccer academies. *The Sport Psychologist*, 28, 137–150.

Moll, T., Jordet, G., and Pepping, G. J. (2010). Emotional contagion in soccer penalty shootouts: celebration of individual success is associated with ultimate team success. *Journal of Sports Sciences*, 28, 983–992. doi:10.1080/02640414.2010.484068.

Morris, J. A. and Feldman, D. C. (1996). The dimensions, antecedents, and consequences of emotional labor. *The Academy of Management Review*, 21, 986–1010.

Mowdey, R. T., Steers, R. M., and Porter, L. W. (1979). The measurement of organisational commitment. *Journal of Vocational Behaviour*, 14, 224–247.

O'Neill, D. F. (2008). Injury contagion in Alpine ski racing: the effect of injury on teammates' performance. *Journal of Clinical Sport Psychology*, 2, 278–292.

Organ, D. W. (1988). *Organisational citizenship behaviour: The good soldier syndrome*. Lexington, MA: Lexington Books.

Pain, M. A., Harwood, C., and Mullen, R. (2012). Improving the performance environment of a soccer team during a competitive season: An exploratory action research study. *The Sport Psychologist*, 26, 390–411.

Paulhus, D. L. and Williams, K. M. (2002). The dark triad of personality: narcissism, machiavellianism, and psychopathy. *Journal of Research in Personality*, 36, 556–563.

Price, M. S. and Weiss, M. R. (2011). Peer leadership in sport: Relationships among personal characteristics, leader behaviours, and team outcomes. *Journal of Applied Sport Psychology*, 23, 49–64.

Reid, C., Stewart, E., and Thorne, G. (2004). Multidisciplinary sport science team in elite sport: Comprehensive servicing or conflict and confusion. *The Sport Psychologist*, 18, 204–217.

Rutten, E., Deković, M., Stams, G. J. J. M., Schuengel, C., Hoeksma, J. B., and Biesta, G. J. J. (2008). On-and off-field antisocial and prosocial behaviour in adolescent soccer players: A multilevel study. *Journal of Adolescence*, 31, 371–387.

Rousseau, D. M. (1989). Psychological and implied contracts in organisations. *Employee Responsibilities and Rights Journal*, 2, 121–139.

Rowold, J. (2006). Transformational and transactional leadership in martial arts. *Journal of Applied Sport Psychology*, 18, 312–325. doi:10.1080/10413200600944082.

Saks, A., Uggerslev, K., and Fassina, N. (2007). Socialization tactics and newcomer adjustment: A meta-analytic review and test of a model. *Journal of Vocational Behaviour*, 70, 413–446.

Schoenewolf, G. (1990). Emotional contagion: Behavioural induction in individuals and groups. *Modern Psychoanalysis*, 15, 49–61.

Shaw, M. E. (1981). *Group dynamics: The psychology of small group behaviour*. New York, NY: McGraw-Hill.

Smith, W. P. and Bordonaro, F. (1975). Self-esteem and satisfaction as affected by unexpected social status placement. *Sociometry*, 38, 223–246.

Tabei, Y., Fletcher, D., and Goodger, K. (2012). The relationship between organisational stressors and athlete burnout in soccer players. *Journal of Clinical Sport Psychology*, 6, 146–165.

Tamminen, K. A. and Crocker, P. R. E. (2013). I control my own emotions for the sake of the team: Emotional self-regulation and interpersonal emotion regulation among female high-performance curlers. *Psychology of Sport and Exercise*, 14, 737–747.

Täuber, S. and Sassenberg, K. (2012). The impact of identification on adherence to group norms in team sports: Who is going the extra mile? *Group Dynamics*, 16, 231–240.

Theeboom, T., Beersma, B., and van Vianen, A. E. (2013). Does coaching work? A meta-analysis on the effects of coaching on individual level outcomes in an organisational context. *The Journal of Positive Psychology*, 9, 1–18.

Totterdell, P. (2000). Catching moods and hitting runs: mood linkage and subjective performance in professional sport teams. *Journal of Applied Psychology*, 85, 848–859.

Totterdell, P., Holman, D., and Niven, K. (2013). Research agenda. In A. Bakker and K. Daniels (eds), *A day in the life of a happy worker* (pp. 150–169). New York, NY: Psychology Press.

Waddington, I., Roderick, M., and Naik, R. (2001). Methods of appointment and qualifications of club doctors and physiotherapists in English professional football: Some problems and issues. *British Journal of Sports Medicine*, 35, 48–53.

Wagstaff, C. R. D. (2014). Emotion regulation and sport performance. *Journal of Sport and Exercise Psychology*, *36*, 401–412. doi: 10.1123/jsep.2013-0257.

Wagstaff, C. R. D. and Weston, N. J. V. (2014). Examining emotion regulation in an isolated performance team in Antarctica. *Sport, Exercise, and Performance Psychology*, *3*, 273–287. doi: 10.1037/spy0000022.

Wagstaff, C. R. D., Fletcher, D., and Hanton, S. (2012a). Positive organisational psychology in sport. *International Review of Sport and Exercise Psychology*, 5, 87–103.

Wagstaff, C. R. D., Fletcher, D., and Hanton, S. (2012b). Positive organisational psychology in sport: An ethnography of organisational functioning in a national sport organisation. *Journal of Applied Sport Psychology*, 24, 26–47. doi:10.1080/104 13200.2011.589423.

Wagstaff, C. R. D., Fletcher, D., and Hanton, S. (2012c). Exploring emotion abilities and regulation strategies in sport organisations. *Sport, Exercise, and Performance Psychology*, 1, 268–282. doi:10.1037/a0028814.

Wagstaff, C. R. D., Hanton, S., and Fletcher, D. (2013). Developing emotion abilities and regulation strategies in a sport organisation: An action research intervention. *Psychology of Sport and Exercise*, 14, 476–487. doi:10.1016/j. psychsport.2013.01.006.

Wagstaff, C. R. D., Neil, R., Mellalieu, S. D., and Hanton, S. (2012). Key movements in directional research in competitive anxiety. *Studies on the Olympic and Paralympic Games*, 1, 143–166.

Wagstaff, C. R. D., Thelwell, R. C., and Gilmore, S. (2015). Sport medicine and sport science practitioners' experiences of organisational change. *Scandinavian Journal of Medicine and Science in Sport*. doi: 10.1111/sms.12340.

Wahrman, R. (1977). Status, deviance, sanctions, and group discussion. *Small Group Behaviour*, 8, 147–168.

Waldron, J. J. and Krane, V. (2005). Whatever it takes: Health compromising behaviours of female athletes. *Quest*, 51, 315–321.

Waldron, J. J., Quinten, L., and Krane, V. (2011). Duct tape, icy hot and paddles: Narratives of initiation into US male sport teams. *Sport, Education and Society*, 16, 111–125.

Weinberg, R. and McDermott, M. (2002). A comparative analysis of sport and business organisations: Factors perceived critical for organisational success. *Journal of Applied Sport Psychology*, 14, 282–298.

Wylleman, P., Alfermann, D., and Lavallee, D. (2004). Career transitions in sport. *Psychology of Sport and Exercise*, 5, 3–5.

# 5 The tripartite efficacy framework in physical activity contexts

*Ben Jackson, Steven R. Bray, Mark R. Beauchamp and Timothy C. Howle*

## Introduction

Since the publication of Bandura's (1977) seminal text, sustained research attention has been devoted toward charting the nature, development, and implications of individuals' confidence in their ability (i.e. self-efficacy). As a result, educators, practitioners, scholars, and students in the field of sport and exercise psychology now have a relatively detailed understanding of the importance of self-efficacy beliefs, the means through which individuals derive (and lose) confidence in their ability, and the diverse consequences with which self-efficacy is associated. Numerous reviews of the self-efficacy literature are available (see, for example, Beauchamp *et al.*, 2012; Biddle *et al.*, 2007; Feltz *et al.*, 2008; Hagger, 2012), and that being the case, rather than (re-)examine the literature on self-efficacy in detail, the primary purpose of this chapter is to consider conceptual and empirical evidence regarding the efficacy beliefs that develop uniquely within interpersonal settings. In particular, our aim is to introduce Lent and Lopez's (2002) tripartite efficacy model, with a specific emphasis on the relational efficacy constructs that exist within this framework, and to provide a synthesis of the tripartite efficacy research that has been conducted to date in physical activity contexts. Relative to our understanding of self-efficacy, much less is known about the relational constructs that exist within the tripartite efficacy model; however, research over the last decade has demonstrated that this framework may be important for understanding behaviour, decision-making, and well-being in relational and group-based pursuits. Prior to reviewing the tripartite efficacy literature, we first provide a brief summary of the conceptual scaffold upon which this model is grounded (i.e. self-efficacy theory).

## Self-efficacy: a brief overview

Self-efficacy refers specifically to an individual's belief in his or her ability to execute the necessary actions required to produce a given attainment (Bandura, 1977). Beyond positive associations with performance attainments

(Moritz *et al.*, 2000), research in sport and exercise has shown that individuals who are more certain regarding their capabilities tend to set more challenging goals (e.g. Boyce and Bingham, 1997; Kane *et al.*, 1996; Theodorakis, 1995), display increased effort (e.g. George, 1994; Hutchinson *et al.*, 2008) and persistence (e.g. Beattie and Davies, 2010; Gao and Newton, 2009), and experience favourable emotional responses (e.g. Hu *et al.*, 2007; Tritter *et al.*, 2013; Welch *et al.*, 2010).

Within individual pursuits, Bandura (1997) identified four primary sources of self-efficacy. Specifically, individuals are theorized to derive confidence in their ability when they accrue enactive mastery accomplishments, observe similar others coping or performing well (i.e. vicarious influences), receive supportive verbal persuasion, and experience optimal physiological and affective states. There is support for Bandura's theorizing regarding these sources of self-efficacy (see Beauchamp *et al.*, 2012; Feltz *et al.*, 2008; Samson and Solmon, 2011); however, our physical activity experiences are supported (or thwarted) by the relationships that we form with others, and focusing solely on the development of *self*-efficacy might obscure the important relational perceptions that develop in interpersonal contexts. For the remainder of this chapter, we turn our attention to the distinct types of efficacy beliefs that emerge alongside self-efficacy within interpersonal and relational scenarios.

## Efficacy beliefs in relational and interpersonal contexts

In seeking to explain individuals' goal-directed behaviour, it is understandable that researchers have often focused on athletes' or exercisers' appraisals regarding their task-related capabilities (i.e. task self-efficacy; see previous section). Importantly though, many of our sport and exercise activities occur in environments that require us to work alongside important others (e.g. within teams, alongside training/playing partners, under coaches/instructors). In such settings, task self-efficacy represents just one construct that exists within an extensive network of efficacy beliefs. In social environments such as group exercise classes or sport teams, individuals harbour beliefs in their abilities to execute tasks independently (e.g. judging the extent to which one is able to perform the necessary actions during the exercise class). However, the interpersonal nature of these experiences invites additional forms of self-efficacy to emerge. For example, exercisers and athletes also develop self-presentational efficacy perceptions reflecting their confidence in their ability to portray a desired image to those with whom they interact (cf. Leary and Kowalski, 1995). Similarly, in interdependent sport teams, athletes not only appraise their abilities to carry out the skills associated with their sport, but also their capability to execute their specific responsibilities associated with their role on the team (i.e. role efficacy; e.g. Bray *et al.*, 2002). These constructs exemplify the range of personal efficacy perceptions – beyond those that relate solely to one's task execution – that individuals hold regarding their own capabilities.

Although interpersonal or team environments can give rise to additional efficacy perceptions reflecting participants' beliefs about their own (i.e. personal) abilities, individuals also develop efficacy appraisals regarding targets *other than themselves* (for an overview, see Beauchamp, 2007). For instance, there exists a relatively well-developed literature in team sport contexts charting the desirable personal and group-level consequences associated with individuals' confidence in their team's ability as a whole (i.e. collective efficacy; for reviews of conceptual and measurement issues, see Chow and Feltz, 2008; Myers and Feltz, 2007). Moreover, those within coactive (e.g. athlete–athlete partnerships) and instructional (e.g. coach–athlete, therapist–client, teacher–student) interactions also reflect upon the capabilities and cognitions of the *individuals* with whom they interact. This premise – that individuals hold efficacy perceptions regarding the significant others with whom they interact – serves as the foundation for Lent and Lopez's (2002) tripartite efficacy model, which we introduce in the following section.

## The tripartite efficacy model: definition and measurement

By integrating the self-efficacy (Bandura, 1997) and interpersonal perception (e.g. Kenny and DePaulo, 1993; Snyder and Stukas, 1999) literature, Lent and Lopez (2002) presented a tripartite (i.e. three-factor) conceptualization for the study of efficacy beliefs within interpersonal and relational scenarios. Central to their model was the notion that individuals make appraisals regarding their own capabilities (i.e. self-efficacy), and that these appraisals are pivotal not only in shaping effective behavioural outcomes (as is the case across all performance contexts), but also in supporting pro-social relationship perceptions. Existing tripartite efficacy investigations have provided some substantiation for this proposal. For instance, researchers have demonstrated that when members of coach–athlete and athlete–athlete sport dyads believe strongly in their own capabilities, this is associated, among other things, with adaptive motivational responses (e.g. Jackson and Beauchamp, 2010; Jackson *et al.*, 2008), elevated commitment to one's relationship (e.g. Jackson *et al.*, 2007), and reduced intra-dyadic conflict perceptions (e.g. Jackson *et al.*, 2011).

In addition to self-efficacy, however, Lent and Lopez (2002) also considered two important relational efficacy constructs that emerge in relationship contexts and that exist alongside, but are unique from, individuals' confidence in their own ability (see Figure 5.1). The first relational efficacy construct upon which we focus our attention is termed *relation-inferred self-efficacy* (RISE). Interpersonal exchanges, such as those that exist within coach–athlete or teacher–student interactions, are characterized by frequent communication (both verbal and non-verbal) between individuals. Lent and Lopez (2002) posited that, as a result of the way in which these interpersonal signals are received and processed, individuals form estimations regarding the confidence that other people have in their ability. RISE, therefore, represents a meta-perception (see Kenny and DePaulo, 1993) regarding one's estimation of another's confidence in one's ability (i.e. person A's estimation of person B's confidence in person A's ability). To illustrate, statements from athletes such as "my coach really believes in me" are indicative of a strong RISE perception on the part of the athlete (in relation to the coach). Given the vagaries that are inherent in the detection and interpretation of interpersonal cues, RISE beliefs may or may not be accurate. Irrespective of the accuracy of the estimation, though, Lent and Lopez asserted that the strength of one's RISE perception is crucial in shaping personal and relational outcomes.

Alongside RISE, the second relational construct that Lent and Lopez (2002) discussed within their tripartite framework is referred to as *other-efficacy*. Other-efficacy beliefs develop as individuals judge the capabilities of those with whom they interact, and relate specifically to the degree of confidence that one person has in another person's capabilities. It is not uncommon, for instance, for members of sport partnerships to speak of the "belief" (or confidence) that they have in their playing partner, or for an exerciser or athlete to praise the various qualities that give them confidence in their instructor/coach. In much the same way that RISE beliefs are vulnerable to distortions or inaccuracies, Lent and Lopez proposed that irrespective of whether one person's other-efficacy beliefs are actually consonant with the target individual's ability, a strong belief in that other person accounts for a range of adaptive task – (e.g. motivation) and social-related (e.g. relationship satisfaction) outcomes.

For the purpose of illustration, and to document the instruments that have been developed for the measurement of RISE and other-efficacy, Table 5.1 presents information regarding the way in which these constructs have been operationalized in existing relational efficacy investigations. In the sections that follow, we draw from Lent and Lopez's assertions and the developing empirical evidence base in order to provide a detailed overview of the inter-relationships between the tripartite constructs, as well as the sources and consequences associated with RISE and other-efficacy. Before doing so, however, it is important that we introduce the concept of proxy efficacy, and clarify the position of this construct relative to the tripartite model.

### Proxy efficacy: a unique type of other-efficacy

Prior to the emergence of "other-efficacy" within the lexicon, scholars had already begun to consider the notion that individuals may develop confidence in others' capabilities. Specifically, in the years leading to (and since) the formalization of the tripartite model, there was (and has been) a gradual accumulation of evidence relating the concept of *proxy efficacy*

Table 5.1 Overview of existing tripartite efficacy and proxy efficacy measurement instruments

| Efficacy belief/s measured | Source | Context | Sample | Example items |
| --- | --- | --- | --- | --- |
| Tripartite efficacy beliefs | Jackson, Whipp et al. (2012) | Physical education | Australian and Singaporean high school students | S-E: Please honestly rate your confidence in your ability at this moment in time to try your hardest in every PE class<br><br>O-E: Please honestly rate your confidence in your PE teacher's ability at this moment in time to motivate you even during hard or unfamiliar activities<br><br>RISE: Please honestly estimate (or guess) how confident your PE teacher is in your ability at this moment in time to try your hardest in every PE class |
| Tripartite efficacy beliefs | Jackson et al. (2011) | Sport | Australian individual-sport athletes | S-E: At this point in time, rate your confidence in your ability to perform all the difficult technical aspects of your sport<br><br>O-E: At this point in time, rate your confidence in your coach's ability to communicate effectively toward you at all times<br><br>RISE: At this point in time, estimate how confident your coach is in your ability to perform all the difficult technical aspects of your sport |
| Tripartite efficacy beliefs | Jackson, Dimmock et al. (2012) | Rehabilitation | Rehabilitation clients enrolled in an exercise programme | S-E: Please honestly rate your confidence in your ability at this moment in time to use the correct technique for all of your exercises<br><br>O-E: Please honestly rate your confidence in your therapist's ability at this moment in time to help you to adhere to your programme at all times<br><br>RISE: Please honestly estimate how confident your therapist is in your ability at this moment in time to use the correct technique for all of your exercises |

| | | | | |
|---|---|---|---|---|
| Other-efficacy | Dunlop et al. (2011) | Exer-gaming | Female university students | Rate your confidence in your partner's ability to step in time with the music |
| Other-efficacy | Beauchamp and Whinton (2005) | Sport | Equestrian riders | Rate your confidence in your horse's ability to display the correct temperament for the level of competition required today |
| Proxy efficacy | Bray et al. (2004) | Exercise | Females in group exercise classes | Exercise choreography: My confidence in my exercise leader's capabilities to include a variety of exercises/moves during the classes over the next month is…<br>Instructional-motivational: My confidence in my exercise leader's capabilities to provide easy-to-follow instructions during the class over the next month is… |
| Proxy efficacy | Bray et al. (2006) | Rehabilitation | Clients in a hospital-based outpatient cardiac rehabilitation programme | Exercise: My confidence in my interventionist's capabilities to include a variety of different exercises in my programme is…<br>Self-regulation: My confidence in my interventionist's capabilities to assist with setting specific goals for how much exercise to do during the upcoming week is… |
| Proxy-efficacy | Shields and Brawley (2006) | Exercise | Exercise class participants | How confident are you that your instructor can help you schedule exercise sessions over the next eight weeks? |

Notes
S-E = self-efficacy.
O-E = other-efficacy.
RISE = relation-inferred self-efficacy.

(for a detailed overview of proxy efficacy research, see Bray *et al.*, 2014). Within self-efficacy theory (Bandura, 1997), a "proxy agent" represents any individual upon whom one relies for help with the regulation of one's behaviour and/or the attainment of one's goals (e.g. the role of a therapist or physician). Thus, the term proxy efficacy was introduced to refer specifically to one's confidence in the capabilities of a proxy agent; the most commonly studied proxy agents within the interpersonal efficacy literature have been physical therapists and exercise instructors (see Bray *et al.*, 2001, 2004, 2006, 2013; Bray and Cowan, 2004; Priebe *et al.*, 2012; Shields and Brawley, 2006; 2007). In the last decade, the literatures on proxy efficacy and other-efficacy have become closely intertwined, and although proxy efficacy was studied prior to other-efficacy, we view proxy efficacy as a specific type of other-efficacy. That is, proxy efficacy represents a form of other-efficacy that is apparent when the perception relates to the capabilities of a proxy agent. On the other hand, it might be argued that other-efficacy perceptions cut more broadly across all relational contexts, and include those perceptions that are not directed specifically at a proxy agent.[1]

## Relationships between the tripartite efficacy constructs

Lent and Lopez (2002) contended that, under most circumstances, individuals' tripartite perceptions operate in a synergistic fashion, noting specifically that favourable RISE and other-efficacy beliefs may augment one's confidence in one's own capabilities (see Figure 5.1). For example, when

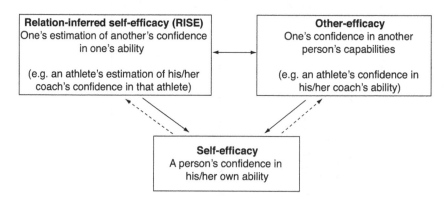

*Figure 5.1* The tripartite efficacy model.

Note
Arrows indicate predictive/associative relationships between tripartite efficacy constructs (positive in nature). Although relational efficacy beliefs are theorized to predominantly act as intra-relationship sources of self-efficacy (Lent and Lopez, 2002), dashed lines from self-efficacy to RISE/other-efficacy indicate that relational perceptions may also be shaped by individuals' confidence in their own ability.

an athlete is highly confident in his/her coach, and feels certain that the coach believes strongly in his/her (i.e. the athlete's) ability, these appraisals should help counter the athlete's self-doubts and contribute to a strong sense of self-efficacy. Although this aspect of the tripartite model has been tested only through observational approaches to date (i.e. via interviews and questionnaires), there is increasing evidence that these intra-relationship perceptions tend to align positively with individuals' confidence in their own ability. For instance, among members of junior athlete–athlete partnerships (Jackson *et al.*, 2007), as well as those within elite coach–athlete and athlete–athlete sport dyads (Jackson *et al.*, 2008; Jackson *et al.*, 2009), qualitative and quantitative analyses have revealed that favourable other-efficacy and RISE perceptions may underpin individuals' confidence in their own ability. More recently, the use of structural equation modelling has demonstrated that high school physical education students report greater confidence in their own ability within their class when they believe that they are being instructed by a highly capable teacher (e.g. Jackson, Whipp, and Beauchamp, 2013; Jackson, Whipp, Chua *et al.*, 2013), and when they infer that their teacher believes strongly in their ability (e.g. Bourne *et al.*, in press). These findings are consistent with those that have been observed for clients' relational efficacy beliefs regarding their therapists within exercise rehabilitation programs (Jackson, Dimmock *et al.*, 2012), as well as undergraduate students' perceptions regarding their physical activity class instructor (Jackson, Myers *et al.*, 2012).

Existing proxy efficacy research highlights further support for the potential efficacy-enhancing properties associated with individuals' confidence in another person's capabilities. In particular, Bray and colleagues' (Bray *et al.*, 2001) cross-sectional analyses showed that fitness class attendees reported greater confidence in their own ability when they were highly confident in their exercise instructor. In a subsequent study, Bray and Cowan (2004) also demonstrated that when cardiac rehabilitation patients strongly endorsed the capabilities of their exercise consultant, this belief prospectively accounted for approximately 30 per cent of the variance in patients' self-efficacy ratings when assessed approximately two months later. Within a college setting, further evidence for the predictive role of proxy efficacy in relation to self-efficacy was provided by Elias and MacDonald (2007), who reported that students were more confident in their own abilities when they believed that their faculty instructors were highly capable.

In order to further advance our understanding of the inter-relations that exist within the tripartite model, theoretically- and/or empirically-driven experimental manipulations are necessary (see, for example, Bray *et al.*, 2013; Dunlop *et al.*, 2011; Priebe *et al.*, 2012) to identify causal pathways between efficacy beliefs. Most notably, although researchers to date have (justifiably) modeled RISE as a predictor of self-efficacy, Lent and

Lopez (2002) noted that the relationship between self-efficacy and RISE is in fact likely to be bidirectional in nature. Indeed, there is ample evidence in the person perception literature for the process of projection, whereby individuals use their own self-views when attempting to infer the ways in which others view them (see Frey and Tropp, 2006; Kenny and DePaulo, 1993). With respect to the tripartite model it is possible that exercisers, for instance, might be guided by the way in which they appraise their own capabilities when estimating how confident their instructor is in their ability, particularly when they have insufficient interpersonal cues upon which to accurately gauge the other person's thoughts (cf. Jussim *et al.*, 1992). In light of this potentially recursive relationship, alongside experimental approaches we would encourage the use of cross-lagged (i.e. multiple time point) designs in future to allow for an examination of reciprocal relations, as well as research that examines the variables that might shape the direction of influence between self-efficacy and RISE (e.g. the level of experience that the perceiver has with the target). Although much is known regarding the wide-ranging affective and behavioural implications associated with self-efficacy (see Beauchamp *et al.*, 2012; Feltz *et al.*, 2008), such work would be invaluable in order to progress our knowledge of the way in which these self-views influence impression formation processes in social exchanges.

### Discrepancies between the tripartite efficacy constructs

As reviewed above, research largely supports the positive associations that are theorized to exist between relational efficacy and self-efficacy beliefs. However, Lent and Lopez (2002) contended that there may be situations in which one's tripartite perceptions become disconnected and that these discrepancies might disrupt task and relationship processes. For example, one can envisage the despondency and frustration that could result when an athlete believes strongly in his/her own ability, but at the same time feels that his/her coach holds a negative impression about his/her capabilities. In addition, it is possible that discordance between self- and other-efficacy might engender anxiogenic responses. In athlete dyads (e.g. rowing pairs), for example, a moderately self-efficacious athlete who is supremely confident in his/her playing partner might experience feelings of pressure in seeking to meet his/her partner's performance standards. Alternatively, the same athlete might be similarly concerned about an upcoming competition if s/he feels that his/her partner is (relatively speaking) less capable and cannot be relied upon to perform at the necessary level.

Although limited in scope, empirical evidence for tripartite efficacy discrepancies does exist. In a recent investigation, Jackson and colleagues (Jackson *et al.*, 2011) recruited 377 regional-, collegiate-, and national-level individual-sport athletes, and used cluster analyses to examine the efficacy profiles that athletes displayed regarding their relationship with their coach. Although the majority of athletes displayed harmonious perceptions characterized by consistently high, moderate, or low self-efficacy, other-efficacy, and RISE beliefs, approximately 20 per cent of the sample displayed a discordant pattern. This discordant profile comprised athletes who, despite lacking confidence in their coach's ability, and estimating that their coach was not highly confident in their ability (i.e. relatively low other-efficacy and RISE), were able to retain relatively strong self-efficacy perceptions. Most notably, analyses revealed that athletes within this profile actually reported the most maladaptive relationship appraisals (i.e. relatively low relationship commitment and satisfaction, relatively high conflict perceptions). In future, it would be worthwhile to examine in more detail (a) the perceiver – (e.g. experience, attachment style, rejection sensitivity) and target-related (e.g. interpersonal behaviour) factors that might give rise to such a discordant profile, (b) the extent to which incongruous efficacy perceptions are prevalent across different sport and exercise settings, and (c) the ways in which such discrepancies might impair personal well-being and relationship dynamics.

## Development and implications of relational efficacy perceptions

In addition to reflecting upon the inter-relationships between the tripartite constructs, and the potential implications arising out of discordant perceptions, Lent and Lopez (2002) provided insight into the means (i.e. sources) through which individuals' relational efficacy beliefs may develop and be revised. Moreover, they articulated how both of the relational efficacy constructs in their model may promote a range of personal and relationship outcomes. In the following sections, we detail Lent and Lopez's proposals regarding the formation and consequences of RISE and other-efficacy beliefs, and overview the recent studies in physical activity contexts – including those with an emphasis on proxy efficacy – that have examined their assertions.

### *Relational-efficacy antecedents*

*RISE*

Lent and Lopez (2002) contended that when attempting to interpret how confident another person is in our ability, we draw from the behavioural cues provided by that individual (see Kenny and DePaulo, 1993). These interpersonal cues include the direct feedback and support that the other person provides, along with the non-verbal behaviour displayed by the interaction partner. In addition, Lent and Lopez noted that individuals might appraise another's confidence in their ability through the performance goals that the other person sets for the perceiver. For example, when a basketball coach selects one of his players to defend against the best player on an opposing team, the athlete may infer the coach believes s/he is up to the task. Conversely, an exercise class member might begin to doubt his/her instructor's confidence in his/her ability if the instructor persistently encourages activities that the exerciser feels are comfortably within his/her reach. Nonetheless, although these overt signals might provide the most direct access to another's thoughts, there are often inconsistencies in others' interpersonal behaviour, and there are also practical difficulties associated with adequately capturing and distilling *all* of the cues provided by the other person (in order to arrive at an accurate judgment). That being the case, RISE perceptions are also theorized to develop in part out of one's own self-views (Kenny and DePaulo, 1993), and accordingly, Lent and Lopez proposed that attributes of the perceiver (e.g. one's confidence in one's own ability) might contribute to one's estimations regarding others' confidence in oneself (see also previous section on projection processes).

Greater empirical attention is needed in order to fully test this aspect of the tripartite model; however, there is some evidence that supports Lent and Lopez's (2002) propositions. Specifically, Jackson and colleagues conducted interviews with members of international-level athlete–athlete (Jackson *et al.*, 2008) and coach–athlete (Jackson *et al.*, 2009) dyads in which participants were asked to reflect upon the formation of their relational efficacy perceptions. Analyses revealed that dyad members believed that the other person in their partnership was highly confident in their ability when that person provided supportive verbal feedback and displayed encouraging body language along with a positive mood. Moreover, RISE beliefs were reinforced for athletes in coach-athlete relationships when they felt that their coach set them challenging goals (e.g. "if he didn't believe in me, then he wouldn't be setting me these goals"). Aside from these interpersonal signals, dyad members also reported that previous successes as a partnership, and a strong belief in their own ability, contributed to favorable RISE appraisals. In terms of other self-perceptions, when athletes were themselves highly motivated, and felt that they had accrued mastery achievements on a personal level, this also encouraged favourable RISE estimations (e.g. "she knows I work hard, and that I have done it in the past, so I think she's confident in me").

Beyond elite sport contexts, preliminary evidence has emerged relating to the factors that predict youth sport participants' RISE beliefs about their instructors and coaches. Saville and colleagues (Saville *et al.*, 2014) interviewed approximately 100 youth sport participants (aged 8–12) about the "things" their coaches did or said that they used to inform their RISE perceptions. Their analyses revealed insight into a number of direct verbal cues (e.g. "I believe you can do this"), as well as various non-verbal cues including being given challenging assignments during games and being selected to lead drills or demonstrate skills in practice. Participants also indicated that they felt that their coaches believed in them when the coach took extra time to show them how to perform a skill, and also by the tone in their coaches' voices or the look in their eyes when they spoke to them. The latter examples are illustrative of the subtle ways of communicating RISE that may be potent and effective, but also unique to relational contexts.

Research in other areas of physical activity has begun to reveal the means through which high school physical education students develop RISE beliefs regarding their teacher's beliefs in their abilities. Specifically, students appear to estimate that their teacher is confident in their ability when they believe that the teacher fosters a highly relatedness-supportive environment (i.e. displays instructional behaviours characterized by warmth, support, attention, and respect; Jackson, Whipp, Chua *et al.*, 2013) and makes use of transformational teaching practices (i.e. actions designed to empower and inspire students; Bourne *et al.*, in press). These predictive effects are encouraging in terms of providing support for Lent and Lopez's (2002) framework and for the development of teacher-mediated interventions that might bolster students' RISE perceptions. However, it is important to caution that these data were collected using observational approaches and, as a result, it is necessary to ascertain whether these relationships remain when examined through a causal methodological design (i.e. through experimental manipulations of the proposed sources).

## Other-efficacy

Drawing from the common determinants of efficacy perceptions (see Bandura, 1997, and earlier section), as well as the origins of interpersonal expectations (see, for example, Snyder and Stukas, 1999), Lent and Lopez (2002) presented a series of antecedents that they believed were central in the formation of individuals' other-efficacy beliefs. Specifically, they contended that other-efficacy beliefs should be bolstered through (a) positive experiences with a target individual (e.g. witnessing the target performing well or displaying desirable characteristics), (b) observing the target interacting well with others, (c) the receipt of positive third party comments (i.e. endorsements) regarding the target's ability, (d) favorable normative comparisons with previous "others" (e.g. comparing one's current partner's strengths against a previous partner's weaknesses), and (e) the use of heuristics tied to social and contextual generalizations (e.g. based on gender, attractiveness, athleticism). Jackson and colleagues' qualitative investigations with members of elite sport dyads provided support for these assertions. Indeed, athletes and coaches endorsed all of the above theorized sources when describing the factors that underpinned their confidence in their athlete, partner, or coach. In addition, Dunlop and colleagues (Dunlop *et al.*, 2011) provided causal insight into the role of performance knowledge and third party information (regarding one's partner) within a coactive task. Specifically, Dunlop and colleagues utilized bogus feedback about a partner's performance on a dance-based task to successfully manipulate participants' other-efficacy beliefs in the direction of the feedback.

Alongside the discrete sources upon which Lent and Lopez (2002) commented (e.g. receiving positive comments, observing an effective performance), there is also evidence to suggest that there may be higher-order factors (i.e. general interactional styles) that shape individuals' other-efficacy perceptions. For instance, athletes in Jackson *et al.*'s (2009) investigation believed strongly in their coach's ability when, over-time, that coach displayed an instructional (e.g. autonomy-supportive) style that was "compatible" with the athlete's preferences. Similarly, students have been shown to report stronger other-efficacy beliefs when they believe that their teacher displays relatedness-supportive (or interpersonally-involving) instructional practices (Jackson, Whipp, Chua *et al.*, 2013). Despite the impetus provided by these findings, researchers have yet to determine the effectiveness of interventions aimed at modifying leader instructional styles (e.g. based on need-supportive practices) in order to enhance followers' other-efficacy perceptions, and this is an important avenue for future study.

In terms of other opportunities for further research in this area, the potential for other-efficacy beliefs to stem from characteristics of the perceiver (rather than the target) is an issue that has yet to be considered. In particular, consistent with the way in which RISE beliefs are theorized to develop, it is possible that other-efficacy perceptions may be partly shaped by aspects of the *perceiver* (see Snyder and Stukas, 1999). For instance, those who are prone to feelings of isolation and rejection (e.g. those scoring highly on neuroticism, rejection sensitivity, and insecure attachment styles), or those who are inflexible and prefer to work on their own (e.g. displaying perfectionist tendencies), may tend to exaggerate others' shortcomings and develop relatively unfavorable expectations regarding their ability. Similarly, it is possible that maladaptive other-efficacy beliefs might arise when certain perceiver traits are paired (i.e. interact) with specific target characteristics. With this in mind, an examination of perceiver traits and attributes (potentially in combination with target characteristics) would progress our understanding of the ways in which personal and situational factors might drive individuals' expectations regarding others' capabilities.

*Proxy efficacy*

Given that it represents a specific type of other-efficacy, the theorized antecedents of proxy efficacy are consistent with those outlined in the previous section (for detailed coverage, see Bandura, 1997; Bray *et al.*, 2014). To date, experimental studies within group exercise (Bray *et al.*, 2004; Priebe *et al.*, 2012) and cardiac rehabilitation (Bray *et al.*, 2013) contexts have demonstrated the methods through which exercisers' and patients' proxy efficacy perceptions may be manipulated. In the first of these investigations, Bray *et al.* (2004, Phase 3) randomly assigned novice exercise class attendees to receive instruction from either a capable, encouraging, attentive, and interactive (i.e. an "enriched") instructor, or from a less socially-engaging instructor who provided only general, technical instruction. Findings showed that, relative to their counterparts in the neutral condition, participants who received the enriched instruction reported greater confidence in their instructor's capabilities.

In a similar vein, Priebe and colleagues (2012) sought to modify novice exercisers' proxy-efficacy perceptions through the provision of a theory-derived efficacy-enhancing message regarding an exercise instructor (cf. Bandura, 1997). Specifically, compared to an attention-control condition (in which the message contained neutral descriptive information regarding the instructor), participants in an experimental group were informed that (a) the instructor was recommended to them by a friend, (b) similar others had experienced success under the instructor, and (c) the instructor created a fun environment that promoted a good experience for those in the class. Despite there being no between-group differences on relevant demographic attributes (e.g. exercise engagement), participants in the efficacy-enhancing message condition reported greater instructor-related proxy efficacy perceptions.

Most recently, Bray *et al.* (2013) invited cardiac rehabilitation patients to read vignettes in which they were encouraged visualize themselves as a patient interacting with an exercise interventionist. By modifying only the nature of the imagined practitioner, Bray and colleagues demonstrated that patients reported greater confidence in the interventionist when that person was described as supportive, helpful, and someone who provided assistance with planning and executing their exercise behaviour, relative to a neutral scenario in which the practitioner was knowledgeable but did not provide a high level of assistance or encouragement. Taken together, this experimental work has begun to provide insight into the behavioural (Bray *et al.*, 2004), persuasion-based (Priebe *et al.*, 2012), and imaginal (Bray *et al.*, 2013) methods that might be utilized in order to create desirable perceptions about the qualities of a proxy agent, and that could be applied to the study of proxy efficacy and other-efficacy in other interaction contexts (e.g. sport, physical education).

### Relational efficacy outcomes

#### RISE and other-efficacy

Although RISE and other-efficacy are shaped by a number of relatively disparate sources, there is some consistency in terms of the implications with which these constructs are theorized to align. Within this section, therefore, we present conceptual and empirical support for the outcomes associated with both relational efficacy constructs (rather than presenting this material separately for each construct as in the previous section). With respect to the broad predictive functions that Lent and Lopez (2002) discussed, they noted that RISE and other-efficacy should both align *indirectly* with a range of desirable outcomes, via their self-efficacy-supporting effects. That is, in cases when individuals hold favorable relational efficacy appraisals, this should bolster their confidence in their own ability, which should in turn promote the various desirable outcomes that accompany self-efficacy. Recent evidence has emerged that provides support for this contention. For example, favorable relational efficacy beliefs among undergraduates regarding their physical activity class instructor have been shown to indirectly support enhanced in-class effort and enjoyment perceptions, through self-efficacy (Jackson, Myers *et al.*, 2012). In addition, when high school students believe that they are being instructed by a highly capable physical education teacher (e.g. Jackson, Whipp and Beauchamp, 2013), and/or infer that their teacher believes strongly in their ability (e.g. Bourne *et al.*, in press), this predicts greater self-efficacy on the part of students, which in turn supports their within-class and leisure-time physical activity engagement. Together, these findings provide preliminary insight regarding the perceptual processes through which RISE and other-efficacy might support downstream affective and behavioural outcomes.

Although the findings reviewed above are indicative of the indirect effects proposed by Lent and Lopez (2002), both relational constructs may also directly predict a range of personal and relationship-oriented variables. With respect to personal outcomes, Lent and Lopez presumed that individuals put forth more effort and experience adaptive emotional responses when they feel they are working with/under a highly capable person (i.e. other-efficacy), and when they feel that their significant other is confident in them (i.e. RISE). Alongside motivational and affective responses, strong relational efficacy perceptions are also likely to promote more adaptive coping efforts during challenging or stressful periods, due to the stress-buffering properties associated with these perceptions. In terms of relational processes, Lent and Lopez described that both constructs independently contribute to stronger relational ties and a more cohesive working alliance between individuals. That is, individuals are assumed to seek out, be more satisfied with, and desire to continue interacting with those about whom they hold strong RISE and/or other-efficacy beliefs. Favourable relational efficacy beliefs may also alleviate conflict and engender inclusionary interpersonal behaviours on the part of the perceiver, such as greater attentiveness, responsiveness, and provision of support.

Many of Lent and Lopez's (2002) proposals regarding outcome variables remain to be tested; little is known, for example, about the putative crisis-coping and support-enabling functions associated with RISE and other-efficacy in sport and exercise. A handful of studies, however, have provided some support for the implications associated with these constructs. In their qualitative work with members of elite athlete–athlete dyads, Jackson *et al.* (2008) reported that when athletes felt that their partner was highly confident in their ability, this encouraged them to (a) feel happier and be more personally motivated, (b) perform effectively, and (c) experience favorable relationship satisfaction and persistence intentions. The outcomes that athletes described for other-efficacy were largely congruent with those observed for RISE, with the notable addition that individuals displayed more open, encouraging communication toward their partner, as well as being more responsive to their partner's feelings, when they believed strongly in their partner's ability. Consistent findings were subsequently observed for members of elite coach–athlete dyads (Jackson *et al.*, 2009), though one novel aspect of this work was that coaches were likely to set more challenging and long-term goals for their athletes when they believed that their athletes were highly capable.

In the first sport-based investigation that utilized quantitative methods to examine the predictive utility of other efficacy in relation to indices of sport performance (Beauchamp and Whinton, 2005), equestrian riders were asked to rate their confidence in their own ability (i.e. self-efficacy), as well as their confidence in their horse's ability (i.e. other-efficacy). Hierarchical regression analyses revealed that riders' confidence in their horse's capabilities explained unique variance in dressage performance beyond the effect of self-efficacy. More recently, it has been demonstrated that members of junior tennis partnerships report greater satisfaction with their relationship when they believe they are working alongside a highly capable partner (Jackson *et al.*, 2007). Within coach-athlete interactions, athletes have also been shown to display a range of desirable outcomes, including enhanced perceptions of relationship quality (Jackson *et al.*, 2010) and commitment (Jackson and Beauchamp, 2010), as well as heightened personal effort (Jackson and Beauchamp, 2010), when they believe strongly in their coach's ability. Interestingly, moderator analysis within both of the above investigations revealed a tendency for these effects to be stronger for athletes than for coaches. For example, despite athletes' relationship satisfaction being strongly predicted by their confidence in their coach, the magnitude of this relationship was significantly weaker for coaches (when considering their confidence in their athlete). In interpreting this trend, it is worth noting that Lent and Lopez (2002) posited that the effects of RISE and other-efficacy might be particularly pronounced for those who are heavily invested in a relationship (e.g. the lower-status/-authority, more-dependent member of the relationship), or for those undergoing challenging periods that might be accompanied by fragile self-perceptions or a lack of personal knowledge (see also Kenny and DePaulo, 1993). These findings support this assertion insofar as athletes occupy the lower-status position within coach–athlete exchanges, and rely on their coach for effective instruction, plans, and guidance. That being the case, relative to the effects associated with coaches' confidence in their athletes, it may be more important (in terms of promoting outcomes for the holder of the perception) for athletes to believe that they are being instructed by a highly capable "leader".

The notion that relational efficacy beliefs might be most salient for those in subordinate positions served as the foundation for a series of recent studies that have focused on the outcomes of other-efficacy and RISE beliefs held by physical therapy clients (in relation to their therapist) and physical education students (in relation to their teacher). Findings from these studies showed that clients' relational efficacy beliefs predicted positive appraisals about their relationship with their therapist (Jackson, Dimmock *et al.*, 2012), and that a high degree of confidence in one's instructor directly predicted greater effort, enjoyment, and overall achievement in undergraduate physical activity classes (Jackson, Myers, *et al.*, 2012). In terms of direct health-related effects, students have been shown to participate in greater leisure-time physical activity when they believe strongly in their physical education teacher's ability (e.g. Jackson, Whipp, Chua *et al.*, 2013), and infer that their teacher is highly confident in their in-class capabilities (e.g. Bourne *et al.*, in press). Although further work is needed to elucidate any mechanisms underpinning this effect, it is possible that favourable perceptions regarding one's physical education teacher might be responsible for driving more adaptive attitudes toward physical activity, which might stimulate greater engagement outside of school.

Beyond observational studies, there are currently few experimental investigations that have targeted the outcomes associated with other-efficacy and RISE. Within their dance-based investigation, however, Dunlop and colleagues (2011) demonstrated that participants in the elevated other-efficacy condition performed significantly better in a subsequent trial than their counterparts who received feedback that had resulted in diminished pre-trial other-efficacy. In addition, a recent study by Bray and colleagues (2013) used an experimental paradigm to investigate the effects of a RISE-enhancing manipulation on children's performance of an effort-based task. All of the participants initially performed a maximum endurance handgrip squeeze using a dynamometer. Following the initial task an "exercise coach" provided half the sample with RISE-enhancing feedback (i.e. "you did great; I believe you are capable of doing even better"), while the others received general praise and encouragement (i.e. "you did great; let's see you try it again"). On the follow-up trial, participants in the control condition improved on their previous performance by 14 per cent whereas those in the RISE-enhanced feedback group bettered their earlier performance by 44 per cent. Clearly, one fruitful avenue for further research in this area would be to continue to manipulate individuals' RISE and other-efficacy beliefs in order to explore in more detail the causal effects (i.e. the range of dependent variables) associated with these constructs.

To this point, we have examined the ways in which relational efficacy beliefs might predict outcomes for the *holder* of the perception. In the methodological literature on dyadic processes, within-person relations such as these are termed *actor effects* (see Kenny *et al.*, 2006). Importantly though, the types of interactions upon which we have focused our attention are all characterized by (varying degrees of) interdependence, whereby individuals exert reciprocal influences upon each other's behaviour and well-being. As a result, it is likely that one person's relational efficacy beliefs might also shape outcomes for the other person in the relationship (e.g. a coach believes strongly in his athlete's ability, which promotes more favourable relationship perceptions on the part of the athlete). These between-person relations are known as *partner effects* (Kenny *et al.*, 2006), and Lent and Lopez (2002) drew from existing work on interpersonal expectations (see Snyder and Stukas, 1999) in order to identify the causal chain through which partner effects might emerge for relational efficacy constructs. This process begins with one person's behaviour and interaction styles being shaped by their relational efficacy beliefs (e.g. providing compliments to a partner who we believe to be highly capable). Subsequently, the other person observes and internalizes these cues (e.g. "my partner's being really supportive"), which then drives outcomes for that individual (e.g. enhanced relationship satisfaction).

In light of the necessity to recruit both dyad members, and the requirement for analytic methods that account for intra-dyadic interdependence, empirical evidence for partner effects in sport and exercise settings is somewhat sparse. Indeed, perhaps the most compelling demonstration of partner effects exists in relation to the role of spousal support during recovery from critical health episodes. In particular, a series of studies have shown that when a spouse believes strongly in his/her significant other's (i.e. the patient's) recovery ability, this helps drive more adaptive recovery outcomes for the patient. For example, Rohrbaugh *et al.* (2004) reported that spouse's confidence in their partner's ability to manage their illness after heart failure contributed significantly to patient survival rates. Similar findings have also been documented with respect to recovery from stroke (Molloy *et al.*, 2008) and acute myocardial infarction (Taylor *et al.*, 1985), insofar as greater spouse confidence in the patient partly accounts for enhanced functional recovery outcomes. Greater attention is required in order to examine these processes in sport and exercise; however, partner effects have been demonstrated for other-efficacy in relation to effort and relationship commitment in coach–athlete dyads (Jackson and Beauchamp, 2010). That is, when one person is highly confident in the other's capabilities, this has been shown to predict enhanced effort and commitment for the other person (i.e. the target of the other-efficacy perception).

There is also evidence in coach–athlete interactions that partner effects may be more pronounced in the direction from coach relational efficacy beliefs to athlete outcomes (rather than from athlete efficacy beliefs to coach outcomes). Specifically, Jackson *et al.* (2010) reported that when coaches believed strongly in their athlete's capabilities, this promoted positive relationship quality appraisals for athletes (i.e. closeness, complementarity; see Jowett, 2007), but the effect from athlete other-efficacy to coach outcomes was significantly weaker in magnitude. These findings again supported Lent and Lopez's (2002) dependence hypothesis, insofar as the direction of influence within dyads is presumed to flow from high- to lower-status individual (see Kelley, 1979; Snyder and Stukas, 1999). In this instance, given that coaches represent the authority figure, athlete outcomes may be highly susceptible to the appraisals that coaches hold regarding their athletes, whereas coach outcomes may not be as reliant upon the relational efficacy beliefs of the lower-status dyad member.

### Proxy efficacy

It is worth noting that there is also evidence regarding the predictive utility of proxy efficacy perceptions. For example, among cardiac rehabilitation patients, individuals' confidence in their exercise instructor's capabilities has been shown to account for post-programme exercise intentions (Bray and Cowan, 2004) and prospective engagement in home-based physical activity (Bray *et al.*, 2006). In addition, Bray *et al.* (2001) reported that, among new exercise class attendees, participants' confidence in their fitness instructor's ability predicted greater class attendance, over and above the effect of self-efficacy. A particularly noteworthy finding within this study was that this predictive effect emerged for exercise initiates only (i.e. those who had no prior experience attending structured exercise classes), lending support to Lent and Lopez's (2002) contention that relational efficacy beliefs may be most pronounced in situations where one's own personal resources are not fully developed.

### Counter-evidence: when theorized outcomes do not emerge

Although support for Lent and Lopez's (2002) proposals continues to develop, counter-intuitive findings have also emerged in the literature, and in this section we turn our attention to some interesting instances in which this is the case. First, despite the majority of outcomes associated with relational efficacy beliefs in Jackson *et al.*'s (2008) investigation being positive in nature, some athletes noted that an extremely strong belief in their partner's ability might actually engender negative affective responses (e.g. anxiety), as well as concern regarding the longevity of the relationship. The qualitative nature of the design did not enable the authors to consider the potential for these effects to be caused by discrepancies between self- and other-efficacy, but it is possible that these concerns might have arisen due to athletes holding a high level of confidence in their partner *at the same time* as experiencing a degree of doubt regarding their own capabilities (e.g. "can I keep up?" "will I let the team down?").

As for RISE, a minority of athletes in Jackson *et al.*'s (2008) study reported that, under some circumstances, unfavourable RISE appraisals regarding their partner might actually motivate them to "prove the other person wrong". We would anticipate that weak RISE inferences would exert a demoralizing influence upon personal motivation, and future research would be worthwhile in order to examine the circumstances under which negative RISE beliefs might activate these opposing motivational effects. Similarly, in light of coaches' typical position of being higher-status relative to their athletes, it is noteworthy that a minority of coaches in Jackson *et al.*'s (2009) coach–athlete investigation reported that their RISE estimations regarding their athlete would have no effect whatsoever upon any personal or relational outcomes. In future, it would be fascinating to explore the dispositional factors that might predispose some coaches to ignore their athlete's confidence in their ability, as well as the instructional styles that such coaches might adopt.

In the previous section, we reported on the desirable actor and partner effects that have emerged (primarily for other-efficacy) within sporting interactions. Within recreational coach–athlete dyads, though, athletes' RISE perceptions have been shown to be inversely related to their relationship commitment and satisfaction (e.g. Jackson and Beauchamp, 2010; Jackson *et al.*, 2010). This finding stands in contrast to Lent and Lopez's (2002) assertions, and further work is needed to explore the occurrence (and prevalence across other contexts) of this effect. One possible reason for this finding is that when athletes believe that their coach is extremely confident in their ability, in some cases this might foster a sense of complacency and the perception that the coach is not pushing the athlete to improve. In turn, this perception might manifest itself for athletes through lowered feelings of commitment to, and satisfaction with, their relationship. Alternatively, it is also possible that when athletes feel that their coach is highly confident in their ability, this promotes athletes' confidence in their own ability, and results in athletes becoming less committed to their current coach as they seek out new opportunities for progression and challenge (e.g. the feeling that they have "outgrown" their coach). Interestingly, in these investigations, athletes' RISE beliefs were also predictive of lower commitment on the part of coaches (i.e. a partner effect), demonstrating that the deleterious within-person effects might be detected and internalized by coaches, resulting in less favorable relational perceptions for both parties.

The research on proxy efficacy has also revealed some contradictory findings. Despite there being a number of positive consequences associated with proxy efficacy (e.g. enhanced self-efficacy, intentions, exercise adherence), negative consequences have also been observed. In particular, studies by Shields and Brawley (2006; 2007) and Bray *et al.* (2006) have shown that greater proxy efficacy is associated with a higher degree of dependence on proxy agents. Although dependence may not be problematic in some situations, results from those studies suggest that people who come to depend more on their proxy agents may be less motivated to exercise if their proxy is not available to help them.

In a general sense, although existing observational studies appear to demonstrate stronger and more consistent support for the predictive effects associated with other-efficacy (in comparison to RISE), preliminary evidence indicates that RISE does appear to be important, at least indirectly, in predicting behavioural and affective responses. On that note, despite a developing understanding regarding the mechanisms (i.e. indirect pathways) through which relational efficacy beliefs may be linked with personal outcomes, further work will undoubtedly help clarify the conditions (i.e. moderator variables) under which these effects are supported, disrupted, or even reversed.

## Future directions and conclusions

Although much of the evidence that has accumulated to date points toward the utility of the tripartite efficacy model (and the relational constructs embedded within the model), there is significant scope for further work in order to better understand the nature of these constructs. Several avenues for future tripartite efficacy research have been articulated in recent reviews (see Beauchamp *et al.*, 2012; Bray *et al.*, 2014), and interested readers are encouraged to consult these sources for a number of worthwhile lines of enquiry. In addition, throughout this chapter we have provided numerous specific suggestions for investigating the development and implications of RISE and other-efficacy, as well as the interrelationships between the tripartite constructs. Within this section, therefore, we draw from relevant conceptual and methodological sources in order to consider some general recommendations for future tripartite efficacy research.

In broad terms, we would encourage investigators to diversify the interaction contexts in which tripartite efficacy research is conducted, not only to expand the knowledge base, but also to explore the generalizability of existing findings. Indeed, there are numerous interpersonal situations in which the role of individuals' relational efficacy perceptions is not well understood. It would be valuable, for instance, to consider how RISE and other-efficacy beliefs relating to physical and social capabilities might develop within peer interactions (see Smith and McDonough, 2008), sibling relationships (see Saelens and Kerr, 2008), and parent–child exchanges (see Carr, 2012). In addition, it would be worthwhile to begin to identify the role of individuals' relational efficacy beliefs in these settings with respect to their own (i.e. actor effects) and others' (i.e. partner effects) experiences and participation in sport and physical activity. On that note, researchers to this point have also investigated only a limited range of all the potential outcomes that Lent and Lopez (2002) described. Future work is warranted that focuses on the social/interpersonal behaviours, self-presentational issues, and social support perceptions that stem from individuals' relational efficacy perceptions. Similarly, it would be worthwhile to determine whether the supportive functions associated with these relational perceptions may be at their most salient during challenging periods in one's sport (e.g. injury recovery, high-pressure competition) or exercise (e.g. joining a new class, participating in a new activity) involvement.

Guided by knowledge of the variables that might moderate efficacy effects (Bandura, 1997; Lent and Lopez, 2002), there is also a need to examine the boundary conditions under which the predictive capacity of RISE and other-efficacy might be modified. It is possible, for example, that favourable RISE beliefs might be particularly crucial for personal well-being and motivation when the other person is believed to be a highly credible source, as well as in situations where an individual is heavily invested in making a favourable impression (e.g. when attending try-outs for a new squad). Similarly, there may be important personal characteristics that limit the deleterious effects associated with negative RISE beliefs (e.g. a high level of resilience), or that predispose individuals to be less likely to suffer when they feel that others do not believe in their ability (e.g. an internal locus of control). It is also important to better understand the situations in which the desirable effects associated with other-efficacy may be reduced. One such situation might arise when athletes believe that their playing partner is highly capable (in terms of task execution), but at the same time (a) hold relatively unfavorable perceptions regarding their partner's personality, (b) believe that their partner is looking to leave the relationship, (c) believe that their partner does not provide them with sufficient opportunities to display their own capabilities, or (d) believe that their own and their partner's goals may be incompatible.

On a conceptual level, there is also a need for greater insight into generality processes associated with individuals' relational efficacy beliefs. The generality principle relates to the extent to which one's efficacy perceptions generalize, or transfer, from one domain to another (Bandura, 1997), and existing tripartite efficacy work has yet to account for such issues given that multiple relationship perspectives (e.g. parent, coach, peer/teammate) have not been incorporated in any single study. Future work that encompasses multiple "targets" in a single investigation would be interesting in determining evidence for cross-target generality (e.g. the extent to which one's RISE beliefs regarding one's coach and playing partner are similar/disparate). This approach would also more faithfully reflect the way that these relational perceptions co-exist in real-world settings, and would allow investigators to understand the relative influence of different significant others. For instance, this method would enable researchers to consider the potential dissonance that might arise when individuals hold conflicting perceptions about those with whom they interact in a given network (e.g. when an athlete feels that her playing partner believes in her ability, but feels that her coach does not).

In order to investigate tripartite efficacy processes across multiple interpersonal scenarios, researchers are also encouraged to make use of the sophisticated design and analytic approaches that are available for the study of dyadic interactions. As outlined by Kenny *et al.* (2006), relational exchanges can be characterized by diverse interaction patterns, which can give rise to substantively different research questions. In one-to-one relationships (e.g. athlete–athlete pairs), for example, where researchers seek to examine how predictor variables for both partners (e.g. other-efficacy) are associated with outcomes for both one's self and/or that person's partner (e.g. relationship satisfaction), actor–partner interdependence modeling is particularly useful (see earlier coverage of actor and partner effects). In addition to such one-to-one interactions, Kenny and colleagues also considered the "*one with many*" design, whereby one individual is paired with multiple "others", but those others are themselves not linked (e.g. a therapist and his patients, a physical trainer who works one-to-one with her separate clients). Despite the prevalence of this kind of interaction in sport and exercise, one with many analyses have yet to be applied to the study of relational perceptions in these contexts. In future, this approach would enable researchers to consider, for example, the way in which a group of exercisers or patients rate the capabilities of their instructor/therapist, as well as the extent to which the instructor/therapist elicits favourable relationship perceptions from those under his/her guidance.

Finally, Kenny and colleagues' (2006) *social relations model* applies to situations in which a group of individuals interact with one another (i.e. creating multiple dyadic linkages). Consider, for example, the reciprocal interactions that take place over the course of a season between the members of an offensive line in an American football team. In this situation, where each person interacts with each other person in the group (i.e. in a round-robin design), it is possible to examine how interpersonal perceptions might be partitioned into actor, partner, and relationship components. To illustrate, if each offensive lineman was asked to rate his confidence in each of the other linemen, it is possible that (a) one person might tend to see all others as being equally capable (actor variance), (b) one person might tend to be rated as equally capable by all others (partner variance), and/or (c) that there is something unique about each rating (relationship variance). Importantly, by applying a social relations lens to the study of relational efficacy, researchers would be able to identify, among other things, the characteristics that predispose individuals to form consistent perceptions about all those with whom they interact, as well as the attributes that tend to elicit favourable impressions from others (see Kenny, 1994).

In sum, as well as encouraging perceptions regarding one's own ability, the relational environments that are prevalent in physical activity settings also stimulate individuals to reflect upon the capabilities of those with whom they interact, as well as the extent to which those others believe the individual to be capable. Despite evidence that these constructs are important in shaping individual and relationship functioning, sustained effort is needed to provide a more thorough understanding of how relational efficacy beliefs develop, as well as their direct and indirect roles in driving health, well-being, and achievement-related outcomes.

## Note

1 We acknowledge that the distinction between who is and who is not a proxy agent may be somewhat nebulous. Indeed, in almost all close relationships – even those in which one proxy agent is clearly present such as in client-therapist interactions – both individuals may at times act as a proxy agent, insofar as both individuals may be required to relinquish some aspect of control and place their behaviour or their goals (to some extent) in the hands of the other. Nevertheless, in light of the way in which these constructs were originally defined, throughout the remainder of this chapter we present proxy efficacy research separately from our coverage of other-efficacy. It is worth noting that when presenting the relevant material, our decisions regarding terminology were guided by that which was used within the original source material (i.e. whether the authors themselves referred to their investigation as a study of proxy efficacy or other-efficacy).

## References

Bandura, A. (1977). Self-efficacy: Toward a unifying theory of behavioural change. *Psychological Review*, 84, 191–215.

Bandura, A. (1997). *Self-efficacy: The exercise of control.* New York, NY: Freeman and Company.

Beattie, S. and Davies, M. (2010). A test of engagement versus disengagement in catastrophe models. *British Journal of Psychology*, 101, 361–371.

Beauchamp, M. R. (2007). Efficacy beliefs within relational and group contexts in sport. In S. Jowett and D. Lavallee (eds). *Social psychology in sport* (pp. 181–193). Champaign, IL: Human Kinetics.

Beauchamp, M. R. and Whinton, L. (2005). Self-efficacy and other-efficacy in dyadic relationships: Riding as one in equestrian eventing. *Journal of Sport and Exercise Psychology*, 27, 245–252.

Beauchamp, M. R., Jackson, B., and Morton, K. L. (2012). Efficacy beliefs and human performance: From independent action to interpersonal functioning. In S. M. Murphy (ed.), *The Oxford handbook of sport and performance psychology* (pp. 273–293). Oxford, U.K.: Oxford University Press.

Biddle, S. J. H., Hagger, M. S., Chatzisarantis, N. L., and Lippke, S. (2007). Theoretical frameworks in exercise psychology. In G. Tenenbaum and R. C. Eklund (eds), *Handbook of sport psychology* (3rd edn, pp. 537–559). Hoboken, NJ: John Wiley.

Bourne, J., Liu, Y., Shields, C. A., Jackson, B., Zumbo, B. D., and Beauchamp, M. R. (in press). The relationship between transformational teaching and adolescent physical activity: The mediating roles of personal and relational efficacy beliefs. *Journal of Health Psychology*.

Boyce, B. A. and Bingham, S. M. (1997). The effects of self-efficacy and goal-setting on bowling performance. *Journal of Teaching in Physical Education*, 16, 312–323.

Bray, S. R. and Cowan, H. (2004). Proxy efficacy: Implications for self-efficacy and exercise intentions in cardiac rehabilitation. *Rehabilitation Psychology*, 49, 71–75.

Bray, S. R., Brawley, L. R., and Carron, A. V. (2002). Efficacy for interdependent role functions: Evidence from the sport domain. *Small Group Research*, 33, 644–666.

Bray, S. R., Brawley, L. R., and Millen, J. (2006). Proxy efficacy and proxy reliance predict self-efficacy and independent home based exercise following supervised cardiac rehabilitation. *Rehabilitation Psychology*, 51, 224–232.

Bray, S. R., Graham, J. D., Saville, P. D., Martin Ginis, K. A., Cairney, J., Marinoff Shuppe, D., and Petitt, A. (2013) "You believe in me?... Maybe I can!": Interpersonal feedback increases relation-inferred self-efficacy (RISE) and effortful performance. *Journal of Sport and Exercise Psychology*, 35, S79.

Bray, S. R., Gyurcsik, N. C., Culos-Reed, S. N., Dawson, K. A., and Martin, K. A. (2001). An exploratory investigation of the relationship between proxy efficacy, self-efficacy and exercise attendance. *Journal of Health Psychology*, 6, 425–434.

Bray, S. R., Gyurcsik, N. C., Martin-Ginis, K. A., and Culos-Reed, S. N. (2004). The proxy efficacy exercise questionnaire: Development of an instrument to assess female exercisers' proxy efficacy in structured group exercise classes. *Journal of Sport and Exercise Psychology*, 26, 442–456.

Bray, S. R., Saville, P. D., and Brawley, L. R. (2013). Determinants of clients' efficacy in their interventionists and effects on self-perceptions for exercise in cardiac rehabilitation. *Rehabilitation Psychology*, 58, 185–195.

Bray, S. R., Shields, C. A., Jackson, B., and Saville, P. D. (2014). Proxy agency and other-efficacy in physical activity. In M. R. Beauchamp and M. A. Eys (eds), *Group dynamics in sport and exercise psychology* (2nd edn, pp. 91–109). New York, NY: Routledge.

Carr, S. (2012). Relationships and sport and performance. In S. M. Murphy (ed.), *The Oxford handbook of sport and performance psychology* (pp. 400–417). Oxford, U.K.: Oxford University Press.

Chow, G. M. and Feltz, D. L. (2008). Exploring new directions in collective efficacy and sport. In M. R. Beauchamp and M. A. Eys (eds), *Group dynamics advances in sport and exercise psychology: Contemporary themes*, (pp. 221–248). New York: Routledge.

Dunlop, W. L., Beatty, D. J., and Beauchamp, M. R. (2011). Examining the influence of other-efficacy and self-efficacy on personal performance. *Journal of Sport and Exercise Psychology*, 33, 586–593.

Elias, S. M. and MacDonald, S. (2007). Using past performance, proxy efficacy, and academic self-efficacy to predict college performance. *Journal of Applied Social Psychology*, 37, 2518–2531.

Feltz, D. L., Short, S. E., and Sullivan P. J. (2008). *Self-efficacy in sport*. Champaign, IL: Human Kinetics.

Frey, F. E. and Tropp, L. R. (2006). Being seen as individuals versus as group members: Extending research on metaperception to intergroup contexts. *Personality and Social Psychology Review*, 10, 265–280.

Gao, Z. and Newton, M. (2009). Examining the mediating role of strategy use on students' motivation and persistence/effort in physical education. *Journal of Sport Behaviour*, 32, 278–297.

George, T. R. (1994). Self-confidence and baseball performance: A causal examination of self-efficacy theory. *Journal of Sport and Exercise Psychology*, 16, 381–399.

Hagger, M. S. (2012). Psychosocial influence. In E. O. Acevedo (ed.), *The Oxford handbook of exercise psychology* (pp. 224–240). Oxford, UK: Oxford University Press.

Hu, L., Motl, R. W., McAuley, E., and Konopack, J. F. (2007). Effects of self-efficacy on physical activity enjoyment in college-aged women. *International Journal of Behavioural Medicine*, 14, 92–96.

Hutchinson, J. C., Sherman, T., Martinovic, N., and Tenenbaum, G. (2008). The effect of manipulated self-efficacy on perceived and sustained effort. *Journal of Applied Sport Psychology*, 20, 457–472.

Jackson, B. and Beauchamp, M. R. (2010). Efficacy beliefs in coach–athlete dyads: Prospective relationships using actor–partner interdependence models. *Applied Psychology: An International Review*, 59, 220–242.

Jackson, B., Beauchamp, M. R., and Knapp, P. (2007). Relational efficacy beliefs in athlete dyads: An investigation using actor-partner interdependence models. *Journal of Sport and Exercise Psychology*, 29, 170–189.

Jackson, B., Dimmock, J. A., Taylor, I. M., and Hagger, M. S. (2012). The tripartite efficacy framework in client-therapist rehabilitation interactions: Implications for relationship quality and client engagement. *Rehabilitation Psychology*, 57, 308–319.

Jackson, B., Grove, J. R., and Beauchamp, M. R. (2010). Relational efficacy beliefs and relationship quality within coach-athlete dyads. *Journal of Social and Personal Relationships*, 27, 1035–1050.

Jackson, B., Gucciardi, D. F., and Dimmock, J. A. (2011). Tripartite efficacy profiles: A cluster analytic investigation of athletes' perceptions of their relationship with their coach. *Journal of Sport and Exercise Psychology*, 33, 394–415.

Jackson, B., Knapp, P., and Beauchamp, M. R. (2008). Origins and consequences of tripartite efficacy beliefs within elite athlete dyads. *Journal of Sport and Exercise Psychology*, 30, 512–540.

Jackson, B., Knapp, P. and Beauchamp, M. R. (2009). The coach-athlete relationship: A tripartite efficacy perspective. *The Sport Psychologist*, 23, 203–232.

Jackson, B., Myers, N. D., Taylor, I. M., and Beauchamp, M. R. (2012). Relational efficacy beliefs in physical activity classes: A test of the tripartite model. *Journal of Sport and Exercise Psychology*, 34, 285–304.

Jackson, B., Whipp, P. and Beauchamp M. R. (2013). The tripartite efficacy framework in high school physical education: Trans-contextual generality and direct and indirect prospective relations with leisure-time exercise. *Sport, Exercise and Performance Psychology*. 2, 1–14.

Jackson, B., Whipp, P. R., Chua, K. L. P., Dimmock, J. A., and Hagger, M. S. (2013). Students' tripartite efficacy beliefs in high school physical education: Within- and cross-domain relations with motivational processes and leisure-time physical activity outcomes. *Journal of Sport and Exercise Psychology*, 35, 72–84.

Jackson, B., Whipp, P. R., Chua, K. L. P., Pengelley, R., and Beauchamp, M. R. (2012). Assessment of tripartite efficacy beliefs within school-based physical education: Instrument development and reliability and validity evidence. *Psychology of Sport and Exercise*, 13, 108–117.

Jowett, S. (2007). Interdependence analysis and the 3+1Cs in the coach-athlete relationship. In S. Jowett and D. Lavallee (eds). *Social psychology in sport* (pp. 15–28). Champaign, IL: Human Kinetics.

Jussim, L., Soffin, S., Brown, R., Ley, J., and Kohlhepp, K. (1992). Understanding reactions to performance feedback by integrating ideas from symbolic interactionism and cognitive evaluation theory. *Journal of Personality and Social Psychology*, 62, 402–421.

Kane, T. D., Marks, M. A., Zaccaro, S. J., and Blair, V. (1996). Self-efficacy, personal goals, and wrestlers' self-regulation. *Journal of Sport and Exercise Psychology*, 18, 36–48.

Kelley, H. H. (1979). *Personal relationships: Their structure and processes.* Hillsdale, NJ: Erlbaum.

Kenny, D. A. (1994). *Interpersonal perception: A social relations analysis.* New York, NY: Guilford Press.

Kenny, D. A. and DePaulo, B. M. (1993). Do people know how others view them? An empirical and theoretical account. *Psychological Bulletin*, 114, 145–161.

Kenny, D. A., Kashy, D. A., and Cook, W. L. (2006). *Dyadic data analysis.* New York: Guilford Press.

Leary, M. R. and Kowalski, R. M. (1995). *Social anxiety.* New York, NY: Guilford Press.

Lent, R. W. and Lopez, F. G. (2002). Cognitive ties that bind: A tripartite view of efficacy beliefs in growth-promoting relationships. *Journal of Social and Clinical Psychology*, 21, 256–286.

Molloy, G. J., Johnston, M., Johnston, D. W., Pollard, B., Morrison, V., Bonetti, D., Joice, S., and MacWalter, R. (2008). Spousal caregiver confidence and recovery from ambulatory activity limitations in stroke survivors. *Health Psychology*, 27, 286–290.

Moritz, S. E., Feltz, D. L., Fahrbach, K. R., and Mack, D. E. (2000). The relation of self-efficacy measures to sport performance: A meta-analytic review. *Research Quarterly for Exercise and Sport*, 71, 280–294.

Myers, N. D. and Feltz, D. L. (2007). From self-efficacy to collective efficacy in sport: Transitional methodological issues. In G. Tenenbaum and R. C. Eklund (eds). *Handbook of sport psychology* (3rd edn, pp. 799–819). Hoboken, NJ: Wiley and Sons.

Priebe, C. S., Flora, P. K., Ferguson, L. J., and Anderson, T. J. (2012). Using efficacy information to manipulate proxy efficacy in novice exercisers. *Psychology of Sport and Exercise*, 13, 562–568.

Rohrbaugh, M. J., Shoham, V., Coyne, J. C., Cranford, J. A., Sonnega, J. S., and Nicklas, J. M. (2004). Beyond the 'self' in self-efficacy: Spouse confidence predicts patient survival following heart failure. *Journal of Family Psychology*, 18, 184–193.

Saelens, B. E. and Kerr, J. (2008). The family. In A. L. Smith and S. J. H. Biddle (eds), *Youth physical activity and sedentary behaviour: Challenges and solutions* (pp. 267–294). Champaign, IL: Human Kinetics.

Samson, A. and Solmon, M. (2011). Examining the sources of self-efficacy for physical activity within the sport and exercise domains. *International Review of Sport and Exercise Psychology*, 4, 70–89.

Saville, P. D., Bray, S. R., Martin Ginis, K. A., Cairney, J., Marinoff-Shupe, D., and Pettit, A. (2014). Sources of self-efficacy and coach/instructor behaviours underlying relation-inferred self-efficacy (RISE) in recreational youth sport. *Journal of Sport and Exercise Psychology*, 36, 146–156.

Shields C. A. and Brawley L. R. (2006). Preferring proxy-agency impact on self-efficacy for exercise. *Journal of Health Psychology*, 11, 904–914.

Shields C. A. and Brawley L. R. (2007). Limiting exercise options depending on a proxy may inhibit exercise self-management. *Journal of Health Psychology*, 12, 663–671.

Smith, A. L. and McDonough, M. H. (2008). Peers. In A. L. Smith and S. J. H. Biddle (eds), *Youth physical activity and sedentary behaviour: Challenges and solutions* (pp. 295–320). Champaign, IL: Human Kinetics.

Snyder, M. and Stukas, A. A. (1999). Interpersonal processes: The interplay of cognitive, motivational, and behavioural activities in social interaction. *Annual Review of Psychology*, 50, 273–303.

Taylor, C. B., Bandura, A., Ewart, C. K., Miller, N. H., and DeBusk, R. F. (1985). Exercise testing to enhance wives' confidence in their husbands' cardiac capabilities soon after clinically uncomplicated acute myocardial infarction. *American Journal of Cardiology*, 55, 635–638.

Theodorakis, Y. (1995). Effects of self-efficacy, satisfaction, and personal goals on swimming performance. *The Sport Psychologist*, 9, 245–253.

Tritter, A., Fitzgeorge, L., Cramp, A., Valiulis, P., and Prapavessis, H. (2013). Self-efficacy and affect responses to sprint interval training. *Psychology of Sport and Exercise*, 14, 886–890.

Welch, A. S., Hulley, A., and Beauchamp, M. R. (2010). Affect and self-efficacy responses during moderate-intensity exercise among low-active women: The effect of cognitive appraisal. *Journal of Sport and Exercise Psychology*, 32, 154–175.

# 6   Choking under pressure

## A review of current debates, literature, and interventions

*Christopher Mesagno, Katharina Geukes and Paul Larkin*

### Introduction

Athletes who "crumble" under the pressure of competition are often defamed, embarrassed, and sometimes ostracized from the sporting community. One Australian elite rower, Sally Robbins, was heavily shunned and vilified by the media and rowing community for a potential choking under pressure episode. Sally was a member of the Australian Women's Eight rowing team competing in the 2004 Athens Summer Olympics. With 500 meters to complete the race and the team in medal contention, Sally stopped rowing, collapsing in the lap of one of her teammates, with her oar dragging in the water because of intense exhaustion, with the team finishing in last place. This episode may have been exacerbated by the reported intense anxiety she was experiencing prior to the well-publicized Olympic final. In fact, this was not the first time extreme anxiety and concomitant exhaustion had befallen on Sally with reports suggesting perhaps it happened up to nine times previously (Wilkins, 2008). After that event, "Lay down Sally (as she was quickly labeled by Australian media and public) ... was derided as a quitter and labeled un-Australian.... The lay down Sally affair ended in misery, defamation lawsuits and recriminations" (Davis, 2008, p. 95).

This type of incidence has led to media speculation about choking so often that Davis (2008), an Australian magazine editor and newspaper reporter, wrote a book explaining many potential choking incidences from elite international competitions. Some choking instances are more easily detectable than others. For example, tennis player Jana Novotna played Steffi Graf in the 1993 Wimbledon women's final, led the match 6–7, 6–4, and had a game point at 4–1 in the third and final set. Novotna lost the game and Steffi Graf won the final five games of the match and the Grand Slam title. Professional golfers Jean Van de Velde and Greg Norman also squandered leads to lose major championships, but in different ways. Van de Velde drastically "lost the plot" in the 1999 British Open after leading the tournament over 71 holes with a 3-shot lead going into the final hole. Off the tee, each of his shots went into the rough, hit the grandstand, in a water hazard, into the greenside bunker, on the green, and finally in the hole for a triple bogey and tie for the lead. Van de Velde eventually lost in a three-person playoff. Greg Norman's 1996 U.S. Masters choking episode was similar because a large lead (i.e. six strokes) diminished, however, this occurred in a round-long (rather than an acute one-hole) collapse and eventual loss to Nick Faldo by five strokes. One reason these situations could be classified as choking episodes is they were based on the person's normal standard of play, rather than on other's success. For example, Novotna's performance deterioration was credited for the choking incident and not because Graf played exceptionally well in the last set to win the tournament. Nevertheless, some researchers (e.g. Buszard *et al.*, 2013) argue that some choking incidents are difficult to determine and confounded because as one player gets worse, the other possibly gets better. Thus, researchers should ensure that intra-individual standards are compared to determine if choking occurred.

## Choking vs. under-performance debate

Most researchers would agree that the above examples are choking experiences since they are referenced in many research articles (e.g. Gucciardi *et al.*, 2010; Mesagno *et al.*, 2008; Wang *et al.*, 2004), however, there are other possible choking episodes that are not as clear. For example, in American football Super Bowl XXV against the New York Giants, Buffalo Bills' field goal kicker Scott Norwood had a 47-yard field goal attempt in the last eight seconds of the game to win the prestigious football game, but the kick drifted past the right upright and the Buffalo Bills lost by one point (Giants 20 – Bills 19). The media, and some researchers (e.g. Beilock and Gray, 2007), would classify this as choking, however, Hill *et al.* (2009) have questioned whether any performance decrement, or a substantial decrease in performance, should be classified as choking. Hill *et al.* argued that cognitive differences may exist between small scale (i.e. under-performance) and substantial (i.e. choking) decreases in performance, and caution should be used when labeling performances a "choke". Based on Hill *et al.*'s argument, then, is missing a 47-yard field goal slightly to the right a big enough decrease in performance to constitute choking? The field goal attempt by Norwood was not a "shank" or a terribly performed kick, so can we classify this as choking or just an under-performance?

The magnitude of performance decrease is only one aspect of performance under pressure that should be considered when determining if choking has occurred. For example, the skill level of the performer (novice vs. expert), whether anxiety increased under pressure, and the difficulty of the attempt are all contextual variables that should be considered before labeling performances as choking. In the Norwood situation, surely a 47-yard field goal was not a "gimme" (i.e. a normally successful kick for goal) and was difficult enough that even without pressure the kick could likely have been missed? Jackson *et al.* (2013) suggested it is important to distinguish between normal performance fluctuations and performances that are significantly worse than normal and likely to be explained by random variation. Thus, random variation could have been a reason for the Norwood incident rather than choking per se.

As a result of the Hill *et al.* (2009) research and because, in the past five years, researchers have not yet investigated whether cognitive differences between under-performance and choking exist, Mesagno and Hill (2013a) instigated a debate about a universally accepted choking definition and the under-performance and choking dichotomy. In one of the first anxiety-related debates within a sport psychology journal issue, a constructive and fruitful debate developed among Mesagno and Hill (2013a, 2013b), Buszard *et al.* (2013), and Jackson (2013) with the researchers disagreeing on how important it may be to investigate the under-performance/choking dichotomy. Mesagno and Hill (2013a) argued for greater clarity in the choking definition with more investigations dedicated to examining if there are cognitive processing differences between under-performance and choking. Buszard *et al.* stated that "researchers should take precautions to avoid falling into the trap of treating choking as a separate phenomenon because of the emotive connotations that it carries and the media hype that it attracts" (p. 279), while Jackson explained that investigations of under-performance and choking should be hypothesis tested to determine if cognitive processes differ. Mesagno and Hill (2013b) then argued that it is important for sport psychology researchers to investigate this dichotomy to allow applied sport psychologists to provide the most effective interventions possible based on the processes involved in choking or under-performance. Nevertheless, all researchers agreed that examination of this dichotomy could advance the quality of the choking literature even though it would be an "enormous challenge" (Buszard *et al.*, 2013, p. 279).

Based on the extant experimental research and existing definitions, Mesagno and Hill (2013a) proposed that choking is "an acute and considerable decrease in skill execution and performance when self-expected standards are normally achievable, which is the result of increased anxiety under perceived pressure" (p. 273). Mesagno and Hill (2013a) conceded that this definition should be modified when researchers determine whether the cognitive processes associated with choking and under-performance are distinct and when the magnitude of a choking episode is determined. Jackson (2013) argued that the Mesagno and Hill definition leads to circular reasoning because it included reference to underlying processes of the phenomenon. Irrespective of the arguments put forward, all researchers involved in the choking definition debate would likely agree that a more universally accepted choking definition is needed.

While there are no universally accepted definitions of choking to date, there are personality characteristics that may intensify athletes' possible inclination to experience choking. The "Lay down Sally" incident highlights how personality characteristics may have contributed to Sally Robbins' performance collapse and the creation of pressure before the 2004 Athens Olympics final. That is, at a press conference following her unsuccessful qualification for the 2008 Beijing Summer Olympic Games, Sally:

> In my personality I like to try and please others.... In trying to please others ... I tried too hard and went beyond my capabilities.... Going beyond my limits in the pressure of the Olympic final led to the collapse at the Olympic Games. In the past four years, I have learned a lot about myself ... I feel I have succeeded because I faced my fears and my weaknesses.
>
> (Walsh and Kogoy, 2008)

Two points should be made about this direct quote: a) By using the word "collapse" in her explanation, Sally understands that she performed far worse than what she is capable in normal, low pressure circumstances, and should be argued as a choking experience, and b) Sally has clearly reflected deeply on her Olympic experience, whereby she explains that personality characteristics that relate to impression management led her to choking. Although Sally suggests that impression management characteristics may have contributed to her demise in the Olympics, researchers have also investigated other personality traits that lead athletes to be more choking-susceptible (i.e. proneness to choking experiences).

## Personality correlates of choking

Within sport, it is only human for athletes to experience both successes and failures during their careers. Yet, journalists, spectators, coaches, sport psychologists, and even athletes tend to hastily ascribe big wins or choking to athletes' general (in-) ability to perform under pressure and provide them with "winner" or "choker" labels. Researchers, however, often search for explanations for both excelling and choking under pressure within stable personal attributes (i.e. athletes' personalities; see Roberts and Woodman, this volume). Accordingly, they assume an outcome-decisive relationship between athletes' personalities and the ability to perform under pressure situations (Markman *et al.*, 2006; Mesagno and Marchant, 2013; Otten, 2009). To date, researchers have found support that trait anxiety and self-confidence (Otten, 2009; Wang *et al.*, 2004), coping (Jordet, 2009; Jordet and Hartman, 2008; Wang *et al.*, 2004), self-consciousness (Baumeister, 1984; Wang *et al.*, 2004), narcissism (Geukes *et al.*, 2012, 2013a; Wallace and Baumeister, 2002; see also Roberts and Woodman, this volume), and dispositional reinvestment (Jackson *et al.*, 2006; Kinrade *et al.*, 2010; Masters *et al.*, 1993; Maxwell *et al.*, 2000; Poolton *et al.*, 2004) are likely characteristics of choking-susceptible athletes.

## Experimental approach

Based on the dispositional approach within personality psychology (Allport, 1966; Funder, 1991, 2001), sport psychology researchers (e.g. Baumeister, 1984; Beilock and Carr, 2001; Masters *et al.*, 1993; Wang *et al.*, 2004) empirically tested that (some particular) personality dispositions or traits, which are defined to be stable over time (Allport, 1966), have predictive validity for performance under pressure and explain inter-individual differences. To investigate the predictive link between personality traits and performance under pressure, researchers generally conduct experiments with two phases (e.g. Lewis and Linder, 1997; Beilock and Carr, 2001; Wang *et al.*, 2004). First, researchers assess participants' respective trait values via questionnaires (e.g. narcissism, fear of negative evaluation, etc.). Second, measures of participants' performances in two situations (i.e. a low-pressure and a high-pressure) are obtained. Correlational or regression analytical analyses are then conducted to determine whether the trait values predict performance (cf. Geukes *et al.*, 2013a). This experimental approach offers the opportunity to differentiate between low-pressure and high-pressure performances with the differences attributed to the absence and presence of pressure, respectively.

## Personality traits that exacerbate choking-susceptibility

### Trait anxiety and self-confidence

To build on the research exploring the relationship between test anxiety and test outcomes in the academic context (Wine, 1971), sport psychologists investigated trait anxiety and self-confidence as potential predictors of performance under pressure (e.g. Otten, 2009; Wang *et al.*, 2004). Trait anxiety was hypothesized to be a critical psychological characteristic leading to substandard performance under pressure and self-confidence was hypothesized to be a positive predictor of performance under pressure, with high self-confidence scorers expected to perform better under pressure than low self-confidence scorers. Researchers investigating these hypotheses found that athletes with high trait anxiety and low confidence are more susceptible to choking. Conversely, athletes with low anxiety levels and high confidence maintain performance under pressure compared to a low-pressure situation (e.g. Baumeister *et al.*, 1985; Baumeister and Showers, 1986; Otten, 2009; Wang *et al.*, 2004). Despite the empirical evidence for the relationship between trait anxiety and self-confidence with performance under pressure, few studies have focused on these trait variables as performance predictors. Mesagno *et al.* (2012), however, investigated an anxiety-related concept, fear of negative evaluation, and its relationship to performance under pressure. Results indicated that athletes who score high on fear of negative evaluation were more likely to experience choking compared to athletes that are low on fear of negative evaluation (Mesagno *et al.*). Nonetheless, the underpinning mechanisms for how anxiety affects performance are not yet fully understood and require further empirical investigation.

## Coping

Athletes' ability to successfully cope with increased anxiety levels as a response to stress and threat may also determine performance quality under pressure (see Crocker *et al.*, this volume). Researchers (e.g. Jordet, 2009; Jordet and Hartman, 2008; Wang *et al.*, 2004) have hypothesized that approach or avoidance coping may influence performance under pressure. Approach coping involves focusing on a particular concern by using direct cognitive effort (Crocker and Graham, 1995). Avoidance coping typically entails directing cognitions away from the threat-related stimulus (Anshel and Weinberg, 1999). Wang *et al.* examined the differential predictive capability of approach and avoidance coping styles to predict choking. During a high-pressure situation, athletes who scored high on approach coping were less accurate than those scoring high on avoidance coping. According to Wang *et al.* approach "copers" ruminate about performance concerns, which may increase perceived threat. Conversely, using video-based footage from World Cup soccer penalty shootouts, Jordet and colleagues (Jordet, 2009; Jordet and Hartman, 2008) found that an escapist self-regulatory coping style and avoidance motivation is likely to increase individuals' susceptibility to choking. Although counterproductive to performance, avoidance coping from the penalty shootouts may provide a break from unpleasant emotions (Jordet and Hartman). These conflicting findings presumably result from different operational indicators of coping styles (i.e. questionnaire-based vs. behavioural; see Mesagno *et al.*, 2011). Although these initial results support the link between coping styles and performance under pressure, further research is required to improve our understanding of how coping mechanisms are linked to performance.

## Narcissism

Narcissists are expected to excel in settings that are challenging and promise support for their perceived grandiosity and contingent admiration (Wallace *et al.*, 2005; Roberts and Woodman, this volume). Even in its subclinical expression, narcissism, a self-confidence-related personality trait, may be a relevant personality disposition for the prediction of performance under pressure (Wallace *et al.*). Initial empirical support for the positive association between narcissism and performance under pressure in sports derives from a study conducted by Wallace and Baumeister (2002; Experiment 3). Participants performed dart throwing in a low-pressure (with only the researcher present) and a high-pressure condition (where the experimenter offered a monetary incentive). Wallace and Baumeister found an interaction between narcissism and pressure, with no differences between high and low narcissists in the low pressure situation but high narcissists outperformed low narcissists under pressure. Geukes *et al.* (2012, 2013a) also found empirical support for a positive relationship between narcissism and performance under pressure (i.e. ball-throwing accuracy), but only when pressure was manipulated in a public manner, involving a comparatively large crowd of spectators (i.e. 1,500 to 2,000). In laboratory-based high-pressure situations, with no obvious opportunity for glory and admiration (Wallace and Baumeister, 2002), narcissism did not significantly contribute to the explanation of high-pressure performance variance (Geukes *et al.*, 2013a, 2013b). Despite a growing body of literature on narcissism and its sub-facets, assessment, and consequences for behaviour and interpersonal perceptions in general (e.g. Ackerman *et al.*, 2011; Back *et al.*, 2013), few studies have specifically tested the predictive validity of narcissism for performance under pressure. Thus, it is worth investigating narcissism to enhance our understanding of its facilitative role, including underpinning processes, in the performance and pressure-context (see also Roberts and Woodman, this volume).

### Self-consciousness

In addition to these anxiety- and self-confidence-related personality dispositions, researchers (e.g. Baumeister, 1984; Baumeister and Showers, 1986; Beilock and Carr, 2001; Lewis and Linder, 1997; Masters, 1992) have found self-consciousness to be a performance-critical trait. In fact, self-consciousness and related traits such as reinvestment (see Masters, 1992) are probably the most thoroughly investigated trait predictors of performance under pressure in sport. Self-consciousness describes individuals' tendency to direct attention either inward or outward and can therefore be further separated into two subcomponents: private self-consciousness and public self-consciousness (Fenigstein *et al.*, 1975). While private self-consciousness refers to the tendency to introspect, with individuals high in private self-consciousness habitually observing inner states and feelings, public self-consciousness describes the awareness of oneself as a social object (i.e. the awareness of being observed and/or evaluated by others [Fenigstein *et al.*, 1975]).

Two plausible but opposing hypotheses have been offered regarding the relationship between self-consciousness and performance under pressure. Initially, Baumeister (1984) found a positive relationship between dispositional self-consciousness and performance under pressure; individuals who scored low on dispositional self-consciousness experienced choking. Baumeister explained that, generally, pressure leads to the state of being self-aware. Given a trait-state intercorrelation between self-consciousness and self-awareness, athletes who score low on dispositional self-consciousness experience a state of being self-aware that is rare and uncommon. Those low in self-consciousness perform poorly under pressure because they are unaccustomed to the state of being self-aware (Baumeister, 1984). Subsequently, however, researchers (e.g. Wang *et al.*, 2004) have hypothesized and also provided empirical support for the contrary argument that athletes habitually high in (private) self-consciousness are susceptible to choking. Wang *et al.* explained that individuals in a state of being self-aware are likely to show poor performances because they tend to place attention on the process of skill execution when attentional shifts to skill execution are not necessary and in the autonomous stage of learning (Fitts and Posner, 1967).

*Dispositional reinvestment*

Dispositional reinvestment refers to individuals' habitual tendencies to consciously control a well-learned skill under pressure (Masters, 1992; Masters *et al.*, 1993). Researchers have found a negative relationship between dispositional reinvestment and performance under pressure (Jackson *et al.*, 2006; Kinrade *et al.*, 2010; Liao and Masters, 2002; Maxwell *et al.*, 2006; Poolton *et al.*, 2004). Individuals who score high on reinvestment are more likely to experience choking because they are predisposed to a self-focus and consciously control skill execution under pressure (Masters and Maxwell, 2008). Masters *et al.* (1993) found a significant negative correlation between scores on the reinvestment scale and performance under pressure in golf putting. Poolton *et al.* found that the accumulation of explicit rules was associated with higher reinvestment scores, which also led to poorer performance under stress. Kinrade *et al.* found that reinvestment scores may predict choking beyond the sport domain into cognitive tasks that challenge working memory capacity. Thus, high reinvestment scores lead to increased use of explicit rules and the likelihood of choking.

Given that self-consciousness and dispositional reinvestment are similar in their conceptualizations and even share several items in their assessment, it would be expectable that researchers have found similar results when investigating the relevance of self-consciousness and reinvestment to performance under pressure, but surprisingly the investigation of the directionality of these associations has revealed conflicting findings (i.e. positive direction: Baumeister, 1984; negative direction: Masters, 1992; Wang *et al.*, 2004). The mixed findings, however, have not challenged the general conviction that self-consciousness is crucial for motor performance under pressure circumstances. To improve our understanding of the relevance of the private and public self-consciousness subscale, Geukes *et al.* (2013a) systematically used the subcomponents of the self-consciousness scale as separate predictors of performance. They found that private self-consciousness is negatively associated with performance under pressure in laboratory-based high-pressure situations (i.e. one to seven spectators), while public self-consciousness is positively related to performance under public pressure (i.e. in front of a large audience of 1,500 to 2,000 spectators). These findings indicate that the relevance of private and public self-consciousness to performance under pressure is situational and depends on the investigated high-pressure situation. The exact mechanism(s) of how private and public self-consciousness influence performance under pressure are not yet understood and require(s) further research.

### Theoretical foundation and critique

Generally, the growing, but still minimal, body of research on the personality/performance under pressure-relationship supports the contention that personality dispositions influence athletes' ability to perform under pressure. Nevertheless, equivocal findings limit researchers' ability to assume stable and reliable predictive effects. Thorough personality-related investigations involve the challenge that the predictor variables (i.e. the personality scores) are relatively stable over time (Allport, 1966) but the criteria (i.e. the performance scores) are situational in nature. Thus, researchers face the difficulty of integrating and explaining the association of two sets of variables that are differently stable over time, due to higher variability (i.e. natural fluctuations) of situational measures. Athletes enter the low- and high-pressure situations with identical expressions on personality traits due to expected trait-stability, but the identical trait expressions are hypothesized to be differently relevant for the situational performance outcomes. Thus, the goal is to identify traits that are crucial for high-pressure performances, while being independent from low-pressure performances (cf. Geukes *et al.*, 2013a).

To explain the situational relevance of personality traits expectation Baumeister (1984), initially, used the trait-state-intercorrelation. Baumeister argued that if the high-pressure situation is, for example, related to the self-consciousness trait, differences on that trait should result in differences on the self-consciousness state (i.e. self-awareness). Subsequently, differences on that state should then influence the situational performance outcomes. More recently, a different explanation was provided that relies on the interaction of person and situation variables: The interactionist principle of trait activation (Tett and Burnett, 2003; Tett and Guterman, 2000). Formalizing the interactionist concept of a person by situation interaction (Bowers, 1973; Kenrick and Funder, 1988; Mischel, 1968, 1977), this principle describes that personality traits are only relevant to situational behaviour and/or performance when the situation (i.e. situational cues or demands) activates these traits. Only if activated, personality traits will have predictive validity for behaviour or performance in that situation. Translated to the prediction of performance under pressure through personality traits (Geukes *et al.*, 2012, 2013a, 2013b), this principle constitutes that personality traits need to be related to the demands of the high-pressure situation and at the same time be unrelated to the demands of the low-pressure situation. Only then, a personality trait is distinctly relevant only to high-pressure but not to low-pressure performance. For example, anxiety becomes activated in the high-pressure but not in the low-pressure condition, therefore, scores on anxiety predict performance only in the high-pressure situation. In the low-pressure situation, anxiety is not significantly associated with performance. Because the identification of personality traits with these exact attributes was the ultimate goal of research on the personality/performance under pressure relationship, the explicit consideration of the trait activation principle appears helpful in providing a sound theoretical basis for what has before been implicitly assumed. Additionally, the trait activation principle motivates researchers to re-address the pressure concept, with a thorough focus on features that create pressure. Behaviour is a result of both the person and situation variables (Funder, 2001), therefore, it is important that the situation variable receives as much attention as the person variable.

Typically, researchers intuitively combined situational factors to at least produce "enough" pressure to induce perceptional changes in athletes, which have often been conducted in laboratory-based, rather than field-based settings. Therefore, it remains questionable how ecologically valid these laboratory-based settings are, compared to real competitions, which typically involve large audiences, personal importance, and career- and identity-relevant consequences. As studies that tested the trait activation principle in laboratory-based and field-settings suggest (cf. Geukes *et al.*, 2013a), these differently public high-pressure conditions differ in pressure intensity (i.e. field-settings induce more state-anxiety than laboratory-based pressure situations) and in their ability to activate personality traits. While private self-consciousness was only relevant in laboratory-based high-pressure situations, public self-consciousness and narcissism were relevant in field-settings. Thus, with the introduction of the trait activation principle (Geukes *et al.*, 2013a; Tett and Guterman, 2000) to the investigation of the personality/performance under pressure-relationship, a broad theoretical basis is provided that not only explains the situational relevance of personality traits to high-pressure performance and the irrelevance of identical traits to low-pressure performance but also the distinct relevance of personality traits to different situations within the high-pressure settings.

As intuitively presumed, sport psychology research has identified athletes' personalities to be a crucial factor when having to perform under pressure. Findings of experimental studies suggest that, generally, athletes who score high on anxiety, fear of negative evaluation, private self-consciousness, and reinvestment, but score low on self-confidence, public self-consciousness, narcissism, and use an approach coping style, experience choking. The good news about the investigation of personality traits, however, is that the results only describe likelihoods. How successful a particular athlete will be in a given high-pressure situation remains a difficult question, requiring a complex, multi-causal, and individual answer. Thus, the excitement that derives from the unpredictability of success and failure in sports adds to the spectacle of sporting events. To date, researchers have only begun to provide a comprehensive answer to the issue of the exact role personality plays in the context of performing under pressure. Therefore, further research re-visiting the pressure concept, re-addressing the ecological validity of sport psychological experiments, and re-testing the situational relevance of personality traits to performance under pressure is required.

## Existing choking models

Personality characteristics have been investigated to determine if athletes are more likely to experience choking, but the causes and mechanisms of choking have led researchers toward examining attention-based models.

### Attentional models of choking

In sport, optimal performance occurs when the athlete voluntarily focuses attention on task-relevant information, processes, and behaviours, while concomitantly ignoring task-irrelevant cues (Nideffer, 1992). According to Nideffer, a voluntary ability to maintain focus on task-relevant cues assists the athlete in remaining motivated towards their best performance output. Attentional models of choking are principally focused around choking being caused by the athlete diverting attention to either internal (i.e. movement-related or emotion-focused) or external (i.e. environmental) irrelevant cues, disrupting task concentration when anxiety levels increase. Researchers have formulated two attention-based models that predominantly apply to choking: *Distraction* and *Self-focus*.

### Distraction model

Sport-related distraction models originated from explanations of poor performance in test anxiety (Wine, 1971). Test anxiety researchers found that poor test-taking performance was due to attention to task-irrelevant (e.g. worry about outcome or the situational demands), rather than task-relevant (e.g. the question being answered) information, which may be a product of the amount of working-memory capacity. Working memory is a short-term memory system that maintains, in an active state, a limited amount of information with immediate relevance to the task while preventing distractions from the environment and irrelevant thoughts (Kane and Engle, 2000). Engle (1996) argued that individual differences for working-memory capacity reflect the capability to use controlled attention to prevent distraction from the environment and interference from events stored in long-term memory. If the ability of working memory to maintain task focus is disrupted by internal or external factors, then performance may suffer. Beilock *et al.* (2004) conducted a study to investigate the influence of pressure in a task in which performers would be susceptible to choking via distraction. The researchers asked individuals to perform easy (low demand on working memory) and difficult (high demand on working memory) math problems in both low- and high-pressure situations. Beilock *et al.* (2004) found that participants who performed difficult math problems (strongly reliant on working memory resources) experienced failure under pressure, which indirectly indicated worrisome thoughts. Beilock *et al.* (2004) concluded that pressure could compromise working memory resources, causing failure via distraction in tasks that rely heavily on working memory.

Distraction-based explanations (e.g. Eysenck and Calvo, 1992; Eysenck *et al.*, 2007; Gucciardi *et al.*, 2010; Hardy *et al.*, 2001; Hill *et al.*, 2010a; Mullen *et al.*, 2005; Oudejans *et al.*, 2011) postulate that choking occurs because attention shifts from task-relevant to irrelevant cues as a result of heightened anxiety. Athletes who experience choking become distracted by task-irrelevant shifts in attention, resulting in the athlete disregarding important task-relevant cues. As conceptualized in the distraction model, choking occurs when worry and explicit self-instruction exceed a threshold of attentional capacity, thereby diminishing the potential attentional space and allocation that enables high-level performance.

While not choking models per se, Processing Efficiency Theory (PET; Eysenck and Calvo, 1992) and Attentional Control Theory (ACT; Eysenck *et al.*, 2007) can be included as distraction models. According to supporters of PET, worry causes a reduction in the storage and processing capacity of the working memory system available, as well as an increment of on-task effort designed to improve performance (Eysenck and Calvo). Accordingly, when individuals encounter an anxiety-inducing situation, increased effort and compensatory strategies are employed. A crucial distinction exists between performance effectiveness (i.e. quality of performance) and processing efficiency (i.e. performance effectiveness divided by effort); the major difference being that anxiety impairs efficiency more than effectiveness (Eysenck and Calvo). As such, increases in anxiety will typically result in detriments in processing efficiency due to extra effort invested in performance and reduced attentional resources. However, performance effectiveness could be maintained or improved with extra effort, or could be impaired despite the extra effort. ACT (Eysenck *et al.*, 2007), a successor of PET, posits that anxiety increases as a result of a valued goal being threatened, which causes attention to be distributed to detecting the source of the threat and deciding how to respond. Consequently, cognitive processing is likely to be diverted from task-relevant stimuli to task-irrelevant cues automatically and irrespective of whether those cues are external (e.g. watching an opponent, attention to crowd behaviour) or internal (e.g. worry) distracters (Eysenck *et al.*, 2007). Advocates of ACT postulated that the inhibition and shifting functions of the central executive of working memory are most adversely affected by anxiety. The inhibition function uses attentional control to resist interference from task-irrelevant stimuli, whereas the shifting function helps attentional control shift and remain focused on task-relevant stimuli. Functional impairment of inhibition and shifting of attentional control disrupts the balance between the goal-directed and stimulus-driven attentional systems (Eysenck *et al.*, 2007).

*Self-focus model*

Advocates of self-focus approaches (e.g. Beilock and Carr, 2001; Jackson *et al.*, 2006; Masters, 1992) have broadly adopted Baumeister's (1984) Automatic Execution Hypothesis, which specifies that choking occurs because the athlete allocates explicit attention to movement execution after anxiety increases. Baumeister conducted a series of studies proposing three hypotheses: increased self-awareness causes decrements in performance, pressure causes decrements in performance, and performance decrements occur in field settings. The first three studies illustrated that increased self-awareness was detrimental to performance. In the final three studies, the hypothesis that pressure decreases performance in an experimental and field based study was confirmed. To expand on Baumeister's concepts, Masters conducted a classic explicit and implicit motor learning study in which participants learned golf-putting through explicit motor learning (i.e. explicit instructions about how to perform the skill) or implicit motor learning (i.e. no explicit instructions provided). Masters' Conscious Processing Hypothesis (or Reinvestment Theory), which was based around motor learning rather than psychological mechanisms, indicates that anxiety encourages attention to shift toward conscious processing of explicit performance rules. Apparently, implicit motor learners performed more automatically under stress than explicit motor learners, due to their lack of "reinvestment" in explicit rules. More specifically, explicit rules were not formed because participants learned implicitly, and therefore were not accessible under stress.

To further investigate the processes involved with self-focused attention and expert performance, Beilock and Carr (2001) sought to document the accessibility of declarative (i.e. formal, rule-based [Anderson, 1987]) knowledge about golf putting with changes in skill level. Beilock and Carr hypothesized that generic knowledge increases as level of skill progresses, whereas episodic knowledge decreases with further expertise. Beilock and Carr found that episodic recollection of specific putts was poor for experts, denoting that skilled putting is encoded in a procedural form that supports performance without the need for constant attentional control and substantiates the contention that self-focusing is not necessary during skilled performance. Beilock and Carr forwarded an explicit monitoring hypothesis (EMH), arguing that awareness of step-by-step procedures when executing well-learned behaviours may disrupt execution of high-level skills. For sensorimotor skills, pressure apparently leads to impractical efforts to consciously control more complex, procedural knowledge that already operate automatically outside of working memory. Jackson *et al.* (2006) extended these findings by explaining that disruptive effects on motor skills occur when an athlete attempts to consciously monitor *and* control movements, rather than monitor movements alone. Thus, advocates of the EMH of choking believe that the combination of monitoring and attempting to control skilled performance leads to choking.

### Distraction or self-focus: research support for both?

After a review of the distraction and self-focus models of choking, the keen reader may wonder which model is the most supported within the research literature. Much of the experimental evidence supports the primary tenets of self-focus explanations (e.g. Beilock and Carr, 2001; Gray, 2004; Gucciardi and Dimmock, 2008; Jackson *et al.*, 2006; Lewis and Linder, 1997; Mesagno *et al.*, 2009). More recent qualitative investigations (e.g. Gucciardi *et al.*, 2010; Hill *et al.*, 2010a; Ouanddejans *et al.*, 2011), however, have questioned the ubiquity of the self-focus model, suggesting that distraction based explanations remain viable. The differences in findings, thus, may be a result of skill level. In sport, researchers have found that novices are likely to experience choking as a result of distraction-based accounts, whereas experts mostly experience choking through self-focused attention (e.g. Beilock *et al.*, 2002). Despite a committed debate about whether and when the distraction or the self-focus model may account for choking as explanation, these two choking models may be less concurrent than researchers have assumed and we have presented thus far.

### Are distraction and self-focus models distinct or do they overlap?

Most choking review papers (including this one) have explained current attention-based choking models as competing theories. But are these choking models distinct or do they overlap in different aspects of the models? Some researchers (e.g. Edwards *et al.*, 2002; Mesagno *et al.*, 2011; Nieuwenhuys and Oudejans, 2012) assert that aspects of the distraction and self-focus models should be integrated. For example, Nieuwenhuys and Oudejans argue that although researchers who have investigated the distraction and self-focus models propose different mechanisms for how anxiety affects movement execution, these models can both be explained through distraction-related methods. That is, when anxiety increases, attention is shifted toward threatening stimuli, ultimately leaving less attentional space for task-relevant information. Thus, for expert performers who experience choking as a result of self-focusing, this is ultimately a type of task-irrelevant focus and can be categorized within distraction models. Other researchers (e.g. Baumeister and Showers, 1986; Buszard *et al.*, 2013) have also suggested that the self-focus and distraction models may overlap. It is important to resolve this debate because if these models in fact overlap, then how will researchers know when self-focus or distraction is the reason for choking effects? If self-focus models of choking sometimes overlap with distraction models when experts are involved, then how can researchers unequivocally suggest that one model is predominantly supported over the other? Baumeister and Showers suggested, "The development of therapeutic techniques for ameliorating choking must wait until this debate (between distraction and self-focus models of choking) is resolved" (p. 377). Even though there is still debate on choking models, investigations on appropriate choking interventions have commenced and continue to be examined.

## Choking interventions

Understanding personality characteristics and choking models does not necessarily translate into prevention of choking at the applied level, but interventions can minimize the possibility of choking. Commonly mentioned choking interventions, which are not theory-matched, include cognitive restructuring, thought stopping, and encouraging athletes to maintain realistic expectations (Anshel, 1995). More recently, Hill *et al.* (2009) asked applied sport psychologists, who were experts in stress and performance, what choking interventions could be used. Suggestions from the experts primarily focused on interventions related to self-confidence building and minimizing expectations such as self-talk regulation, goal setting, and imagery. Although many choking interventions have been proposed (see Beilock and Gray, 2007; Jackson *et al.*, 2013; Hill *et al.*, 2010b for the most recent reviews), to date, only minimal applied sport psychology techniques have been empirically tested. The interventions discussed here are those labelled as choking interventions in the research even without the clarification of cognitive differences between underperformance and choking (see earlier choking debate section).

Initially, researchers (e.g. Beilock and Carr, 2001; Lewis and Linder, 1997; Reeves *et al.*, 2007) included interventions as secondary components in published choking studies. For example, using simulation (also called acclimatization) training, Lewis and Linder (1997) used a video camera to simulate and familiarize participants with pressure. Lewis and Linder hypothesized that, if pressure adaptation is trained and the athlete becomes familiar with the pressure adaptation, then the performer may maintain performance under pressure. The hypothesis was confirmed with the simulation trained (called the self-awareness adapted) group performing more accurately in golf putts than a non-adapted self-awareness group under pressure. Similar to Lewis and Linder, and using self-consciousness training as a secondary purpose of the study, both Beilock and Carr (2001) and Reeves *et al.* (2007) found that self-consciousness training also reduced choking effects.

More recently, Oudejans and Pijpers (2009, 2010) conducted acclimatization studies with the primary purpose to examine whether training with mild anxiety could prevent choking. Oudejans and Pijpers' (2009) conducted two experiments (with tasks of basketball and dart throwing) that examined whether training with anxiety can prevent choking. In both studies, low- and high-pressure tests were completed during the pre- and post-intervention tests. The intervention consisted of groups completing a five week acclimatization training period, whereby the experimental group practiced with pressure but the control group did not. Oudejans and Pijpers (2009) found that acclimatization training improved performance in the post-test compared to the control group, indicating the simulation training was effective for improving performance under pressure, irrespective of the task used within either experiment. Nieuwenhuys and Oudejans (2011) have also replicated this finding.

From the aforementioned simulation training studies, it seems that acclimatization training is an effective method to ameliorate choking, however, a recent study provides contradictory evidence. Beseler *et al.* (in review) replicated Oudejans and Pijpers' (2009) study with Australian football players and with minimal changes to their pressure manipulations. Although a limitation of Beseler *et al.*'s study was a small sample size (as was Oudejans and Pjipers' study), there was no significant advantage for the acclimatization training group under pressure compared to a no acclimatization training group. Beseler *et al.* suggested that, apparently, adapting athletes to increased self-awareness may be counterproductive and could create a conditioned response for athletes to continue to increase self-awareness in real-world pressure situations, which may lead to decreases in performance under pressure. Acclimatization training was an initial attempt at minimizing choking effects by reducing the anxiety-related effects, however, was not theory-matched to choking research. Theory matched interventions have led researchers to investigate the amelioration of choking through distraction or self-focus approaches.

### Distraction-based interventions

Distraction-based interventions are founded under the guise that optimal sport performance is maintained when a task-relevant focus of attention is maintained on important cues prior to and during skill execution. Based on anecdotal and research evidence, Mesagno and colleagues (i.e.

Mesagno *et al.*, 2008; Mesagno and Mullane-Grant, 2010) believed that a pre-performance routine (PPR) could help to maintain task-relevant attention while disregarding task-irrelevant information under pressure. According to Moran (1996), a PPR is a sequence of task-relevant thoughts and actions an athlete systematically engages in prior to performance of a sport skill. In an initial test of the efficacy of the PPR intervention, Mesagno *et al.* conducted a single-case design study with three "choking-susceptible" athletes to determine if a PPR could help maintain appropriate attentional control under pressure. Mesagno *et al.* (2008) found that an extensive PPR helped the athletes improve performance by an average of 29 per cent under pressure to an initial, high-pressure phase with no intervention. Considering the many PPR components included for the participants in Mesagno *et al.*'s (2008) study, such as a deep breath and concentration cues, Mesagno and Mullane-Grant (2010) then conducted a study to determine which PPR component was likely the most beneficial to performance under pressure. Experienced Australian football players were asked to complete 20 kicks at a scoring zone in low- and high-pressure phases. Prior to the high-pressure phase, participants were assigned to one of four PPR intervention groups (i.e. extensive PPR, deep breath, cue word, and temporal consistency), or a pressure control who received no intervention. The extensive PPR group was educated about a PPR with many components (similar to the Mesagno *et al.* study), the deep breath group took deep breaths, the cue word group was educated about appropriate concentration words, and the temporal consistency group was instructed to count to five before each attempt. Results indicated that even though anxiety significantly increased during the high-pressure compared to the low pressure phase, the extensive PPR group improved performance under pressure the most, with the other groups' performance improving, but the pressure control group decreasing performance. Thus, although an extensive PPR may be beneficial to performance under pressure, it appears that even counting to five consistently may also have beneficial effects on performance under pressure.

### Self-focus based interventions

A central tenet of decreasing choking effects based on self-focus models is to minimize the accumulation of explicit knowledge during skill acquisition to reduce the likelihood of reinvestment occurring, irrespective of the amount of knowledge accumulated. Some interventions have decreased reinvestment by investigating different types of learning directly, while other researchers have attempted to divert attention away from self-focusing thoughts in other ways.

Explicit motor learning can accelerate skill acquisition through early stages of learning, however, it is also associated with inferior performance under pressure, whereas implicit motor learning provides slower methods of learning but skill execution does not break down under pressure (Masters, 1992). To accelerate motor skill learning while minimizing explicit rules, Masters and colleagues created analogy motor learning as a choking intervention. Masters (2000) suggested that analogy learning uses biomechanical metaphors to teach complex actions (e.g. hitting a table tennis backhand as if "throwing a frisbee"). In their initial study, Liao and Masters (2001) taught a table tennis forehand to novice players via explicit motor learning or analogy motor learning (i.e. participants were asked to draw a right-angled triangle when performing the forehand). Liao and Masters found that the analogy motor learning group maintained performance under pressure and accumulated less explicit knowledge in comparison to the explicit motor learning group, which was provided rules about skill execution during training. Furthermore, the rate at which learning occurred was similar for both groups, which indicates that analogy motor learning can match explicit motor learning benefits for learning rate and pressure resilience. These findings have also been replicated and extended (e.g. Lam *et al.*, 2009; Poolton *et al.*, 2006) indicating the robustness of this intervention especially for novice athletes.

Researchers have recently found that compared to groups that have been trained using explicit motor learning methods, participants that are trained with visual gaze strategies can also help to alleviate choking. That is, quiet eye trained participants learn more quickly and are more resilient under pressure than those trained through explicit motor learning (Vine and Wilson, 2010). Quiet eye is defined as the final visual fixation toward a relevant target prior to the initiation of a movement (Vickers, 2007). More recently, Vine *et al.* (2013) examined whether quiet eye training may foster a more implicit motor learning approach to help decrease the likelihood of choking. Novice golfers participated in baseline, training, and test phases of an experiment where they completed 320 training putts in one of three groups: quiet eye, analogy learning, or explicit learning groups. The quiet eye group viewed a video of an expert who exhibited optimal quiet eye functioning, the analogy learning group were instructed using a grandfather clock analogy for golf putting, and the explicit learning group received six technical coaching instructions about the mechanics of golf putting. Direct comparison between these three groups indicated that the quiet eye group performed more accurately than the analogy learning group in the retention test and more accurately in the pressure test than both the groups; the quiet eye group developed greater attention control as reflected in longer quiet eye periods. The quiet eye group also reported less explicit rules than the explicit learning group. Apparently, quiet eye training may be a form of implicit motor learning that can help to limit the explicit knowledge accumulated over time and reduce choking effects for novices. Wood and Wilson (2011) have also extended the benefits of quiet eye training into experienced soccer players. After a seven-week training programme for soccer penalty kicks, the quiet eye trained athletes had better visual attention control, and were more accurate than a control group who practiced without instructions; the quiet eye group also maintained this higher performance under a penalty shootout. Thus, it seems quiet eye training may be beneficial for novices and experts alike.

Outside novice athletes, researchers have also developed interventions for skilled athletes who have already accumulated explicit knowledge during the learning processes to minimize reinvestment under pressure. Researchers (e.g. Beilock *et al.*, 2002; Lewis and Linder, 1997; Masters, 1992) have found that athletes who use a dual-task under pressure have a reduced likelihood of self-focusing and thus improve performance under pressure. Mesagno *et al.* (2009) explained, however, that asking athletes to count backwards from 100 by 3's (as is completed with some choking research) is not a practical task that would be accepted by athletes when performing under pressure. Thus, other practical and applied interventions have been examined to alleviate choking.

Using principles associated with successful dual-task interventions and applied sport psychology methods, Mesagno *et al.* (2009) used music as a dual-task to alleviate choking in choking-susceptible athletes. Similar to Mesagno and colleagues (2008), Mesagno *et al.* (2009) used a single-case design to determine whether music that incorporates common sport psychology and performance enhancement constructs (e.g. cognitive restructuring, humor, and relaxation) can improve performance under pressure. Mesagno *et al.* (2009) found that focusing attention on the words of a song during basketball free-throw shooting improved performance under pressure compared to a high-pressure phase without a music intervention. It appears that using task-irrelevant dual-tasks are beneficial to performance under pressure, however, additional methods of decreasing the likelihood of self-focusing are needed.

Based on external focus research that indicates concentrating on external effects of movements facilitates functionality (e.g. Wulf and Prinz, 2001), Land and Tenenbaum (2012) investigated whether a task-relevant secondary task could help alleviate choking. Land and Tenenbaum (2012) asked skilled and novice golfers to perform golf putts in low- and high-pressure conditions using either a golf-specific or irrelevant letter generation dual-task (similar to previous research). In the golf-specific secondary task, participants were asked to indicate the moment the club struck the golf ball by saying "hit" aloud at ball contact. Results indicated that both secondary tasks alleviated choking in skilled golfers. While both interventions were beneficial to performance under pressure, the golf-specific task is a more practical and applied secondary task for on-course performance. As a result, coaches and athletes may be more enthusiastic to incorporate this intervention into concentration methods.

Outside of assisted motor learning and dual task paradigms, German researchers have created a novel, behavioural intervention based on motor control and brain hemisphere activation principles. For example,

Beckmann *et al.* (2013) investigated whether brain hemisphere-priming could prevent choking. Beckmann *et al.* rationalized that athletes who experience choking as a result of self-focused attention increase their left brain hemisphere activity when under pressure, which is responsible for language production and is linked to cognitive stages of motor learning, and detrimental to motor skill execution. Apparently, increasing the right brain hemisphere activation through brain hemisphere priming using contralateral motor movements could decrease choking (Beckmann *et al.*). In three inter-linked studies with soccer penalty shots, taekwondo kicks, and badminton serves, squeezing a soft ball in their left hand for 30 seconds prior to performance under pressure led to superior performance compared to a control group who squeezed the soft ball in the right hand. Although novel and theory based, one limitation of the Beckmann *et al.* study was that the anxiety manipulation was only marginally effective in two out of the three inter-connected studies. The initial study on soccer penalty kicks was the only study that increased both cognitive and somatic anxiety, with the other two studies only providing marginally significant increases in somatic anxiety from low- to high-pressure phases. Caution should be used in interpreting these choking results especially considering the current debates within choking literature about definitions and the minimal increases in anxiety from pre- to post-phases of these studies. Arguably, these results may not transfer to real world situations or those that create additional anxiety under perceived pressure. Furthermore, the Beckmann *et al.* studies may have limited generalizability to sports that do not have stoppages in play (e.g. some team sports) to allow players to use the suggested squeezing technique to its full advantage. Thus, other interventions that use the same principles as the Beckmann *et al.* (2013) study with consideration for sport specific demands should be developed.

## Future research directions

In this chapter, we have provided fundamental information about choking from personality characteristics that correlate with choking to possible interventions that may help alleviate choking. Within this discussion we have also developed topics for debate to further advance choking research. A logical discussion point now is to suggest possible future research directions for innovative and motivated researchers to examine.

It is obvious from this chapter and from the discussion ignited by Mesagno and Hill (2013a) that, within sport especially, the cognitive, biomechanical, and performance outcome differences between underperformance and choking should be investigated to determine whether these labels are different in their underlying choking mechanisms. Although this is still a contentious issue and debates about whether the dichotomy is important are only now surfacing, we believe that deciphering between choking and underperformance is important for the advancement of choking research. Irrespective of what is identified with this dichotomy, further development of a universally accepted operational definition is also needed to advance the choking literature.

Several studies have verified that researchers can induce choking behaviour within controlled, experimental conditions (e.g. Baumeister, 1984; Beilock and Carr, 2001; Masters, 1992), however, researchers have not yet demonstrated that the personality characteristics, models of choking, and choking interventions found in experimental conditions are ecologically valid. Archival data (Clark, 2002; Wells and Skowronski, 2012) among professional golfers in actual Professional Golfers Association (PGA) tournaments have found equivocal evidence for whether choking occurs, yet controlled field studies should be conducted for more direct, robust evidence of choking in real-world situations. Although real-world settings provide a logistically difficult medium to control confounding variables, understanding whether laboratory based experiments can be validated in real-world situations, especially with choking interventions, is important. If researchers can show real-world intervention studies can alleviate choking, sport psychologists could provide evidence-based choking interventions for athletes to improve performance under pressure and the usability of these sport psychology techniques for possible choking-susceptible athletes.

Distraction models of choking indicate that when anxiety increases attention shifts occur to threat related stimuli automatically, which results in decreases in performance. Distraction models may encompass many possible distractions, and researchers are yet to pinpoint the origins of the possible threat. That is, what is the origin of the threat by which anxiety increases when choking occurs? One anxiety-based choking model that has recently been proposed for the origins of the anxiety increase, which also needs additional research attention, is the self-presentation model (Mesagno *et al.*, 2011). Mesagno *et al.* (2011) suggested that anxiety increases during choking because certain personality characteristics (e.g. fear of negative evaluation, public self-consciousness), combined with the athlete being highly invested in sport, predispose the athlete to continuous concerns about making a positive impression on others, leading to self-presentation, which are behaviours aimed at conveying an image of self to others (Schlenker, 1980). Mesagno *et al.* (2011) believe that self-presentation leads to either the distraction or self-focus models of choking (explained as self-monitoring techniques), but whether the self-presentation perspective should be integrated with the attention-based models, included as a distraction model, or provided as a stand-alone model is for future researchers to verify and test.

Considering the person by situation interaction may determine human behaviour and sport performance, one could easily assume that the applicability of the choking models depends on this interaction. Thus, to predict if and how athletes experience choking, researchers need person-related information to determine the person main effect, situation-related information to determine situation main effect, and the interaction-related information to ascertain person by situation interaction effects. The picture becomes even more complex when we consider existing task-related differences; the person by situation interaction can be supplemented by the task-variable resulting in a person by situation by task interaction. Thus, using intensive longitudinal within- and between-subject designs will provide researchers the opportunity to disentangle and improve our understanding of these main, and interaction, effects. Furthermore, interactions could be investigated for mean performance as outcome variable, but also for the variability of high-pressure performance. Increased variability of performance under pressure has often been hypothesized (e.g. Gray, 2011), but has not yet received considerable research attention. Increased performance variability per se would be a good explanation for performance decreases (i.e. under-performances) compared to low-pressure performances. Finally, further development and testing of theory-matched interventions that are both practical and user friendly for athletes during actual competitions are always welcomed within future choking investigations. If self-presentation explanations of choking is tested and supported, then future research should also focus on more clinical-based sport psychology interventions.

## Conclusions

This chapter included a review of the choking under pressure literature as explained through sport-related research. Current choking debates, personality characteristics that predispose athletes to choking, explanation of choking models, common choking interventions, and future choking research directions were all discussed. In our review, we have attempted to highlight the common debate issues in the choking literature to help the reader understand current choking topics. These debate topics should not only fuel future choking research, but should also promote other constructive disagreement within the choking research community in order to promote more robust, experimental and ecologically valid research. Ultimately, if debate and future research can be initiated and developed, it should benefit athletes who experience, applied sport psychologists who work with athletes who experience, and researchers who investigate, choking under pressure.

## References

Ackerman, R. A., Witt, E. A., Donnellan, M. B., Trzesniewski, K. H., Robins, R. W., and Kashy, D. A. (2011). What does the Narcissistic Personality Inventory really measure? *Assessment*, 18, 67–87.

Allport, G. W. (1966). Traits revisited. *American Psychologist*, 21, 1–10.

Anderson, J. R. (1987). Skill acquisition: Compilation of weak-method problem solutions. *Psychological Review*, 94, 192–210.

Anshel, M. H. (1995). Anxiety. In T. Morris and J. Summers (eds), *Sport psychology: Theory, applications and issues* (pp. 29–62). Brisbane, Australia: John Wiley and Sons.

Anshel, M. H. and Weinberg, R. S. (1999). Re-examining coping among basketball referees following stressful events: Implications for coping interventions. *Journal of Sport Behaviour*, 22, 141–161.

Back, M. D., Küfner, A. C. P., Dufner, M., Gerlach, T. M., Rauthmann, J. F., and Denissen, J. J. A. (2013). Narcissistic admiration and rivalry: Disentangling the bright and dark sides of narcissism. *Journal of Personality and Social Psychology*, 105, 1013–1037.

Baumeister, R. F. (1984). Choking under pressure: Self-consciousness and paradoxical effects of incentives on skillful performance. *Journal of Personality and Social Psychology*, 46, 610–620.

Baumeister, R. F. and Showers, C. (1986). A review of paradoxical performance effects: Choking under pressure in sports and mental tests. *European Journal of Social Psychology*, 16, 361–381.

Baumeister, R. F., Hamilton, J. C., and Tice, D. M. (1985). Public versus private expectancy of success: Confidence booster or performance pressure? *Journal of Personality and Social Psychology*, 48, 1447–1457.

Beckmann, J., Gröpel, P., and Ehrlenspiel, F. (2013). Preventing motor skill failure through hemisphere-specific priming: Cases of choking under pressure. *Journal of Experimental Psychology: General*, 142, 679–691.

Beilock, S. L. and Carr, T. H. (2001). On the fragility of skilled performance: What governs choking under pressure? *Journal of Experimental Psychology: General*, 130, 701–725.

Beilock, S. L. and Gray, R. (2007). Why do athletes choke under pressure? In G. Tenenbaum and R. C. Eklund. (eds), *Handbook of sports psychology* (3rd ed., pp. 425–444). Hoboken, NJ: Wiley and Sons.

Beilock, S. L., Carr, T. H., MacMahon, C., and Starkes, J. L. (2002). When paying attention becomes counterproductive: Impact of divided versus skill-focused attention on novice and experienced performance of sensorimotor skills. *Journal of Experimental Psychology: Applied*, 8, 6–16.

Beilock, S. L., Kulp, C. A., Holt, L. E., and Carr, T. H. (2004). More on the fragility of performance: Choking under pressure in mathematical problem solving. *Journal of Experimental Psychology: General*, 133, 584–600.

Beseler, B., Mesagno, C., Young, W., and Harvey, J. (in review). Igniting the pressure acclimatization training debate: Contradictory evidence from Australian football. Submitted to *Journal of Sport Behaviour*.

Bowers, K. S. (1973). Situationism in psychology – An analysis and a critique. *Psychological Review*, 80, 307–336.

Buszard, T., Farrow, D., and Masters, R. S. W. (2013). What is the "significance" of choking in sport? A commentary on Mesagno and Hill. *International Journal of Sport Psychology*, 44, 278–280.

Clark, R. D., III. (2002). Do professional golfers "choke"? *Perceptual and Motor Skills*, 94, 1124–1130.

Crocker, P. R. E. and Graham, T. R. (1995). Emotion in sport and physical activity: The importance of perceived individual goals. *International Journal of Sport Psychology*, 26, 117–137.

Davis, T. (2008). *Choke! Sporting flops, fiascos and brain explosions*. Crow's Nest, Australia: Arena.

Edwards, T., Kingston, K., Hardy, L., and Gould, D. (2002). A qualitative analysis of catastrophic performance and the associated thoughts, feelings, and emotions. *The Sport Psychologist*, 16, 1–19.

Engle, R. W. (1996). Working memory and retrieval: An inhibition-resource approach. In J. T. E. Richardson, R. W. Engle, L. Hasher, R. H. Logie, E. R. Stoltzfus, and R. T. Zacks (eds), *Working memory and human cognition* (pp. 89–119). New York: Oxford University Press.

Eysenck, M. W. and Calvo, M. G. (1992). Anxiety and performance: The Processing Efficiency Theory. *Cognition and Emotion*, 6, 409–434.

Eysenck, M. W., Derekshan, N., Santos, R., and Calvo, M. G. (2007). Anxiety and cognitive performance: Attention Control Theory, *Emotion*, 7, 336–353.

Fenigstein, A., Scheier, M. F., and Buss, A. H. (1975). Public and private self-consciousness: Assessment and theory. *Journal of Consulting and Clinical Psychology*, 43, 522–527.

Fitts, P. M. and Posner, M. T. (1967). *Human performance.* Belmont CA: Brooks-Cole.

Funder, D. C. (1991). Global traits: A Neo-Allportian approach to personality. *Psychological Science*, 2, 31–39.

Funder, D. C. (2001). Personality. *Annual Review of Psychology*, 52, 197–221.

Geukes, K., Mesagno, C., Hanrahan, S. J., and Kellmann, M. (2012). Testing an interactionist perspective on the relationship between personality traits and performance under public pressure. *Psychology of Sport and Exercise*, 13, 243–250.

Geukes, K., Mesagno, C., Hanrahan, S. J., and Kellmann, M. (2013a). Activation of self-focus and self-presentation traits under private, mixed, and public pressure. *Journal of Sport and Exercise Psychology*, 35, 50–59.

Geukes, K., Mesagno, C., Hanrahan, S. J., and Kellmann, M. (2013b). Performing under pressure in private: Activation of self-focus traits. *International Journal of Sport and Exercise Psychology*, 11, 11–23.

Gray, R. (2004). Attending to the execution of a complex sensorimotor skill: Expertise differences, choking, and slumps. *Journal of Experimental Psychology: Applied*, 10, 42–54.

Gray, R. (2011). Links between attention, performance pressure, and movement in skilled motor action. *Current Directions in Psychological Science*, 20, 5, 301–306.

Gucciardi, D. F. and Dimmock, J. A. (2008). Choking under pressure in sensorimotor skills: Conscious processing or depleted attentional resources? *Psychology of Sport and Exercise*, 9, 45–59.

Gucciardi, D. F., Longbottom, J., Jackson, B., and Dimmock, J. A. (2010). Experienced golfers' perspectives on choking under pressure. *Journal of Sport and Exercise Psychology*, 32, 61–83.

Hardy, L., Mullen, R., and Martin, N. (2001). Effect of task-relevant cues and state anxiety on motor performance. *Perceptual and Motor Skills*, 92, 943–946.

Hill, D. M., Hanton, S., Fleming, S., and Matthews, N. (2009). A re-examination of choking in sport. *European Journal of Sport Science*, 9, 203–212.

Hill, D. M., Hanton, S., Matthews, N., and Fleming, S. (2010a). A qualitative exploration of choking in elite golf. *Journal of Clinical Sport Psychology*, 4, 221–240.

Hill, D. M., Hanton, S., Matthews, N., and Fleming, S. (2010b). Choking in sport: A review. *International Review of Sport and Exercise Psychology*, 3, 24–39.

Jackson, R. C. (2013). Babies and bathwater: Commentary on Mesagno and Hill's proposed re-definition of "choking". *International Journal of Sport Psychology*, 44, 281–284.

Jackson, R. C., Ashford, J. J., and Norsworthy, G. (2006). Attentional focus, dispositional reinvestment and skilled performance under pressure. *Journal of Sport and Exercise Psychology*, 28, 49–68.

Jackson, R. C., Beilock, S. L., and Kinrade, N. P. (2013). "Choking" in sport: Research and implications. In D. Farrow, J. Baker, and C. MacMahon (eds), *Developing sport expertise: Researchers and coaches put theory in to practice.* (2nd edn, pp. 177–194). London: Routledge.

Jordet, G. (2009). When superstars flop: Public status and choking under pressure in international soccer penalty shootouts. *Journal of Applied Sport Psychology*, 21, 125–130.

Jordet, G. and Hartman, E. (2008). Avoidance motivation and choking under pressure in soccer penalty shootouts. *Journal of Sport and Exercise Psychology*, 30, 450–457.

Kane, M. J. and Engle, R. W. (2000). Working-memory capacity, proactive interference, and divided attention: Limits on long-term memory retrieval. *Journal of Experimental Psychology: Learning, Memory, and Cognition*, 26, 336–358.

Kenrick, D. T. and Funder, D. C. (1988). Profiting from controversy: Lessons from the person situation debate. *American Psychologist*, 43, 23–34.

Kinrade, N., Jackson, R. C., and Ashford, K. J. (2010). Dispositional reinvestment and skill failure cognitive and motor tasks. *Psychology of Sport and Exercise*, 11, 312–319.

Lam, W. K., Maxwell, J. P., and Masters, R. S. W. (2009). Analogy versus explicit learning of a modified basketball shooting task: Performance and kinematic outcomes. *Journal of Sports Sciences*, 27, 179–191.

Land, W. and Tenenbaum, G. (2012). An outcome-and process-oriented examination of a golf-specific secondary task strategy to prevent choking under pressure. *Journal of Applied Sport Psychology*, 24, 303–322.

Lewis, B. P. and Linder, D. E. (1997). Thinking about choking? Attentional processes and paradoxical performance. *Personality and Social Psychology Bulletin*, 23, 937–944.

Liao, C. and Masters, R. S. W. (2002). Self-focused attention and performance failure under psychological stress. *Journal of Sport and Exercise Psychology*, 24, 289–305.

Markman, A. B., Maddox, W. T., and Worthy, D. A. (2006). Choking and excelling under pressure. *Psychological Science*, 17, 944–948.

Masters, R. S. W. (1992). Knowledge, knerves, and know how: The role of explicit versus implicit knowledge in the breakdown of a complex sporting motor skill under pressure. *British Journal of Psychology*, 83, 530–541.

Masters, R. S. W. (2000). Theoretical aspects of implicit learning in sport. *International Journal of Sport Psychology*, 31, 343–358.

Masters, R. S. W. and Maxwell, J. (2008). The Theory of Reinvestment. *International Review of Sport and Exercise Psychology*, 1, 160–184.

Masters, R. S. W., Polman, R. C. J., and Hammond, N. V. (1993). 'Reinvestment': A dimension of personality implicated in skill breakdown under pressure. *Personality and Individual Differences*, 14, 655–666.

Maxwell, J. P., Masters, R. S. W., and Eves, F. F. (2000). From novice to no knowhow: A longitudinal study of implicit motor learning. *Journal of Sports Sciences*, 18, 111–120.

Maxwell, J. P., Masters, R. S. W., and Poolton, J. M. (2006). Performance breakdown in sport: The roles of reinvestment and verbal knowledge. *Research Quarterly for Exercise and Sport*, 77, 271–276.

Mesagno, C. and Hill, D. M. (2013a). Definition of choking in sport: Reconceptualisation and debate. *International Journal of Sport Psychology*, 44, 267–277.

Mesagno, C. and Hill, D. M. (2013b). Choking under pressure debate: Is there chaos in the brickyard. *International Journal of Sport Psychology*, 44, 288–293.

Mesagno, C. and Marchant, D. (2013). Characteristics of polar opposites: An exploratory investigation of choking-resistant and choking-susceptible athletes. *Journal of Applied Sport Psychology*, 25, 72–91.

Mesagno, C. and Mullane-Grant, T. (2010). A comparison of different pre-performance routines as possible choking interventions. *Journal of Applied Sport Psychology*, 22, 343–360.

Mesagno, C., Harvey, J. T., and Janelle, C. M. (2011). Self-presentational origins of choking: Evidence from separate pressure manipulations. *Journal of Sport and Exercise Psychology*, 33, 441–459.

Mesagno, C., Harvey, J. T., and Janelle, C. M. (2012). Choking under pressure: The role of fear of negative evaluation. *Psychology of Sport and Exercise*, 13, 60–68.

Mesagno, C., Marchant, D., and Morris, T. (2008). A pre-performance routine to alleviate choking in "choking-susceptible" athletes. *The Sport Psychologist*, 22, 439–457.

Mesagno, C., Marchant, D., and Morris, T. (2009). Alleviating choking: The sounds of distraction. *Journal of Applied Sport Psychology*, 21, 131–147.

Mischel, W. (1968). *Personality and assessment*. New York, NY: Wiley.

Mischel, W. (1977). The interaction of person and situation. In D. Magnusson and N. Endler (eds), *Personality at the crossroads: Current issues in interactional psychology* (pp. 333–352). Hillsdale, NJ: Erlbaum.

Moran, A. P. (1996). *The psychology of concentration in sport performers: A cognitive analysis*. London: Taylor and Francis.

Mullen, R., Hardy, L., and Tattersal, A. (2005). The effects of anxiety on motor performance: A test of the conscious processing hypothesis. *Journal of Sport and Exercise Psychology*, 27, 212–215.

Nideffer, R. M. (1992). *Psyched to win*. Champaign, IL: Leisure Press.

Nieuwenhuys, A. and Oudejans, R. R. D. (2011). Training with anxiety: Short- and long-term effects on police officers' shooting behaviour under pressure. *Cognitive Processing*, 12, 277–288.

Nieuwenhuys, A. and Oudejans, R. R. D. (2012). Anxiety and perceptual-motor performance: Toward an integrated model of concepts, mechanisms, and process. *Psychological Research*, 76, 747–759.

Otten, M. (2009). Choking vs. clutch performance: A study of sport performance under pressure. *Journal of Sport and Exercise Psychology*, 31, 583–601.

Oudejans, R. R. D. and Pijpers. (2009). Training with anxiety has a positive effect on expert perceptual-motor performance under pressure. *The Quarterly Journal of Experimental Psychology*, 62, 1631–1647.

Oudejans, R. R. D. and Pijpers, J. R. (2010). Training with mild anxiety may prevent choking under higher levels of anxiety. *Psychology of Sport and Exercise*, 11, 44–50.

Oudejans, R. R. D., Kuijpers, W., Kooijman, C. C., and Bakker, F. C. (2011). Thoughts and attention of athletes under pressure: Skill-focus or performance worries? *Anxiety, Stress and Coping*, 24, 59–73.

Poolton, J. M., Masters, R. S. W., and Maxwell, J. (2006). The influence of analogy learning on decision making in table tennis: Evidence from behavioural data. *Psychology of Sport and Exercise*, 7, 677–688.

Poolton, J. M., Maxwell, J., and Masters, R. S. W. (2004). Rules for reinvestment. *Perceptual and Motor Skills*, 99, 771–774.

Reeves, J., Tenebaum, G., and Lidor, R. (2007). Choking in front of the goal: The effects of self-consciousness training. *International Journal of Sport and Exercise Psychology*, 5, 240–254.

Schlenker, B. R. (1980). *Impression management: The self-concept, social identity, and interpersonal relations*. Monterey, CA: Brooks/Cole.

Tett, R. P. and Burnett, D. D. (2003). A personality trait-based interactionist model of job performance. *Journal of Applied Psychology*, 88, 500–517.

Tett, R. P. and Gutermann, H. A. (2000). Situation trait relevance, trait expression, and cross-situational consistency: Testing a principle of trait activation. *Journal of Research in Personality*, 34, 397–423.

Vickers, J. N. (2007). *Perception, cognition and decision training: The quiet eye in action*. Champaign, IL: Human Kinetics.

Vine, S. J. and Wilson, M. R. (2010). Quiet eye training: Effects on learning and performance under pressure. *Journal of Applied Sport Psychology*, 22, 361–376.

Vine, S. J., Moore, L. J., Cooke, A., Ring, C., and Wilson, M. R. (2013). Quiet eye training: A means to implicit motor learning. *International Journal of Sport Psychology*, 44, 367–386.

Wallace, H. M. and Baumeister, R. F. (2002). The performance of narcissists rises and falls with perceived opportunity for glory. *Journal of Personality and Social Psychology*, 82, 819–834.

Wallace, H. M., Baumeister, R. F., and Vohs, K. D. (2005). Audience support and choking under pressure: A home disadvantage? *Journal of Sports Sciences*, 23, 429–438.

Walsh, C. and Kogoy, P. (2008, May 2). Robbins finally answers that question. *The Australian*. Retrieved from www.theaustralian.com.au/archive/news/robbins-finally-answers-that-question/story-e6frg7y6-1111116221468.

Wang, J., Marchant, D. B., and Morris, T. (2004). Coping style and susceptibility to choking. *Journal of Sport Behaviour*, 27, 75–92.

Wang, J., Marchant, D. B., Morris, T., and Gibbs, P. (2004). Self-consciousness and trait anxiety as predictors of choking in sport. *Journal of Science and Medicine in Sport*, 7, 174–185.

Wells, B. M. and Skowronski, J. J. (2012). Evidence of choking under pressure on the PGA tour. *Basic and Applied Social Psychology*, 34, 175–182.

Wilkins, P. (2008). *Don't rock the boat: The untold story of the women's rowing eight Olympics debacle*. Sydney: ABC Books.

Wine, J. (1971). Test anxiety and direction of attention. *Psychological Bulletin*, 76, 92–104.

Wood, G. and Wilson, M. R. (2011). Quiet-eye training for soccer penalty kicks. *Cognitive Processing*, 12, 257–266.

Wulf, G. and Prinz, W. (2001). Directing attention to movement effects enhances learning: A review. *Psychonomic Bulletin and Review*, 8, 648–660.

# 7 Transformational leadership behaviour in sport

*Calum A. Arthur and Peter Tomsett*

## Introduction

Transformational leadership is often cited as the most widely used theory of leadership in the organisational psychology domain (cf. Lowe and Gardner, 2000). Indeed, Lowe and Gardner reported that one third of the research appearing in *The Leadership Quarterly* between 1990 and 2000 was about transformational or charismatic leadership. We conducted a Web of Knowledge search using 'Transformational leadership' in the title term, which produced 824 citations with 90 of those having a 2013 publication date. The same search for other prominent leadership theories such as path goal theory, servant leadership, and leader-member-exchange, produced 28, 122, and 303 articles respectively. There have also been 7 meta-analyses conducted on transformational leadership that have examined transformational leadership in relation to factors such as, leader effectiveness (Judge and Piccolo, 2004; Lowe *et al.*, 1996), gender (Eagly *et al.*, 2003), personality (Bono and Judge, 2004), and school leadership (Chin, 2007; Leithwood and Sun, 2012). Transformational leadership has been shown to predict a wide range of individual and organisational outcomes across a diverse range of contexts including military (Bass *et al.*, 2003; Dvir *et al.*, 2002; Hardy et al., 2010), business (Barling *et al.*, 1996; Judge and Piccolo, 2004; Kelloway *et al.*, 2012), education (Chin, 2007; Leithwood and Sun, 2012), public sector (Rafferty and Griffin, 2004), parenting (Morton *et al.*, 2011), and sport (Arthur *et al.*, 2011; Callow *et al.*, 2009; Charbonneau *et al.*, 2001; Rowold, 2006; Smith *et al.*, 2012). There has also been a number of field-based experimental studies that have been conducted in a number of different contexts including business (Barling *et al.*, 1996; Mullen and Kelloway, 2009), military (Arthur and Hardy, 2014; Dvir *et al.*, 2002; Hardy *et al.*, 2010), teaching (Beauchamp *et al.*, 2011), and sport (Vella *et al.*, 2013a). Clearly transformational leadership has been an influential theory in the leadership literature. However, transformational leadership has received relatively little attention in the sport and exercise psychology literature (cf. Hoption *et al.*, 2008). Indeed, in our review we located only 14 empirical research papers that examined transformational leadership in a sport setting (when we refer to sport we are referring to coach, captain, peer, or exercise leaders).

## A brief history of transformational leadership

Bass' (1985) theory of transformational leadership extended the work of theorists such as Weber (1924/1947), Berlew (1974), Downtown (1973), House (1977) and Burns (1978). A common factor of these theorists are that they all referred to, or explicitly delineated, a distinct component of leadership that involved inspiring followers via charismatic or emotional appeals that normally included some sort of vision component. Bass integrated these theories (and others) to create transformational leadership theory. Transformational leadership theory posits that transformational leaders inspire followers via emotional appeals to achieve their full potential by transcending their own self-interest for the better of the team or organisation. This is in contrast to the earlier behavioural approaches that described leadership as a transactional process whereby incentives and punishments were used to gain compliance; this is often referred to as transactional leadership. In his seminal works Bass stated that 'To sum up, we see the transformational leader as one who motivates us to do more than we originally expected' (p. 20). Bass delineated three primary inter-related factors by which such effects are theorised to be obtained.

1   By raising our level of awareness, our level of consciousness about the importance and value of designated outcomes, and ways of reaching them.
2   By getting us to transcend our own self-interest for the sake of the team, organisation, or larger polity.
3   By altering our need level on Maslow's (or Alderfer's) hierarchy or expanding our portfolio of needs and wants.

(Bass, 1985, p. 20)

A fundamental proposition of transformational leadership theory is that it builds on, or adds to, the effects of transactional leadership (Judge and Piccolo, 2004). This is referred to as the augmentation hypothesis. In contrast with Burns's original theorising that leaders are transactional or transformational, implicit within the augmentation hypothesis is that leaders will use both transactional and transformational leadership styles. Indeed, Bass suggests that transactional leadership forms the base upon which transformational leadership exerts its influence (Bass, 1998), thereby implying that without transactional leadership transformational effects may not be possible (Judge and Piccolo, 2004). The role that transactional leadership is proposed to play is one of building trust by consistently honouring transactional arrangements. In general the augmentation hypothesis has received support in the transformational leadership literature (Bass *et al.*, 2003; Judge and Piccolo, 2004).

## Transformational leadership in sport

To the best of the current authors knowledge Zacharatos *et al.* (2000) was the first empirical research article to be published that examined transformational leadership in sport teams. This study examined the influence of parental transformational leadership on the transformational leader behaviours displayed by their children in a sport setting. Since this first study, the sport coaching literature had somewhat of a lethargic uptake of transformational leadership research with the following seven years producing only another three research papers. However, since 2007 there has been a steady increase in the number of research articles appearing in journals with ten articles appearing in the past six years, six of these articles having a 2013 publication date. The growth of transformational leadership research in sport might be described as having a slow start but has quickly gained momentum in recent years. Indeed, if current rate of growth continues, transformational leadership research in sport might emulate that of the organisational psychology literature where it is the most popular leadership theory in that domain. However, popularity does not necessarily mean quality and it is important that the transformational leadership theory when applied to sport learns from almost three decades of research that has been conducted in the organisational psychology literature. Of course the primary tenets of the organisational psychology literature should be, to some extent, replicated in the sporting context, but as a discipline we need to ensure we take on board the lessons learned from the organisational psychology literature and extend transformational leadership theory into the sporting arena. Thus far the research in sport has been what one might call a mixed bag of research with regard to contexts examined, sport types, gender, analytical techniques, and research design. The current chapter will briefly review the research conducted in sport to date (see Table 7.1 for list of studies reviewed), some key themes that emerge from this review will be discussed in relation to future directions, and lastly a recent model of transformational leadership that is expressed as the provision of vision, support, and challenge will be described.

### Predictive relationships in sport

In our review of the area we managed to locate 14 empirical research articles that have used transformational leadership to underpin the research (as displayed by the coach, captain, or peers). Generally the sport psychology literature has emulated that in the organisational psychology literature in that transformational leadership is nearly always positively related to positive outcomes and negatively related to negative outcomes. For example, coaches or captains that are rated as being more transformational by their athletes have been shown to have more cohesive teams (Callow *et al.*, 2009; Smith *et al.*, 2012), more positive developmental outcomes (Vella *et al.*, 2013b), higher levels of collective efficacy (Price and Weiss, 2013), increased levels of intrinsic motivation (Charbonneau *et al.*, 2001), increased well-being and need satisfaction (Stenling and Tafvelin, 2013), more satisfied with the their coach (Rowold, 2006), more empowered and display more organisational citizen behaviours (Lee *et al.* 2013), less aggression (Tucker *et al.*, 2010), greater levels of attendance (Rowold, 2006), and performance (Charbonneau *et al.*, 2001). Furthermore, the augmentation hypothesis has also been demonstrated in sport (Rowold, 2001). Overall the results in sport psychology have generally supported the predictive relationships often found in the organisational psychology literature. These results have been demonstrated on what one might call the classic transformational leadership outcomes such leader inspired extra effort (Arthur *et al.*, 2011; Rowold, 2001) and satisfaction related variables (Rowold, 2001), however, the results have also been demonstrated on somewhat less researched outcomes in the transformational leadership literature such as aggression (Tucker *et al.*, 2010).

Whilst the majority of the results in the sport and exercise psychology literature have emulated that of the organisational psychology literature one study demonstrated results are not typical of the literature (Beauchamp *et al.*, 2007). Beauchamp *et al.* (2007) demonstrated that transformational leadership was not associated to exercise-related efficacy beliefs (efficacy related to scheduling, over-coming barriers, and within class capabilities) in a group of female exercisers who were attending a structured ten-week exercise programme. This result was evidenced regardless of the experience level of the exercisers. Furthermore, contingent reward was related to exercise related beliefs in the inexperienced exerciser group but not the experienced group. It would appear that transformational leadership is perhaps not as important in an exercise setting. This is an excellent example that demonstrates that the simple transplanting of transformational leadership into a sport and exercise domain will not necessarily emulate the organisational psychology literature

To date there has only been one published field-based experimental study examining the efficacy of a transformational leadership intervention in sport (Vella *et al.*, 2013a). This study conducted a pilot test of transformational leadership training on an Australian sample of youth soccer coaches. A quasi-experimental design was employed to evaluate the efficacy of a transformational leadership training programme. The athlete outcomes in this study were assessed using the Youth Experience Survey for Sport (MacDonald *et al.*, 2012), which assessed the developmental experiences of youth athletes. The results demonstrated that the transformational leadership training positively impacted athlete perceptions of their coach's transformational leader behaviours and also athlete reported developmental experiences when compared to a control group. Whilst this study is an important first step in developing intervention programmes in sport, further research should seek to replicate the findings in different populations, including high performance samples, and in a range of different sport and exercise settings.

Thus far the populations that have been examined in sport have been fairly heterogeneous with North American (Charbonneau *et al.*, 2001; Tucker *et al.*, 2010; Zacharatos *et al.*, 2000), Asian (Arthur *et al.*, 2011; Lee *et al.*, 2013), Australian (Vella *et al.*, 2012, 2013b), and European (Callow *et al.*, 2009; Rowold, 2006; Smith *et al.*, 2012) all being represented. The samples have also had varying performance levels of athletes that include recreational (Vella *et al.* 2013b), university-level athletes (Callow *et al.*, 2009; Tucker *et al.*, 2010), and mixed samples that have included regional, national, and international athletes (Arthur *et al.*, 2011). However, only one study has been conducted in an exercise setting (Beauchamp *et al.*, 2007) and the majority of the sport transformational leadership research has been conducted with youth or young adult populations. Furthermore, the participation level of the athletes has also tended be of a lower level with professional or elite populations yet to be fully examined.

Whilst the transformational leadership research in sport to date has furthered our understanding and provides a good base to work on there are many areas that require further research attention. For example, greater variety of sport types, populations, demographics including age, participation level, and gender (of athlete and coach) all require further research in sport. Antecedent factors of transformational leadership have also received virtually no attention, with the notable exception of the Zacharatos *et al.* (2000) study. Antecedent factors refer to what conditions facilitate the emergence of transformational leadership; these may include for example, the personality of the leader, personality of the follower, context, and situation. There are also a number of broader issues that emerged from this review of the sport transformational leadership literature; 1) nearly all the studies reviewed used either cross-sectional or quasi longitudinal designs; 2) common method bias issues are apparent in nearly all of the research; and 3) multilevel analyses is rarely used. These aspects plus a number of generic issues are discussed in the following sections.

### Over reliance on correlational designs

Like the organisational psychology literature, there has been an over reliance on correlational designs adopted in sport psychology. To date there has been only one experimental study published in sport (Vella *et al.*, 2013a). Dumdum *et al.* (2002) sum up the organisational psychology literature stating that, 'Any researcher going through the coding exercise

Table 7.1 Transformational leadership research in sport

| Authors and year | Journal | Sample | Measure | Dependent variables | Same source | Multilevel analyses |
|---|---|---|---|---|---|---|
| Zacharatos et al. (2000) | The Leadership Quarterly | Canadian youth sport | MLQ-5X | Parental TLB related to athlete TLB. Athlete TLB related to effective, satisfying and effort evoking. | Yes and No | No |
| Charbonneau et al. (2001) | Journal of Applied Social Psychology | Canadian university students | MLQ | Intrinsic motivation mediates the relationship between coaches TLBs and performance. | Yes and No | No |
| Rowold (2006) | Journal of Applied Sport Psychology | German recreational karate | MLQ-5X | TLBs predict perceptions of coach effectiveness, satisfaction with coach, extra effort, and training sessions attended per month. | Yes | No |
| Beauchamp et al. (2007) | Journal of Health Psychology | UK female exercisers | MLQ | TLBs did not predict exercise related self-efficacy in either initiates or experienced exercisers. Contingent reward predicted exercise related self-efficacy in initiates but not experienced exercisers. | Yes | No |
| Callow et al. (2009) | Journal of Applied Sport Psychology | UK university students Ultimate frisbee | DTLI | TLBs predicted athlete perceptions of cohesion. High performance expectations and individual consideration predicted task cohesion in high performers, and fostering acceptance of group goals and high performance expectations predicted task cohesion in low performers. | Yes | No |

| Study | Journal | Sample/Sport | Measure | Findings | | |
|---|---|---|---|---|---|---|
| Tucker et al. (2010) | The Leadership Quarterly | North American youth ice hockey | GTL | Transformational coaches less likely to endorse aggression. Transformational leadership negatively predicted incidents of player aggression that was mediated by team-level aggression. | Yes | No |
| Arthur et al. (2011) | Journal of Sport and Exercise Psychology | Mixed youth sample (Chinese, Malay, Indian) International and regional athletes Mixed sports | DTLI | TLBs related to extra effort. However, athlete narcissism moderated the relationship between fostering acceptance of group goals and high performance expectations such that high narcissist were less positively influenced by these TLBs. | Yes | Yes |
| Vella et al. (2012) | The Sport Psychologist | Australia youth soccer | DTLI | Modified DTLI for youth – High performance expectations subscale was removed from DTLI. | Yes | |
| Smith et al. (2013) | Psychology of Sport Exercise | UK University students Ultimate frisbee | DTLI | The relationship between TLB and task cohesion was mediate by intra team communication. | Yes | Yes |
| Price et al. (2013) | Journal of Applied Sport Psychology | North American female youth soccer | MLQ-5X | Peer and coach transformational leadership influence on perceived competence, enjoyment, intrinsic motivation, cohesion, and collective efficacy. Peer TLB predicted cohesion Coach TLB predicted competence, enjoyment, cohesion, and collective efficacy. | Yes | No |

continued

Table 7.1 Continued

| Authors and year | Journal | Sample | Measure | Dependent variables | Same source | Multilevel analyses |
|---|---|---|---|---|---|---|
| Stenling and Tafvelin (2013) | Journal of Applied Sport Psychology | Swedish youth competitive floorball (regional and international) | TTQ | The relationship between transformational leadership and wellbeing was mediated by need satisfaction | Yes | No |
| Vella et al. (2013b) | Physical Education and Sport Pedagogy | Australian adolescent soccer | DTLI | Coach transformational leadership was related to athlete developmental variables. | Yes | No |
| Lee et al. (2013) | International Journal of Sport Science and Sport Coaching | Male Korean handball | MLQ | Coach TLB predicted athlete psychological empowerment and organisational citizen behaviours. | Yes | No |
| Vella et al. (2013a) | International Journal of Sports Science and Coaching | Australian adolescent soccer | DTLI | Quasi-experiment. Results suggested that the transformational leadership intervention positively impacted athlete perceptions of coach transformational behaviour and athlete personal developmental variables. | Yes | No |

Note
Research articles not conducted directly on sport coaches, peers, or captains were omitted. For example, Kent and Chelladurai (2001) examined the leadership of athletic directors and their effects on employees. Tucker et al.'s (2006) study was conducted in a sport context but was not included as it examined antecedents of coach perceptions of transformational refereeing in ice hockey. Beauchamp and colleagues' work with parental (e.g. Morton et al., 2011a) and schoolteacher (Beauchamp et al., 2010; Beauchamp et al., 2010; Beauchamp et al., 2010) transformational leadership was also omitted.

cannot help but be struck by the fact that there are still too few experimental studies...' (p. 62). Consequently, there is a clear need for more experimental designs (both field and lab based) to be utilised within the sport transformational leadership literature.

### Common method bias

Common method bias refers to variance that is attributable to the method of measurement rather than the constructs of interest (Podsakoff *et al.*, 2003). Podsakoff *et al.* suggested that common method bias is one of the main sources of measurement error in behavioural research. Whilst there are many causes of common method bias, in relation to the transformational leadership research in sport the most salient feature is when studies use the same source for criterion and predictor variables. That is, research studies that only collect self-report data from athletes for all of the study variables. For example, a typical research objective might be to examine the relationship between athlete perceptions of their coach's transformational leader behaviours and outcomes such as self-confidence, motivation, group cohesion etc. Common method variance becomes a problem when all the variables are collected using self-report format from the same athletes. Nearly all the research in the sport and exercise psychology literature has this problem. The simplest and cleanest way of removing common method effects is to use different sources for the predictor and criterion variables. For example, use informant reports for the criterion variables, of course leadership could be measured via other sources than athlete report but this has inherent problems associated with it. However, it is not always possible or desirable to use informant reports because the research maybe interested in athlete perceptions at both the criterion and predictor levels. When this is the case there are procedures that can be employed to reduce the effects of common method bias; these can be broadly separated into two groups, research design, and statistical procedures. Podsakoff *et al.* provides an excellent detailed description of what common method bias is, what causes it, and how to try and reduce it in research.

A summary of Podsakoff *et al.*'s recommendations includes trying to create temporal, psychological, or methodological separation between measures. Creating a temporal separation involves building a time lag into the administration of the questionnaires, for example, giving a five-minute break between questionnaires or separating data collection by days. Psychological separation includes providing a cover story that makes it appear that the predictor and criterion variables are not connected. Using different response formats (e.g. likert scales, semantic differential) can also help to create psychological distance. Counter balancing of questionnaires may also help to reduce any priming effects that may occur. Protecting anonymity and reducing evaluation apprehension, for example, explaining that there are no right or wrong answers are all procedures that can be used to reduce the impact of common method bias.

Statistical solutions include partial correlation procedures, which involves partialling out the assumed variance, associated with the common method effect. Three types of variables that can be used for this purpose are partialling out social desirability or general affectivity, partialling out a 'marker variable', or partialling out a general factor score. The partialling out of social desirability and affectivity are believed to remove variance that is associated with participant's tendency to answer in a socially desirable manner and their current mood state respectively. A marker variable is a variable that is theoretically unrelated to all of the research variables, thus any correlations between the study variables and the marker variable will be to some extent due to common method bias. Therefore, partialling out the variance of the marker variable will theoretically remove the variance associated with same source data. The general factor covariate technique involves conducting exploratory factor analyses of all the study variables where the scale score for the first un-rotated factor is calculated and partialled out. For a full detailed discussion of common method bias please see (Podsakoff *et al.*, 2003).

To sum up transformational leadership research in sport would benefit from considering common method factors. The best way to avoid common method bias is to collect data from different sources. In terms of transformational leadership research this will normally involve using other sources for the criterion variables. However, when this is not possible trying to reduce the impact of common method variance would seem prudent.

## Multilevel analyses

Multilevel data structures have been discussed in the leadership literature for decades and it has become the norm to analyse leadership data using multilevel techniques. A special issue of *The Leadership Quarterly* was published in 2002 that was entirely devoted to multilevel analyses and complex data structures in relation to leadership research. This special issue is a good resource for any researcher interested in incorporating multilevel analyses into their leadership work. With regards to the sport psychology literature there have been calls for researchers to give consideration to multilevel analyses in their work. For example, Myers and Feltz (2007) stated in relation to the collective efficacy literature 'In most instances, multilevel modelling is likely to be the optimal framework for analysing collective efficacy data' (p. 810), they further stated 'These rationales to impose single level models should be judged insufficient in most instances in the future' (p. 810). The rationales they were referring to were not having collected enough teams to enable multilevel analyses, or by claiming that the individual level of analyses was the focal research question.

Examination of the transformational leadership literature in sport reveals a worrying statistic; only two of the 14 studies employed a multilevel framework in their main analyses. This is especially worrying because the rational for using multilevel analyses in leadership research are similar, if not more compelling than that of collective efficacy research. Whilst a full discussion of multilevel analyses is beyond the scope of the current chapter, a brief non-technical practical guide outlining the basic features of multilevel analyses is provided. There are numerous excellent resources available that provide a full discussion of multilevel analyses (e.g. Hox, 2010) and readers are referred to these for more details.

Leadership research is inherently multilevel, that is, athletes are nearly always nested within teams and or coaches. This is problematic for three broad reasons. First, relationships can and do occur at more than one level, the individual level (often referred to as level 1) and the group level (often referred to as level 2), there can also be more than two levels, for example, a three-level model would be athletes (level 1) nested within teams (level 2) with teams nested in sports (level 3). However, the level is sometimes not straightforward and there are times when the levels may not always be clearly defined as in 'cross-classified models'. An example of a cross-classified model in sport would be when some athletes play for more than one team (e.g. some athletes from a school team may also represented the regional team). Second, variables can be measured at different levels, for example, individual perceptions of leader behaviours (level 1) and team performance (level 2); and third, an assumption that underlies analyses of variance is that all observations are independent. However, this assumption is almost never met in transformational leadership research. This is because transformational leadership is nearly always measured by follower perceptions of their leader's behaviours, thus, if a leader has multiple followers rating them then these observations are clearly not independent. Consequently, if research designs involve collecting data from multiple athletes that rate the same coach then this design feature alone necessitates that multilevel issues require consideration. There are of course many more reasons why multilevel frameworks would be the optimum approach, please refer to the specialised multilevel sources for these (e.g. Hox, 2010). The following is a simplified non-technical outline of a procedure that can be adopted when designing and implementing transformational leadership research in sport.

First of all it is necessary to determine if the sample is likely to have a multilevel structure (e.g. non-independence of observations, players nested within teams, and or variables measured at more than one level). The next decision to make is to determine how large the sample should be (how many athletes, coaches, and number of athletes per coach). Unfortunately, there is no simple answer to this question as it depends on numerous other factors (e.g. if one is interested in fixed models, cross-level interactions, or random effects models). However, Hox (2010) provides a rule of thumb that at least 30 groups with 30 individuals per group is reasonable if the research focus is on a model with fixed parameters only. The practical application of this rule in sport is immediately problematic because some teams (probably most teams) will not have 30 athletes in them. The team-level data should not be problematic in most research designs because collecting data from 30 teams should be achievable. However, the more elite the sample becomes, typically the fewer teams there are. For example, if one was interested in examining transformational leadership in professional-level English cricket teams, there are only 18 teams and thus there is a problem. In this situation a reasonable approach to the multilevel level issue maybe to include a rationale for why so few teams are available and the steps that have been taken to model or control for the nested nature of the data.

After the sample size issues have been resolved and the data collected the next stage is the analysis. Typically, the analytical procedures will start by generating some descriptives about the groupness of the data, or in other words, to what extent the variance in the data set is attributable to group membership. A typical statistic that one might wish to report with regard to groupness is the interclass correlation coefficient (ICC). This is simply the proportion of the group level variance to total variance and is expressed as a ratio or a percentage. This statistic (and others) is typically used to decide whether the groupness of the data merits a multilevel approach. That is, whether the nested nature of the data is ignorable or not. However, there is no consensus with regard to what an ICC should or should not be for multilevel analyses. None the less, in terms of leadership research where non-independence of observations is evident (i.e. coaches are rated by multiple athletes) then even a low ICC will likely warrant a multilevel framework to be adopted because the assumption of independence is still violated.

Following the descriptives regarding the groupness of the data there is one more 'screening' process to go through prior to conducting the main analyses. This stage investigates the nature of the particular multilevel model that should be specified. There are two aspects to this, (1) whether the intercepts should be fixed or random, and (2) whether slopes should be fixed or random. Multilevel analyses differ from normal regression analyses in that the intercept can be specified to be fixed (this is identical to normal regression analyses) or the intercepts can be random, that is, every group in the sample will have their own intercept value, if the sample contains 30 groups there will be 30 intercepts. To determine which model should be specified from an empirical perspective (theoretical considerations should also play a role here) two models are run, one with the intercepts fixed and one with the intercepts free to vary. Statistical packages such as MLwiN provide a *deviance* score, which indicates how well a model fits the data, with lower scores indicating better fit. The deviance score can then be used to perform a chi-square test between the models to test whether the random model fits the data significantly better than the fixed model (at one degree of freedom). If the random intercept model fits the data significantly better than the fixed model then a random intercept model should specified. Conversely, if the fits are no different or the fixed model fits the data better the fixed model should be specified. It is important to note that at this stage the regression slopes are all fixed to be parallel. In the case of a random intercept model with 30 teams there will be 30 parallel regression slopes modelled in the analyses, in the fixed intercept model (and fixed slope) there will be just one average regression slope modelled (identical to normal regression analyses).

The second part of the screening phase refers to whether the regression slopes should be fixed or random. In normal regression analyses the average regression slope is calculated resulting in an average slope for the entire sample. However, multilevel analyses allows for each group's slope to vary (i.e. random). If the sample has 30 groups then there will be 30 regression slopes that are free to vary. This means that some groups may have steep positive slopes, other groups might have shallow positive slopes and yet other groups may have flat slopes or even negative slopes. In essence there could be situations where the relationship between variables may be determined by group membership. This part of the analyses essentially tests whether slopes differ between groups in a meaningful way and should thus be modelled in the analyses. That is, is the observed relationship between the variables the same for each group or does it vary between groups? This can be crudely thought of as testing for an interaction between the regression slopes (i.e. to what degree do the regression slopes deviate from being parallel). In more advanced uses of multilevel analyses the question of whether the relationship between two variables is impacted by group membership might be the research question in itself. However, for basic multilevel modelling with regard to which model should be specified an identical procedure that was employed to determine whether the intercepts should be fixed or random is applied to the slopes, only this time it is to two degrees of freedom. If the chi square test reveals that the random slopes model fits the data significantly better than the fixed slopes model then the random slope model should be specified. Conversely, if there is no difference between the random slope and fixed slope models or the fixed slope model fits the data significantly better the fixed slope model should be specified. The main analyses are now ready to be run.

It is important to note that there are far more details and complexities to multilevel analyses that have not been addressed in this brief practical guide. For example, cross-level interactions, multilevel mediation analyses, moderation analyses, repeated measures designs, multilevel growth analyses, and multilevel confirmatory factor analyses. For sport examples of multilevel mediation (see Smith *et al.*, 2012), moderation (see Arthur *et al.*, 2011), multilevel confirmatory factor analyse (see Myers *et al.*, 2010; Myers and Beauchamp, 2011), and multilevel longitudinal analyses (see, Ntoumanis *et al.*, 2012).

Another factor that needs to be considered when conducting multilevel analyses is whether to centre the data around the grand mean or the group mean. The centring decision is complex and one that is not without its controversies (e.g. Enders and Tofighi, 2007). The centring method adopted will dramatically impact the results of the multilevel model. A discussion of centring is beyond the scope of the current chapter. For detailed discussions of centring see (Enders and Tofighi, 2007), for a sport related discussion on centring see (Myers *et al.*, 2010), and for a practical application in a research paper please see Smith *et al.* (2012).

## Measurement

There have been a large number of questionnaires developed to measure transformational leadership. For example, the Multifactor Leadership Questionnaire and its various forms (MLQ-5X; Avolio and Bass, 1995), Transformational Leadership Inventory (TLI; Podsakoff *et al.*, 1990), Rafferty and Griffin Scale (Rafferty and Griffin, 2004), Global Transformational Leadership (Carless *et al.*, 2000), Differentiated Transformational Leadership Inventory (DTLI; Callow *et al.*, 2009; Hardy *et al.*, 2010), Safety Specific Transformational Scale (Barling *et al.*, 2002), Transformational Parenting Questionnaire (TPQ; Morton *et al.*, 2011a), and Transformational Teaching Questionnaire (TTQ; Beauchamp *et al.*, 2010). The most widely used measure is the MLQ-5X (Avolio and Bass, 1995). Broadly speaking the various questionnaires can be categorised according to whether they were developed in a specific context (e.g. DTLI and TPQ) or were developed across contexts (e.g. MLQ-5X), whether they measure transformational leadership as global construct (e.g. MLQ-5X and TTQ) or as a differentiated construct (e.g. TLI and DTLI). Furthermore, Barling *et al.* (2002) developed a transformational leadership scale that was designed to measure transformational leadership in reference to a specific set of behaviours, in this case safety-related behaviours. Thus far the transformational leadership in sport research has made use of four different transformational leadership scales; MLQ-5X has been used in six papers, DTLI has also been used in six papers, and the TTQ and GTL have both been used once in the sport coaching transformational leadership research. Of the measures that have been used in sport only the DTLI conceptualises transformational leadership as a differentiated construct and as yet no measure has been developed that targets specific behaviours or values.

The MLQ has undergone many revisions since its conception in 1985. The early versions of the MLQ (Bass, 1985) consisted of three behaviours that were considered transformational: charismatic leadership – leadership that instils pride, faith, and respect, shows a special gift for seeing what is really important, and demonstrates a sense of mission; intellectual stimulation – leadership that provides ideas which result in a rethinking of issues that had never been questioned before and that enables subordinates to think about old problems in new ways; and individualised consideration – leadership that delegates assignments to provide learning opportunities, gives personal attention to neglected members, and treats each subordinate as an individual. The early versions of the MLQ have been criticised on both theoretical and empirical grounds. Hunt (1991) and Yukl (1999) suggested that the early versions of the MLQ bundled together leader behaviours, leader attributions, and leader outcomes, and Yukl suggested that the separate leader behaviours often contained more than one conceptually distinct construct. For example, Yukl suggested that individualised consideration contained two main behaviours that were theoretically distinct, namely, supportive leadership and developmental leadership. More recently, Rafferty and Griffin (2006) found empirical evidence that supported this claim. In response to these criticisms, Bass and his colleagues further developed the MLQ resulting in the MLQ-5X (Avolio and Bass, 1995). Essentially, the major conceptual and measurement changes Bass and Avolio (1995) made to the MLQ was to delineate the charisma scale into idealised influence (behaviour), idealised influence (attributed) and inspirational motivation. The transformational leader behaviours included in the MLQ-5X (Avolio and Bass) are: idealised influence (attributed) – refers to the socialised charisma of the leader, whether the leader is perceived as being confident and powerful, and whether the leader is focused on higher order ideals and ethics; idealised influence (behaviours) – refers to charismatic actions of the leader that are centred on values, beliefs, and a sense of mission; inspirational motivation – refers to the ways in which the leader energises his/her followers by viewing the future with optimism, stressing ambitious goals, projecting an idealised vision, and communicating to followers that the vision is achievable; intellectual stimulation – gets followers to question the tried and true ways of solving problems, encourages them to question the methods they use to improve upon them; and individualised consideration – focuses on understanding the needs of each follower and works continuously to get them to develop to their full potential. The MLQ-5X also measures transactional leadership, namely, contingent reward – behaviour that clarifies reward contingencies and rewards them when achieved, management by exception (active) – the leader attends to follower behaviours and takes corrective action if the if followers fail to meet the standards, management by exception (passive) – the leader waits for problems to arise before taking corrective action. The ninth leader behaviour that is contained in the MLQ-5X is laissez-faire leadership, which is a form of non-leadership and leader inaction. The above nine-factor model is often referred to as the full range leadership model (e.g. Bass and Bass, 2008). Both the longevity of the MLQ-5X and its wide use across contexts attest to its value and the contribution it has made to the research literature. The MLQ-5X is nearly always used as global a representation of transformational leadership in the research literature.

The DTLI was first developed in a British military context in an endeavour to create a contextually relevant differentiated transformational leadership scale. In developing the DTLI Hardy *et al.* (2010) combined aspects of the TLI and the MLQ-5X. The DTLI was based primarily on the TLI with some additions from the MLQ-5X. The TLI was adopted as the base measure because the TLI offered most promise with respect to creating a differentiated scale. Hardy *et al.* noted two minor weaknesses regarding the TLI as it related to the British military context. First, the vision construct in the TLI was deemed to be quite narrow and related more to an organisational vision rather than individually based visions. However, Avolio and Bass's (1995) conceptualisation of inspirational motivation is broader and incorporates the articulation of an exciting vision, inspiring others with this vision, and also expressing that followers can achieve the vision. Consequently, the vision component in the TLI was replaced by a sub-dimension that was based on Avolio and Bass's conceptualisation of inspirational motivation. The individual support dimension in the TLI was also deemed to be relatively narrow that related mostly to showing consideration of individual's feelings and needs, whereas the measurement of individual consideration in the MLQ-5X contains two broad areas, namely, consideration of individual needs and also behaviours which are focused on follower development. The resulting behaviours contained within the DTLI were: inspirational motivation (Avolio and Bass) – developing and articulating a positive vision of the future, inspiring others to achieve that vision, and expressing belief that followers could achieve the vision; provides an appropriate role model (Podsakoff *et al.*, 1990) – behaviour by the leader that sets an example for others to follow which is consistent with the values that the leader/organisation espouses; fosters acceptance of group goals (Podsakoff *et al.*, 1990) – behaviour by the leader aimed at promoting cooperation among followers, getting them to work together towards a common goal, and developing teamwork; high performance expectations (Podsakoff *et al.*, 1990) – behaviour by the leader that demonstrates his or her expectations for excellence in followers; intellectual stimulation (Podsakoff *et al.*, 1990) – behaviour by the leader that challenges followers to re-examine old problems in new ways; individual consideration (Avolio and Bass, 1995) – behaviour by the leader that recognises individual differences and demonstrates concern for the development of followers; and contingent reward (Podsakoff *et al.*, 1990) – provision of positive reinforcement to followers in return for appropriate follower behaviour. Contingent reward was included because, although it is a transactional rather than a transformational behaviour, it has been identified as an important predictor of group potency and performance in military settings (Bass *et al.*, 2003).

The DTLI has subsequently been modified to reflect a sporting (Callow *et al.*, 2009), higher education (Mawn *et al.*, 2012), and expedition leadership context (McElligott *et al.*, 2012). The DTLI has been shown to have good psychometric and predictive validity in adult and youth populations (Arthur *et al.*, 2012; Callow *et al.*, 2009; Smith *et al.*, 2013). However, the DTLI has also been demonstrated to have questionable psychometric properties in an Australian youth soccer setting (Vella *et al.*, 2012). Specifically, the high performance expectations subscale was claimed to be problematic with the removal of this sub-scale resulting in stronger fit statistics *(Vella et al.*, 2012). Whilst the removal of the high performance expectations subscale resulted in a better fitting model this result was only obtained on a single sample and was not confirmed in a different sample. Furthermore, evidence of the predictive and concurrent validity of the high performance expectations scale requires further testing. It is also important to note that empirical evidence exists in a sport setting that high performance expectations is important in predicting outcomes including communication (Smith *et al.*, 2012), cohesion (Callow *et al.*, 2009; Smith *et al.*, 2012), and leader inspired extra effort (Arthur *et al.*, 2011). Notably, the Arthur *et al.* (2012) study was conducted in a youth sport setting with a mean age of 14.28 years where the DTLI demonstrated good psychometric properties and high performance expectations predicted significant variance in leader-inspired extra effort. From a theoretical perspective, high performance expectations form a central role in Bass's (1985) original theorising of transformational leadership and also forms a central role in the theorising of Podsakoff *et al.* (1990). Indeed, Bass and Bass (2009) stated that 'Transformational leaders motivate their followers to do more than the followers originally intended and thought possible. The leader *sets challenging expectations* and achieves higher standards of performance [emphasis added].' (p. 618).

The notion of challenge is clearly embedded within the transformational process. It is suggested that the subscale not fitting in a particular sample is not necessarily evidence that the behaviour is inconsistent with the theory or does not apply in a particular context. Rather, it might not be the theoretical relevance of the behaviour that is problematic but it might be a problem with the items that were designed to tap the behaviour. Whilst there appears to be problems with the high performance expectations subscale in an Australian youth soccer setting more work is required before this scale is removed from the DTLI. Until more evidence has been accumulated it would seem prudent to include the high performance expectations subscale in future research that will enable more work to be done with regards to the validity of this component of transformational leadership.

### Global vs. differentiated conceptualisations of transformational leadership

Related to the above discussion on measurement is the level at which transformational leadership is conceptualised, that is, as a global construct, reduced factor structure, or fully differentiated. The most popular conceptualisation of transformational leadership in the research literature has been to use a global construct. Global conceptualisations have been demonstrated to be valid across a wide range of contexts and measures (Antonakis *et al.*, 2003; Bass *et al.*, 2003; Beauchamp *et al.*, 2010; Morton *et al.*, 2011b). The dimensions of transformational leadership are considered to be mutually reinforcing, therefore representing transformational leadership as a single global construct is consistent with the theory. However, whilst global representations of transformational leadership are clearly valid and will be appropriate in some contexts there are certain limitations and assumptions that are apparent when adopting this conceptualisation.

Global conceptualisations of transformational leadership assume that all the separate leader behaviours will have similar effects on all outcome variables. This assumption is somewhat counter-intuitive. For example, why should individual consideration have the same effect as high performance expectations? Indeed, there is research evidence that suggests that different behaviours differentially affect outcomes. For example, Podsakoff *et al.* (1990) demonstrated that whilst the majority of the leadership behaviours examined in their study demonstrated hypothesised relationships, some crucial differences were evidenced; specifically, that intellectual stimulation was negatively related to trust and satisfaction. A further study by Podsakoff *et al.* (1996) revealed that intellectual stimulation, and high performance expectations were both positively related to role conflict and high performance expectations was negatively related to general satisfaction. In the same study, high performance expectations were positively related to courtesy. In another study, Rafferty and Griffin (2004) found that intellectual stimulation was positively related to affective commitment and continuance commitment, but that vision was negatively related to continuance commitment and role breadth self-efficacy. Dumdum *et al.* (2002) reported that the different leader behaviours analysed in their meta-analyses displayed different magnitudes of relationships with the outcome variables included. For example, attributed charisma was shown to have a corrected correlation of .57 with job satisfaction whereas intellectual stimulation was shown to have a corrected correlation of .21 with job satisfaction. Collectively, these results suggest that the different leader behaviours may have different relationships with outcome variables, and the nature of these relationships may depend on context as well as the nature of the outcome variables measured. Adopting a global conceptualisation of transformational leadership will obscure these subtleties.

On a more general note a criticism that has been levelled at the leadership literature as a whole is the oversimplification of the domain (see for example, Antonakis *et al.*, 2003; House and Aditya, 1997). Indeed, Antonakis *et al.* (2003) warns '... that going to simpler models [of leadership] will push leadership research and training in the wrong direction in the same way that earlier two-factor models of leadership did at Ohio State and Michigan.' (p. 285). Emulating the sentiment of Antonakis *et al.* (2003), Yukl (1999) suggests that relying on two factor models of leadership (e.g. transformational/ transaction) fails to properly examine the underlying components of these factors. Furthermore, in regard to leadership training Antonakis *et al.* suggested that global constructs of leadership will be of limited use because feedback on transformational leadership in general will be less focused and will likely therefore be less effective than interventions based on more detailed feedback. For example, it is suggested that 'you need to be more transformational' will be of less use to leaders than 'you need to pay attention to the individual needs of your followers'.

In conclusion, transformational leadership is a very large domain that encompasses a wide array of different behaviours, characteristics, and situations. Whilst there are strong theoretical and empirical grounds for adopting a global representation there are also strong theoretical and empirical grounds for adopting a differentiated representation of transformational leadership. The choice of which particular conceptualisation is adopted in research programmes would appear to be influenced by the nature of the research question. For example, if the research is interested in generic transformational effects in a new area of theoretical development then perhaps the initial theorisation could be around generic transformational leadership effects. However, a more fine-grained approach utilising a differentiated conceptualisation might be warranted to further explore the nuances of the relationships. With regards to leadership intervention programmes it would appear that a more differentiated approach would be beneficial. For example, aside from the practical benefits of more focused feedback a reasonable question to ask is whether all the different transformational leader behaviours can be equally well taught. That is, individual consideration might be relatively straightforward to teach but the charismatic or visionary components may not lend themselves as well to being developed. It would seem prudent to explicitly align the theoretical question with the specific conceptual model of transformational leadership that is adopted. With regards to the transformational leadership research in sport there appears to be questionnaires that perform well as differentiated conceptualisation (e.g. DTLI) and questionnaires that perform well as a global construct (e.g. MLQ-5X). Furthermore, a recent adaptation of the TTQ (Beauchamp *et al.*, 2010) by Stenling and Tafvelin (2013) to reflect a sport-coaching context would also seem to offer some promise with regard to a global conceptualisation of transformational leadership in the sport coaching literature.

### Contextual and situational moderators

As articulated earlier in this chapter transformational leadership has been shown to be effective across a diverse range of contexts and national boundaries. Indeed, Bass (1997) stated that, 'Evidence supporting the transactional-transformational leadership paradigm has been gathered from all continents except Antarctica – even offshore in the North Sea.' (p. 130). In the same article Bass further states that

> to refute transactional-transformational distinction will require finding conditions, cultures, and organisations in which trust between the leader and led are unimportant and the led have no concern for self-esteem, intrinsic motivation, consistency in self-concept, actions taken for the leader, or meaningfulness in their work and lives.
>
> (p. 137)

However, the universality, or the extent to which transformational leadership *is* universal has been called into question by some researchers (e.g. Yammarino and Dubinsky, 1994). This has either been articulated as the identification of boundary conditions (Yammarino and Dubinsky, 1994) or the search for situational and contextual moderator variables (Lim and Ployhart, 2004; Yukl, 1999). In relation to the universality of transformational leadership Yukl stated that,

> The search for situational moderator variables may be more successful if directed at specific types of transformational behaviour. Even if there is always some type of transformational behaviour that is relevant for effective leadership, not every type of transformational behaviour will be relevant in every situation.
>
> (p. 291)

In essence this line of research seeks to examine variables that will either increase the likelihood of transformational leadership occurring (antecedents), or moderate the effectiveness of transformational leadership. Despite various calls from researchers (e.g. Avolio, 2007; Yukl, 1999) to examine this area there are still relatively few published studies (in either the organisational or the sport psychology literature) that have sought to identify factors that moderate the impact of transformational leadership. There have been a small number of studies appearing in the research literature that have examined potential moderating variables, for example, narcissism (Arthur *et al.*, 2011), performance context (Lim and Ployhart, 2004), and trust climate (Menges *et al.*, 2011) have all been shown to moderate the relationship between transformational leadership and follower outcomes but still only a small number of variables have been tested.

Moderators of the leadership effectiveness relationship can generally fall under two broad categories, contextual moderators and situational moderators. Contextual moderators refer to the setting in which the research is conducted in. For example, a context could be defined by sport, military, education, and business boundaries; the context could also be defined by national boundaries (European, North American, Asian, etc.); or within sport such as sport type (e.g. rugby, gymnastics, football, etc.). Whereas situational moderators refer to boundaries that are defined by factors that occur within the same context but under different circumstances. For example, training vs. competition; after a defeat vs. after a victory; just before a cup final vs. a pre-season friendly etc. The situational moderators could also refer to factors such as personality, gender, participation level, and age. The important aspect here is identifying under what conditions and with whom is transformational leadership likely to be more or less effective. In sport two studies have been published that have identified performance level (Callow *et al.*, 2009) and follower narcissism (Arthur *et al.*, 2011) as moderators of the transformational leadership effectiveness relationship. However, there are many other contextual and personality variables that may be of relevance in a sport setting. For example, transformational leadership may more positively impact less optimistic athletes because they may require greater expressions of belief in them from their coach than their more optimistic counterparts. Alternatively, if a differentiated approach to transformational leadership is adopted the more supportive transformational leader behaviours (e.g. individual consideration) maybe more beneficial for less optimistic athletes than their more optimistic counterparts. Other personality variables that may be worth considering are trait anxiety, self-esteem, reward sensitivities, social affiliation, and goal orientation. Furthermore, there are likely to be circumstances where context and situation will interact to determine the effectiveness of transformational leadership. For example, the effectiveness of transformational leadership may be determined by an interaction between situation (competition vs. practice) and athlete personality (e.g. narcissism). These sorts of questions would inevitably involve some more complex analyses such as three-way interaction designs (see also Roberts and Woodman, this volume, for a discussion of the interaction between situation and personality).

### Potential negative effects of transformational leadership

Whilst the majority of the research literature focuses on the positive effects of transformational leadership the potential for transformational leadership to have negative effects has received very little research attention in the organisational psychology literature (Eisenbeiss and Boerner, 2013) and no study has examined the potential negative effects in a sport coaching context. However, there seems to be potential for transformational leadership, in some situations, and with some people, to have potential negative effects. For example, (Yukl, 1999) suggested that transformational leadership could cause burnout by overly engaging the emotions of followers. Burnout is an important consideration within sport (Eklund and Cresswell, 2007) and thus research into this area would seem warranted. Furthermore, transformational leadership may in some circumstances lead to an over reliance on the leader or dependence on the leader. Research into potential negative effects of transformational leadership in sport would seem warranted.

### Vision support and challenge

An applied conceptualisation of transformational leadership comprising vision, support and challenge, was developed in a military setting by Hardy *et al.* (2010). The vision, support and challenge model was developed as a meta-cognitive model that was theorised to represent what it is that transformational leaders provide their followers with. The model was developed in an applied setting in order to make transformational leadership more accessible and has been used to underpin two interventions in the military (Hardy *et al.*, 2010; Arthur and Hardy, 2014). The basic notion is that transformational leaders provide their followers with a positive vision of the future, provide the necessary support in order to achieve the vision, or at least to instil a sense of belief in their followers that the vision is attainable, and to provide appropriate levels of challenge in order to achieve the vision. Vision is defined *as the extent to which athletes have an inspirational and meaningful future image of themselves in their sport.* Support is defined as the *extent to which emotional, esteem, informational, and tangible support is provided or is perceived as being available when needed.* Challenge is defined as *an understanding of what needs to be done in order to achieve goals and the gap between current state and a future desired sate, with the implicit assumption that the larger the discrepancy the more challenged followers are.* The vision, support, challenge model has been discussed in a sport setting (Arthur *et al.*, 2012) but has yet to be empirically tested. However, a recent qualitative study by Hodge *et al.* (2014) that was conducted in an elite sport setting supported the transformational leadership model and vision, support, and challenge. In the interviews that were conducted with the elite level coaches' vision, support, and challenge emerged from the data. The vision, support, challenge model of transformational leadership would appear to offer some promise in a sport setting and particularly at the elite level. Further research into the applied usefulness and empirical bases of the vision, support, and challenge model in sport is required.

### Summary

Applying transformational leadership theory to the sport leadership context appears to offer some promise in helping to understand the complex world of sport leadership. Indeed the theory may help to generate a better understanding of what it is that makes great coaches great. Furthermore, the theory may also shed some light on the processes and mechanisms by which great leaders have their impact on teams and followers. Sport maybe a particular fruitful area for developing theory on contextual and situational moderators because of the many different sports, settings, and performance levels that exists within the world of sport.

# References

Antonakis, J., Avolio, B. J., and Sivasubramaniam, N. (2003). Context and leadership: An examination of the nine-factor full-range leadership theory using the multifactor leadership questionnaire. *Leadership Quarterly*, 14, 261–295. doi:10.1016/S1048–9843(03)00030–4.

Arthur, C. A. and Hardy, L. (2014). Transformational leadership: a quasi-experimental study. *Leadership and Organisation Development Journal*, 35, 38–53. doi:10.1108/LODJ-03-2012-0033.

Arthur, C. A., Hardy, L., and Woodman, T. (2012). Realisng the olympic dream: Vision, support, and challenge. [null] *Reflective Practice Intrenational and Multidisciplinary Perspectives*, 13, 399–406. doi:10.1080/14623943.2012.670112.

Arthur, C. A., Woodman, T., Ong, C. W., Hardy, L., and Ntoumanis, N. (2011). The role of athlete narcissism in moderating the relationship between coaches' transformational leader behaviours and athlete motivation. *Journal of Sport and Exercise Psychology*, 33, 3–19.

Avolio, B. J. (2007). Promoting more integrative strategies for leadership theory-building. *American Psychologist*, 62, 25–33. doi:10.1037/0003–066X.62.1.25.

Avolio, B. J. and Bass, B. M. (1995). *Multifactor leadership questionnaire*. Mind Garden Inc.

Avolio, B. J. and Bass, B. M. (1995). Individual consideration viewed at multiple levels of analysis: A multi-level framework for examining the diffusion of transformational leadership. *The Leadership Quarterly*, 6, 199–218.

Barling, J., Loughlin, C., and Kelloway, E. K. (2002). Development and test of a model linking safety-specific transformational leadership and occupational safety. *Journal of Applied Psychology*, 87, 488–496. doi:10.1037//0021–9010.87.3.488.

Barling, J., Weber, T., and Kelloway, E. K. (1996). Effects of transformational leadership training on attitudinal and financial outcomes: A field experiment. *Journal of Applied Psychology*, 81, 827–832. doi:10.1037/0021–9010.81.6.827.

Bass, B. M. (1997). Does the transactional-transformational leadership paradigm transcend organisational and national boundaries? *American Psychologist*, 52, 130–139. doi:10.1037/0003–066X.52.2.130.

Bass, B. M. (1998). *Transformational leadership: Industrial, military, and educational impact*. Mahwah, NJ: Lawrence Erlbaum & associates.

Bass, B. M. and Bass, R. (2009). *The bass handbook of leadership: Theory, research, and managerial applications*. SimonandSchuster.com.

Bass, B. M., Avolio, B. J., Jung, D. I., and Berson, Y. (2003). Predicting unit performance by assessing transformational and transactional leadership. *Journal of Applied Psychology*, 88, 207–218. doi:10.1037/0021–9010.88.2.207.

Bass, M. B. (1985). *Leadership and performance beyond expectations* (4th edn). New York: Free Press.

Beauchamp, M. R., Barling, J., Li, Z., Morton, K. L., Keith, S. E., and Zumbo, B. D. (2010). Development and psychometric properties of the transformational teaching questionnaire. *Journal of Health Psychology*, 15, 1123–1134. doi:10.1177/1359105310364175.

Beauchamp, M. R., Barling, J., and Morton, K. L. (2011). Transformational teaching and adolescent self-determined motivation, self-efficacy, and intentions to engage in leisure time physical activity: A randomised controlled pilot trial. *Applied Psychology-Health and Well being*, 3, 127–150. doi:10.1111/j.1758–0854.2011.01048.x.

Beauchamp, M. R., Welch, A. S., and Hulley, A. J. (2007). Transformational and transactional leadership and exercise-related self-efficacy – an exploratory study. *Journal of Health Psychology*, 12, 83–88. doi:10.1177/1359105307071742.

Berlew, D. E. (1974). Leadership and organisational excitement. *California Management Review*, 17, 21–30.

Bono, J. E. and Judge, T. A. (2004). Personality and transformational and transactional leadership: A meta-analysis. *Journal of Applied Psychology*, 89, 901–910. doi:10.1037/0021–9010.89.5.901.

Burns, J. (1978). *Leadership*. New York, NY: Harper & Row.

Callow, N., Smith, M. J., Hardy, L., Arthur, C. A., and Hardy, J. (2009). Measurement of transformational leadership and its relationship with team cohesion and performance level. *Journal of Applied Sport Psychology*, 21, 395–412.

Carless, S. A., Wearing, A. J., and Mann, L. (2000). A short measure of transformational leadership. *Journal of Business and Psychology*, 14, 389–405. doi:10.1023/A:1022991115523.

Charbonneau, D., Barling, J,. and Kelloway, E. K. (2001). Transformational leadership and sports performance: The mediating role of intrinsic motivation. *Journal of Applied Social Psychology*, 31, 1521–1534. doi:10.1111/j.1559–1816.2001.tb02686.x.

Chin, J. M. (2007). Meta-analysis of transformational school leadership effects on school outcomes in taiwan and the USA. *Asia Pacific Education Review*, 8, 166–177.

Downtown, J. V. (1973). *Rebel leadership*. New York, NY: Free Press.

Dumdum, U. R., Lowe, K. B., and Avolio, B. J. (2002). A meta-analyses of transformational and transactional leadership correlates of effectiveness and satisfaction. In B. J. Avolio and F. J. Yammarino (eds), *Transformational and charismatic leadership: The road ahead* (pp. 35–66). JAI Press, Amsterdam.

Dvir, T., Eden, D., Avolio, B. J., and Shamir, B. (2002). Impact of transformational leadership on follower development and performance: A field experiment. *Academy of Management Journal*, 45, 735–744. doi:10.2307/3069307.

Eagly, A. H., Johannesen-Schmidt, M. C., and van Engen, M. L. (2003). Transformational, transactional, and laissez-faire leadership styles: A meta-analysis comparing women and men. *Psychological Bulletin*, 129, 569–591. doi:10.1037/0033–2909.129.4.569.

Eisenbeiss, S. A. and Boerner, S. (2013). A double-edged sword: Transformational leadership and individual creativity. *British Journal of Management*, 24, 54–68. doi:10.1111/j.1467–8551.2011.00786.x.

Eklund, R. C. and Cresswell, S. L. (2007). Athlete burnout. In G. Tenenbaum and R. C. Eklund (eds), *Handbook of sport psychology* (3rd edn, pp. 621–641). John Wiley & Sons: NJ.

Enders, C. K. and Tofighi, D. (2007). Centering predictor variables in cross-sectional multilevel models: A new look at an old issue. *Psychological Methods*, 12, 121–138. doi:10.1037/1082–989X.12.2.121.

Hardy, L., Arthur, C. A., Jones, G., Shariff, A., Munnoch, K., Isaacs, I., and Allsopp, A. J. (2010). The relationship between transformational leadership behaviours, psychological, and training outcomes in elite military recruits. *Leadership Quarterly*, 21, 20–32. doi:10.1016/j.leaqua.2009.10.002.

Hodge, K., Henry, G. and Smith, W. (2014). A case study of excellence in elite sport: Motivational climate in a world. *The Sport Psychologist*, 28, 60–74.

Hoption, C., Phelan, J., and Barling, J. (2008). Transformational leadership in sport. In M. R. Beauchamp and M. A. Eys (eds), *Group dynamics in exercise and sport psychology: Contempoary themes* (1st edn, pp. 45–60). New York: Routledge.

House, R. (1977). A 1976 theory of charismatic leadership. In J. G. Hunt and L. L. Larson (eds), *Leadership: The cutting edge.* Carbondale, IL: Southern Illinois University Press.

House, R. J. and Aditya, R. N. (1997). The social scientific study of leadership: Quo vadis. *Journal of Management*, 23, 409–473. doi:103–370–564.

Hox, J. J. (2010). *Multilevel analysis; techniques and applications quantitative methodology series* (2nd edn). Routledge: NY.

Judge, T. A. and Piccolo, R. F. (2004). Transformational and transactional leadership: A meta-analytic test of their relative validity. *Journal of Applied Psychology*, 89, 755–768. doi:10.1037/0021–9010.89.5.755.

Kelloway, E. K., Turner, N., Barling, J., and Loughlin, C. (2012). Transformational leadership and employee psychological well-being: The mediating role of employee trust in leadership. *Work and Stress*, 26, 39–55. doi:10.1080/02678373.2 012.660774.

Kent, A. and Chelladurai, P. (2001). Perceived transformational leadership, organisational commitment, and citizenship behaviour: A case study in intercollegiate athletics. *Journal of Sport Management*, 15, 135–159.

Lee, Y., Kim, S., and Joon-Ho, K. (2013). Coach leadership effect on elite handball players' psychological empowerment and organisational citizenship behaviour. *International Journal of Sports Science & Coaching*, 8, 327–342. doi:10.1260/ 1747–9541.8.2.327.

Leithwood, K. and Sun, J. (2012). The nature and effects of transformational school leadership: A meta-analytic review of unpublished research. *Educational Administration Quarterly*, 48, 387–423. doi:10.1177/0013161X11436268.

Lim, B. C. and Ployhart, R. E. (2004). Transformational leadership: Relations to the five-factor model and team performance in typical and maximum contexts. *Journal of Applied Psychology*, 89, 610–621. doi:10.1037/0021–9010.89.4.610.

Lowe, K. B. and Gardner, W. L. (2000). Ten years of the leadership quarterly: Contributions and challenges for the future. *Leadership Quarterly*, 11, 459–514. doi:10.1016/S1048–9843(00)00059-X.

Lowe, K. B., Kroeck, K. G., and Sivasubramaniam, N. (1996). Effectiveness correlates of transformational and transactional leadership: A meta-analytic review of the MLQ literature. *Leadership Quarterly*, 7, 385–425. doi:10.1016/ S1048–9843(96)90027-2.

MacDonald, D. J., Cote, J., Eys, M., and Deakin, J. (2012). Psychometric properties of the youth experience survey with young athletes. *Psychology of Sport and Exercise*, 13, 332–340. doi:10.1016/j.psychsport.2011.09.001.

Mawn, L., Hardy, J., Callow, N., and Arthur, C. (2012). Transformational leadership in higher education: Developing a measure. *International Journal of Psychology*, 47, 707–707.

McElligott, S. J., Arthur, C. A., and Callow, N. (2012). The impact of transformational leadership behaviours on self-esteem in the youth expedition context. *Journal of Sport and Exercise Psychology*, 34, S260–S261.

Menges, J. I., Walter, F., Vogel, B., and Bruch, H. (2011). Transformational leadership climate: Performance linkages, mechanisms, and boundary conditions at the organisational level. *Leadership Quarterly*, 22, 893–909. doi:10.1016/j.leaqua.2011.07.010.

Morton, K. L., Barling, J., Rhodes, R. E., Masse, L. C., Zumbo, B. D., and Beauchamp, M. R. (2011). The application of transformational leadership theory to parenting: Questionnaire development and implications for adolescent self-regulatory efficacy and life satisfaction. *Journal of Sport & Exercise Psychology*, 33, 688–709.

Mullen, J. E. and Kelloway, E. K. (2009). Safety leadership: A longitudinal study of the effects of transformational leadership on safety outcomes. *Journal of Occupational and Organisational Psychology*, 82, 253–272. doi:10.1348/096317908X325313.

Myers, N. D. and Beauchamp, M. R. (2011). Coaching competency and satisfaction with the coach: A multilevel structural equation model. *Journal of Sport and Exercise Psychology*, 33, S173–S173.

Myers, N. D. and Beauchamp, M. R. (2011). Coaching competency and satisfaction with the coach: A multilevel structural equation model. *Journal of Sport and Exercise Psychology*, 33, S173–S173.

Myers, N. D. and Feltz, D. L. (2007). From self-efficacy to collective efficacy in sport: Transitional methodological issues. In G. Tenenbaum and R. Eklund (eds), *Handbook of sport psychology* (pp. 799–819). Hoboken, NJ, US: John Wiley & Sons Inc.

Myers, N. D., Brincks, A. M., and Beauchamp, M. R. (2010). A tutorial on centering in cross-sectional two-level models. *Measurement in Physical Education and Exercise Science*, 14, 275–294.

Myers, N. D., Chase, M. A., Beauchamp, M. R., and Jackson, B. (2010). Athletes' perceptions of coaching competency scale II-high school teams. *Educational and Psychological Measurement*, 70, 477–494. doi:10.1177/0013164409344520.

Ntoumanis, N., Taylor, I. M., and Thogersen-Ntoumani, C. (2012). A longitudinal examination of coach and peer motivational climates in youth sport: Implications for moral attitudes, well-being, and behavioural investment. *Developmental Psychology*, 48, 213–223. doi:10.1037/a0024934.

Podsakoff, P., MacKenzie, S., Lee, J., and Podsakoff, N. (2003). Common method biases in behavioural research: A critical review of the literature and recommended remedies. *Journal of Applied Psychology*, 88, 879–903. doi:10.1037/0021-9101.88.5.879.

Podsakoff, P. M., MacKenzie, S. B., Moorman, R. H., and Fetter, R. (1990). Transformational leader behaviours and their effects on followers' trust in leader, satisfaction, and organisational citizenship behaviours. *The Leadership Quarterly*, 1, 107–142. doi:10.1016/1048-9843(90)90009-7.

Price, M. S. and Weiss, M. R. (2013). Relationships among coach leadership, peer leadership, and adolescent athletes' psychosocial and team outcomes: A test of transformational leadership theory. *Journal of Applied Sport Psychology*, 25, 265–279. doi:10.1080/10413200.2012.725703.

Rafferty, A. E. and Griffin, M. A. (2004). Dimensions of transformational leadership: Conceptual and empirical extensions. *Leadership Quarterly*, 15, 329–354. doi:10.1016/j.leaqua.2004.02.009.

Rafferty, A. E. and Griffin, M. A. (2006). Refining individualized consideration: Distinguishing developmental and supportive leadership. *Journal of Occupational and Organisational Psychology*, 79, 37–61. doi:10.1348/096317905X36731.

Rowold, J. (2006). Transformational and transactional leadership in martial arts. *Journal of Applied Sport Psychology*, 18, 312–325. doi:10.1080/10413200600944082.

Smith, M. J., Arthur, C. A., Hardy, J. T., Callow, N., and Williams, D. (2012). Transformational leadership and task cohesion in sport: The mediating role of intrateam communication. *Psychology of Sport and Exercise*, 14, 249–257.

Tucker, S., Turner, N., Barling, J., and McEvoy, M. (2010). Transformational leadership and childrens' aggression in team settings: A short-term longitudinal study. *Leadership Quarterly*, 21, 389–399. doi:10.1016/j.leaqua.2010.03.004.

Tucker, S., Turner, N., Barling, J., Reid, E., and Elving, C. (2006). Apologies and transformational leadership. *Journal of Business Ethics*, 63, 195–207. doi:10.1007/s10551-005-3571-0.

Vella, S. A., Oades, L. G., and Crowe, T. P. (2012). Validation of the differentiated transformational leadership inventory as a measure of coach leadership in youth soccer. *Sport Psychologist*, 26, 207–233.

Vella, S. A., Oades, L. G., and Crowe, T. P. (2013a). A pilot test of transformational leadership training for sports coaches: Impact on the developmental experiences of adolescent athletes. *International Journal of Sports Science & Coaching*, 8, 513–530.

Vella, S. A., Oades, L. G., and Crowe, T. P. (2013b). The relationship between coach leadership, the coach-athlete relationship, team success, and the positive developmental experiences of adolescent soccer players. *Physical Education and Sport Pedagogy*, 18, 549–561. doi:10.1080/17408989.2012.726976.

Weber, M. (1924). Legitimate authority and bureaucracy. *Organisation Theory: Selected Readings* (pp. 3–15). London: Penguin.

Weber, M. (1947). *The theory of social and economic organisation*. New York: Oxford University Press.

Yammarino, F. J. and Dubinsky, A. J. (1994). Transformational leadership theory – using levels of analysis to determine boundary-conditions. *Personnel Psychology*, 47, 787–811. doi:10.1111/j.1744-6570.1994.tb01576.x.

Yukl, G. (1999). An evaluation of conceptual weaknesses in transformational and charismatic leadership theories. *Leadership Quarterly*, 10, 285–305. doi:10.1016/S1048-9843(99)00013-2.

Zacharatos, A., Barling, J., and Kelloway, E. K. (2000). Development and effects of transformational leadership in adolescents. *Leadership Quarterly*, 11, 211–226. doi:10.1016/S1048-9843(00)00041-2.

# 8 Qualitative methods and conceptual advances in sport psychology

*Brett Smith, Nick Caddick and Toni Williams*

## Introduction

The use of qualitative methods in sport psychology is increasing (Culver *et al.*, 2012). But, what has this increase in qualitative methods done for sport psychology research? Our aim in this chapter is twofold; (1) to briefly survey the state of the field and comment on the conceptual advancements made with the increasing use of qualitative methods, and; (2) to guide future conceptual advancements by exploring how qualitative methods might be used better within sport psychology. In line with these aims, we first highlight the trend towards interviews as the dominant method of data collection in sport psychology research. We then highlight several criticisms that have been levelled at interview research – including our own work – in order to signal how interviews might be used better to conceptually advance the field of sport psychology. Next, we outline several worthwhile but under-utilised methods of data collection and suggest how an expansion of methods would advance the field of sport psychology conceptually. Finally, we offer some concluding thoughts on qualitative conceptual advances in sport psychology.

## Interviews in qualitative sport psychology research

Sport psychology researchers, it seems, like to interview athletes. A recent 'decade review' of qualitative research in sport psychology journals revealed that 78.1 per cent of studies from 2000–2009 used interviews (most often 'semi-structured' ones) as a method of data collection (Culver *et al.*, 2012). The reasons for this dominance of interviews are perhaps understandable; when done well, they can result in good, rich, storied data from athletes about their sport experiences over time and across contexts. They can also be a relatively direct way of collecting such data (e.g. by simply asking the athletes themselves 'what's it like?') whilst simultaneously allowing athletes the flexibility to narrate their experiences as they see fit. Accordingly we do not wish to jettison the use of interviews in sport psychology. Indeed, we have used them – and continue to use them – in our own research. Rather, we seek to highlight a number of problems/ criticisms of interviewing which, if ignored, could limit future conceptual advances in sport psychology. Many of these criticisms can be applied to ourselves and our own research over the years. Therefore, as we become increasingly reflexive about our own use of interviews, we seek to highlight how interviewing can be used to conduct better qualitative research in sport psychology.

The first problem with interviews concerns their use as a way to understand athletes' individual lived experiences. For some (e.g. Potter and Hepburn, 2005), using interviews to understand lived experience is problematic as it wrongly assumes that the nature of experience can be accurately and pristinely described by the individual him or herself. In particular, it is often assumed that lived experience derives from within the mind of the individual, flowing *outwards* from the person into the world through talk. This view of lived experience as individual and 'in the mind' typically reflects a cognitivist perspective. Cognitivism emphasises individual mental processes as the basic object of psychological study, typically conceiving of the mind as an 'information processor'. Consistent with this emphasis on internal, individual processes, sport psychology interviews are often framed by a desire to understand what Potter and Hepburn (2005) refer to as 'POBAs'; Perceptions, Opinions, Beliefs, and Attitudes. For example, researchers might typically ask athletes to describe their perceptions of 'feeling stressed', 'thinking tough', or possibly even their attitudes towards their 'coach–athlete relationships'. However, trying to understand lived experience solely through interviewing athletes about their POBA's prevents a more multidimensional understanding of athletes' lives and thus restricts conceptual advances. The reasons for this are unpacked below.

In cognitivism, psychological concepts like motivation, mental toughness, and resilience are assumed to originate from and reside within the mind of the individual athlete. This assumption has been critiqued in the recent sporting literature. Smith (2013a), for example, described how the concept of resilience derives from the relationships *between* people, rather than from an individual's mental interior. As Smith suggested, 'we come to self-awareness and self-knowledge (e.g. about resilience) in the context of our interactions and relations with others.' (p. 146). The relational psychology (Gergen, 2009) perspective that framed Smith's approach provides an alternative to cognitivist understandings of resilience that may help to advance the conceptual basis of this and other phenomena in sport psychology. A relational perspective emphasises humans as fundamentally 'relational beings', with concepts of 'mind' and 'mental processes' understood as emerging from *relationships between* people, rather than from individual persons (Gergen, 2009). Accordingly, sport psychology researchers using interviews to collect data may need to become more cautious/reflexive about positioning POBAs as 'things' that people 'have' somewhere inside their individual minds and which, in turn, can be represented in transparent ways through talk.

One response to the problem of assuming that an interview can capture individual, lived experience in a transparent or mirror like way that we (e.g. Caddick and Ryall, 2012; Phoenix and Smith, 2011; Smith, 2013a, 2013b) and others (e.g. Douglas and Carless, 2009; McMahon and Penney, 2013) have adopted is to think of methods like interviewing as a technique for illuminating the role of culture and relationships in shaping lived experience. Athletes are immersed within sporting cultures and sub-cultures which inevitably help to constitute their psychological experiences in sport. Sporting cultures and sub-cultures powerfully shape athletes' lived experiences in sport, influencing what they *can* do, what they *ought* to do, and what they *must not* do. For instance, sport culture can help promote the use of performance enhancing drugs to carry on training whilst injured, encourage athletes to make personal sacrifices for the good of their team, or to dedicate their entire lives to the pursuit of a singular athletic goal. Accordingly, sport cultures have great potential to influence the ways in which athletes think, feel, and act in the realm of sport, yet culture is often glossed over by researchers emphasising individual experiences in interview research. How, then, might this be reversed? What approaches might help orientate our attention to culture and how cultures constitute our experiences?

There are a number of approaches that use interviews to understand the role of culture in shaping athletes' lived experience in sport (Smith and McGannon, in press). One example is narrative inquiry (Phoenix & Orr, 2014; Smith and Sparkes, 2009a, 2009b; Sparkes and Smith, 2009). Narrative inquiry examines the stories people tell about their sporting experiences, and the effects that certain stories can have *on*, *in*, and *for* athletes' lives and psychological worlds. A key assumption of narrative inquiry is that people organise their experiences into narratives and assign meaning to them through storytelling. Moreover, the stories athletes use to assign meaning to their experiences are not simply personal creations, but are borrowed and adapted from the dominant storylines provided by the sporting cultures in which they are immersed (Smith and Sparkes, 2009a; Sparkes *et al.*, 2012). For this reason, narrative enables us to turn a cultural lens on interviewing and broaden our view of athletes' lived experiences. As Smith and Sparkes (2009a) suggested:

> Given our personal stories are constituted through narratives that society and culture make available, then, as Riessman (1993) points out, *socio-cultural life* 'speaks itself' through an individual's story. For this reason, rather than leaving the social unexamined or in the background, narratives may illuminate and foreground the multifaceted forms of socio-cultural life and the different ways they can operate in our sporting and physically (in)active lives.
>
> (p. 6; emphasis in original)

An example of this type of research in sport psychology is provided by Douglas and Carless (2009). These authors used interviews to explore two women's stories of athletic career transition out of professional sport. Exploring how culture 'spoke itself' through these women's stories, they examined the influence of a cultural 'performance narrative' upon the women's identity and well-being as they transitioned out of sport. As described by Douglas and Carless, the performance narrative consists of:

> A story of single-minded dedication to sport performance to the exclusion of other areas of life and self. Within the plot of the performance narrative, winning, results, and achievements are pre-eminent and link closely to the storyteller's mental well-being, identity, and self-worth.
>
> (p. 215)

Douglas and Carless identified the performance narrative as by far the culturally preferred narrative within elite sport. For the two women in their study, this cultural narrative exerted a powerful influence upon their lives, complicating their transition out of sport and resulting in significant damage to health and well-being when the performance narrative ceased to 'fit' their lives. The research by Douglas and Carless conceptually advances the area of career transitions in sport psychology by showing 'how the personal process of withdrawal [from sport] is necessarily affected by socio-cultural and historical factors' (p. 226); and not, therefore, located solely within the individual.

The second problem with interviews involves focusing exclusively on *what* athletes say (i.e. content) whilst neglecting to consider that *how* they say it (i.e. form) is also important to describing their sporting experiences. As noted by Culver *et al.* (2012), the majority of interview research in sport psychology focuses primarily on content. Focusing on content grants primacy to athletes' descriptions of *what* their lived experiences *are*, often in an attempt to refine researchers' conceptual understandings of sporting phenomena. This has notably been the case with regard to concepts central to the area of 'high performance' psychology such as confidence, motivation, resilience, flow, stress and anxiety, and mental toughness. Researchers investigating such concepts have tended to focus on athletes' perceptions of what these concepts *are* and how they are cultivated or experienced. For example, in relation to the concept of flow, Sparkes and Partington (2003) note that producing definitive lists, components, and characteristics that define the experience of flow has been of central concern. However, focusing exclusively on the '*whats*' of interviews, can mean the equally important '*hows*' of talk are neglected.

*How* athletes tell stories in interviews necessarily shapes the meaning of their lived experiences and what gets communicated to the interviewer. For example, how someone structures the language they use to convey an experience (e.g. the metaphorical language used to explain something) inevitably shapes how that experience is communicated and understood. How athletes actually *express* what they say is important too, for example with a shout, a nod, or a silence; so the popular expression goes, 'it's not what you said, it's the way you said it!' A focus on the *hows* of storytelling in interviews thus shifts from the content of what is said, to understanding the structures of the story being told and how these shape the meanings of participants' experiences. Therefore, rather than ask 'what does the story tell us about X?' the broad question becomes, 'how is X constructed in the telling?' Exemplars of sport psychology research exploring *how* athletes talk in interviews are rare. However, one detailed and instructive example can be found in the work of Sparkes and Partington (2003) on the concept of flow.

The third problem with interviews relates to flooding the interview with social science jargon and the agendas and categories of the researcher (Potter and Hepburn, 2005). The specific questions that researchers ask, along with the broader topics and lines of questioning they pursue, are often dominated by their own concern with understanding a particular concept in greater detail. Accordingly, they might ask athletes about their resilience, mental toughness, flow experiences, or even about their ego-oriented motivation. The problem here is that participants are asked to frame their responses in terms of the *researcher's* concepts; concepts which may not exist for the participants themselves. One reason why this can be problematic is that the participant might simply not understand what they are being asked. However, a deeper problem is that participants tend not to think about their everyday experiences in terms of social scientific concepts. As such, when participants are asked to describe their experiences using the researcher's concepts, they may be subtly coerced into dressing their experience up in terms which have little meaning or relevance to their lives. As Potter and Hepburn (2005) put it:

> At its most basic these issues present us with the possibility that a piece of interview research is chasing its own tail, offering up its own agendas and categories and getting those same agendas and categories back in a refined or filtered or inverted form.
>
> (p. 293)

One possible response to this problem for researchers who wish to retain the strengths of interviews as a method of data collection is to become more reflexive about the phrasing of their questions and possibly to adopt a more 'unstructured' style of interviewing in which the researcher follows the participant's lead. Unstructured interviews hand control over to the participant and grant them the freedom to describe events, emotions and behaviours in messy and more detailed ways (Sparkes and Smith, 2014). However, there is another possible response that sidesteps the issue of flooding the interview with the researcher's concepts and categories by turning to 'naturally occurring data'. This is where 'the activity being recorded would have happened as it would have anyway; it is not got up by the researcher, for example by way of an open-ended interview' (Potter and Hepburn, 2005, p. 301). Again, examples in sport psychology are rare. One exception is the work of Zucchermaglio and Alby (2012). These authors conducted a narrative analysis of team meetings of a professional soccer team both before and after matches over a two-month period. The 'data' they were exploring (e.g. discussions between coaches and players) would have taken place anyway, regardless of their involvement as researchers. Zucchermaglio and Alby were thus able to consider how different narrative forms were used by the coaches when planning and assessing performance before and after matches. They then examined the impact of these narrative forms on players' actions and behaviours:

> Narratives provided a shared frame in which the coach made suggestions, underlined errors, sanctioned wrong behaviour and oriented the players towards the behaviour he wanted from them. Such regular occasions for sharing may have had an important bearing also on the fact that the team won the championship that year.
>
> (p. 467)

The research by Zucchermaglio and Alby thus provides an innovative example of how 'naturally occurring data' can be used to make conceptual advances in sport psychology.

The fourth problem with interviews, intimately connected to the problem of lived experience, concerns an under-appreciation of the interview itself as *co-constructed* between interviewer and interviewee. Rather than interviewing being seen as an *individual* event in which the task is to understand just the interviewee and what they simply say, the interview needs to be understood as an inescapably *social* event. It is an *interaction* between at least two people – the teller and the listener – that profoundly influences the data collected. As Randall and Phoenix (2009) put it, 'Stories are told in particular situations to particular listeners for particular reasons' (p. 126). Moreover, exactly *how* the teller's story unfolds (as well as *what* they include and exclude from that story) is shaped by a range of interpersonal factors and how people respond to a story (Smith and Sparkes, 2011). Most obviously, the phrasing of questions and the particular line of questioning the interviewer adopts will influence how the teller's story emerges. The teller may also wish the listener (interviewer) to perceive them in certain ways, adapting their story and the language used to express it accordingly. Still other factors influence the storytelling process such as the how people were recruited for the study, the participant's situation and life circumstances at the time of the interview, and the teller's reconstruction of memories (perhaps distant ones) in line with the present concerns of the interview (Randall and Phoenix, 2009). None of these features of interviewing are necessarily problematic for qualitative sport psychology researchers. Indeed, since we are 'finite' beings, unable to extricate ourselves from the process of data collection, this is simply how it is. Such features of interviewing should, however, lead the researcher to a greater appreciation of the *inter-subjective context* of interviews, and to become more reflexive about their role in the co-construction of the data (Randall and Phoenix, 2009; Sparkes and Smith, 2014).

One possible response (not a solution) to this issue is to include more of the interviewer's talk in the published research. This increases transparency and helps the reader understand how a particular story or quote emerged within the interview. Consider, for example, the following interview exchange taken from Smith's (2013b) research on disability and leisure-time physical activity:

INTERVIEWER: Are there any other reasons you keep exercising?

MATT: Sure. Appearance a little. I certainly don't want to get a belly, I'm too disciplined for that anyhow. But I exercise mainly because I feel I should, to care for my health, and there are added benefits like more function and independence. That's huge for me. It's meant I've been able to work in a demanding job and get my self-worth back as a man. Every man needs to work and exercising has given me more energy, more independence, which means I can work, and work harder, and can now contribute to society. (p. 115)

Including the interviewer's questions helps to show how the data was co-constructed between teller and listener. However, appreciating the inter-subjective context of the interview goes beyond this simple practice. As Smith *et al.* (2005) explain:

Undoubtedly it is good practice to reinsert the interviewer into the analysis ... but this is a peripheral part of a greater problem which is the separation of relatively short extracts of text from the context of the whole interview encounter for analytic purposes. The responses of the interviewee at a particular juncture do not just relate back to the last few utterances of the interviewer and not just to the last question that was asked. They are built up out of the whole history of the research encounter: how they were recruited, what they were told the interview was about, what happened before the tape recorder was switched on, the continuous dynamics (not just conscious) between interviewee and interviewer. This cannot all be represented in the text and so it becomes part of the researcher's responsibility to reflect on these effects and trace them in the context of the whole, providing evidence from the record.

(p. 312)

Understanding the inter-subjective context of interviews therefore means that sport psychology researchers should strive to understand how they have shaped and ultimately *co-authored* their participants' stories (Randall and Phoenix, 2009), and what effect this has had on their understanding of the topic under investigation.

The fifth problem of interviews, related to the issue of co-construction, involves how the interviewer handles trust and rapport within the interview. Most qualitative research textbooks suggest that researchers should always aim to establish trust and rapport to encourage participants to 'open up' about their lives. This can be important, yet there are dangers too. For example, close rapport with participants can shut off lines of inquiry just as it might open up others. Furthermore, it is often suggested or presupposed that to understand others, to attain knowledge and to do so in ethically admirable ways, we should empathise with our participants by imaginatively putting ourselves in the place of the other. However, to assume that we *can* put ourselves in place of another is problematic because it suggests we can transcend our differences with the participant and truly know what it is like to be them. But this is elusive and ethically dangerous (see Smith, 2008). What this means is that a researcher can empathise and use their imagination, but if they do, they cannot think they can put himself or herself in another person's place and truly imagine being them. If they do they risk denying the difference between self and other.

As an example of when trust and rapport can be useful in interviews, consider the following excerpt from one of the authors' (Nick Caddick) reflexive research journal. The excerpt was recorded following an interview that Nick conducted with a military combat veteran named Eric (pseudonym) as part of Nick's doctoral research exploring the effects of surfing in the lives of combat veterans diagnosed with post-traumatic stress disorder (PTSD) (see Caddick, Smith & Phoenix, 2015 and in press). Eric had just shared his highly emotional story of combat-related PTSD:

> When Eric had finished telling his story, I made sure to thank him sincerely for talking so openly about his experiences. During the interview, I had sat there respectfully allowing his story to unfold – prompting when necessary – but often deadly silent as Eric slowly recalled the horrors he had encountered and the misery of his suffering. Eric told me later that talking openly was a big deal for him as he tends not to let people in: 'I don't trust no fucker!' Why, then, had he trusted me with his story? Talking with Eric after the interview, he said there was something about me that was easy to open up to. He said he felt as though he could tell me these things – not that I would understand – but perhaps that I might appreciate them. I am heartened that Eric has extended this confidence to me, and I feel privileged to have witnessed stories that many civilians are not permitted to share.

As this excerpt suggests, trust and rapport as part of the emerging relationship between interviewer and interviewee were crucial to how the story eventually unfolded (and even that it was told in the first place). The ability to cultivate trust and rapport during interview encounters is a useful skill for qualitative researchers to develop. However, as noted, researchers also need to guard against over-rapport and the dangers of empathising too closely with participants. As such, Sparkes and Smith (2014) thus offer the following guideline:

> When appropriate, seek to establish rapport and empathy in order to build trusting relationships so that participants are more willing to be 'open' about their lives. Be mindful of over-rapport and, in turn, becoming too familiar and overlooking matters that need to be problematised. Also be wary of attempting to empathise with participants by imaginatively putting yourself in the place of them. This is elusive and a problem as there is a risk of projecting one's own fears, interests and values onto the other.
>
> (p. 95)

The final problem of interviewing concerns the issue of truth. As Randall and Phoenix (2009) put it, 'truth becomes an issue for researchers in sport the moment we find ourselves wondering what it is the people whom we interview are telling us' (p. 125). Much traditional qualitative work in sport psychology tends to assume that interviews grant us direct, unmediated access to the truth of participants' experiences. However, this view is problematic on multiple levels. First, it assumes that '*theory-free knowledge*' can be achieved. That is to say, researchers can somehow discover the participant's mental/social reality in ways that are independent of their interests, purposes, and languages used – we can step outside our own experiences and history and discover the truth uninfluenced, uncontaminated, by whom we are. However, none of this can be done. Whilst we accept that there are physical beings out there moving around in time and space and uttering in interviews what we can call data, our or anybody else's interpretations/descriptions of these movements and utterances are not out there in the sense of being independent of our interests and purposes. This is because who we are is crucial to how we see the world, and standing outside of our own experiences and history is beyond us as humans. Hence, we can't achieve theory-free knowledge: neither our participants nor we as researchers can be a transparent reporter of some independent domain and be a 'truthful' witness of a world independent of our interpretation of it (Sparkes and Smith, 2014).

A second issue with truth in interviewing has to do with the language participants use to express their experiences. It is often assumed that participants' words are an accurate reflection of their lived experiences; that they are simply and faithfully reporting what happened. However, once again this view is problematic. This is because language structures our thoughts and actually constitutes, rather than reflects, our experiences. For instance, by choosing to describe an experience in this way, not that, the meaning of that experience is altered both for the participant describing the experience, and the researcher attempting to understand it. The participant's choice of words forecloses certain meanings that could potentially be attributed to experience whilst ushering others in. This is the case even for the most articulate of research participants. This is not to say that participants are being deliberately deceptive or are prone to misrepresenting their experience through their stories. Rather, it is a recognition that language is no clear and transparent medium for describing experience, and that our choice of language strongly influences the meaning of what is conveyed and understood. As such, we can't rely on words to give us access to the truth.

Another issue with truth relates to method. A common assumption is that methods (such as interviewing) when properly followed will enable us to access the truth of participants' experiences. One reason (as stated above) why this assumption is misguided is because interviewing relies fundamentally on the use of language. A further reason is that methods are not the neutral and independent tools they are often considered to be for objectively conducting research. Methods are useful, yet they are human constructions, and dependent then on us. In other words, people construct methods and we construct them in line with our particular interests, purposes, and so on. As such, methods are not neutral nor can they secure procedural objectivity. Given this, methods cannot then help us out in terms of making contact with the truth independent of us. This leaves us once again with the position in which we started: we have to just accept we cannot, no matter how hard we try, know if the participant is really telling the truth as it is. This is just how it is.

Accepting that we cannot discover the truth of our participants' experiences, however, does not mean that we should abandon the issue of truth or that simply 'anything goes'; that just any claims about a participant's life and experiences are as good as any others. What it does mean is that we need to ask more sensitive questions about truth and begin to reconsider how 'truth' is conceptualised in qualitative sport psychology interviews. Following Smith (1989, 2009), we can start by saying that truth is a contingent social agreement. As Smith (1989) put it, 'truth – or what we come to accept as true in terms of intentions, purposes, and meanings – is the result of socially conditioned agreement, arising from dialogue and reasoned discourse' (p. 171).

Furthermore, as part of treating truth as a contingent social agreement, we need to be sensitive to the constitutive function of language. As noted, what the participant says in an interview does not reflect the truth of past experience. Their words create and re-create the very events they reflect upon. In this sense, what they say becomes their experience, and feels for them truthful and meaningful at that particular time. As Frank (2013) notes,

The truth of stories is not only what *was* experienced, but equally what *becomes* experience in the telling and its reception. The stories we tell about our lives are not necessarily those lives as they were lived, but these stories may become our experience of those lives.... Life moves on, stories change with that movement, and experience changes. Stories are true to the flux of experience, and the story affects the direction of that flux.

(p. 22)

As such, 'what is the truth of participants' experiences?' is not a meaningful question for qualitative sport psychology researchers. Rather, researchers should consider 'how do participants' experiences come to be accepted as true, and in what contexts, times, places, and cultures are these experiences made meaningful?'

## Potentials of diversification in sport psychology research methodologies

In this section, we propose a range of alternatives to interviewing that may help to diversify and enrich the field methodologically. Different methods in qualitative research that are employed in other academic disciplines, but somewhat underutilised within sport psychology, will be examined for their potential to generate data that can conceptually advance the field. We will focus on observational methods, visual methods and the use of the internet as tools for data collection, interpretation and (re)presentation. These methods can be used in conjunction with, or as an alternative to the standard interview method to enhance our understanding of the relational and cultural aspects of athletes' psychological worlds. Thus, we do not advocate abandoning interviews. Rather, we seek a more reflexive approach to interviews grounded partly in the problems identified above plus seek, in what follows, to expand our repertoire of methods for collecting data (see also Smith and Caddick, 2012; Sparkes and Smith, 2014).

### Observational methods

Observation is one method that can advance the field of sport psychology as it enables the researcher to reconceptualise the difference between what is *said* in interviews, and what is *done* in elite sport practice. Furthermore, observational methods enable the examination of peoples' lives in *real time* and 'record the mundane, taken-for-granted, and unremarkable (to participants) features of everyday life that interviewees might not feel were worth commenting on' (Sparkes and Smith, 2014, p. 100).

Observational methods as data collection involve perceiving the workings of people, culture and society through one's senses and documenting these in field notes. The difference with participant observation is that the researcher *participates* (physically, cognitively, socially, sensually, and/or emotionally) in the daily lives and culture of the participants (Sparkes and Smith, 2014). It is, however, difficult to distinguish between observation and participant observation as the researcher can take on a range of roles within the field. These include:

- Complete observer – the researcher does not actively participate but observes what occurs and how (non-participant observation).
- Observer as participant – the researcher mostly observes but may have a minor role in participating in the field.
- Participant as observer – the researcher participates in the daily activities of the social group whilst still observing.
- Complete participant – the researcher immerses themselves in the culture of the social group and observes whilst fully participating.

These different roles are not static but exist along a continuum as the researcher may move between positions during data collection. Within observational settings field notes include, but are not limited to; what is going on, commenting on the people in the field, where and when the social interactions take place and why this is happening (Sparkes and Smith, 2014). Additionally, to account for the different roles researchers can adopt in the field, they must be reflexive about how they have influenced the data collected in their notes.

Observational methods are typically used within ethnographic research, but are not exclusive to this tradition. Observation is a suitable method for data collection within ethnography because this tradition is concerned with the exploration over time of the culture of a particular group from the perspective of the group members. Observation is however also employed within other traditions such as phenomenology and narrative inquiry. Phenomenology is the study of a phenomena (appearances/lived experiences), through how they are perceived by the actors involved. Narrative inquiry on the other hand is the examination of the stories people tell to make meaning of their life (Sparkes and Smith, 2014). Participant observation can benefit research in sport psychology in these traditions by providing a contextual understanding of peoples' relations, actions and emotions. This is because observational methods permit a much lengthier and more 'involved' engagement in the field and therefore allow for processes to be examined over time. An additional strength of this method of data collection is that it can be a route to *knowing people* rather than *knowing about them* (Sparkes and Smith, 2014).

The use of observational methods within sport psychology has been suggested as a method for 'enhancing our understanding of the psychology of athletes' sport experiences and diversifying research tactics in sport psychology' (Krane and Baird, 2005, p. 87). In particular, ethnographic research in sport psychology could be prolific in evaluating applied sport psychology interventions and enhancing multicultural understandings of psychological concepts (Krane and Baird, 2005). Unlike some more novel techniques (discussed below), the use of observation is evident in recent sport psychology literature. For example, Cowan *et al.*'s (2012) study on coaching shows how observation can be used to make conceptual advances. Cowan *et al.* employed an instrumental case study to investigate how self-determination theory (SDT) could inform soccer coaching practices with disadvantaged youth. Using non-participant observation of the coaching sessions, video footage and field notes, enabled the authors to gain an understanding of the context within which coaches and participants interacted. The authors then employed semi-structured interviews to discuss and further clarify the participants' reaction to coaching.

The combination of methods in Cowan *et al.*'s (2012) study facilitated a 'comprehensive and plausible picture of the coaches and participants' experiences' (p. 371). The use of qualitative methods and observation in particular provided an alternative perspective of SDT-based coaching to the dominant quantitative based assumptions within the literature. For example, as Cowan *et al.* explained, 'the mixed consequences of a controlling interpersonal style was a common theme in the data, and goes beyond the proposal that controlling behaviour leads to negative outcomes' (pp. 370–371). Accordingly, through observation this research conceptually advanced the field by providing a body of evidence highlighting the impact of 'situation-specific' factors on SDT-based coaching. The conceptual status of SDT-based coaching is thus enhanced by warnings against broadly promoting autonomy support and reproving controlling coaching.

Another example of the use of observational methods to conceptually advance the field can be seen in the ethnography by Shilling and Bunsell (2009) on female bodybuilders. The aim of their research was to explore and portray the values, practices and norms of the lived experiences of the marginalised group that is female bodybuilders. The observational aspect of ethnography was suitable to uncover the *way of life* of these bodybuilders. This is because the primary researcher, Tanya, became an *insider* of this culture:

> During the period of the study she immersed herself in the routines of this lifestyle by training, dieting and interacting with female bodybuilders. While not regarding herself as a bodybuilder, Tanya was sufficiently strong to gain the respect of these women when working out with them, while not being so visibly muscular that she was unable to pass as an 'ordinary user' to other gym members and to those friends and family members she interviewed.
>
> (p. 144)

As this extract highlights, Tanya was acting the role of complete participant. This in itself was beneficial to the research project. The fact that

Tanya was female, and of approximately the same age as the female body-builders, meant that she could make initial contact with the participants. Subsequently, Tanya's commitment to weight training convinced the other bodybuilders that she was sympathetic to, and serious in her efforts to understand a culture normally ostracised by others (Shilling and Bunsell, 2009). By utilising observational methods the authors were able to explore the issues concerned with experiences of body building and how these female bodybuilders constructed their identities. This example highlights how observational methods can conceptually advance the field by facilitating access to cultures that are not easily permeated by *outsiders* to that culture.

### Diaries

A diary is a frequently kept record of thoughts, feelings and ideas about personal experiences and observations. A diary could therefore be a useful methodological tool for data collection as it allows participants to report on experiences *as they are lived*. In other words, diaries offer the potential to conceptually advance the field by collecting 'rich data that may not have been gained using alternative methods such as interview due to its reliance on retrospective recall' (Day and Thatcher, 2009, p. 250).

Keeping a diary is an act of *self-writing* where the 'writer engages in active self-creation by transcribing personal reflections and experiences onto paper, thus gaining self-knowledge, gathering and recording information and creating a permanent record of his life' (MacKay and Dallaire, 2013b, p. 187). The use of diaries and the act of reflective writing has been shown within sport psychology research to offer multiple bene-fits to elite athletes. Fletcher and Wilson (2013) explored the use of reflec-tive diaries during competition as a self-help tool for elite cricket players. They found that self-writing was beneficial in that it offered the cricketers 'a heightened sensibility for personal reflection; offering valuable oppor-tunities for cathartic release; and facilitating participants to overcome neg-ative experiences' (p. 282). Whilst the use of diaries as a therapeutic tool is well established in psychology for such reasons like cathartic release, the use of a diary as a methodological tool for data collection is limited within the field (Day and Thatcher, 2009).

One example of the use of diaries in qualitative research is offered by Day and Thatcher (2009). They explored the use of a handwritten daily participant diary as a tool for data collection regarding stress in athletes. The diary was a suitable method of data collection for a number of reasons. First, participants were able to complete diary entries soon after important events as they could take them to training and competitions. This limits the timeframe between the experience and the participants' recall of that experience. Second, keeping a diary for the duration of a training period or competition season permits a longitudinal study design.

This allows for the examination of changes over time. Third, written accounts in diaries provide an insight into how each athlete interprets an event and makes meaning of their experiences. In other words, 'by ascribing meaning, the diary keeper allows the reader a personal insight into their own rationalizations of actions' (Day and Thatcher, 2009, p. 250). Lastly, participants were able to write about sensitive or confidential information which they may not have felt comfortable to discuss in an interview setting.

Whilst the use of a diary can provide a rich source of information that may be unobtainable or inaccessible through an interview, there is one potential drawback. In this instance the researcher has no control over the diary entries and relies on the participant to complete them at the required time point and with sufficient depth and detail. Day and Thatcher (2009) suggest that to overcome this, the researcher needs to encourage their participants to complete their diary entries and show an interest in their accounts. The duration of time the participants are expected to complete the diary needs to be negotiated so as to not place excessive demands on the participants. This should help alleviate response fatigue when filling in the diary and will be dependent upon the phenomenon under investigation. However, as elite athletes are often used to filling in training diaries, they may be an easily accessible method of data collection for future sport psychology research.

### Visual methods

The use of visual methods to *collect* data rather than just *represent* data is growing within qualitative research in general. However, despite growth in visual methods in other social science disciplines, its use as a tool to offer a different way of seeing the world has been underutilised in sport psychology.

Despite this, there are a number of reasons why sport psychology researchers might consider using visual methods. First, visual methods utilise a range of different visual media such as photography, paintings, drawings, videography, drama, and dance to generate, interpret and communicate knowledge. These methods are able to 'embrace emotional, sensory, embodied and imaginative ways of knowing that lead to richer knowledge production and communication processes' (Blodgett *et al.*, 2013, p. 312). Second, visual methods provide a much needed supplement, and in some cases alternative, to the dominance of language-based research methods in qualitative sport psychology research. Third, visual methods address the ocular. In other words, collecting and examining images is important because 'images can act on, in, and for us in powerful ways, shaping how are we able to see, how are we allowed to see, what is to be seen, what is not seen, and what we do and don't do' (Sparkes and Smith, 2014, p. 105). Lastly, given the potential power of visual methods to *do* things and affect us in various ways, they can be examined as both as a *topic* (analysing what the image may do both *for* and *on* us) or a *resource* (when using visual material to explore a specific issue).

Whether using visual methods as a topic or a resource, there are various forms of visual data to be considered. *Found visual data* is concerned with images and representations that are already available in the field. In sport psychology research this would include media images, magazine articles and photos, newspaper images, and posters. Another form of collecting visual data is via *respondent-generated* and *researcher-generated* methods. Through the medium of film, photography, and drawing to name but a few, either the participant or researcher can produce images that represent an experience (Phoenix, 2010). In the case of participant-created 'auto-photography', the participant can be asked to take person-ally meaningful photographs relating to a specific research question or purpose. *Co-constructed visual data* on the other hand is where the researcher and participant collaborate to produce visual material together. Here, both parties invest in the process and outcome of the project making this a suitable method for participatory action research (PAR; Schinke *et al.*, 2013; Sparkes and Smith, 2014).

PAR is a tradition of qualitative research that is committed to facilit-ating social or institutional change and actively involves participants in the research process and product. The knowledge created through PAR is thought to be more powerful as it is collaboratively produced through action. Visual methods in this context may also be referred to as participa-tory methods because they 'facilitate participants in finding their own lan-guage to articulate what they know and help them put words to their ideas and share understandings of their worlds, thereby giving participants more control over the research process' (Enright and O'Sullivan, 2012, p. 36). Participants may also find visual methods more engaging as the practical activities can provide a more enjoyable means of generating data.

One example where more than one respondent-generated visual data is utilised in research is provided by Enright and O'Sullivan (2012). They evaluated the use of photovoice and timelining together in PAR with young people. The use of *Photovoice*, or what is commonly referred to also as *autophotography*, is a method whereby participants are given the oppor-tunity to take photos and then discuss them openly. In this instance stu-dents were asked to take photos of various aspects of their lives including their experiences of physical activity. *Timelining* on the other hand is a drawing-based method that visually represents how a participant makes sense of experience over time. Here, the participant draws a temporal graph that plots both positive and negative experiences of a specific subject as it changes over time. For example, timelining in Enright and O'Sullivan's research involved students plotting critical incidents that had either positively or negatively impacted their engagement with physical activity using drawings and written texts. Unlike photos, timelining gave the students the opportunity to engage in their history of physical activity by identifying these critical moments over time.

Photovoice and timelines were used to support and enhance, rather than replace, interview and observational methods of data collection. This point was of importance to Enright and O'Sullivan as 'Neither the photographs nor the timelines were ever allowed speak for themselves. The images, both photographs and timelines, only became meaningful through the interpretative work of the participants' (pp. 49–50). Being able to discuss and understand what may lie outside of the photographs and beyond the timeline impacted upon the researchers' interpretations of this data. Additionally, photographs and timelines allowed access to knowledge that might not be possible through conventional methods. Participants were able to express their experiences outside of the boundaries set by language:

> They supported sense-making, in that the dialogue they promoted required participants to engage critically with what they had photographed, made, drawn, said or written. In these conversations, participants examined their beliefs, assumptions and their patterns of behaviour. In telling and hearing each other's stories of disengagement they came to reassess their lives and their individual and collective relationship with physical education and physical activity.
>
> (p. 49)

Through the use of visual methods and PAR, sport psychology practitioners may be able to access previously undiscovered or neglected knowledge by working *with* rather than *on* athletes.

The use of visual methods can also conceptually advance the field of sport psychology by capturing a multi-dimensional, embodied and nuanced understanding of a lived experience which may otherwise remain absent or ineffable (Phoenix, 2010). In other words, visual methods may provide an insight into groups or communities that are inaccessible solely through verbal means. One use of visual methods has been to enhance conceptual understandings of the sporting experiences of marginalised, non-Western cultural groups. This is in response to a call for researchers to design approaches to research that are methodologically and epistemologically in line with these cultures and to 'embrace local ways of knowing' (Blodgett *et al.*, 2013, p. 314). For example, McHugh *et al.* (2013) used photovoice as a single visual method to provide Aboriginal youth with the opportunity to share their culturally situated knowledge of sport. In this instance a photovoice approach was requested by the participants as 'such approaches are founded on the assumption that community members are experts of their own experiences and are able to develop their own relevant research agendas' (p. 294). Moreover, the photos that represented participants' layered meanings embedded within sport were discussed through *talking circles*; a storytelling experience which has sacred meaning to Indigenous cultures. As McHugh *et al.* concluded, the use of photovoice therefore afforded a unique opportunity to engage with Aboriginal youth:

> This research makes a contribution to the sport literature in that the often overlooked expertise of Aboriginal youth has been highlighted. This research also makes a methodological contribution to the sport literature in that it provides a practical example of how youth can be actively engaged in research through participatory approaches. Not only did the youth optimise on an opportunity to share their knowledge but, possibly more importantly, they requested and enjoyed the photovoice approach.
>
> (p. 307)

Expanding upon the use of photography in PAR, Blodgett *et al.* (2013) employed an arts-based method to explore the experiences of young Aboriginal athletes who relocated to pursue sporting opportunities, thus enhancing conceptual understandings within this population (see also Blodgett *et al.*, 2011). In particular, the authors explored how 'mandala' drawings could facilitate gaining locally resonant knowledge. Mandala drawings are a culturally relevant art form and therefore offer a 'culturally affirming space for Aboriginal athletes to share sport experiences' (p. 312). Photovoice may then be combined with interviews to enable the participant to reflect upon the details (colour, shape, size, content etc.) of their drawing, to share and interpret how it relates to their sporting experiences. This visual method was beneficial in creating knowledge on sport relocation that was more accessible and relevant at the community level than traditional forms of data collection and presentation. Drawing mandalas was a method of conducting research that played on the strengths and capabilities of the Aboriginal youth, rather than solely relying on words and talk. Moreover the mandala drawings acted as a tool to generate a more holistic understanding of their experiences and facilitate different ways of knowing about these experiences that were aligned with their culture (Blodgett *et al.*, 2013).

As these examples highlight, conducting research through visual methods has the potential to conceptually advance the field of sport psychology. As noted by Enright and O'Sullivan (2012) 'Rethinking how knowledge is produced and what role our participants play in the production, interpretation and dissemination of this knowledge could be methodologically beneficial' (p. 51). Similarly, for Phoenix (2010) the use of visual images in sport 'have the ability to construct and convey arguments whilst powerfully indicating the multiple meanings embedded within' (p. 94). In other words, sport psychology researchers need to consider whether the psychological ideas they are exploring can be expressed and represented visually, to gain an understanding of a concept that words alone cannot provide. Additionally, participants may also find visual methods more engaging as the practical activities can provide a more enjoyable means of generating data.

### The internet

The internet is not only a *tool* to collect data, but can be a *place* and *way of being, of* and *for* scholarly study. Many people interact with the internet acting as computer-mediated beings, broadcasting through social media, blogs, webcams, and so on. The internet therefore provides a unique (re) presentation of an individual's self as it is lived through and reconstructed by people (Sparkes and Smith, 2014). There are various approaches to using the internet for conducting research. A *virtual ethnography* is a study of virtual worlds. It is an online ethnography of internet sites whereby the researcher does not solely observe, but actively participates, in website chats, Facebook, Twitter, email exchanges and so on. Another approach to researching through the internet is *expanded ethnography*. This method-ology differs from a virtual ethnography by exploring people's online worlds (i.e. websites, blogs, social media) *and* their offline everyday lives. Therefore, as Sparkes and Smith (2014) explained, expanded ethno-graphy can enrich sport psychology research by:

> Attending to people's everyday life and social interaction as taking place on and through the internet, therefore not only dissolving any 'real' versus 'virtual dichotomy, but also highlighting how people use the internet as they go about their everyday lives.
>
> (p. 112)

There are a myriad of data sources to choose from when conducting inter-net research. One source of data that is a popular online (re)presentation is that of internet *blogs*. Blogs are multimedia texts that can include a range of written and visual media such as photography, videography, music and so forth. They are characterised by an instant form of website communication published by the author whereby readers are able to leave feedback. Using blogs as a method of data collection has many benefits that can be applied to sport psychology research to conceptually advance the field. First a blog is easily accessible and instantaneously provides a substantial amount of data. Secondly, as many blogs contain archived information they are also suitable for longitudinal research and therefore allow for social processes and changes to be examined over time. Third, the global use of the internet means that blogs can be used to access parti-cipants that are geographically and socially removed from the researcher (Sparkes and Smith, 2014).

There are further practical benefits of using blogs and 'cyber voices' in sport psychology research. Whilst these benefits have yet to be cashed in within sport psychology itself, work in other disciplines exemplifies the practical advantages of internet-based research. For example, work by Rich (2006) in the area of health psychology shows how the internet can be used to explore how people manage anorexia as both illness and identity. During her ethnography the participants revealed that the internet provided a space in which they could interact with other people with eating disorders. The internet therefore offers a virtual community whereby alternative identities and narratives can be constructed. By examining virtual interactions it is possible for the researcher to explore the social dynamics of these alternative spaces. As discussed in the first section of this chapter, athletes inhabit socio-cultural worlds that inescapably shape their lives and psychological experiences in sport. Using the internet is one avenue through which sport psychology researchers can explore how athletes experience these worlds and act out their identities online. Therefore, by studying athletes' online worlds, we can further explore how athletes understand both themselves and their bodies (MacKay and Dallaire, 2013a).

Given there are a lack of examples in sport psychology, as recommended by Smith and McGannon (in press), we have crossed boundaries into another discipline to show the value of internet research. One example of this type of research in sport is provided by MacKay and Dallaire's (2013a) study of young female skateboarders. They examined the discourses that these female skateboarders (known as Skirtboarders) employed when producing their own sport coverage via an internet blog. Their study focused on how the use of a personal blog can allow athletes to produce their own posts which can challenge the dominant discourses circulating in the mainstream media. All posts including text, photos, videos, responses and comments were subjected to a discourse analysis. Exploring the texts produced by these women led to an understanding of how they constructed their bodies and gendered identities in opposition to dominant media portrayals of female athletes. Indeed, the blog offered an outlet for the women to challenge the female stereotypes found in mainstream media (re)presentations of sportswomen:

> This project has generated a deeper understanding of the new ways in which women are acting out their gender identities through new media texts. The Skirtboarders illustrate how young women can transform their own experiences and actively engage in the technological decision-making processes that affect the construction of their subjectivities.
>
> (p. 19)

As demonstrated by MacKay and Dallaire (2013a), the use of blogs is of interest to researchers because they offer a unique platform which fosters dialogue between the blog creator and their users. In a follow up study,

MacKay and Dallaire (2013b) interviewed members of the Skirtboarders crew to explore their interpretations of the blog. A prior analysis of the blog enabled the researchers to use this information when questioning why the participants made the blog, and how they made sense of it. The interviews revealed that the Skirtboarders aimed to create an accurate online depiction of who they were and to produce 'a distinction between mainstream and alternative media's sexualized images of women in their sport and what they consider to be the experiences of "real" female athletes' (p. 183). The blog produced by the Skirtboarders therefore goes beyond the domain of self-writing as seen with a diary. In this instance, their blog was used as a social cause to promote female skateboarding. Building on these examples, sport psychology researchers may be able to use the internet as a tool to deepen their understanding of how psychological concepts are socially and culturally constructed and (re)presented by athletes.

## Conclusion

In this chapter, we have presented a number of alternative methods that sport psychology researchers could use to conceptually advance the field. These methods can be used as both a supplement to, or as an alternative to the interview within sport psychology research. Whilst we believe these methods offer the opportunity to conceptually advance the field of sport psychology, delving into novel methods should not be undertaken lightly. Researchers need to demonstrate an understanding of the epistemological and theoretical underpinnings that inform all methods. They also need to make informed and justified rationales for their choice of method(s) within the field. Using different methods to collect data as a supplement or alternative to interviews should not be seen as a way to triangulate the data. Instead, these methods should be used to gather original data, giving further depth to the phenomenon under investigation, and therefore conceptually advancing the field. We hope this chapter stimulates researchers to be more reflexive about interviewing and equally to think carefully about using other methods to enhance our understandings of sport psychology.

## References

Blodgett, A. T., Coholic, D. A., Schinke, R. J., McGannon, K. R., Peltier, D., and Pheasant, C. (2013). Moving beyond words: Exploring the use of an arts-based method in Aboriginal community sport research. *Qualitative Research in Sport, Exercise and Health*, 5, 312–331.

Blodgett, A., Schinke, R., Smith, B., Peltier, D., and Pheasant, C. (2011). Exploring vignettes as a narrative strategy for co-producing the research voices of Aboriginal Community. *Qualitative Inquiry*, 17, 522–533.

Caddick, N. and Ryall, E. (2012). The social construction of mental toughness – A Fascistoid ideology? *Journal of the Philosophy of Sport*, 39, 137–154.

Caddick, N., Smith, B., and Phoenix, C. (2015). The effect of surfing and the natural environment upon the well-being of combat veterans: A qualitative study. *Qualitative Health Research*, 25, 76–86.

Caddick, N., Smith, B., and Phoenix, C. (in-press). Male combat veterans' narratives of PTSD, masculinity, and health. *Sociology of Health and Illness*.

Cowan, D. T., Taylor, I. M., McEwan, H. E., and Baker, J. S. (2012). Bridging the gap between self-determination theory and coaching soccer to disadvantaged youth. *Journal of Applied Sport Psychology*, 24, 361–374.

Culver, D., Gilbert, W., and Sparkes, A. (2012). Qualitative research in sport psychology journals: The next decade 2000–2009 and beyond. *The Sport Psychologist*, 26, 261–281.

Day, M. and Thatcher, J. (2009). 'I'm really embarrassed that I'm telling you this but…' Reflections on using qualitative diaries in research. *Qualitative Research in Psychology*, 6, 249–259.

Douglas, K. and Carless, D. (2009). Abandoning the performance narrative: Two women's stories of transition from professional sport. *Journal of Applied Sport Psychology*, 21, 213–230.

Enright, E. and O'Sullivan, M. (2012). 'Producing different knowledge and producing knowledge differently': rethinking physical education research and practice through participatory visual methods. *Sport, Education and Society*, 17, 35–55.

Fletcher, T. and Wilson, A. (2013). The transformative potential of reflective diaries for elite English cricketers. *Leisure/Loisir*, 37, 267–286.

Frank, A. W. (2013). *The wounded storyteller: Body, illness and ethics* (2nd edition). Chicago, IL: University of Chicago Press.

Gergen, K. (2009). *Relational being*. Oxford: Oxford University Press.

Krane, V. and Baird, S. M. (2005). Using ethnography in applied sport psychology. *Journal of Applied Sport Psychology*, 17, 87–107.

MacKay, S. and Dallaire, C. (2013a). Skirtboarder net-a-narratives: Young women creating their own skateboarding (re)presentation. *International Review for the Sociology of Sport*, 48, 171–195.

MacKay, S. and Dallaire, C. (2013b). Skirtboarders.com: Skateboarding women and self-formation as ethical subjects. *Sociology of Sport Journal*, 30, 173–196.

McHugh, T. L., Coppola, A. M., and Sinclair, S. (2013). An exploration of the meanings of sport to urban Aboriginal youth: A photovoice approach. *Qualitative Research in Sport, Exercise and Health*, 5, 291–311.

McMahon, J. and Penney, D. (2013). (Self-) surveillance and (self-) regulation: Living by fat numbers within and beyond a sporting culture. *Qualitative Research in Sport, Exercise and Health*, 5, 157–178.

Phoenix, C. (2010). Seeing the world of physical culture: The potential of visual methods for qualitative research in sport and exercise. *Qualitative Research in Sport and Exercise*, 2, 93–108.

Phoenix, C. and Orr, N. (2014). Pleasure: A forgotten dimension of ageing and physical activity. *Social Science and Medicine*, 115, 94–102.

Phoenix, C. and Smith, B. (2011). Telling a (good?) counterstory of aging: Natural bodybuilding meets the narrative of decline. *The Journals of Gerontology Series B: Psychological Sciences and Social Sciences*, 66, 628–639.

Potter, J. and Hepburn, A. (2005). Qualitative interviews in psychology: Problems and possibilities. *Qualitative Research in Psychology*, 2, 281–307.

Randall, W. and Phoenix, C. (2009). The problem with truth in qualitative interviews: reflections from a narrative perspective. *Qualitative Research in Sport, Exercise and Health*, 1, 125–140.

Rich, E. (2006). Anorexic dis(connection): managing anorexia as an illness and an identity. *Sociology of Health and Illness*, 28, 284–305.

Riessman, C. (1993). *Narrative analysis*. London: Sage.

Schinke, R., Smith, B., and McGannon, K. (2013). Pathways for community research in sport and physical activity: Criteria for consideration. *Qualitative Research in Sport, Exercise and Health*, 5, 460–468.

Shilling, C. and Bunsell, T. (2009). The female bodybuilder as a gender outlaw. *Qualitative Research in Sport, Exercise and Health*, 1, 141–159.

Smith, B. (2008). Imagining being disabled through playing sport: The body and alterity as limits to imagining others' lives. *Sport, Ethics and Philosophy*, 2, 142–157.

Smith, B. (2013a). Sporting spinal cord injuries, social relations, and rehabilitation narratives: An ethnographic creative non-fiction of becoming disabled through sport. *Sociology of Sport Journal*, 30, 132–152.

Smith, B. (2013b). Disability, sport and men's narratives of health: A qualitative study. *Health Psychology*, 32, 110–119.

Smith, B. and Caddick, N. (2012). Qualitative methods in sport: A concise overview for guiding social scientific research. *Asia Pacific Journal of Sport and Social Science*, 1, 60–73.

Smith, B. and McGannon, K. (in press). Sociology and psychology in sport studies: Crossing boundaries. In R. Giulianotti (ed.). *Routledge Handbook of the Sociology of Sport*. London: Routledge.

Smith, B. and Sparkes, A. (2009a). Narrative inquiry in sport and exercise psychology: What can it mean, and why might we do it? *Psychology of Sport and Exercise*, 10, 1–11.

Smith, B. and Sparkes, A. C. (2009b). Narrative analysis and sport and exercise psychology: Understanding lives in diverse ways. *Psychology of Sport and Exercise*, 10, 279–288.

Smith, B. and Sparkes, A. C. (2011). Multiple responses to a chaos narrative. *Health: An Interdisciplinary Journal for the Social Study of Health, Illness and Medicine*, 15, 38–53.

Smith, J. (1989). *The nature of social and educational inquiry: Empiricism versus interpretation*. Norwood, NJ: Ablex Publishing Corporation.

Smith, J. (2009). Judging research quality: From certainty to contingency. *Qualitative Research in Sport, Exercise and Health*, 1, 91–100.

Smith, J. A., Hollway, W., and Mishler, E. G. (2005). Commentaries on Potter and Hepburn, 'Qualitative interviews in psychology: Problems and possibilities. *Qualitative Research in Psychology*, 2, 309–325.

Sparkes, A. C. and Partington, S. (2003). Narrative practice and its potential contribution to sport psychology: The example of flow. *The Sport Psychologist*, 17, 292–317.

Sparkes, A. C and Smith, B. (2005). When narratives matter. *Medical Humanities*, 31, 81–88.

Sparkes, A. C and Smith, B. (2009). Men, spinal cord injury, memories, and the narrative performance of pain. *Disability & Society*, 23, 679–690.

Sparkes, A. C. and Smith, B. (2014). *Qualitative research in sport, exercise and health sciences. From process to product*. London: Routledge.

Sparkes, A. C., Perez-Samaniego, V., and Smith, B. (2012). Social comparison processes, narrative mapping, and their shaping of the cancer experience: A case study of an elite athlete. *Health: An Interdisciplinary Journal for the Social Study of Health, Illness and Medicine*, 16, 467–488.

Zucchermaglio, C. and Alby, F. (2012). Planning and assessing performance through narratives in soccer team meetings. *Qualitative Research in Sport, Exercise and Health*, 4, 459–469.

# 9 Advances in quantitative analyses and their implications for sport and exercise psychology research

*Nikos Ntoumanis, Athanasios Mouratidis,
Johan Y. Y. Ng and Carme Viladrich*

Author Note: The last three authors are listed in an alphabetical order. Each author had the overall responsibility of one of the main sections of the chapter, but all authors edited the entire chapter.

## Introduction

A cursory examination of all the major sport and exercise psychology (S&E) journals over the last three decades shows that most researchers in this field utilize quantitative methodologies to analyse their data. In the 1980s and 1990s regression analysis, exploratory factor analysis, and (Multivariate) Analysis of Variance (MANOVA and ANOVA) were the most frequently used statistical tests. Biddle *et al.*'s' (2001) overview of quantitative (and qualitative) issues in S&E psychology research identified a number of controversial topics and offered suggestions for new procedures and new statistical analyses. However, since the publication of this article there have been significant advances in statistical analyses for social sciences and psychology research; these have been facilitated by the development of new and in some cases specialized software. S&E psychologists have generally done well in keeping up with such advances by making more appropriate use of existing tests or utilizing new ones. Nevertheless, there are still examples in the literature of poor or inappropriate applications of statistical methods.

Hence, the purpose of this chapter is to provide a brief introduction and overview of advances in existing statistical techniques (i.e. mediation tests and meta-analysis), as well as to demonstrate the utility of somewhat new but underutilized techniques (exploratory structural equation (ESEM) and bifactor modelling, multilevel modelling for longitudinal data) which have superior capabilities compared to "traditional" statistical techniques employed by many S&E psychologists. The utility of such advances in offering new or more methodologically vigorous ways for theory testing is discussed throughout the chapter. Due to space restrictions, in this chapter we are selective in identifying advances in only a few statistical analyses. Our choice was guided by the fact that some of these techniques are widely used in the S&E field (e.g. mediation tests) or have the ability to supplement or even replace existing widely used analyses (e.g. multilevel modelling instead of repeated measures analysis of variance to analyse change). We offer only a brief introduction to each of the topics we discuss in this chapter and we refer the readers to additional sources for more detailed explanations and examples.

## Mediation analysis

Mediation analysis is a very popular statistical technique among psychologists (Rucker *et al.*, 2011). This is not surprising since, in its simplest form, this analysis attempts to explain how one variable explains the relationship between two other variables. Many theories of psychology postulate mediating processes. For example, self-determination theory (SDT; Deci and Ryan, 2002) suggests that three basic psychological needs (e.g. athlete autonomy, competence and relatedness) mediate the relationship between perceptions of the social environment (e.g. how unsupportive a coach is) and human functioning (e.g. athlete psychological ill-being). In the S&E psychology literature mediation analysis has been widely used to test both direct and indirect pathways by which independent variable(s) predict dependent variables. Such testing, when underpinned by sound methodology and theory, is crucial in moving beyond a mere description of antecedents and outcomes, and toward an understanding of the mechanisms and processes by which such outcomes occur. Thus, such testing can aid the development and refinement of conceptual frameworks.

The Baron and Kenny (1986) article on mediation analysis has been a reference point for many psychologists (including S&E psychologists) when conducting mediation analysis. Baron and Kenny proposed four steps for testing for mediation. Figure 9.1 illustrates the use of these steps

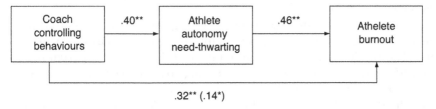

Note: * $p < .05$, ** $p < .01$

*Figure 9.1* Testing the mediation of athlete ($n=284$) autonomy need thwarting in the relationship between athlete perceptions of coach controlling behaviours and athlete reports of sports burnout using the Baron and Kenny (1986) four-step approach.

Note
* $p<.05$.
** $p<.01$.

by showing how athlete perceptions of controlling coach behaviours (e.g. pressuring language, intimidation techniques; Bartholomew *et al.*, 2010) predict athlete reports of burnout from their sport via the thwarting of their basic need for autonomy (Bartholomew *et al.*, 2011). In other words, the model tests whether controlling coach behaviours predict athlete feelings of burnout possibly because such behaviours undermine one of their basic human needs.

Using the Baron and Kenny four-step approach, mediation testing involves the following sequence.

Step 1: Test whether controlling coach environment predicts burnout. This step establishes the total predictive effect of the independent variable (IV) on the dependent variable (DV).

Step 2: Test whether controlling coach environment (IV) predicts the mediator (M) of autonomy need thwarting.

Step 3: Test whether autonomy need thwarting (M) predicts burnout (DV), whilst statistically partialling out coach environment. In other words, both the IV and the M are simultaneous predictors of the DV.

Step 4: Using the output from the analysis in Step 3, examine how much the effect of controlling coach behaviours (IV) on burnout (DV) is reduced in Step 3 when compared to the same effect in Step 1.

Baron and Kenny (1986) suggested that when the IV to DV effect in Step 4 is reduced to zero, then evidence of complete mediation is provided. When this effect is reduced somewhat compared to the same effect in Step 1, then evidence of partial mediation is shown. In the 1986 paper, full and partial mediation were defined in terms of statistical significance; full mediation was evident when the direct effect in Step 3 became non-significant, and part mediation was inferred when this effect was reduced but it was still significant. However, given that regression path coefficients are affected by sample size, Kenny (e.g. see his website: http://davidakenny.net/cm/mediate.htm#BK) subsequently dropped the reference to statistical significance.

Based on this four-step approach, three regression analyses were run in SPSS, and the standardized path coefficients are summarized in Figure 9.1. The results indicate that autonomy need thwarting is a partial mediator of the relationship between controlling coach behaviours and athlete burnout. This is because all four steps are met and also Step 4 indicates that the direct effect is reduced from $\beta = .32$ in Step 1 to $\beta = .14$ in Step 3 (but remains significant).

The four-step approach has been heavily criticized on a number of grounds (for a detailed technical discussion and explanation, see Preacher and Hayes, 2008; Rucker *et al.*, 2011). For example, it has been questioned whether a total effect needs to exist between the IV and DV as a prerequisite to establish mediation (see Step 1), as significant indirect effects can be present in the absence of significant total or direct effects. Further, the terms partial and full mediation have been labeled as unhelpful and potentially hindering theory testing and development, as they imply additional mediators (when such might not exist) or no additional mediator (when such might exist). Hence, the emphasis on mediation analysis has shifted from testing the four-step approach to testing the size of the indirect effect of the IV on the DV via the M. In the example of Figure 9.1, the indirect effect of controlling coach behaviours on burnout via psychological need thwarting is equal to the product of the two direct effects: $\beta = .40 \times .46 = .18$. This is equivalent to the reduction in the direct effect from Step 1 to Step 3: $\beta = .32 \times .14 = .18$.

Using the Sobel test (Sobel, 1982), one can employ normal theory statistics to establish the statistical significance of the indirect effect. However, it has been shown that this test is not appropriate for small sample sizes (Preacher and Hayes, 2008). The currently accepted procedure is to use bootstrapping to construct confidence intervals (CI) around the estimate of the indirect effect. Bootstrapping makes no assumptions about normal distribution and estimates the indirect effect in a number of samples randomly drawn from the original sample. One can construct 95 per cent CI (preferably bias-corrected CI which can be asymmetric around the mean estimate) using the estimates of the indirect effect provided by bootstrapping; if the zero is outside the CI, one can claim evidence of an indirect effect being in operation (Preacher and Hayes). Andrew Hayes has developed the PROCESS macro for SPSS and SAS (available from www. afhayes.com/introduction-to-mediation-moderation-and-conditional-process-analysis.html#process), as well as the PROCESS custom dialog box for SPSS, which can be employed to estimate direct and indirect effects. Using PROCESS, the lower and upper values of the bias-corrected 95 per cent CI of the indirect effect ($\beta = .18$) of coach controlling behaviours on athlete burnout are .13 and .28, respectively. Given that zero is not included in the interval, this provides evidence of an indirect effect from controlling behaviours on burnout via autonomy need thwarting. Preacher and Kelly (2011) present effect size indices for quantifying the magnitude of indirect effects.

PROCESS can easily accommodate the simultaneous testing of multiple mediators, which cannot be done with the four-step approach when tested via regression analysis. This is very important given that many psychological theories and models propose more than one mediator variable. Testing several mediators simultaneously allows the examination of specific indirect effects via each mediator, while controlling for the effects of other mediators. When mediator variables are correlated with each other, the total indirect effect in the multiple mediator model will not equal the sum of the indirect effects when each mediator is tested in separate analysis. Furthermore, when mediator variables are highly intercorrelated this might result in some indirect effects being non-significant due to multicollinearity (or even have opposite sign effects compared to when they are tested on their own, due to suppression).

In Figure 9.2 we present a multiple mediation model that is a more accurate representation of self-determination theory's (Deci and Ryan, 2002) proposition that all three needs (autonomy, competence, and relatedness) can potentially mediate the relationship between social environment influence and individual psychological functioning. In this model, three thwarted psychological needs are tested as simultaneous mediators of the effects of coach controlling behaviours on athlete burnout. The results indicate that the total standardized indirect effect via the three needs is $\beta = .26$ (as opposed to $\beta = .53$ when the indirect effects from single mediator models are summed; this is because the three needs have correlations ranging from $r = .48$ to $r = .66$). Interestingly, the indirect effect via autonomy is $\beta = .13$ (whereas in the single mediator model was $\beta = .18$); the indirect effects via competence and relatedness are smaller ($\beta = .09$ and $\beta = .04$, respectively). Preacher and Hayes (2008) recommend the reporting of unstandardized indirect effects and their 95 per cent bias-corrected CI (as opposed to $p$ values): autonomy ($b = .07$; lower bound (LB) = .03; upper bound (UB) = .12) competence ($b = .05$; LB = −.01; UB = .10) and relatedness ($b = .02$; LB = .01; UB = .07). Notice that only the CI for autonomy does not include zero. Further, if one was to use the Sobel test, the indirect effect via competence would have been judged as significant (at $p = .021$). Together the indirect effects from all three needs equal about 83 per cent of the total effect from coach behaviours on burnout (total indirect effect $b = .15$; total effect $b = .18$). Together these results indicate that autonomy need thwarting mediates the effect of controlling coach behaviours on athlete burnout symptoms, even after controlling for the thwarting of the other two psychological needs. The indirect effects of the other two mediators are weaker. Figure 9.2 presents the direct effects only.

In sum, the indirect effect method helps theory testing and development by examining mediating (indirect) effects even when direct effects are not evident (e.g. due to measurement error or low power), by avoiding the unnecessary and often misleading distinction between partial and total mediation, and by helping the decomposition and comparison of specific indirect effects in complex models involving potentially several independent, mediator and dependent variables. In this chapter we focused on testing for mediation with regression analysis; however, both the four-step and the indirect approach can also be tested via structural equation modelling, which unlike regression analysis, can accommodate the simultaneous testing of multiple dependent variables and can correct for measurement error by including item indicators of latent variables. The software Mplus offers the same capabilities as PROCESS (in terms of reporting specific indirect effects and the bootstrapped CI of these effects) and can be used to test complex mediation models with latent variables. However, note that structural equation modelling typically requires a much larger sample than regression analysis.

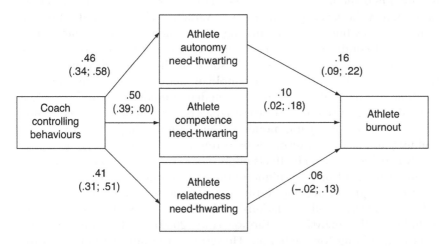

*Figure 9.2* Testing a multiple mediation model showing the role of athlete (*n*=284) autonomy, competence, and relatedness need thwarting in the relation-ship between athlete perceptions of coach controlling behaviours and athlete reports of sports burnout.

Note
Values in brackets indicate the lower and upper bounds for the 95% bootstrapped CI. Unstandardized coefficients and their bootstrapped CI are presented. Indirect effects and their bootstrapped CI are reported in the text. The effects of the three needs on athlete burnout control for coach controlling behaviours.

Preacher and Hayes (2008) discuss a number of issues surrounding mediation, which are in fact not new (e.g. causality, effect size, power, distal vs. proximal mediators). For example, to make a causal argument regarding mediation, there should be a temporal space that separates the variables along the sequence (IV, M, and DV) *and* that any spurious or omitted covariates should be controlled for (see also Antonakis *et al.*, 2000, on the issue of endogeneity and testing for causal claims). In cases where all variables are measured repeatedly over time, Selig and Preacher (2009) give examples of advanced statistical techniques that can be used to examine mediation. Further, experimental manipulation of the IV and in some circumstances the M makes a stronger case for causal mediation effects. In the S&E psychology field, most mediation tests are conducted with cross-sectional data. In such cases, the ordering of the variables into IV, M and DV is based on relevant theory and models, but causal infer-ences cannot and should not be drawn. Mediation analysis can also be conducted with multilevel models to examine mediation at different levels of the hierarchy. More information is provided by Preacher *et al.* (2011) and Zhang *et al.* (2009).

S&E psychologists will do well to utilize more two techniques linked to mediation. Both techniques can be easily tested with PROCESS. The first is moderated mediation and occurs when the size of an indirect effect varies across the levels of a moderator variable. This has implications in terms of theory building, as mediating effects might not be constant across a variety of conditions, leading to underestimation or overestimation of such effects if observed across only some of the levels of a moderator. Curran *et al.* (2013) provide an example of moderated mediation in sport psychology. The second technique is mediated moderation and is evident when the interactive effect of two variables on an outcome variable is indirect via a mediator. Again, moderated mediation is important for theory building and testing in terms of detecting interaction effects (and not to falsely conclude that such effects might not exist); unfortunately there are no applications of this technique in the S&E psychology literature. Lastly, it is worth highlighting that testing for a suppression variable (i.e. a variable that increases the relationship between an IV and a DV when included in the analysis; MacKinnon *et al.*, 2000) involves the same procedures as testing for mediation. However, if the indirect effect has the same sign as the total effect, the included variable is viewed as a mediator, whereas if the indirect effect has the opposite sign, it is considered as a suppressor. Preacher and Hayes (2008) suggest that theories are more complete when they consider both mediator and suppressor variables that can affect the IV-DV relationship.

## Exploratory structural equation and bifactor modelling

To date the most popular measurement model for psychological scales in the sport and exercise psychology literature has been the independent clusters model for confirmatory factor analysis (ICM-CFA, Marsh *et al.*, 2010; McDonald, 1999). According to this model (Figure 9.3 ICM-CFA), clusters of items are univocal, and not perfectly reliable indicators of separable but often-correlated factors. Consequently, the factor loading of an item reflects the impact of a single factor on the item. In other words, each item in a cluster shows convergent validity with all items in the same cluster and discriminant validity with respect to the items from other clusters. A latent variable or factor is thus easily interpretable as a linear combination of its indicators, corrected for unreliability. These factors are expected to show discriminant validity and display differential relations with other variables in their nomological network (AERA *et al.*, 1999).

Usually, authors using ICM-CFA test whether a model with the predicted number of factors fits the observed data and whether all items show statistically significant and sizeable factor loadings on their hypothesized factor. However, two assumptions implied by this approach are that all cross-loadings should be zero and all residuals should be uncorrelated. Additionally, in most cases, both items and factors are considered continuous, normally distributed, linearly related variables (e.g. Brown, 2006). In many cases these assumptions are untested by researchers.

In this scenario, the benefit of easily interpretable factors can be offset by the cost of poor or invalid results due to unmet assumptions. As a consequence, it is very common to obtain solutions with poor fit but with no specific source of misfit (Asparouhov and Muthén, 2009). Further, when indicator cross-loadings exist in the data but are set to zero in the analysis, the correlations between factors will be inflated, thus compromising the discriminant validity of factors (Asparouhov and Muthén, 2009; Morin and Maiano, 2011). Similarly, when correlations among residuals are not zero but are constrained by the analysis to zero, the widely used Cronbach's alpha coefficient is likely to be inflated, thus compromising the claim of alpha being the lower bound of reliability (e.g. Raykov, 2001). No matter how controversial it remains, item parceling (collapsing indicators to form new but fewer indicators) does not adequately solve these issues (Marsh *et al.*, 2013).

A better solution when the assumptions of ICM-CFA are not met is to use more appropriate/less restrictive measurement models that are still compatible with theory. For example, one can define item response theory

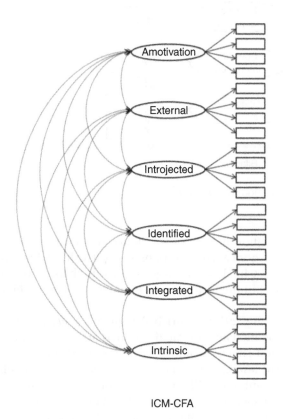

ICM-CFA

*Figure 9.3* Measurement models.

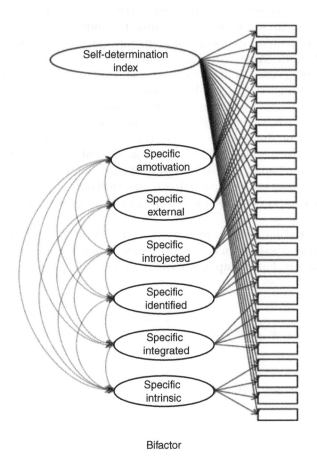

Bifactor

*Figure 9.3* Measurement models *continued.*

models for nonlinear relationships between items and factors, or use latent class analysis for categorical latent variables (e.g. Hoyle, 2012; Skrondal and Rabe-Hesketh, 2004;). For the purposes of this chapter, we will discuss two alternatives within the factor analysis framework, namely bifactor models and ESEM.

Bifactor models (e.g. Reise, 2012; Viladrich, Ntoumanis *et al.*, 2013) are particularly suited to accommodate correlated residuals arising from multifaceted concepts or method effects. Examples of multifaceted concepts are widespread in achievement testing (e.g. general and domain-specific intelligence factors, Lakin and Gambrell, 2012) and are also present in personality research (e.g. general and specific factors or facets, Chen *et al.*, 2012). In S&E psychology, the motivation regulations advanced by SDT (Deci and Ryan, 2002) is an example of a multifaceted concept (see below). Regarding

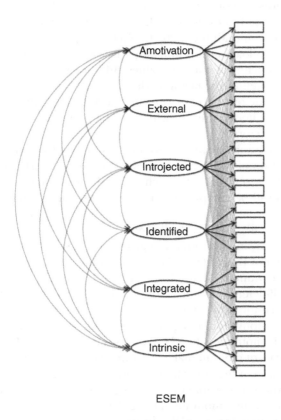

ESEM

*Figure 9.3* Measurement models *continued.*

method effects, one well-known example is the use of positively and negatively worded items in order to better sample a single concept and/or to avoid response biases (e.g. Motl *et al.*, 2000). In bifactor models (Figure 9.3 Bifactor), all items in a scale are seen as indicators of both one general factor and specific (also called domain, facet or group) factors defined by clusters of these items. The relationship between the general and the specific factors is set to 0. Consequently, the factor loadings of one item on the general and specific factors reflect the independent impact of both general and specific concepts on this item, respectively (Bruner *et al.*, 2012). Compared to second-order factor models, the general factor is conceptually similar to the second-order factor and the specific factors resemble the disturbances of the first-order factors, making it easier to study the effect of specific factors on external variables (Chen *et al.*, 2006).

ESEM models (Figure 9.3 ESEM, Asparouhov and Muthén, 2009; Myers, Chase *et al.*, 2011; Viladrich, Appleton *et al.*, 2013) were developed to accommodate factor cross-loadings that are different from zero. Conceptually, items are seen as indicators of more than one, often correlated, factors. The model is sometimes described as exploratory factor analysis with confirmatory elements (Asparouhov and Muthén, 2009). Each group of items loads on its target factor and the loadings on non-target factors are supposed to be lower but are freely estimated at non-zero values. Additionally, the factors can be correlated. Consequently, the factor loadings of one item reflect the direct impact of each factor on the item, and the calculation of the total effects of one factor on an item requires including effects of this factor via its correlation with other factors.

To illustrate the bifactor and ESEM models, we present results obtained with the Spanish adaptation of the Behavioural Regulations in Sport Questionnaire (BRSQ, Viladrich *et al.*, 2011), which originally was tested via an ICM-CFA. These results will be compared to those obtained from bifactor and ESEM analyses.

The BRSQ (Lonsdale *et al.*, 2008) is a self-report measure of the motivation regulations that underpin behavioural engagement in sport activities according to SDT (Deci and Ryan, 2002). According to this theory, motivation regulations lie on a continuum that reflects the degree to which behavioural engagement is self-determined. Six motivational regulations can be distinguished along the continuum. These are (in decreasing order of self-determination): intrinsic motivation, integrated, identified, introjected and external regulations and amotivation (see Deci and Ryan for details). Inter-correlations between adjacent motivational regulations along the continuum are expected to be higher than the associations between the regulations that are more distal. Moreover, it is possible to obtain a general measure of relative self-determination for the motivational regulations assessed by the BRSQ, the self-determination index (SDI), using the following formula: SDI = $-2 \times$ external $-2 \times$ introjected $+1 \times$ identified $+1 \times$ integrated $+2 \times$ intrinsic (Lonsdale *et al.*, 2009). In the nomological network of SDT (see Ntoumanis, 2012, for a summary), the more self-determined motivation regulations are supposed to be related to positive outcomes (e.g. vitality), whereas less self-determined motivations relate to maladaptive outcomes (e.g. anxiety). Details on the procedure and questionnaires employed are given in Viladrich *et al.* (2011).

Goodness of fit indices for the three models are displayed in Table 9.1. All models fit relatively well (cf. Marsh *et al.*, 2010), with ESEM displaying the best fit.

Parameter estimates are shown in two separate tables. Factor loadings are displayed in Table 9.2, and intercorrelation between motivation-related factors from the three models, as well as correlations between these factors and external variables (vitality and anxiety) are displayed in Table 9.3. All factor loadings and correlation coefficients above .12 were statistically significant with $p < .05$, and all below .08 were statistically null. Values between these showed $p$ values between .05 and .10 depending on their standard errors.

*Table 9.1* Goodness of fit indices

|  | $\chi^2(df)$ | $p$ | CFI | TLI | RMSEA (90% CI) |
|---|---|---|---|---|---|
| ICM-CFA | 877.724 (273) | .000 | .920 | .905 | .062 (.057, .067) |
| Bifactor | 685.166 (248) | .000 | .942 | .924 | .055 (.050, .060) |
| ESEM | 351.897 (183) | .000 | .978 | .960 | .040 (.034, .046) |

Note
CFI = Comparative Fit Index, TLI = Tucker-Lewis Index, RMSEA = Root Mean Square Error of Approximation, CI = Confidence Interval for RMSEA.

Parameter estimates from ICM-CFA factor analysis which postulated six intercorrelated first-order factors, led to four main conclusions: (a) all items had high loadings on their target factors, (b) the correlations among the factors were compatible with expectations, and (c) correlations with vitality showed the expected pattern from negative to positive when moving along the motivational continuum from the low to the more self-determined end, whereas (d) correlations with competitive anxiety showed the reverse pattern. Thus, Viladrich *et al.* (2011) concluded that the Spanish version of BRSQ had adequate psychometric properties, except for the somewhat poor discriminant validity between adjacent factors, some of which had correlations as big as .80.

The bifactor model postulated one general factor with all items contributing to the definition of this factor in a pattern compatible with the definition of SDI. Observed results were compatible as the general factor showed negative loadings for the items that measure less self-determined factors and positive loadings for the items that measure more self-determined factors. Further, there were higher absolute loadings for the items that reflect motivation at the extreme end of the continuum than for items that reflect motivation toward the center of the continuum. Each item also loaded on a specific factor and all specific factors were intercorrelated, as in ICM-CFA.

The general factor showed the expected positive correlation with vitality and negative correlation with competitive anxiety. Controlling for the general factor, the items were good indicators of the expected specific factors, which in turn conformed to the expected pattern of correlations among themselves and with the external variables. The only exceptions were the correlations between intrinsic motivation and vitality and competitive anxiety, which were slightly lower than expected. Thus, these results indicate that when a researcher is interested in the predictive effects of both a general SDI factor as well as the specific factors tapped by the BRSQ, the bifactor model provides a measurement framework for testing such effects. Lack of discriminant validity between specific factors was still a concern, particularly between the external and introjected specific factors, and between the identified and integrated specific factors.

Table 9.2 Standardized factor loadings

| ITEM | ICM-CFA | BIFACTOR | | ESEM | | | | | |
|---|---|---|---|---|---|---|---|---|---|
| | | GEN | SPEC | AM | EX | IJ | ID | IG | IM |
| AM1 | .672 | -.592 | .314 | **.703** | -.189 | .133 | .041 | -.147 | -.070 |
| AM2 | .710 | -.512 | .489 | **.764** | -.075 | .077 | -.003 | .035 | -.049 |
| AM3 | .884 | -.675 | .544 | **.772** | .178 | -.016 | -.014 | -.030 | -.041 |
| AM4 | .758 | -.405 | .727 | **.462** | .261 | .187 | -.052 | .071 | -.080 |
| EX1 | .678 | -.232 | .671 | -.060 | **.356** | .400 | .124 | -.013 | -.212 |
| EX3 | .835 | -.553 | .605 | .311 | **.535** | .124 | -.042 | .000 | -.075 |
| EX5 | .612 | -.390 | .472 | .009 | **.605** | .039 | .093 | -.079 | -.111 |
| EX7 | .655 | -.140 | .715 | .009 | **.410** | .256 | .193 | .076 | -.158 |
| IJ1 | .781 | -.055 | .791 | .166 | .059 | **.658** | .007 | .165 | -.018 |
| IJ2 | .787 | -.048 | .799 | .258 | .027 | **.648** | .025 | .123 | .073 |
| IJ3 | .638 | -.284 | .572 | .117 | .419 | **.251** | .091 | -.054 | .035 |
| IJ4 | .755 | -.087 | .753 | -.001 | .368 | **.595** | -.026 | -.011 | .131 |
| ID1 | .568 | -.022 | .645 | .261 | .147 | -.297 | **.705** | .089 | .095 |
| ID2 | .707 | .173 | .678 | -.164 | -.066 | .338 | **.461** | .112 | .017 |
| ID3 | .679 | .217 | .621 | -.094 | .131 | -.173 | **.723** | .015 | .117 |
| ID4 | .705 | .180 | .672 | -.096 | -.052 | .213 | **.510** | .108 | .054 |
| IG1 | .789 | .635 | .478 | -.047 | .065 | .064 | -.143 | **.657** | .296 |
| IG2 | .755 | .471 | .602 | -.021 | -.001 | .024 | -.017 | **.925** | -.112 |
| IG3 | .714 | .443 | .561 | .053 | -.050 | -.087 | .204 | **.661** | -.003 |
| IG4 | .648 | .329 | .574 | -.076 | -.184 | .200 | .440 | **.220** | .028 |
| IM1 | .854 | .725 | .431 | -.176 | .012 | .009 | -.039 | .236 | **.612** |
| IM2 | .895 | .751 | .470 | -.094 | -.049 | -.086 | .014 | .161 | **.725** |
| IM3 | .766 | .482 | .635 | -.056 | -.112 | .120 | .102 | -.134 | **.865** |
| IM4 | .722 | .378 | .739 | .031 | -.051 | .147 | .115 | -.042 | **.736** |

Note

AM = Amotivation, EX = External Regulation, IJ = Introjected Regulation, ID = Identified Regulation, IG = Integrated Regulation, IM = Intrinsic Motivation. Items are identified by the two letters related to the construct they are intended to measure followed by an ordinal number. In ICM-CFA 6 factors were specified and all free loadings are printed in the ICM-CFA column. In bifactor analysis one general and 6 specific factors were specified and all specific factor loadings are printed in the SPEC column. In ESEM, 6 factors were specified; factor loadings that were freely estimated are displayed in bold, whereas all cross-loadings were targeted to be close to zero using target rotation. Cross-loadings with unexpected values are underlined.

Lastly, the parameter estimates for ESEM showed that, in spite of factor loadings being freely estimated, every item in BRSQ had a higher factor loading on its target factor than in non-target factors, except three items (see Table 9.2). There were seven more items with cross-loadings of absolute values around .30. Overall, at least 170 out of 180 factor loadings were consistent with theoretical expectations. The pattern of correlations between the motivation factors, and between these factors and the external variables were very similar to those obtained in ICM-CFA. However, the interesting result was that ESEM helped to obtain better discriminant validity among factors, because the factor correlations, between .31 and .54 in absolute value, were substantially lower than those obtained in ICM-CFA.

*Table 9.3* Correlations among motivational variables, competitive anxiety, and vitality

|  | *SDI* | *AM* | *EX* | *IJ* | *ID* | *IG* | *IM* | *VITALITY* |
|---|---|---|---|---|---|---|---|---|
| **ICM-CFA** | | | | | | | | |
| External | – | .723 | | | | | | |
| Introjected | – | .555 | .796 | | | | | |
| Identified | – | −.102 | .225 | .393 | | | | |
| Integrated | – | −.277 | .023 | .294 | .725 | | | |
| Intrinsic | – | −.534 | −.404 | −.044 | .505 | .718 | | |
| Vitality | – | −.224 | −.186 | −.008 | .311 | .450 | .400 | |
| Anxiety | – | .253 | .222 | .174 | .048 | −.007 | −.087 | −.176 |
| **BIFACTOR** | | | | | | | | |
| Amotivation | .000 | | | | | | | |
| External | .000 | .630 | | | | | | |
| Introjected | .000 | .646 | .802 | | | | | |
| Identified | .000 | .104 | .373 | .438 | | | | |
| Integrated | .000 | .364 | .450 | .517 | .797 | | | |
| Intrinsic | .000 | −.035 | −.086 | .096 | .485 | .426 | | |
| Vitality | .165 | −.158 | −.096 | .018 | .284 | .449 | .406 | |
| Anxiety | −.227 | .129 | .127 | .141 | .101 | .179 | .105 | −.176 |
| **ESEM** | | | | | | | | |
| External | – | .474 | | | | | | |
| Introjected | – | .268 | .371 | | | | | |
| Identified | – | −.023 | .080 | .311 | | | | |
| Integrated | – | −.226 | .031 | .258 | .421 | | | |
| Intrinsic | – | −.415 | −.278 | −.079 | .273 | .543 | | |
| Vitality | – | −.160 | −.215 | .019 | .285 | .408 | .366 | |
| Anxiety | – | .243 | .216 | .114 | .056 | −.017 | −.064 | −.176 |

Note
SDI = Self Determination Index, AM = Amotivation, EX = External Regulation, IJ = Introjected Regulation, ID = Identified Regulation, IG = Integrated Regulation, IM = Intrinsic Motivation, Anxiety = Competitive Anxiety.

How can researchers choose between the three models described in this section? The underlying theoretical framework (are the models conceptually plausible?) and the specific research goals should be considered. If the researcher is primarily interested in multifaceted constructs (e.g. motivational regulations), then the ICM-CFA would be a suitable measurement model. However, if the researcher is interested in modelling separately what the multifaceted constructs have in common (e.g. SDI) and their specificities, then the bifactor model is suitable. According to Reise (2012), ICM-CFA correlated factor models and second-order models are good candidates for consideration of bifactor modelling. Further, provided that ICM-CFA model doesn't fit, researchers should elucidate whether items are univocal indicators of their factors with correlated residuals (bifactor models), or should crossload on several factors and have independent residuals (ESEM). Expert judgment is needed in order to decide which of these interpretations is more appropriate for a particular theory, instrument and/or population.

As a practical guide, comparing ESEM to ICM-CFA results should be routinely carried out as they test the assumption of cross-loadings being zero (e.g. Skrondal and Rabe-Hesketh, 2004). Bifactor models should be considered when mutlifaceted concepts or method effects are known or suspected (Reise, 2012). Finally, global comparison of different models (ICM-CFA, bifactor, and ESEM) should be preferred to the exploratory use of modification indices within a particular model in order to improve model fit (Asparouhov and Muthén, 2009).

Some important issues should be taken into consideration when examining the models outlined in this section. First, the ICM-CFA model is nested within both models and consequently, tests of differential fit are encouraged (Reise, 2012; Skrondal and Rabe-Hesketh, 2004). Second, some caution should be taken when interpreting results, due to the fact that some technical issues need to be further explored. Among them, are issues related to sample size and power (Muthén and Muthén, 2002; Myers, Ahn *et al.*, 2011), rotation indeterminacy (i.e. multiple rotation criteria which give substantially different results, Schmitt and Sass, 2011) and statistical behaviour of goodness of fit indices in ESEM (Marsh *et al.*, 2010). Third, the necessity of ESEM models is still under discussion (e.g. see Herman and Pfister, 2013 versus Marsh *et al.*, 2010), bifactor models are claimed to be easily over-interpreted in the literature (Revelle and Wilt, 2013), and in some areas, discriminant validity of the constructs has been improved by constructing entirely new questionnaires that better conform to the ICM-CFA model (e.g. Pelletier *et al.*, 2013).

Future research needs to further explore these issues. Further, Bayesian factor analysis and Bayesian structural equation modelling could be also utilized in sport and exercise psychology literature. Such approaches represent a generalization of ESEM with prior knowledge of parameter estimates being included in the model, thus helping to solve the rotation uncertainty and being able to accommodate both cross-loadings and correlated residuals (Muthén and Asparouhov, 2011).

## Multilevel modelling for longitudinal data

The multilevel analytical approach is particularly useful in analysing data from longitudinal designs, including diary studies (e.g. Gagne *et al.*, 2003). Such designs are considered to contain different levels of hierarchically structured data with the repeated measures nested within individuals. This nesting structure can be extended to accommodate higher-order nesting; for instance, repeated measures nested within exercisers, nested within groups. For simplicity reasons, the present discussion will be constrained to a two-level model only.

Compared to more traditional types of analyses (e.g. repeated-measures ANOVA/MANOVA), multilevel modelling has some important advantages that renders it more attractive. First, unlike (M)ANOVA multilevel analysis enables us to test whether a construct may relate differently to other constructs at different levels of analyses. For instance, we may expect that competitive state anxiety is more strongly related to athletes' performance at the within-person level and more weakly related at the between-person level, perhaps because of athletes' individual differences in coping skills. Second, unlike (M)ANOVA multilevel analysis let us directly test the extent to which the within-person association between state anxiety and sport performance varies across a sport season as a function of other within- or between-person variables, such as athletes' personal characteristics (e.g. achievement motives, fear of failure, or perfectionism).

Third, multilevel analysis can handle missing observations at the intrapersonal level utilizing all available data, thus rendering unnecessary the listwise deletion that is used in (M)ANOVA. This feature is especially important for longitudinal studies as attrition rates or other types of missing observations are quite common. Fourth, multilevel models seem to provide less biased estimates (under maximum likelihood estimation) for values missing at random (MAR), a less restrictive and more realistic assumption compared to the assumption that values are missing completely at random (MCAR), upon which repeated-measures (M)ANOVA is based (Hox, 2010). Fifth, compared to (M)ANOVA, multilevel analysis may overcome the computation problems arising when the repeated measurements for each individual outnumber the measurements per individual (Snijders, 1996). Also, in contrast to (M)ANOVA, multilevel models do not need to rely on the sphericity assumption – namely, that all differences in scores between consecutive assessments have the same variance (Quené and Van den Bergh, 2004).

The consideration and treatment of time is an additional advantage of the multilevel approach over repeated-measures (M)ANOVA. While the latter requires data collection at fixed occasions, and preferably equally spaced ones, multilevel analysis is more flexible as it can analyse equally well observations that have been collected at varying occasions (Bryk and Raudenbush, 2001). This is an important advantage because in longitudinal studies practical problems may arise and data collection may occur at different times for different people.

The above points clearly illustrate that multilevel modelling has several advantages over repeated-measures (M)ANOVA. In multilevel models time is considered as an observed predictor and can be modeled, like any other predictor, at the intrapersonal level, as either fixed or random, depending on the theory that guides one's research. We can treat the slope for time (i.e. the relation of time to the dependent variable) as fixed if we expect a similar pattern of change across time for all participants. For example, we might expect an increase in all athletes' competitive state anxiety as the day of a crucial game approaches (assuming that we expect all athletes to cope with anxiety in the same way); in contrast we can treat the slopes as randomly varying if we make the (more sensible) hypothesis that the trajectory of state anxiety may vary from athlete to athlete (perhaps due to individual differences in coping skills).

Also, depending on the research question and available time points, time can be modeled as a linear, curvilinear or polynomial predictor. This possibility allows researchers to treat time in a more flexible way. For instance, while time may be estimated as a linear predictor of the skills development of novice athletes, it makes sense to hypothesize that such a trajectory will follow a non-linear pattern with the rate of development becoming more flattened after an initial period of training. Furthermore, one can examine the cross-level interactions between time (or any other within-person predictor) and between-person characteristics. For example, via cross-level interactions we can test whether the non-linear change of skills development among athletes will differ as a function of athletes' quality of motivation – we may want to test whether athletes with higher quality of motivation show less "flattening pattern" across time, compared to athletes with a lesser quality of motivation.

In the remainder of this section we provide a working example with real data to show the usefulness and the flexibility of multilevel analysis for longitudinal designs. We refrain from presenting extended technical details and mathematical formulae; the interested reader may consult various sources that discuss these aspects in depth (e.g. Bryk and Raudenbush, 2001; Hox, 2010; Stoel and Garre, 2011).

We use a three-wave data with a sample of 416 Greek middle school students in physical education (PE) to illustrate some basic applications of multilevel modelling. For the purposes of this example, we present data on students' gender, amotivation and feelings of psychological need thwarting during PE, drawing from SDT (Deci and Ryan, 2002). The repeated measures of amotivation and need thwarting constituted the intrapersonal level (level 1) as they were nested within individuals (the interpersonal level or level 2). The purpose of this illustration is multifold: (a) to determine the variance of amotivation lying at the intrapersonal and interpersonal level; (b) to analyse the intrapersonal fluctuation (i.e. the trajectories) of amotivation towards PE throughout a school year, (c) to examine the association between amotivation and psychological need-thwarting also throughout the school year, (d) to test for gender differences in the mean levels of amotivation, and (e) to test whether gender moderates the trajectories of amotivation and the relation between amotivation and need-thwarting.

We first checked for the assumptions of normality and homogeneity of variance of level 1 residuals (Hox, 2010), but due to space constraints we do not present the results here. Then, we examined an unconditional model (i.e. a model with no predictors) to determine the variance of amotivation distributed at the intrapersonal and interpersonal level (see Table 9.4; Model 1). Using the formula determining the intraclass correlation coefficient (ICC) provided by Bryk and Raudenbush (2001) ($r_{0j} / [e_{ij} + r_{0j}]$), we find that about two thirds of the variance of amotivation lie at the intrapersonal level (i.e. $0.83 / [0.83 + 1.70]$), suggesting marked differences in amotivation across the three waves of assessment within individuals. Also, the intercept shows that students reported an average score of 2.23 points of amotivation on a 1 (Strongly disagree) to 5 (Strongly agree) scale.

We then examined whether the intrapersonal variation of amotivation could be modeled as a linear function of time. We centered time by assigning the value of 0 for the first time point (T1), and the values of 1 and 2 for T2 and T3, respectively. Depending on the research question, we can center time at different waves (e.g. at T3). We assumed that the slope of time would be random as opposed to fixed; that is, we assumed that the fluctuation of amotivation across time would vary from person to person.

The results of this model appear in Table 9.4 (Model 2a). As can be noticed, time ($\beta_{10\,\text{time-linear}} = 0.45$, SE $= 0.05$, $p < .01$) emerged as significant predictor. This coefficient suggests that students reported, on average, about half a point of amotivation higher between two consecutive measurement times. Inclusion of need-thwarting and time resulted in a decrease of the intra-personal variation of amotivation (from 1.70 points down to 1.05 points). Using the formula provided by Bryk and Raudenbush (2002) (i.e. $[\tau_{00} - \tau_{01}] / \tau_{00}$ where $\tau_{00}$ and $\tau_{01}$ represent the residual variance from the unconditional (i.e. no predictor model and the conditional model, respectively) we can estimate that the variance explained by time is 38.2%.

Two issues deserve attention in Model 2a. First, the value of the intercept has substantially changed from the unconditional model. This is because the intercept now represents the average score of amotivation at T1 (given the centering for time) rather than the average score of amotivation across the three assessment waves. Second, there was a considerable

Table 9.4 Estimating amotivation towards PE as function of time (gender and psychological need-thwarting among Greek adolescent students (n=416))

| Fixed effects | Amotivation | | | | | |
| --- | --- | --- | --- | --- | --- | --- |
| | Unconditional | Intrapersonal predictors | | | Intra- & Interpersonal predictors | |
| | Model 1 | Model 2a | Model 2b | Model 2c | Model 3a | Model 3b |
| Intercept, $\beta_{00}$ | 2.23 (0.06) | 1.78 (0.06) | 1.84 (0.06) | 1.84 (0.06) | 2.11 (0.09) | 1.99 (0.10) |
| *Intrapersonal predictors* | | | | | | |
| Time linear $\beta_{10}$ | – | 0.45** (0.05) | 0.11 (0.12) | 0.14 (0.12) | 0.14 (0.12) | 0.17 (0.19) |
| Time quadratic $\beta_{20}$ | – | – | 0.17** (0.06) | 0.15* (0.06) | 0.15* (0.06) | 0.24** (0.09) |
| Need-thwarting $\beta_{30}$ | | – | – | 0.37** (0.06) | 0.38** (0.07) | 0.30** (0.08) |
| *Interpersonal predictors* | | | | | | |
| Gender $\beta_{01}$ | | | | | –0.57** (0.11) | –0.31* (0.12) |
| *Cross-level interactions* | | | | | | |
| Time linear X gender $\beta_{11}$ | | | | | | –0.02 (0.24) |
| Time quadratic X gender $\beta_{21}$ | | | | | | –0.21† (0.12) |
| Need-thwarting X gender $\beta_{31}$ | | | | | 0.21 (0.13) | |
| *Random effects* | | | | | | |
| Intercept $r_{0j}$ | 0.83 | 0.82** | 0.83** | 0.91** | 0.92** | 0.90** |
| Slope of time (linear) $r_{1j}$ | – | 0.46** | 0.47** | 0.41** | 0.41** | 0.37** |
| Level-1 residual $e_{ij}$ | 1.70 | 1.05 | 1.03 | 0.98 | 0.98 | 0.97 |
| *Model fit* | | | | | | |
| Degrees of freedom (*df*) | 2 | 4 | 4 | 4 | 4 | 4 |
| $\chi^2$ | 4546.99 | 4369.97 | 4368.09 | 4321.69 | 4300.84 | 4279.05 |
| $\Delta\chi^2$ (from Model 1)/$\Delta df$ | – | 88.51** | 89.45** | 112.65** | 123.08** | 133.97** |

Notes
† p=.08.
* p<.05.
** p<.01.

variability from student to student in the slope for time (i.e. the change of amotivation across the three measurement waves). With the aid of formulae of Bryk and Raudenbush (2002), we find that the confidence interval of the probability is .95 that the change in scores of amotivation lies between −0.88 and 1.78 ($\beta_{10\,time\text{-}linear} = 0.45 \pm [1.96 \times \sqrt{0.46}]$), suggesting that for some students amotivation decreased rather than increased. Given this wide range, it is prudent to examine other intrapersonal predictors that could further explain the intrapersonal variance in the changes of amotivation (and thus narrow the range of plausible scores of amotivation changes across time).

We then explored whether the changes of amotivation followed a non-linear trajectory. The type of non-linear changes that can be examined depends on the number of repeated measurements. For three repeated measures only quadratic change (but with a fixed slope for the quadratic term) can be explored. For data with four repeated measures quadratic change (with a random slope) and cubic change (with a fixed slope) can be also explored. In general, for $m$ measurements, we can apply polynomials of degree $m-2$ with random slopes or polynomials of degree $m-1$ with the slope of the higher-order term being fixed (Snijders and Bosker, 1999). In our example, we introduced a quadratic term for time in addition to the linear term, but with a fixed slope for the quadratic term (and a random slope for the linear term). Obviously, assessing quadratic change with a random slope is preferable, unless one expects a uniform pattern of change across all individuals, however, for this example we only had three waves of data. The model with the quadratic changes (Model 2b) showed an even better fit and revealed that the changes in amotivation mainly occurred from T2 to T3 as there was a statistically significant acceleration across time in the reported scores of amotivation.

We then tested the degree to which need thwarting could explain any additional variance of amotivation at the intrapersonal level over and above the intrapersonal changes in amotivation across time. This model (Model 2c) showed that regardless of changes of amotivation across time, need thwarting was positively related to amotivation ($\beta_{10\,need\text{-}thwarting} = 0.37$, $SE = 0.06$, $p < .01$). Unlike time however, we fixed the slope of need-thwarting because otherwise the model could not converge. However, in general it is perfectly plausible to also treat the effect of a time-varying predictor as random, if model convergence can be achieved.

We proceeded with a model in which we tried to explain the between-athlete differences in the intercept (i.e. the score of amotivation at T1) and the slopes (i.e. the covariation between amotivation and need-thwarting and the average changes in amotivation as a function of time). In our example, we used gender as such an explanatory between-student variable. Gender was dummy-coded (0 = males; 1 = females) and was entered uncentered so that the intercept would represent the average score of amotivation for male students. We could also have grand-mean centered gender; in such case the intercept would have represented the mean for amotivation for the whole sample, if the proportion of males and females in the sample was the same. Such an option is preferable for samples with unequal distribution between males and females (or other dummy-coded variables) and for models with continuous predictors (see Enders and Tofighi, 2007).

With regard to explaining between-athlete differences in the intercept, inclusion of gender (see Model 3a) revealed that females reported, on average, less amotivation (by 0.57 points) than males. We also tested whether gender would moderate the (intrapersonal) relationship between amotivation and need-thwarting and the trajectories (i.e. the changes across time) of amotivation. To do so, we included cross-level interaction terms between gender on the one hand and time and need-thwarting on the other. This model (Model 3b) showed no statistically significant cross-level effects, although there appears to be a trend for females to report less amotivation from T2 to T3 ($\beta_{31\,time\text{-}quadratic} = -0.21$, $p = .08$).

The above example illustrates how longitudinal data can be analysed through multilevel modelling. This approach can be also used in more complex designs – for instance when there are (a) multiple intrapersonal and interpersonal predictors, (b) higher-order levels (such as classrooms) or (c) two-way interactions (either within the same level or across different levels). Future research in S&E psychology can benefit from even more sophisticated applications of multilevel modelling. For example, future studies could use a multivariate multilevel approach with latent factors thereby including multiple item indicators, multiple dependent variables, and multiple mediators within the same growth model (see Muthén and Asparouhov, 2011). Such analysis is rather rare in the sport and exercise psychology literature but is appropriate given the interdependencies of the psychological constructs under investigation in this literature. Similarly rare in the sport and exercise psychology literature is the use of multilevel models that combine heavily skewed binary outcomes to predict distal outcomes (e.g. the likelihood of using performance-enhancing drugs) by using continuous predictors (e.g. the reasons for doing so; Muthén and Asparouhov).

## Meta-analysis

The goal of quantitative empirical research is to obtain estimates of population parameters from sample statistics. However, sample statistics are prone to various types of error (e.g. sampling error, error of measurement, range restriction in the independent variable; Hunter and Schmidt, 2004). As a solution, when a relatively large number of empirical studies within a particular field are conducted, researchers can employ meta-analysis to provide an estimate that is closer to the population value. Meta-analysis is often called "analysis of analyses". The "raw data" for meta-analysis are the results of empirical (primary) studies. The logic behind meta-analysis is this: although results of primary studies are affected by errors that either inflate or deflate effect sizes, when there is a sufficiently large amount of studies, the weighted average of the test statistic (e.g. correlation coefficient) across the primary studies will be a close estimate of the real effect size. S&E psychologists have employed meta-analysis for many years (e.g. Hausenblas *et al.*, 1997, Marshall and Biddle, 2001, Ntoumanis and Biddle, 1999) and its usage is growing. The purpose of this section is to provide a background of this technique and describe some of the recent developments in conducting and reporting meta-analytic studies.

Different methods of meta-analysis allow corrections for different types of errors. There are two main approaches for conducting meta-analysis, namely fixed effect and random effect model meta-analyses (Hedges and Olkin, 1985). Fixed effect models have the assumption that variations in effect sizes across primary studies are only affected by sampling error. In contrast, random effect models assume that effect sizes also vary due to factors such as measurement errors, dichotomization of variables (e.g. changing a continuous variable to a "high" vs. "low" variable) and range restrictions (e.g. when all respondents scored very high on a variable). Readers may refer to Borenstein *et al.* (2011) for a detailed description of the two approaches. In this chapter we will focus on methods related to the random effect model, and in particular the approach suggested by Hunter and Schmidt (2004), as it is one of the most common approaches used by S&E psychology researchers.

Typically, conducting a meta-analysis involves the following steps: (1) Setting inclusion and exclusion criteria; (2) Searching the literature for primary studies to include; (3) Coding study information in the retrieved studies; (4) Conducting the meta-analysis by calculating effect sizes; (5) Testing for the homogeneity of these effect sizes and identifying possible moderators for heterogeneous effect sizes; and (6) Other follow-up analyses. In this chapter, we will focus on steps 4 to 6.

Hunter and Schmidt (2004) have identified eleven sources of error in primary studies, but researchers utilizing the Hunter and Schmidt meta-analytic approach most often make corrections for sampling and measurement errors only, given that information for such errors can be relatively easily obtained from primary studies. The effect size is estimated by the weighted average of coefficients (usually Pearson correlation or Cohen's *d*, depending on whether the focus of the analysis is on relations between variables or differences between means) from the included studies. Stronger weights will be given to effect sizes from studies with larger sample sizes and measures with better reliability coefficients (e.g. Cronbach alphas). Apart from estimating the effect size, a 95 per cent CI of this measure is drawn. When the CI does not include 0, a real effect is said to exist.

Results of meta-analysis are often presented using forest plots (Lewis and Clarke, 2001). For example, Figure 9.4 represents an analysis, extracted from Ng *et al.* (2012) examining the relation between autonomy need satisfaction and intrinsic motivation, both constructs from SDT. Forest plots present effect sizes (in this case, the Pearson correlation) and the corresponding 95 per cent CIs of included studies. Relative sample sizes are represented by different box sizes for each study. The combined effect size (and the corresponding CI) across all studies, or effect sizes combined across meaningful subgroups – in the case of Figure 9.4 studies with different research designs – are shown using diamonds.

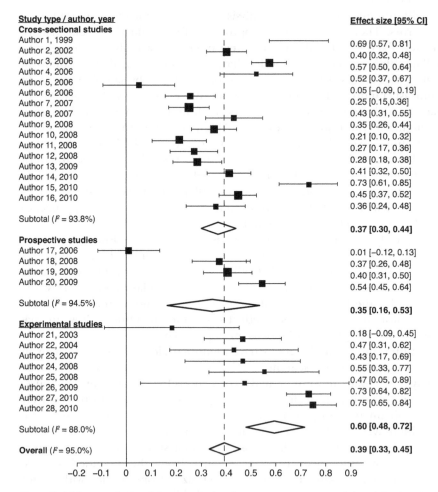

*Figure 9.4* Meta-analysis of the association between autonomy need satisfaction and intrinsic motivation.

Note
This analysis was extracted from Ng *et al.*'s (2012) study.

One potential problem when conducting meta-analysis is that many journals and reviewers favour studies with significant results as opposed to non-significant results, leading to publication bias (Rosenthal, 1979). To counteract this problem, researchers have suggested calculating the "fail-safe number" (FSN). Essentially, the FSN is the number of studies with null findings required to reduce the effect size to a value considered to be insignificant to the researcher (e.g. a small effect size). In cases when the FSN is a lot larger than the number of included studies, the researcher may conclude that the effects found are not very likely to be due to publication bias. Using the Ng *et al.* (2012) example, 82 studies with null findings lost due to publication bias are required to reduce the effect size of the association between autonomy need satisfaction and intrinsic motivation to a value of .10 (i.e. a small effect size).

Possible publication bias can also be detected using funnel plots (see Figure 9.5 for an example). In funnel plots, the effect sizes reported in primary studies are plotted against their standard errors. When publication bias is present, the funnel plot will be asymmetric, with very few studies having large standard errors and small effect sizes (i.e. the lower left corner). In contrast, when no publication bias exists, the plot should be symmetric around the line representing the weight-averaged effect size. However, FSN and funnel plots involve somewhat subjective interpretations. Hence, researchers have proposed other methods or statistical

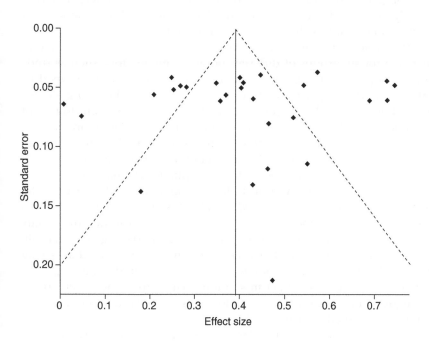

*Figure 9.5* Funnel plot with pseudo 95% confidence limits.

procedures to address the problem of publication bias in meta-analytic estimations (e.g. Macaskill *et al.*, 2001, Schimmack, 2012), but no single method has emerged as the golden standard; the FSN's and funnel plots remain to be the most common methods used and reported.

After estimating effect sizes, the next step is to examine whether these are consistent ("homogeneous") across the primary studies. Researchers have suggested different homogeneity tests. One widely used test is the $I^2$ (Higgins *et al.*, 2003). Specifically, the $I^2$ is an estimate of the proportion of inconsistency (or "heterogeneity") due to real variations in effect sizes (i.e. variation potentially due to the operation of moderator variables). The $I^2$ is presented in form of percentages. Higgins *et al.* proposed 25 per cent, 50 per cent, and 75 per cent as values denoting low, moderate, and high heterogeneity, respectively. In our example the $I^2$ was 95 per cent, meaning 95 per cent of the variation in the effect size between autonomy need satisfaction and intrinsic motivation was caused by real differences, and only 5 per cent of the variation could be attributed to chance. In other words, very high heterogeneity was found in this effect size.

When effect sizes are found to be heterogeneous, moderator analysis should be conducted. Essentially, this analysis involves separating primary studies into meaningful subgroups based on possible moderators (e.g. age, sex, study design). For each level of the moderator (e.g. male and female), separate effect sizes are calculated. 95 per cent CIs of these effect sizes are then compared. If these intervals do not overlap, researchers may conclude that the variable (e.g. sex) is a moderator of the whole sample effect size and can explain the heterogeneity in that effect size.

In the presented example, as heterogeneity was found, effect sizes were calculated for subgroups of different potential moderators, such as study design and participant age. For example, when studies were grouped by study design, the 95 per cent CI of the effect size of studies using a cross-sectional design ($\rho = .37$, 95 per cent CI [.30, .44]) was different to that of experimental studies ($\rho = .60$, 95 per cent CI [.48, .72]). Therefore, we may conclude that the relation between autonomy need satisfaction and intrinsic motivation is moderated by the design of the primary studies.

Besides assessing bias across studies (e.g. publication bias), researchers should also check for bias within studies that may affect effect sizes in the primary studies (e.g. Higgins *et al.*, 2011). Effect sizes may vary across studies of varying methodological rigour. Researchers can rate the quality of primary studies based on a list of pre-defined criteria (e.g. whether validated measures were used). For each criterion, a study is rated as having either high or low risk of bias to the effect size under investigation. Researchers may then conduct moderator analysis to test whether studies with higher, in contrast to those with lower, risks of bias is a source of variation in obtained effect sizes.

The meta-analytic techniques described so far can examine the relation between only two variables at a time. However, many S&E psychology researchers want to test the relation between a network of variables. To address this limitation, researchers have combined meta-analysis with path analysis. Specifically, researchers first generate a correlation matrix of all variables of interest using the meta-analytic techniques described above to correct for various types of error. This matrix is then used as the input for the path analysis. For example, in Figure 9.6 a path analysis model was evaluated based on a correlation matrix involving the variables of autonomy support, competence, autonomy, relatedness, and psychological well being, derived from Ng *et al.*'s (2012) meta-analysis. The variables included in the path analysis are free from measurement error because this is usually corrected in the preceding meta-analysis.

Researchers have also designed guidelines for conducting and reporting results of meta-analysis, such as the PRISMA checklist (Moher *et al.*, 2009). Adhering to such guidelines helps to enhance the clarity and scientific rigour of a meta-analysis. Further, in the last decade or so, researchers have proposed other meta-analytic techniques as alternatives to existing methods. One example is conducting meta-analysis using multilevel modelling techniques (Van den Noortgate and Onghena, 2003). Essentially, multilevel techniques are used to estimate the proportion of variation in effect sizes due to sampling error and real variations (therefore providing a measure of homogeneity). If heterogeneity is suggested, moderators are coded as higher-level variables and the variance that can be attributed to differences in moderators can be examined using multilevel modelling algorithms. The multilevel modelling approach to meta-analysis allows researchers to conduct moderator analyses that cannot be easily done using a random effects model. For example, the multilevel approach allows the testing of continuous moderators. Further, given that often some authors might have conducted several studies within a research

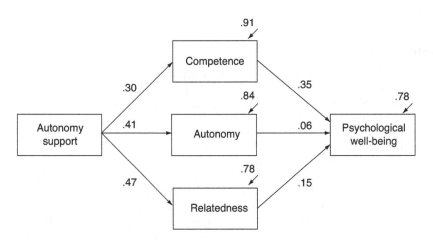

*Figure 9.6* A structural equation model based on meta-analysed correlations.

area, it is possible to do homogeneity testing and subsequent moderator analyses to account for author interdependency by using a three-level analysis with primary studies at level one, nested within the author of the study at level two, and the moderator of interest at level three. This method may be more appropriate for certain research questions or moderators, and can be pursued in future S&E research.

## Concluding thoughts

The purpose of this chapter was to introduce the reader to some of the recent advances in statistical techniques (mediation analysis and meta-analysis) that are widely employed in the sport and exercise psychology literature, as well as to present statistical techniques (ESEM, bifactor modelling, and multilevel modelling for longitudinal data) that are somewhat rare in this literature. The aim was to present a non-technical introduction to all these topics, as well as identify some recommendations and future applications for each of these techniques. However, we must warn the reader that the application of these techniques should not be uncritical or based on how "fashionable" or "impressive" they appear to be. Theory should guide the selection of appropriate statistical tests, as was particularly illustrated on the section on ESEM and Bifactor Modelling. Equally, we urge researchers not to avoid studying these techniques because they appear complex, feel they do not have the necessary background in measurement and statistics, or are unfamiliar with the software needed to perform such analyses. We concur with Sharpe (2013) that the challenge of this age is to close the communication gap between quantitative methodologists and substantive researchers by introducing advances in statistical methodology in a nontechnical manner. We hope this chapter makes a small contribution to this effort.

## References

American Educational Research Association (AERA), American Psychological Association (APA) and National Council on Measurement in Education (NCME) (1999). *Standards for Educational and Psychological Testing*, Washington, DC: American Psychological Association.

Antonakis, J., Bendhanan, S., Jacquart, P. and Lalive (2000). On making causal claims: A review and recommendations. *The Leadership Quarterly*, 21, 1086–120. doi: 10.1016/j.leaqua.2010.10.010.

Asparouhov, T. and Muthén, B. (2009). Exploratory structural equation modelling. *Structural Equation Modelling*, 16, 397–438. doi: 10.1080/10705510903008204.

Baron, R. M. and Kenny, D. A. (1986). The moderator-mediator variable distinction in social psychological research: Conceptual, strategic, and statistical considerations. *Journal of Personality and Social Psychology*, 51, 1173–82. doi: 10.1037/0022-3514.51.6.1173.

Bartholomew, K., Ntoumanis, N., Ryan, R. M. and Thøgersen-Ntoumani, C. (2011). Psychological need thwarting in the sport context: Assessing the darker side of athletic experience. *Journal of Sport and Exercise Psychology*, 33, 75–102.

Bartholomew, K., Ntoumanis, N. and Thøgersen-Ntoumani, C. (2010). The controlling interpersonal style in a coaching context: Development and initial validation of a psychometric scale. *Journal of Sport and Exercise Psychology*, 32, 193–216.

Biddle, S. J., Markland, D., Gilbourne, D., Chatzisarantis, N. L. D. and Sparkes, A. C. (2001). Research methods in sport and exercise psychology: Quantitative and qualitative issues, *Journal of Sports Sciences*, 19, 777–809. doi: 10.1080/026404101317015438.

Borenstein, M., Hedges, L. V., Higgins, J. P. T. and Rothstein, H. R. (2011). *Introduction to Meta-Analysis*. Chichester, UK: Wiley.

Brown, T. (2006). *Confirmatory factor analysis for applied research*. New York, NY: The Guilford Press.

Bruner, M., Nagy, G. and Wilhelm, O. (2012). A tutorial on hierarchically structured constructs. *Journal of Personality*, 80, 798–846. doi: 10.1111/j.1467-6494.2011.00749.x.

Bryk, A. S. and Raudenbush, S. W. (1992). *Hierarchical linear models*. Newbury Park, CA: Sage.

Chen, F. F., Hayes, A., Carver, C. S., Laurenceau, J. P. and Zhang, Z. (2012). Modelling general and specific variance in multifaceted constructs: A comparison of the bifactor model to other approaches. *Journal of Personality*, 80, 219–51. doi: 10.1111/j.1467-6494.2011.00739.x.

Chen, F. F., West, S. G. and Sousa, K. H. (2006). A comparison of bifactor and second-order models of quality of life. *Multivariate Behavioural Research*, 41, 189–225. doi: 10.1207/s15327906mbr4102_5.

Curran, T., Hill, A. P. and Niemiec, C. P. (2013). A conditional process model of children's behavioural engagement and behavioural disaffection in sport based on self-determination theory. *Journal of Sport and Exercise Psychology*, 35, 30–43.

Deci, E. L. and Ryan, R. M. (eds) (2002). *Handbook of self-determination research*, Rochester: University Rochester Press.

Enders, C. G. and Tofighi, D. (2007). Centering predictor variables in cross-sectional multilevel models: A new look at an old issue. *Psychological Methods*, 12, 121–38. doi: 10.1037/1082-989X.12.2.121.

Gagné, M., Ryan, R. M. and Bargmann, K. (2003). Autonomy support and need satisfaction in the motivation and well-being of gymnasts. *Journal of Applied Sport Psychology*, 15, 372–90. doi: 10.1080/10413200390238031.

Hausenblas, H. A., Carron, A. V. and Mack, D. E. (1997). Application of the theories of reasoned action and planned behaviour to exercise behaviour: A meta-analysis'. *Journal of Sport and Exercise Psychology*, 19, 36–51.

Hedges, L. V. and Olkin, I. (1985). *Statistical methods for meta-analysis*. New York, NY: Academic Press.

Herman, A. and Pfister, H.-R. (2013). Simple measures and complex structures: Is it worth employing a more complex model of personality in Big Five inventories? *Journal of Research in Personality*, 47, 599–608. doi: 10.1016/j.jrp.2013.05.004.

Higgins, J. P. T., Altman, D. G. and Sterne, J. A. C. (2011). Assessing risk of bias in included studies. In J. P. T. Higgins and S. Green, (eds), *Cochrane Handbook for*

*Systematic Reviews of Interventions.* The Cochrane Collaboration. Version 5.1.0 (updated March 2011). Available at: www.cochrane-handbook.org.

Higgins, J. P. T., Thompson, S. G., Deeks, J. J. and Altman, D. G. (2003). Measuring inconsistency in meta-analyses. *British Medical Journal*, 327, 557–60. doi: 10.1136/bmj.327.7414.557.

Hox, J. J. (2010). *Multilevel analysis: Techniques and applications* (2nd edn). Mahwah, NJ: Erlbaum.

Hoyle, R. H. (ed.) (2012). *Handbook of structural equation modelling.* New York, NY: The Guilford Press.

Hunter, J. E. and Schmidt, F. L. (2004). *Methods of meta-analysis: Correcting error and bias in research findings.* Thousand Oaks, CA: Sage Publications, Inc.

Lakin, J. M. and Gambrell, J. L. (2012). Distinguishing verbal, quantitative, and figural facets of fluid intelligence in young students. *Intelligence*, 40, 560–70. doi: 10.1016/j.intell.2012.07.005.

Lewis, S. and Clarke, M. (2001). Forest plots: Trying to see the wood and the trees. *British Medical Journal*, 322, 1479–80. doi: 10.1136/bmj.322.7300.1479.

Lonsdale, C., Hodge, K. and Rose, E. A. (2008). The Behavioural Regulation in Sport Questionnaire (BRSQ): Instrument development and initial validity evidence. *Journal of Sport and Exercise Psychology*, 30, 323–55.

Lonsdale, C., Hodge, K. and Rose, E. (2009). Athlete burnout in elite sport: A self-determination perspective. *Journal of Sports Sciences*, 27, 785–95. doi: 10.1080/02640410902929366.

MacKinnon, D. P., Krull, J. L. and Lockwood, C. M. (2000). Equivalence of the mediation, confounding and suppression effect. *Prevention Science*, 1, 173–81. doi: 10.1023/A:1026595011371.

Macaskill, P., Walter, S. D. and Irwig, L. (2001). A comparison of methods to detect publication bias in meta-analysis. *Statistics in Medicine*, 20, 641–54. doi: 10.1002/sim.698.

Marsh, H. W., Lüdke, O., Muthén, B., Asparouhov, T., Morin, A. J. S., Trautwein, U. and Nagengast, B. (2010). A new look at the big five factor structure through exploratory structural equation modelling. *Psychological Assessment*, 22, 471–91. doi: 10.1037/a0019227.

Marsh, H. W., Lüdtke, O., Nagengast, B., Morin, A. J. S., Trautwein, U. and Von Davier, M. (2013). Why item parcels are (almost) never appropriate: Two wrongs do not make a right-Camouflaging misspecification with item-parcels in CFA models. *Psychological Methods*, 18, 257–84. doi: 10.1037/a0032773.

Marshall, S. and Biddle, S. H. (2001). The transtheoretical model of behaviour change: A meta-analysis of applications to physical activity and exercise. *Annals of Behavioural Medicine*, 23, 229–46. doi: 10.1207/S15324796ABM2304_2.

McDonald, R. P. (1999). *Test theory: A unified treatment.* Mahwah, NJ: Lawrence Erlbaum Associates.

Moher, D., Liberati, A., Tetzlaff, J. and Altman, D. G. (2009). Preferred reporting items for systematic reviews and meta-analyses: The PRISMA statement. *British Medical Journal*, 339, 332–6. doi: 10.1136/bmj.b2535.

Molt, R. W., Conroy, D. E. and Horan, P. M. (2000). The Social Physique Anxiety Scale: An example of the potential consequence of negatively worded items in factorial validity studies. *Journal of Applied Measurement*, 1, 327–45.

Morin, A. J. S. and Maiano, C. (2011). Cross-validation of the short form of the physical self-inventory (PSI-S) using exploratory structural equation modelling

(ESEM). *Psychology of Sport and Exercise*, 12, 540–54. doi: 10.1016/j.psych-sport.2011.04.003.

Muthén, B. and Asparouhov T. (2011). Beyond multilevel regression modelling: Multilevel analysis in a general latent variable framework. In J. Hox and K. Roberts (eds), *Handbook of advanced multilevel analysis* (pp. 15–40), New York: Taylor and Francis.

Muthén, B. and Asparouhov, T. (2012). Bayesian structural equation modelling: A more flexible representation of substantive theory. *Psychological Methods*, 17, 313–35. doi: 10.1037/a0026802.

Muthén, L. K., and Muthén, B. O. (2002). How to use a Monte Carlo study to decide on sample size and determine power. *Structural Equation Modelling*, 9, 599–620. doi: 10.1207/S15328007SEM0904_8.

Myers, N., Ahn, S. and Jin, Y. (2011). Sample size and power estimates for a confirmatory factor analytic model in exercise and sport: A Monte Carlo approach. *Research Quarterly for Exercise and Sport*, 82, 412–23. doi:10.1080/02701367.2011.10599773.

Myers, N. D., Chase, M. A., Pierce, S. W. and Martin, E. (2011). Coaching efficacy and exploratory structural equation modelling: A substantive-methodological synergy. *Journal of Sport and Exercise Psychology*, 33, 779–806.

Ng, J. Y. Y., Ntoumanis, N., Thøgersen-Ntoumani, C., Deci, E. L., Ryan, R. M., Duda, J. and Williams, G. C. (2012). Self-determination theory applied to health contexts: A meta-analysis. *Perspectives on Psychological Science*, 7, 325–40. doi: 10.1177/1745691612447309.

Ntoumanis, N. (2012). A self-determination theory perspective on motivation in sport and physical education: Current trends and possible future research directions. In G. C. Roberts and D. C. Treasure (eds), *Motivation in sport and exercise: Volume 3* (pp. 91–128), Champaign, IL: Human Kinetics.

Ntoumanis, N. and Biddle, S. J. H. (1999). Affect and achievement goals in physical activity: A meta-analysis. *Scandinavian Journal of Medicine and Science in Sports*, 9, 315–32. doi: 10.1111/j.1600–0838.1999.tb00253.x.

Pelletier, L. G., Rocchi, M. A., Vallerand, R. J., Deci, E. L. and Ryan, R. M. (2013). Validation of the revised sport motivation scale (SMS-II). *Psychology of Sport and Exercise*, 14, 329–41. doi: 10.1016/j.psychsport.2012.12.002.

Preacher, K. J. and Hayes, A. F. (2008). Asymptotic and resampling strategies for assessing and comparing indirect effects in multiple mediator models. *Behaviour Research Methods*, 40, 879–91. doi: 10.3758/BRM.40.3.879.

Preacher, K. J. and Kelley, K. (2011). Effect size measures for mediation models: Quantitative strategies for communicating indirect effects. *Psychological Methods*, 16, 93–115. doi: 10.1037/a0022658.

Preacher, K. J., Zhang, Z. and Zyphur, M. J. (2011). Alternative methods for assessing mediation in multilevel data: The advantages of multilevel SEM. *Structural Equation Modelling*, 18, 161–82. doi:10.1080/10705511.2011.557329.

Preacher, K. J., Zyphur, M. J. and Zhang, Z. (2010). A general multilevel SEM framework for assessing multilevel mediation. *Psychological Methods*, 15, 209–33. doi: 10.1037/a0020141.

Quené, H. and van den Bergh, H. (2004). On multi-level modelling of data from repeated measures designs: A tutorial. *Speech Communication*, 43, 103–21. doi: 10.1016/j.specom.2004.02.004.

Raykov, T. (2001). Bias of coefficient alpha for fixed congeneric measures with correlated errors. *Applied Psychological Measurement,* 25, 69–76. doi: 10.1177/01466216010251005.

Reise, S. P. (2012). The rediscovery of bifactor measurement models. *Multivariate Behavioural Research,* 47, 667–96. doi: 10.1080/00273171.2012.715555.

Revelle, W. and Wilt, J. (2013). The general factor of personality: A general critique. *Journal of Research in Personality,* 47, 493–504. doi: 10.1016/j.jrp. 2013.04.012.

Rosenthal, R. (1979). The "file drawer problem" and tolerance for null results. *Psychological Bulletin,* 86, 638–41. doi: 10.1037/0033–2909.86.3.638.

Rucker, D. D., Preacher, K. J., Tormala, Z. L. and Petty, R. E. (2011). Mediation analysis in social psychology: Current practices and new recommendations. *Social and Personality Psychology Compass,* 5, 359–71. doi: 10.1111/j.1751–9004.2011.00355.x.

Schimmack, U. (2012). The ironic effect of significant results on the credibility of multiple-study articles. *Psychological Methods,* 17, 551–66. doi: 10.1037/a0029487.

Schmitt, T. A. and Sass, D. (2011). Rotation criteria and hypothesis testing for exploratory factor analysis: Implications for factor pattern loadings and interfactor correlations. *Educational and Psychological Measurement,* 71, 95–113. doi: 10.1177/0013164410387348.

Selig, J. P. and Preacher, K. J. (2009). Mediation models for longitudinal data in developmental research. *Research in Human Development,* 6, 144–64. doi:10.1080/15427600902911247.

Sharpe, D. (2013). Why the resistance to statistical innovations? Bridging the communication gap. *Psychological Methods,* 18, 572–82. doi: 10.1037/a0034177.

Skrondal, A., and Rabe-Hesket, S. (2004). *Generalized latent variable modelling: multilevel, longitudinal, and structural equation models.* London: Chapman and Hall/CRC.

Snijders, T. (1996). Analysis of longitudinal data using the hierarchical linear model. *Quality and Quantity,* 30, 405–26. doi: 10.1007/BF00170145.

Snijders, T. and Bosker R (1999). *An introduction to basic and advanced multilevel modelling.* London: Sage.

Sobel, M. E. (1982). Asymptotic confidence intervals for indirect effects in structural equation models. *Sociological Methodology,* 13, 290–312. doi: 10.2307/270723.

Stoel, R. D. and Garre, F. G. (2011). Growth curve analysis using multilevel regression and structural equation modelling. In J. Hox and K. Roberts (eds), *Handbook of advanced multilevel analysis* (pp. 97–111). New York: Taylor and Francis.

Van den Noortgate, W. and Onghena, P. (2003). Multilevel meta-analysis: A comparison with traditional meta-analytical procedures. *Educational and Psychological Measurement,* 63, 765–90. doi: 10.1177/0013164403251027.

Viladrich, C., Appleton, P. R., Quested, E., Duda, J., Alcaraz, S., Heuzé, J. P., Fabra, P., Samdal, O., Ommundsen, Y., Hill, A. P., Zourbanos, N. and Ntoumanis, N. (2013). Measurement invariance of the Behavioural Regulation in Sport Questionnaire when completed by young athletes across five European Countries. *International Journal of Sport and Exercise Psychology,* 11: 384–94. doi:10.1080/1612197X.2013.830434.

Viladrich, C., Ntoumanis, N., Quested, E., Appleton, P. R. and Duda, J. L. (2013). *Measuring basic need satisfaction: Alternatives to confirmatory factor analysis when the three needs are highly correlated.* Presented at the 5th International Conference on Self-Determination Theory, Rochester, NY.

Viladrich, C., Torregrosa, M., and Cruz, J. (2011). Psychometric quality supporting the Spanish adaptation of the behavioural Regulation in Sport Questionnaire [Calidad psicométrica de la adaptación española del Cuestionario de Regulación Conductual en el Deporte]. *Psicothema*, 23, 786–94.

Zhang, Z., Zyphur, M. J. and Preacher, K. J. (2009). Testing multilevel mediation using hierarchical linear models: Problems and solutions. *Organisational Research Methods*, 12, 695–719. doi: 10.1177/1094428108327450.

# 10 Epilogue

*Lew Hardy*

When I was invited to write this epilogue, the Editors gave me the same brief that they had given the other chapter Authors in this book. This was to take a stance on what I personally felt were key potential issues or themes for the field that had been raised in each chapter, with a view to offering a "steer" to the sport and exercise psychology readership on where we should perhaps be heading as a discipline. This inevitably implies that I engage in some sort of critical analysis of the chapters, and I hope that I will not be considered disloyal, or too biased and egocentric, if I sometimes disagree with key themes that the chapter Authors have identified.

## Chapter 1: Contemporary personality perspectives in sport

Having provided an overview of the rather difficult history that personality research in sport has endured, the Authors move beyond the popular Big 5 personality factors, to provide a detailed review of more recent research on perfectionism, optimism, mental toughness, narcissism, and alexithymia. The Authors adopt a very strong interactionist perspective throughout. Unsurprisingly, I was especially pleased to read the Authors' critical discussion of the "one size fits all" principle that seems to pervade much of the psychological skills literature. In this discussion, the Authors highlight evidence which suggests that different personality types might benefit more, or less, from training in specific psychological skills. Similarly, the Authors extend the person x situation interactionist perspective that other Authors in this book have proposed to discuss personality x psychological skills, and personality x personality interactions.

I must confess that, having been a co-author on some of the research that is reviewed, I have perhaps even more personal bias regarding this chapter than I generally have (and I am not short in that particular department). Nevertheless, I particularly enjoyed the sections on optimism, narcissism, and alexithymia which have not been extensively researched in sport. I also like the strong theoretical slant that pervaded the whole chapter, and the hint of dark underpinnings that may lurk behind narcissism and alexithymia. I often wonder if the current fashion for apparently believing that "a happy performer will be a great performer" is not actually staring in the wrong direction. On a more critical note, one could question whether goal orientations research might not have been worth at least a mention, but no doubt the Authors would quite correctly point out that that has been extensively reviewed elsewhere.

Finally, I could not help noticing how infectious the Authors' enthusiasm for their subject was, and I was left with the feeling that there were lots of exciting questions waiting to be answered across this domain. This chapter should be essential reading for anyone starting up in personality research in sport.

## Chapter 2: Coping in sport

Twenty years ago, Dan Gould, Graham Jones, and I reviewed the literature on coping in sport for a book we were writing (Hardy *et al.*, 1996). It was a disappointing review, in that the quality of the evidence available was very weak. I really enjoyed reading the present chapter and seeing how much the field has come on in those intervening years. I think the Authors have done an excellent job of pulling together a very balanced, but critical, review of research that has been conducted using very disparate methodologies, and different theoretical orientations, to capture what we know and what we need to explore next.

After dealing with the usual conceptual and measurement issues, I liked the emphasis that the Authors placed on the explanatory power of mediating and moderating studies, again drawing attention to the need to move beyond "main effects models" of life. I especially liked the section on within and between person levels of analysis that are so important in this particular domain, grounded as it is in Lazarus and Folkman's (1984) conceptualisation of coping as a "constantly changing process". There were plenty of other things that resonated for me as well. For once, I enjoyed reading a scientific discussion of gender and cultural differences (complete with moderator effects), instead of what seems to be the more usual atheoretical or political discussion of such effects.

Finally, I thought the section on coping effectiveness was outstanding. The need for future research to consider the full breadth of coping (both emotionally and behaviourally, in both the short and the long term) was very well articulated. No assumptions were made about the global dominance of approach coping (another main effects model of the world), or about what it means to be adaptive or maladaptive, and the possibility of performance-health trade-offs was discussed. I did just wonder if there might be some mileage to be had in making links between the discussion of coping resources and Baumeister's work on self-control (Baumeister *et al.*, 2007; Muraven and Baumeister, 2000), but that is probably "nit-picking" in so thorough a piece of work. I applaud the Authors: Job well done...

## Chapter 3: The five self-determination mini-theories applied to sport

Before commencing this particular commentary, I must confess that I have a personal bias against self-determination theory. Despite the fact that self-determination theory has generated a lot of empirical support for some very useful and quite complex ideas, in my personal opinion, its foundations stand on unjustified assumptions, inconsistent arguments, and untestable hypotheses. It also seems to be regarded by its proponents as some sort of religion that cannot be challenged, rather than a scientific theory awaiting contradiction.

With such a strong personal bias, it would be surprising if the following comments were entirely reasonable. Nevertheless, I have to say that the author has done a good job of clarifying what exactly the various sub-theories of self-determination theory say, and identifying further ways in which the sub-theories might be applied to sport. There is an occasional lack of clarity in the section on basic psychological needs theory about whether the author is referring to the magnitude of psychological needs or the magnitude of need satisfaction, but otherwise I thought the review did an excellent job of clarifying the predictions of the theories. I also thought that the author raised some very interesting questions from the different sub-theories.

I particularly like the discussion of whether the controlling aspect of competition or the loss of competence following defeat in competition caused reduced intrinsic motivation, and the discussion of how self-determination in coaches might impact their behaviour towards their athletes. I regret the fact that the vast majority of research on self-determination theory does not consider objective performance or focus upon high-level performers, but that is hardly the author's fault, and it is not really surprising given the positive humanistic psychology underpinnings of self-determination theory. In truth, I thought the present review was very balanced, if a little uncritical of the basic tenets of the theory.

As regards the key issues area that future research should address, I confess that I think we need to challenge some of the basic tenets of self-determination theory and find out exactly how robust the five sub-theories really are, and what the boundary conditions of the sub-theories are, rather than simply accept them as true and try to work out how to apply them to sport. For example, are humans "fundamentally inclined towards growth" (p. 3 of Chapter 3)? And, if they are, why does such growth manifest itself as "an innate tendency to engage in activity for its own sake and without external prompts (p. 3 of Chapter 3)". From where I am sat, psychological growth implies that the behavioural/performance outcome of activities is important, so that growth-related activities cannot be intrinsically motived. As another example, are all individuals "predisposed to internalise extrinsically driven behaviour so that it becomes integrated with one's true sense of self"? Surely, there are some circumstances in individuals reject such extrinsically regulated behaviour? What are the boundary conditions for such changes? As a final example, in basic psychological needs theory, what exactly is a *basic* psychological need? Why exactly are there only three of them? And why exactly are these three basic psychological needs the only personal characteristics in the whole of psychology that do not demonstrate individual differences? Recent research by Schuler and colleagues (Schuler *et al.*, 2010, 2013) seems to question the universality principle of basic psychological needs theory.

I guess I will not be getting that invitation to the next self-determination theory conference after all...

## Chapter 4: Organisational psychology in sport

As one of the Authors on the first research paper to be published on organisational psychology in sport (Woodman and Hardy, 2001), I was looking forward to reading this chapter. I am pleased to say that I was not disappointed. The Authors present a wide ranging but thorough review of the considerable developments that have been made in this area over the last 10–15 years. I had several (constructive) thoughts whilst reading the chapter, including the following. First, the sections on emotional regulation, emotional contagion, and emotional labour raised a number of issues that could have implications for the development of psychosocial capital in sport organisations, and it would be good to understand more about the development of such assets and the causal links between them. Second, high-level sport in the twenty-first century is indeed a global business and the further study of organisational commitment and socialisation would probably be attractive to research users in this area. Third, because the globalisation of high-level sport is a relatively recent phenomena, many sport organisations are currently confronted with a need to engage in major programmes of organisational change. Consequently, there is both a need and an opportunity for further research into climate, culture, and structural change. Fourth, I have a warning. We could spend many research hours and years re-inventing much of what is already known and generalisable from organisational psychology research in non-sport organisations and calling it new. This would be a grave error. We need to focus on researching the genuine unknowns as we move forward, whilst attempting to develop more robust causal designs wherever possible.

Finally, I had a very specific thought for the cognoscenti. The High Performance Environments model described in Jones *et al.* (2009) was developed and empirically tested by Mark Gittins for his PhD. His thesis (Gittins, 2010) was unfortunately never published because Mark moved onto other things as soon as it was completed. However, it is probably worth a read for those interested in this area.

## Chapter 5: Tripartite efficacy framework in physical activity contexts

Given the complexity and cyclical nature of self-other perceptions, it is little wonder that the study of relationships in sport is a relatively recent phenomena. Reading this chapter reminded me of some sort of party game ... he thinks that I think that he thinks that I think that he thinks.... It seems likely that the cyclical process of self- and other perception could continue endlessly. Yet, in their thorough review, the Authors present a coherent and convincing argument (despite very limited causal evidence) that performers' other efficacy and relation-inferred efficacy (RISE) beliefs are an important influence upon not only their own self-efficacy but also upon a host of other relationship and performance related cognitions and behaviours. Clearly, there is a need for researchers in the area to develop more causally robust designs, but the two sections that I found most interesting were the discussions of efficacy discrepancies and boundary conditions/moderator effects.

Gaining a greater understanding of the perceiver-related and target-related characteristics that exacerbate such discrepancies would seem to be a high priority for future research given the host of negative relationship variables that appear to be affected by such discrepancies. I found it especially interesting that the Authors identified attachment styles as a likely candidate. Consideration of psychodynamic perspectives is relatively rare in sport psychology research and this would seem to be an obvious place to remedy that. The Authors' conclusion that "junior" partners are most susceptible to other efficacy effects would seem to reinforce this view.

As always, I found the discussion of boundary conditions and moderator effects especially interesting. The Authors draw attention to the fact the some athletes might find that very high RISE beliefs induce doubts about their own ability, and I couldn't help wondering what the boundary conditions are for athletes deriving positive motivational effects from a lack of RISE (e.g. elite performers responding to media criticism by demonstrating increased motivation "to prove them wrong"). I think these would both be very interesting lines for future research to pursue.

## Chapter 6: Choking under pressure

A key element that appears to underpin this chapter is the notion that researchers need to differentiate between what the Authors term *underperformance* and *choking*. If the purpose of this proposition was to differentiate between performance loss that is due to pressure or competitive stress and performance loss that is due to other causes, then I would totally agree. However, that appears not be the key distinction. Rather it appeared to me that the key distinction that was being made was to do with the magnitude of performance loss. The Authors propose that we should adopt Mesagno and Hill's (2013) definition that choking is "an acute and considerable decrease in skill execution and performance when self-expected standards are normally achievable, which is the result of increased anxiety under perceived pressure" (p. 273). I have to concede that I do not really see the point in re-writing the "rule book" inserting "acute and considerable decrease" and "self-expected" everywhere that it previously stated "decrease" and "expected". One approach that may be useful here in supporting this clarification in nomenclature is the incorporation of catastrophe models (e.g. Hardy and Parfitt 1991; Hardy *et al.*, 1996), which to the best of my knowledge are the only models of choking that predict a "considerable decrease" (discontinuity) in the performance of choking athletes.

I also felt the adoption of a broader perspective when discussing models of choking in this chapter may also be of value to researchers. For example, additional attentional models such as ironic effects theory (Wegner, 1994) are worthy of consideration and, if major performance loss is a key aspect of choking, such loss is likely to be caused by motivational or social psychological factors as by attentional factors (Hardy and Parfitt, 1991). Indeed, it seems to me highly likely that such motivational and cognitive processes interact to determine whether and to what extent somebody chokes under pressure (see, for example, Hardy and Mullen, 2001). That aside, I liked the call for more research on personality and individual differences in choking.

Personally, I have always felt that choking is probably caused by a number of different processes and that some of these processes will be more prevalent in some performance environments and others will be more prevalent in other environments (cf. Hardy *et al.*, 1996; Hardy and Mullen, 2001). I also think there is sufficient evidence for us to have at least a reasonable idea of what some of these generic processes underpinning choking might be. However, we know much less about individual differences in athletes' predispositions to "lose" these key processes when they are under pressure. Recent multi-disciplinary research that includes psychophysiological, perceptual, and biomechanical measures of performance under pressure (e.g. Gray, 2013; Mullen *et al.*, 2005; Pijpers *et al.*, 2005) might add to our understanding of all of these issues.

Similarly, I would reinforce the interactionist perspective taken throughout the chapter by the Authors. Life is indeed unlikely to be a set of main effects. It might be nice and simple to consider it as such, but it is almost certainly not ecologically valid to do so.

Finally, the Authors quite correctly call for choking interventions to be more directly linked to theoretical explanations of choking. However, I was therefore rather surprised by their apparent claim that acclimatisation interventions were "not theory-matched to choking research". Acclimatisation training may not be linked to the narrow range of cognitive theories discussed by the Authors, but its focus on habituating the stress response is directly linked to a very large body of behavioural psychology dating back over the best part of a century (Levine, 1978; Meichenbaum, 1985). Furthermore, I was also rather surprised to read the Authors' discussion of pre-performance routines as though they were a recent invention without any reference to the original work by Boucher (e.g. Boutcher and Crews, 1987; Boucher, 1990) on the use of such routines as a theory driven intervention to reduce choking.

In conclusion, there is much to like about this chapter and the issues that the Authors discuss, but I could not help feeling that some additional important foundational research could have been discussed. For example, there was no mention at all of the research on appraisal (e.g. Jones *et al.*, 2009) and directional interpretations of anxiety (Jones *et al.*, 1994; Jones and Swain, 1992), which can be directly linked to both theory and intervention. Furthermore, Jones and Swain's original paper on directional interpretations is probably one of the most cited papers on stress and performance in sport. Instead the Authors appear to have chosen to focus on recent research that in many instances has only really "reinvented the wheel". Perhaps this is an old man's view of the world, but my call to the readership would be to use multi-disciplinary, interactionist, paradigms to build on (as opposed to overlook) previous research to explore the individual differences in the large number of processes underpinning choking.

## Chapter 7: Transformational leadership behaviour in sport

Transformational leadership has been extensively researched for over 25 years in organisational and management psychology, but has only recently received attention in the sport psychology literature. The Authors give an overview of the history of transformational leadership and then review the limited volume of transformational leadership research that has been conducted in sport. They raise a number of important measurement, methodological, and conceptual issues for researchers in the area to consider.

The fact that there is an issue regarding the differentiated measurement of transformational leadership has always rather baffled me. Basically, I have never understood how proponents of global measures can hypothesise that such sub-constructs as personalised support and high performance expectations should be positively correlated to one another and share the same relationship with other dependent variables. I can only assume that proponents of global models adopt that position because of the somewhat bewildering array of different sub-dimensions of transformational leadership that have been proposed by proponents of differentiated models. The fact is that, although there does seem to be some agreement on the broad underpinnings of transformational leadership, there are nearly as many different differentiated models as there are transformational leadership researchers. Perhaps the vision, support, challenge model introduced by the Authors may simplify this problem in sport; although one cannot help suspecting it may only meet with resistance from organisational psychology researchers who seem to be just about "transformational leadershipped out", and may consider it to be yet another variant on the basic differentiated model.

I liked the discussion of potential moderator variables, which echoes the call from Masagno, Geukes, and Larkin in the chapter on choking. Leadership researchers in organisational settings have been calling on researchers to consider contextual and follower variables for a number of years (see, for example, Yukl, 1999). In a similar vein, I liked the Authors' call for researchers to consider the potential negative effects of transformational leadership in future research. Clinical psychologists often talk about their clients experiencing functional difficulties because they have "overplayed strengths", and I can see how a similar issue could arise in transformational leadership if a "one size fits all" approach was taken.

I liked the Authors' discussion of methodological limitations in current research into transformational leadership, many of which generalise across many domains of our discipline. Some organisational and applied psychology journals no longer consider manuscripts reporting cross-sectional data, or studies based on single source data, and simply give them a desktop rejection. This is a sobering thought for all researchers in sport and exercise psychology, since I suspect that most of our highly rated sport and exercise psychology journals currently contain a substantial proportion of such papers.

The Authors call for a greater use of multi-level analysis also struck a chord with me. As the Authors point out, data obtained from sports performers will almost always have some sort hierarchical structure to it, and I cannot see regular analyses of variance and multiple linear regression analyses holding much sway in the future … five years? Ten years? Oh, alright, … we are a fairly conservative lot, perhaps twenty years at the most!

## Chapter 8: Qualitative methods and conceptual advances in sport psychology

The Authors start by presenting a detailed critique of the perils of interview-based qualitative research as frequently performed in sport and exercise psychology. As someone who has never really understood the logic of using content analysis to reduce rich qualitative data to some sort of hierarchical list, this critique was as refreshing as it was much-needed. I confess to sometimes feeling that the discussions of reality, experience, and truth, slipped a little too close philosophical nihilism; but the basic message that interview-based research in sport and exercise psychology is frequently poorly done and ignores the philosophical roots of naturalistic enquiry was very clear.

Having identified a substantial number of ways in which researchers could improve their use of interviews in qualitative research, the Authors identify an equally substantial number of alternative and/or supplementary methods that can be used. These include observation, diaries, visual methods, and the internet. I particularly liked the examples that were used of research that had been conducted using visual methods and the internet because I thought they offered some generally original ways of enhancing understanding.

If I had one concern when reading the chapter, it was a question about when does creative data collection become an act of gratuitous voyeurism that denies participants the right to be informed that they are participants? This is probably most relevant in complete participant observation studies when researchers must ethically balance two mutually antagonistic priorities: (1) their desire to immerse themselves in a culture in such a way as to not change the nature of the cultural group being studied; and (2) the rights of people to not have their private lives invaded and exposed (even if anonymously) to the rest of the world. I found myself asking the question "what exactly is the difference between a spy and a participant observer who does not declare his/her true identity to the group being observed?" The only answer I could come up with was that the spy reported the data to a smaller community of users … I found this a cause for some concern…

I especially liked the Authors' recommendation to use multiple methods in their qualitative research and would go further and recommend that researchers use both qualitative and quantitative methods in their study of research questions. Although the philosophical underpinnings of these two research methods are very different, there seems no reason why researchers should not be able to grasp both philosophies and behave in accordance with those different philosophies in different contexts. Perhaps the Authors would argue that such a dualist perspective is impossible, but if psychological patients with dissociative identity disorder, or bipolar disorder, can have such dualist perspectives, there must be some hope that at least some sport and exercise psychology researchers could do it…

## Chapter 9: Advances in quantitative analyses and their implications for sport and exercise psychology research

In this chapter, the Authors attempt to introduce readers to some recent advances in statistical techniques that can be used in sport and exercise psychology. They cover some very impressive ground: Preacher and Hayes (2008) approach to mediation analysis; exploratory structural equation and bi-factor modelling; the use of multi-level modelling to analyse multivariate repeated measures data; and Hunter and Schmidt's (2004) approach to meta-analysis. I applaud the Authors' boldness in challenging and encouraging their fellow researchers to adopt these techniques. I have a PhD in pure mathematics, and almost 40 years' experience of teaching statistics, and I learned a lot from this chapter. Despite the complexity of the material, I think the Authors did an excellent job of making it accessible to readers.

Perhaps inevitably, the sections that most impressed were those about which I knew least. However, I have read quite a lot of "promotional" research papers on exploratory structural equation modelling and found them nowhere near as convincing as the present exposition. The use of bifactor modelling was new to me and I found it very helpful. I also really liked the sections on the use of multi-level modelling for the analysis of multivariate repeated measures data. This is definitely not to say anything negative about the sections on mediation analysis and meta-analysis. They are both excellent. It was just that I knew rather more about the material discussed in these sections than I did about the material presented in the others.

Any criticisms I had were minor niggles about things I would have liked to have had a little more information about: item response theory models and latent class analysis, rotation indeterminacy, and rotation uncertainty in the section on exploratory structural equation and bifactor modelling; and a conceptual description of how $I^2$ is computed in the section on meta-analysis. But, as I said, these are trivial criticisms and I think this chapter will encourage many sport and exercise psychology researchers who were formerly statistical "wall flowers" to engage in a bit of statistical "dirty dancing", so to speak.... The Authors have my sincere congratulations.

## Concluding remarks

In the preceding sections, I have attempted to provide some critical analysis of each chapter together with some personal views about issues that might influence the direction that future research might take. Given my character, it is inevitable that this epilogue is at least slightly egocentric. Nevertheless, I most sincerely hope that readers will have found it interesting and constructive, and that none of the Authors whose work I have commented on will feel personally slighted by any criticisms that I may have made.

## References

Baumeister, R. F., Vohs, K. D., and Tice, D. M. (2007). The strength model of self-control. *Current Directions in Psychological Science*, 16, 351–355.

Boutcher, S. H. (1990). The role of performance routines in sport. In J. G. Jones and L. Hardy (eds), *Stress and performance in sport* (pp. 231–245). Chichester, UK: John Wiley.

Boutcher, S. H. and Crews, D. J. (1987). The effect of pre-shot routine on a well-learned skill. *International Journal of Sport Psychology*, 18, 30–39.

Gittins, M. (2010). *Developing and validating a high performance environment model.* Unpublished PhD thesis, Bangor University.

Gray, R. (2013). Being selective at the plate: Processing dependence between perceptual variables relates to hitting goals and performance. *Journal of Experimental Psychology: Human Perception and Performance*, 39, 1124–1142.

Hardy, L. and Mullen, R. (2001). Performance under pressure: A little knowledge is a dangerous thing? In P. R. Thomas (ed.), *Optimising performance in golf* (pp. 245–263). Brisbane: Australian Academic Press.

Hardy, L. and Parfitt, C. G. (1991). A catastrophe model of anxiety and performance. *British Journal of Psychology*, 82, 163–178.

Hardy, L., Jones, J. G., and Gould, D. (1996). *Understanding psychological preparation for sport: Theory and practice of elite performers.* Chichester: John Wiley.

Hunter, J. E. and Schmidt, F. L. (2004). *Methods of meta-analysis: Correcting error and bias in research findings.* Thousand Oaks, CA: Sage Publications, Inc.

Jones, G. and Swain, A. B. J. (1992). Intensity and direction as dimensions of competitive state anxiety and relationships with competitiveness. *Perceptual and Motor Skills*, 74, 467–472.

Jones, G., Hanton, S., and Swain, A. B. J. (1994). Intensity and interpretation of anxiety symptoms in elite and non-elite sport performers. *Personality and Individual Differences*, 17, 657–663.

Jones, M. V., Meijen, C., McCarthy, P. J., and Sheffield, D. (2009). Challenge and threat states in athletes. *International Review of Sport and Exercise Psychology*, 2, 161–180.

Lazarus, R. S. and Folkman, S. (1984). *Stress appraisal and coping.* NY: Springer.

Levine, S. (1978). Cortisol changes following repeated experiences with parachute training. In H. Ursin, E. Baade and S. Levine (eds). *Psychobiology of stress – A study of coping men* (pp. 51–56). NY: Academic Press.

Meichenbaum, D. (1985). *Stress inoculation training.* NY: Pergamon.

Mesagno, C. and Hill, D. M. (2013). Definition of choking in sport: Reconceptualisation and debate. *International Journal of Sport Psychology*, 44, 267–277.

Mullen, R., Hardy, L., and Tattersall, A. (2005). The effects of anxiety on motor performance: A test of the conscious processing hypothesis. *Journal of Sport and Exercise Psychology*, 27, 212–225.

Muraven, M. and Baumeister, R. F. (2000). Self-regulation and depletion of limited resources: Does self-control resemble a muscle? *Psychological Bulletin*, 126, 247–259.

Pijpers, J. R., Oudejans, R. R., and Bakker, F. C. (2005). Anxiety-induced changes in movement behaviour during the execution of a complex whole-body task. *Quarterly Journal of Experimental Psychology*, 58A, 421–445.

Preacher, K. J. and Hayes, A. F. (2008). Asymptotic and resampling strategies for assessing and comparing indirect effects in multiple mediator models. *Behaviour Research Methods*, 40, 879–91.

Schuler, J., Brandstatter, V., and Sheldon, K. M. (2013). Do implicit motives and basic psychological needs interact to predict well-being and flow? Testing a universal hypothesis and a matching hypothesis. *Motivation and Emotion*, 37, 480–495.

Schuler, J., Sheldon, K. M., and Frohlich, S. M. (2010). Implicit need for achievement moderates the relationship between felt competence and subsequent motivation. *Journal of Research in Personality*, 44, 1–12.

Wegner, D. M. (1994). Ironic processes of mental control. *Psychological Review*, 101, 34–52.

Woodman, T. and Hardy, L. (2001). A case study of organisational stress in elite sport. *Journal of Applied Sport Psychology*, 13, 207–238.

Yukl, G. (1999). An evaluation of conceptual weaknesses in transformational and charismatic leadership theories. *Leadership Quarterly*, 10, 285–305.

# Index

Page numbers in *italics* denote tables, those in **bold** denote figures.